Planning for Human Systems

Planning for Human Systems

Essays in Honor of

Russell L. Ackoff

Edited by

Jean-Marc Choukroun and

Roberta M. Snow

Published by the Busch Center, the Wharton School of the University of Pennsylvania.

Distributed by the

UNIVERSITY OF PENNSYLVANIA PRESS   Philadelphia

Permission is acknowledged to reprint previously published material:

From Albert O. Hirschman, *Essays in Trespassing: Economics to Politics and Beyond.* Copyright © 1981 by Cambridge University Press. Reprinted by permission.

From Björn Hettne, *Development Theory and the Three Worlds.* Copyright © 1990 by Longman Scientific and Technical. Reprinted by permission of Longman Group UK.

From Diana Crane, *Invisible Colleges.* Copyright © 1972 by the University of Chicago Press. Reprinted by permission.

Library of Congress Cataloging-in-Publication Data
Planning for human systems: essays in honor of Russell L. Ackoff /
    edited by Jean-Marc Choukroun and Roberta M. Snow.
        p. cm.
    Includes bibliographical references and index.
    ISBN 0-8122-3128-7
    1. Human capital—Planning. 2. System analysis. 3. Operations
research. I. Ackoff, Russell Lincoln, 1919– . II. Choukroun,
Jean-Marc. III. Snow, Roberta M., 1955– .
HD4904.7.P55 1992
658.4'03—dc20   91-45087
                                                          CIP

Contents

Section III: Systems Thinkers and Systems Applications

Section IV: Decision Making and Problem Solving: Purposeful Action Within Systems

Acknowledgments

The idea of publishing a "festschrift" honoring Russ Ackoff was first suggested by Tom Saaty a number of years ago. This seemed to be a particularly fitting tribute to a man whose prolific writing had had so much influence on so many people, and it was with great enthusiasm that this project was taken on at the Busch Center and Social Systems Sciences Department of the Wharton School. We felt that, within reason, everyone who had had a direct and significant relationship with Russ—friend, colleague, client, student—should have the opportunity to make a contribution. This turned out to be both a blessing and a curse: blessing because we were able to include a broad cross section of the people touched by Russ over the years; curse because this commitment to voluntary participation made it nearly impossible to enforce deadlines and adhere to a tight schedule.

We apologize to the early contributors who had to wait until now before seeing their work in print. Hopefully, it was worth the wait since the result is a book of contributions whose diversity is a reflection of Russ's broad, far-ranging, and lasting influence.

A negative side effect of the passage of time is that it can invalidate or contradict certain statements or conclusions made by some of the contributors. This is particularly true when dealing with global social, economic, and political issues. The recent developments in world politics and East-West relations are cases in point. Several chapters in the book touch on those issues and would, in some cases, probably reach different conclusions were they to be rewritten today. We feel, however, that their more important value lies in the methodological contributions made, and they should be read in this spirit.

To succeed, a project of this nature needs the help and cooperation of many people and organizations. We would like to express our deep gratitude to all of them. The various contributors should be thanked first, since without them there would be no book. We particularly want to thank those who submitted their papers early and had to wait, wondering whether the project would ever be completed.

Publication was made possible through a generous grant from Anheuser-Busch Companies. Bernard Krief Consultants USA also contributed financially. The Department of Management at the Wharton School helped in the preparation of the graphics and figures and in other aspects of manuscript preparation. The Busch Center and Social Systems Sciences Department also covered some of the production expenses. The University of Pennsylvania Press took care of the publication on the Busch Center's behalf and is handling the distribution. We wish to extend our deeply felt gratitude to all of these organizations for their help and generosity.

Introduction

Russell Lincoln Ackoff has been a thinker and practitioner whose ideas and activities have had a global impact. This volume is a small tribute from his friends and colleagues. To the reader unfamiliar with Ackoff's work, it might seem an odd collection of disparate pieces. This is not the case. It is a series of writings, each of which grew out of an intimate involvement with Ackoff at significant points in his career. Together they accurately reflect the constantly evolving nature of his contributions in a number of fields.

To set each paper in its appropriate perspective, an overview of Ackoff's development is required. Not only does this provide a framework for understanding this volume, but it also provides insight into how the collegial relationships reflected herein have contributed to progress in a number of disciplines.

Ackoff's ideas have their roots in American pragmatism. As a student in the 1940s, he was profoundly affected by a professor of Philosophy at the University of Pennsylvania, Edgar Arthur Singer, Jr., who had been the assistant to William James during his own student years at Harvard. He instilled in the young Ackoff the notions that philosophy was more than an intellectual exercise and that ideas and abstraction are of the world and should play a role in its progress and development.

During his students years he began collaborating with two young members of the Philosophy Department, Thomas A. Cowan and C. West Churchman. Together they began to develop in detail three aspects of Singer's work: (1) that the practice of philosophy or "applied" philosophy was necessary for philosophy to develop as a discipline; (2) that the effective application required philosophy to borrow or "sweep in" conceptual tools from other disciplines because science is a system of related points of view; and (3) that philosophy should turn itself foremost to the treatment of the most difficult problems, social issues. These foci served as the basis of their theoretical writing and, more importantly, as the basis of their first experiments in application.

In 1946 Ackoff and Churchman organized an informal research group that included other students and faculty members called "The Institute of Experimental Method." Among the projects undertaken by the group was a seminal investigation of the measurement of consumer interest. As their collaborative relationship developed, Ackoff and Churchman's vision of appropriate application of philosophy became more sophisticated.

Their next activity was to find an appropriate "home," a context in which they could put into practice their ideas. Ackoff, followed by Churchman, was given an appointment in the Philosophy Department of what is now Wayne State University. They were later joined by Cowan, who took a position on Wayne's Law School faculty. At first, a sympathetic dean supported the idea of establishing an Institute of Applied Philosophy. However, others in the faculty and administration were less enthusiastic about what was then considered by many a radical and unscholarly activity.

During this period Ackoff and Churchman began to develop an appreciation of the emerging British model of operational research. (The term "operational research" became "operations research" in its American version.) An outgrowth of wartime technical projects, operational research was a systemic approach to problem solving involving interdisciplinary teams with a common knowledge of scientific method. This new focus provided the team with a new institutional opportunity in 1951. The Case Institute of Technology, now Case Western Reserve University, offered them appointments to develop an operations research group.

One year later, they had succeeded in establishing the first doctoral program in operations research. Peter Fishburn, a contributor to this volume, was a student. So were Shiv Gupta and J. Sayer Minas, who, together with Ackoff, wrote *Scientific Method: Optimizing Applied Research Decisions,* the first text in the field.

Throughout the 1950s the group at Case became world leaders in the development of operations research. During this time Ackoff began to establish lasting personal and professional relationships with noted British operational researchers. Among these are Stafford Beer, Rolfe Tomlinson, Brian Haley, and John Friend, all of whom discuss the impact of Ackoff's thinking on their own work in this festschrift. It was also during this period that he began a professional relationship with Britton Harris, an urban planner who brought operations research techniques into that field.

During the 1950s and 1960s, Ackoff began to apply Singer's principle of "sweeping in" and continued to build his concept of applied philosophy. While still a student he, along with Churchman and Cowan, was introduced to Carl Jung's writings in psychology. The group had begun to apply Jungian concepts to the understanding of human behavior. They realized that Jung's model complemented Singer's notion of system. In particular, the concepts of introversion and extroversion were key to describing how an individual behaves in relationship to the environment around him. Through his association with British social scientist Eric Trist and later with his Australian colleague Fred Emery, Ackoff began to develop and refine the Singerian notion of system further. In particular, he began to reexamine human behavior as "purposeful" or "teleological" within the confines of a natural and social environment.

In the 1950s and 1960s programs in operations research, many modeled after the one at Case, were institutionalized in universities as well as in industry. In 1958, Churchman moved to the University of California at Berkeley and established a new group working in the field. Richard O. Mason and Ian Mitroff were among his early students in this setting.

In 1964, Ackoff moved almost all that remained of the Case group, including faculty, students, and research projects, to his alma mater, the University of Pennsylvania. He did not find a home in the philosophy department. Instead, the group was based within the more pragmatic Wharton School. The academic enterprise became part of the Department of Statistics and Operations Research, while the research activities were housed within the Management Science Center.

Throughout this period of intense intellectual development—at the University of Pennsylvania, at Wayne State, at Case Institute, in Britain, where he spent a great deal of time, and at other stops along the way—Ackoff developed and implemented a simple yet powerful model of academic education and research. The development of knowledge relevant to real-world problems could not be divorced from those problems. Academic education and research had to be intimately involved in the problems they were meant to address.

With this philosophy of learning, Ackoff could only reject the traditional ivory-tower model. Instead, he viewed the real world as the laboratory in which to experiment. This led to a series of associations with corporations and government organizations in a never-ending search for innovation in problem solving. Among these, the most remarkable has undoubtedly been Anheuser-Busch.

Ackoff began his association with the world's largest brewer in 1959. As documented in the two contributions by August A. Busch III and Leon Pritzker in this book, it started as a research assignment in capacity forecasting. Thirty years later, Ackoff is still intimately involved with the company and the impact he has had during that period would take another volume to document. Suffice it to say that it went well beyond his initial assignment and that it helped shape not only Anheuser-Busch as it is today but the whole field of corporate planning as it is practiced today.

During the 1960s Ackoff began to question the direction that operations research as a discipline was taking. Its institutionalization, he felt, had limited its development. Those working in the field seemed to have lost their original goal: to solve management problems. Instead, they devoted themselves to the development of technical mathematical tools. Ackoff became fond of saying that they seemed to be more interested in finding problems to fit their tools instead of developing new techniques to fit their problems. Moreover, in becoming a discipline, those in operations research lost their interest in learning from and "sweeping in" ideas from other areas of science.

This disquiet led Ackoff to take a deeper look into the process of problem solving. He realized that the complicated problems that faced managers could well be understood from a systems perspective. Instead of trying to break them down through the process of analysis to a series of discrete problems easily solved with existing techniques, Ackoff sought to move away from this reductionism. He returned to his intellectual roots and used William James's description of reality as a "great buzzing confusion" to set the framework for his own view of how problems should be defined and treated.

Ackoff went on to conceptualize reality as a set of interacting systems, complex and dynamic. Within this systemic reality problems were also viewed as interactive systems—or "messes." He began to see the role of the problem solver as one of understanding and managing the mess without breaking it down through analysis and destroying the relationships that defined it as a system. At the same time Ackoff began to examine the role of the scholar as problem solver. Problem solving was a form of applied philosophy. Going back to Singer, he took the position that it was the role of those working in the field to develop and apply methodology for treating systems of problems, or messes, *holistically*. Ackoff viewed himself no longer as an operations researcher, but as a systems scientist.

During this period Hasan Ozbekhan and Eric Trist became part of Wharton's faculty in operations research. They too believed that a systems approach going beyond traditional methods and techniques was more appropriate for understanding and treating problems facing organizations. In 1973, Ackoff and these colleagues left the operations research department and formed a new experimental program based on systems principles. It was called Social Systems Sciences. In addition to the standing faculty, the department drew upon distinguished adjuncts and visitors including C. West Churchman, Stafford Beer, Donald Schon, and Ignacy Sachs.

When Eric Trist joined the faculty, the Management Science Center became the Management and Behavioral Science Center to reflect the research perspective he brought to the group. He was also named its chairman. When the new experimental program was formed it was decided to divide the center. The Busch Center was created to provide research opportunities directly related to the academic program. The Management and Behavioral Science Center maintained an informal link with the program; its emphasis was clinical and organization behavior, and work was carried out primarily in not-for-profit and public sector settings. Several students from the Social Systems Sciences program developed research and career agendas based on their experiences in the center. Among these were Burton Cohen and Thomas Gilmore. The group also developed strong ties with Canadian scholars interested in systems planning. One of the most notable is Michel Chevalier.

The Busch Center, on the other hand, emphasized corporate strategic planning and organization design. Thomas Cowan returned to the University of Pennsylvania at this point to become a consultant with the center. He also participated in the academic program providing students with the philosophical and methodological foundations of systems science.

As the academic and research programs grew, Ackoff again sought to expand his notion of system. He realized that corporations and other large organizations existed within complex environments. The social and political environment then became the object of the study for the systems scientist.

In the early 1970s Ackoff began to build strong ties with systems-oriented institutions in other parts of the world. Most notable of these were relationships with Mexican and prerevolutionary Iranian planning and research groups. In both of these instances the groups were interested in development planning on the national as well as on the corporate level. Soon Mexican and Iranian colleagues and students began to work in formal relationships with the Social Systems Sciences department and the Busch Center. Elsa Vergara Finnel's paper on creativity, Jaime Jimenez's on a rural development project, and Raúl Carvajal's theoretical review resulted from their relationships with

Ackoff as a mentor. The contribution by Ali Geranmayeh and Jamshid Gharajedaghi provides general insight into the principles used in systemic development strategies.

The program and center began to attract more foreign nationals. By the mid-1970s it became an international center for systems education and research. Jamshid Gharajedaghi became the director of the Busch Center. Aron Katsenelinboigen, a Soviet economist and systems theorist, joined the faculty. William Smith from Britain and Paramjit Sachdeva from India were also students during this period, and both were employed by the World Bank. Their contributions offer examples of systems principles employed to analyze international organizational settings.

Russell Ackoff's peripatetic career led him to many stimulating settings. A loyal student of Singer's, he integrated or "swept in" diverse theoretical perspectives to build his notion of systems science. However, this volume is not intended to provide an overview of Ackoff's own work. It is intended to show that not only did he learn from his colleagues and students, but he gave generously to them as well. Each piece illustrates how Ackoff's insights have been "swept in" in the Singerian tradition to enrich different areas of theory and practice. They are "messy" in the best sense of the word; each is an attempt to understand the complexity of the world and its problems.

Section I
Russell Ackoff and Anheuser-Busch: The Story of a Model Relationship

The relationship between Ackoff and Anheuser-Busch is probably without parallel in American corporate history. What started as a specific research assignment grew into an all-encompassing collaboration of joint learning and innovation. This relationship encapsulates the essence of what Ackoff's philosophy of learning is all about: relevant knowledge, real-time problem-solving, real-world experimentations, learning from doing, the undivisible marriage between theory and practice.

Two individuals at Anheuser-Busch have played central roles in this long association: August A. Busch III, now chairman and chief executive officer of Anheuser-Busch Companies but a young manager at the time the collaboration began; and Leon Pritzker, a fellow graduate student at the University of Pennsylvania whose lifelong friendship and intellectual kinship with Ackoff were further strengthened when he joined Anheuser-Busch a few years after the relationship started.

The two papers in this section, which they have authored, chronicle the more than thirty years of this association. As a real-life account of Ackoff's ideas in practice, they are an indispensable complement to the conceptual and theoretical discussions of the subsequent sections.

Chapter 1
Russell L. Ackoff and Anheuser-Busch: I. The Influence of the Man on the Organization

August A. Busch III[1]

Introduction

The organization now known as Anheuser-Busch Companies, Inc., traces its history to 1852. It started as a brewer of beer, and although there are significant areas of diversification, brewing remains the primary activity. My great-grandfather, Adolphus Busch, created a tradition of brewing excellence which continues to this day. He also created a tradition of innovation—which may appear to be but has not been, for us, a contradiction in terms—which also continues to this day. He introduced the refrigerated railroad car, which ultimately made the existence of national brewers possible in the United States. He led the advance of bottling technology. He created enormously powerful concepts of sales promotion that identified the house of Anheuser-Busch early on as a marketing innovator.

The tradition of innovation continued over the four generations of leadership of Anheuser-Busch. My father, August A. Busch, Jr., introduced modern methods of statistical quality control to the company. And under his leadership, Russell L. Ackoff started his association with Anheuser-Busch in 1959 and has continued an extraordinarily intensive, productive, and fruitful relationship with the company for more than thirty years.

It should be noted that Anheuser-Busch was a "successful" company at the time the association with Ackoff began. It had regained market share leadership in the brewing industry in the United States in 1957—two years before the association began—and has not lost it

Reprinted with permission from *Systems Practice*, Volume 3, Number 2, 1990. Copyright © 1990 by Plenum Publishing Corporation.

since. Its market share in 1957 was 7.17%, based on sales of 6,116,077 barrels of beer.

In 1988, our beer market share was 41.10%, based on sales of 78,505,877 barrels. Although it is impossible to trace precise causal relationships, it is a straightforward and relatively simple task to show that Ackoff's contribution to this growth was real and considerable. In my view, this statement does not diminish the contribution that literally thousands of people have made to Anheuser-Busch's growth. The entire work force, led by able managers and executives, is responsible for the growth. Yet this growth would not have taken place if we did not have our traditions of quality and innovation, if we had not already achieved a measure of success, and if we did not have Russ Ackoff. (More precisely if we did not have the talents, the insights, and, yes, the argumentative skills that Russ possesses, we would have been missing some key ingredients for our long-term success.)

How the Relationship Started

It may be of some interest to know just how the relationship between Russ Ackoff and Anheuser-Busch started. In 1959, some of Anheuser-Busch's senior executives recognized the need for outside help to develop the marketing function. Television had come of age; the techniques of sales promotion had reached a high level of sophistication. American industry was marching into an era when marketing became the primary corporate function, and Anheuser-Busch wanted to join the parade.

In the view of these executives, a necessary condition for success in marketing was to have adequate capacity. And because the costs of adding capacity were high, there was a need for accurate forecasts of demand. These same executives had also learned about the new discipline of Operations Research (OR) and determined that they would find an OR group both competent and interested in applying that discipline to marketing. Their search ended at the Case Institute of Technology, where there was a group headed by C. West Churchman and Russ Ackoff. However, the terms of the initial engagement were not what these executives had in mind. They wanted help in forecasting. Russ and his colleagues offered rather to help with the decisions that led to the need for a forecast as well as the decisions that would follow from a forecast. This definition was accepted on behalf of Anheuser-Busch, and a thirty-year relationship began.

Russ Ackoff's Contributions: A Summary

Introduction

It would take a lengthy study—far beyond the scope of this paper—to catalog and evaluate the specific contributions made by Russ over a 30-year period. Some occurred, I believe, not because of any specific technical input but rather because of the strength of his character and the force of his personality. It is a credit to us that we were willing to accept an argumentative and sometimes even combative approach to problem-solving. Although there were times when it didn't seem so, both the company and Russ developed as a result of the sharp and intensive way he defended his position—more than occasionally.

Some of the growth of Anheuser-Busch can be traced back to Russ's recommendations regarding corporate structure. He provided the impetus for the establishment of a Corporate Planning Department and he was very instrumental in its staffing. About half of the senior management positions—what we term "policy committee executives"—have been filled by these corporate planners.

Russ developed his ideas about corporate planning while working with us and other companies. We have helped in the development, and we have been a significant beneficiary of the fruits of this development. For us, corporate planning is a continuous, interactive process guided by some rather permanent values and by a vision of what we want Anheuser-Busch to be. We reexamine our values and our vision periodically. This planning process is the keystone of our management process, and a major source of our effectiveness.

Russ has introduced the concept of dialectic into our planning process. Where an issue produces suggested courses of action that are uncertain and risky, we organize teams, each of which is assigned to defend an alternative. Out of the clash of ideas and evidence, we select a course of action—not necessarily any of the alternatives that have been brought forth.

In the succeeding sections of this paper, I present brief accounts of what Russ has contributed in the areas of logistics, marketing—particularly advertising—corporate planning, environmental issues, alcoholism, and corporate organization.

I must add that when I speak of what Russ has contributed, I do not mean to slight the contributions of his colleagues and graduate students. Over the years, Russ has directed perhaps 100 people in teams organized to study specific issues at Anheuser-Busch.

Logistics

Two areas are worthy of mention. The decision as to where to locate the next new brewery was the first problem Russ worked on. Out of this effort has come a linear programming-based transportation model that provides a set of alternative locations. The difficult task of picking the specific site still remains, and Russ has contributed to specific selections.

The keystone of Anheuser-Busch's logistics system is the Requirements Planning/Inventory Programming system. The twenty-five years of continual improvement came from our staff. It has helped us a great deal in making our beer production closer to level throughout the year, despite the large seasonal variation in sales and consumption. This system has given us additional utilization of capacity equivalent to what we would now obtain from two new breweries of average size.

An important element of the system is what Russ described in the 1960s as a "Marketing Early Warning System" (MEWS). As it has evolved today, it is a great deal more than a forecasting system. We track product movement through our three-tier distribution system (brewer–wholesaler–retailer) on a very frequent basis. Some movements are tracked daily. It is a system that permits us not only to react to sudden emergencies but also to be proactive in our distribution planning.

Marketing

In the 1960s, Russ convinced us to experiment with the issue of how much to spend on advertising. We conducted some large-scale experiments that put—in terms of what some of us thought we knew—a considerable part of our market share at risk. We learned a great deal about how much advertising to do as well as how often to do it. We also learned something about the relative effectiveness of various types of media. And in the process, we saved a great deal of money—money that helped us fund some capacity expansion from retained earnings.

In the 1970s Russ turned his attention to the content of our advertising. In collaboration with Fred Emery, Russ developed a theory of beer-drinker types. Field studies determined the proportion of beer drinkers of each type. The pyschological profiles of these types suggested the kind of advertising that might appeal to them most. Effective advertising campaigns continue to be run based on this research.

Corporate Planning

Russ has taught us to differentiate among goals, objectives, and ideals. Our goals are set forth in the annual, five-year-base corporate plan, the first year of which becomes the corporate budget. Our long-term objectives and ideals (very long-term) are defined during planning conferences that occur at least twice a year. Russ has been an active participant in these conferences for a very long time.

Environmental Issues

Russ has helped us greatly in defining the responsibilities of our company to society. One area of concentration for him and for us is that of solid waste disposal in general. We have also focused on the issue of reducing the quantity of litter on our streets and highways. I believe that our company has taken a position of leadership. We have supported research—some of it under the direction of Russ and all of it with his urging—on solid waste disposal. We have had an even more direct role in research on the abatement of litter. There has been a substantial reduction of litter on the highways in the United States over the past twenty years, and I believe that our research that was instrumental in the creation of the "Pitch-In" campaign contributed to the overall reduction of litter.

Alcoholism

Understanding alcoholism and contributing to the reduction in the frequency both of alcoholism itself and of its consequences, particularly automobile accidents, have been significant initiatives for Anheuser-Busch over the past ten years. Russ has led the efforts and has helped us formulate our policies. These policies are summarized in a pledge we made to the American people.

We at Anheuser-Busch pledge:
To continue to expand our efforts to increase awareness among the consumers of our products to the dangers of irresponsible drinking.
To maintain substantial funding for research and treatment programs to address the needs of the chronic abuser.
To support legislative and regulatory proposals that focus on the problem of alcohol abuse, without unfairly penalizing responsible drinkers.
And to uphold the right of the American public to consume our products responsibly.
Irresponsible consumption is a serious problem—but it is a problem that can be addressed through a cooperative effort of the public and private sectors to develop realistic and workable programs.

Corporate Organization

Russ and his colleagues have helped us to formulate our policies concerning corporate organization and corporate organizational behavior. They have urged us to extend the concept of our work force as a "human resource" to be highly valued. They stimulated the introduction of quality-of-work life programs.

Final Note

As the paper has made apparent, Russ has influenced the growth and the development of Anheuser-Busch in many ways. He and I have also had a very close personal relationship. I first met him in my early twenties, when I was learning the business. He has been an advisor, a mentor, and a friend. His influence on my life and on the course of events at Anheuser-Busch has been profound and positive.

Note

1. Anheuser-Busch Companies, Inc., One Busch Place, St. Louis, Missouri, 63118.

Chapter 2
Russell L. Ackoff and Anheuser-Busch: II. The Influence of the Organization on the Man

Leon Pritzker[1]

Introduction

Russ Ackoff was about forty years old when he began his association with Anheuser-Busch in 1959. Thus, in tracing the influence of that association on his intellectual and professional development, one should examine two extremely active and productive periods in his life—the time before the relationship began and the time after. Russ brought a great deal to the party but so did Anheuser-Busch. The consequences for his personal development and for the development of management and systems science and of the practice associated with these disciplines were significant and positive.

Indeed my main purpose in preparing this paper is to encourage someone more qualified than me to undertake a full-scale study of the relationship between Russ and Anheuser-Busch. There are important lessons to be learned not only by management science and systems science practitioners, but also by theoreticians eager to test their models and theories in laboratories that Russ has demonstrated can be established in the "real world." The most important objective of such a full-scale study, however, is to contribute to the ongoing debate of how universities should be organized and how the faculty and students should relate to the world around them.

My background both qualifies me and disqualifies me as the author of this paper. I have been privileged to be a friend and colleague of Russ for forty-three years, encompassing most of the period before and all of the period after the start of the relationship with Anheuser-Busch. I have been an employee of Anheuser-Busch for twenty-two

Reprinted with permission from *Systems Practice*, Volume 3, Number 2, 1990. Copyright © 1990 by Plenum Publishing Corporation.

years. Indeed, it was Russ who introduced me to the company. I have been a coauthor of one of his papers (Ackoff and Pritzker 1951). I have written a chapter for one of his books (Ackoff 1953). He joined me for a brief period at the U.S. Bureau of the Census. I joined his group at the Case Institute for a year. And throughout the years—as Russ will attest—I have been both a severe critic and an ardent admirer. Therefore, let the reader beware.

Intellectual Development Prior to 1951

Although, not surprisingly, one can find changes in Russ Ackoff's system of values and beliefs over a forty-year period, there has been an underlying consistency. Furthermore, these values and beliefs have been—to a surprising degree in retrospect—the foundation of specific research and consulting programs. He has held to them at times with considerable passion, even when it has led to ruptures with colleagues and clients. Russ has not been the model of the cool, aloof, dispassionate, and "objective" scientist. Rather he has been intensely involved in the "messes" and problems with which he has been asked to deal. He has been the model of the committed, partisan investigator. This is a model that he would espouse as necessary and relevant in the arenas in which he has been working.

What were the main components of his value system prior to 1951? My personal association with him suggests the following: (1) a deep appreciation and intuitive understanding of design, structure, and organization in the most general sense of these terms; (2) a conception of the methodology of science that substitutes teleology for reductionism as the road to truth; (3) a conviction that both science and society can be better served by interdisciplinary research; and (4) a conviction that experimentation was not only feasible but also necessary in social science and management science.

Russ received his undergraduate education in architecture from the University of Pennsylvania. I believe that his deep appreciation of design was both a cause and a consequence of this initial vocational choice. I also suspect that his strong adherence to an antireductionist position on issues of scientific methodology had its origins in his growing attachment to design as an underlying, unifying process for most human activities. One sees the primary role that he has given to design in the specific work he did for Anheuser-Busch and in his long-term development as a systems theorist and practitioner, which in turn was influenced by the work at Anheuser-Busch.

Russ abandoned architecture for philosophy, in particular the philosophy of science, at about the time he received his degree in architecture. He became a student of C. West Churchman, who was a disciple of Edgar A. Singer, Jr. Singer, who had been a student of William James and thus nurtured in the philosophy of pragmatism, devoted much of his intellectual life to an effort to make teleology scientifically respectable. Singer called his program "experimentalism." [See, for example, Singer (1959).] The focus of the graduate work was a dissertation written *jointly* by Russ and West Churchman. The dissertation was an effort to establish the foundations of behavioral and social science on the basis of rigorously defined concepts such as "purpose" and "intention." Those early years of graduate study are described in a paper that appeared in this journal (Ackoff 1988). The product of these years is also seen in some of the work Russ did for Anheuser-Busch, which in turn influenced the further development of this approach.

As indicated in the paper that appeared in this journal (Ackoff 1988), the commitment to interdisciplinary research began in the early years at the University of Pennsylvania. An informal organization called the "Institute of Experimental Method" was set up with the program of promoting interdisciplinary research. The distinguished American statistician W. Edwards Deming was one of the members. It did not "get off the ground," but it did influence how Russ went about organizing his professional practice.

The commitment to experimentation grew out of his graduate education, the "Institute," and his very early association with what he regarded as inadequate research practice in the social sciences. The fact that Russ persuaded Anheuser-Busch to underwrite actual, large-scale marketing experiments demonstrates the strength of his convictions and his tenacity in promoting them.

The Early Operations Research Period: 1951–1958

Russ has told the story of how he and West Churchman were introduced to Operations Research (OR) and the Case Institute of Technology in 1951 (Ackoff 1988). They were instrumental in founding the Operations Research Society of America. Along with Leonard Arnoff, they authored the first major textbook on Operations Research (Ackoff et al. 1957). Russ became an outstanding practitioner of Operations Research as applied to business and industry. It is of interest to note that the Operations Research group established by Russ and

West at Case Institute was part of the Systems Research Center, which also contained the Systems Engineering Department headed by Donald Ekman. Russ and West entered the OR arena with a systems orientation based on their philosophical outlook. This was strengthened by the association of the two groups.

Russ and his group had a number of large corporations as clients before Anheuser-Busch came on the scene. As an adjunct to his teaching and writing, Russ began a successful consulting and applied research practice. He developed a modus operandi that had some distinctive features that can only be labeled "Ackovian." (I was privileged to be a member of his group during the academic year 1954–55—a year of great excitement and exhilaration for me.)

Russ used the facilities and resources of his clients to create an amalgam of a clinic and a laboratory. This was used not only for the benefit of his clients but also for the training of his clients' personnel, his graduate students, his colleagues, and himself. As a general rule, he operated only at the highest organizational levels.

There was considerable benefit to Case Institute and to the rapidly growing field of Operations Research from this. Russ and his colleagues produced the first doctorates in Operations Research in the United States. A significant number of books and journal articles authored by members of the group appeared. And, throughout all of this period, Russ remained methodologically oriented rather than technique oriented. He was far more concerned with purposes and objectives and with methods of evaluative inquiry rather than with linear programming, queuing, inventory models, etc.

In the sections that follow, I attempt to associate some major emphases of Russ's professional career by relating them to periods of time in his relationship with Anheuser-Busch. The chronology is very imprecise. Some developments began much earlier; others ended much later. The chronology does, however, capture the essence of Russ's career.

The Early Years with Anheuser-Busch: 1959–1962

Anheuser-Busch engaged Russ on the basis of his background in applied industrial Operations Research. Russ would regard "applied" Operations Research as a redundant term. I have employed it because Russ did become disenchanted and disillusioned with OR in the 1970s. When the *Journal of the Operations Research Society of America* (JORSA) became a vehicle for publishing exercises in intermediate-level mathematics and could not be changed, Russ became disaffected. That disaffection arose because of his basic philosophy regarding science and also, I suspect, because JORSA and a substantial proportion of its constituency were not meeting the needs either of his clients, such as Anheuser-Busch, or society in general.

The period 1959–62 was when the brewery location models and the requirements planning/inventory programming system had their initial development as indicated by August Busch in the preceding paper. During this period, Russ continued to learn and to teach the need for "enlarging the system." One does not locate breweries simply on the basis of minimizing transportation costs. There are a host of other considerations, among them marketing, relations with state and local governments, and labor relations.

The period was one of growing mutual trust and respect that led to the extraordinary thirty-year relationship, which still continues.

Relationship with Anheuser-Busch: 1963–1970

The principal focus of the relationship was on the marketing function. The major research emphases on the quantity and content of advertising have been described in the preceding paper. The impact on Anheuser-Busch was substantial. The influence was also substantial the other way round. A doctoral dissertation on the question of quantity of advertising came out of the research. It was expanded into a significant book on quantitative theories in advertising (Rao 1970).

The work on the content of advertising based on a psychological typology developed by Russ was one of the factors that ultimately led him to reexamine his doctoral dissertation. It was a long and complicated path that involved collaboration with Fred Emery, who was during this period engaged in the study of alcoholism and drinking behavior at the Tavistock Institute of Human Relations. The final outcome was a jointly authored book, *On Purposeful Systems,* which went far, far beyond the research on beer-drinker types, but whose genesis can be traced to the opportunity for collaboration afforded by Anheuser-Busch (Ackoff and Emery 1972).

The research on the quantitative aspects of advertising and on the content side (i.e., the beer-drinker typology) was also summarized in two papers that Russ coauthored (Ackoff and Emshoff 1975). These papers were rewritten by Russ and provided two chapters in his book, *The Art of Problem Solving* (Ackoff 1978). Russ clearly drew upon the Anheuser-Busch experience in formulating his distinction between "mess" and "problem" and in developing his concept of a systems approach to problem solving.

Relationship with Anheuser-Busch: The 1970s

The principal focus shifted from marketing to corporate planning. Russ played an important role in establishing Anheuser-Busch's Corporate Planning Department in 1967. He did make contributions to the design of planning methods and to the content of the plans themselves from that point on. In the 1970s, however, Russ turned to the planning function—*attacked* might be a better word—with his customary intensity. The evolution of his thinking can be seen in the books and articles that he wrote and that were published during the decade. The process actually started before 1970 with *A Concept of Corporate Planning* (Ackoff 1970) and continued with *Redesigning the Future* (Ackoff 1974) and *Creating the Corporate Future* (Ackoff 1981a). These books, and a number of papers on the subject, were influenced by his work at Anheuser-Busch, to be sure, but Russ also drew heavily from his work with other companies and with governments.

The basic ideas that came out of his work on planning, namely, (1) an interactive planning process, and (2) an appropriate organization setting, were also influenced by his increasing involvement with systems science and systems practice. Anheuser-Busch provided some rather generous financial support that was perhaps a necessary condition for Russ to make the move from Operations Research to Management Science to Systems Science. I return to this below.

The 1970s also saw Russ becoming involved with two related, major corporate concerns of Anheuser-Busch, solid waste disposal and litter abatement. As indicated in the preceding paper, Russ helped Anheuser-Busch take a socially responsible position in this area. The company helped establish the rather short-lived National Center for Resource Recovery and was instrumental afterward in establishing a university department dealing with these matters in the School of Engineering at the University of Pennsylvania. Professor I. Zandi, the first National Center Professor, started *The Journal of Resource Management and Technology*. Both the professorship and the journal came about because Russ took a leadership role.

Relationship with Anheuser-Busch: The 1980s

Russ has continued his active interest in both planning and marketing at Anheuser-Busch. However, in terms of the influence of the company on him, two other areas have been more prominent, namely, organization and alcoholism.

Eric Trist, the British social psychologist, was an important influence in the 1960s and 1970s in the development of the knowledge and interest that Russ displayed in the field of organizational behavior. Trist joined Russ in working on some problems at Anheuser-Busch in this area. Out of their collaboration—supported to a large degree by Anheuser-Busch—came further development of the ideas that Russ incorporated in his work with other clients, notably at Alcoa (Ackoff and Deane 1984), and in his writing on systems in which the organizational aspects took on additional importance. The concept of the "lowerarchical" as contrasted to the hierarchical organization is one of the more intriguing developments that came out of this work.

The verdict is not yet in on the work that Russ and his colleagues have been doing in the field of alcoholism. The work is continuing. It has significant implications for public policy and for the prevention and treatment of alcoholism. Russ has, as usual, been an iconoclast. Although there has not yet been any serious effort at paying attention to his work, that will surely come. Our society is becoming sensitized not only to the problems of alcoholism but also to the fact that current remedies are at best inadequate.

Anheuser-Busch's Support

In over thirty years of practice, Russ has compiled a very distinguished list of clients, among which are a significant number of American "Fortune 500" companies as well as large corporations and governmental agencies around the world. The client with whom he has had the most intense, the most extensive in areas of business functions and the most long-continued relationship is Anheuser-Busch Companies. Although in a number of areas outlined above, one can trace a direct connection between his work for Anheuser-Busch and his intellectual development, Anheuser-Busch and its staff cannot take credit for all of it. Russ has always had one foot in academia, and doubtless much came from his reading and his direct association with his colleagues in that arena. Other clients provided opportunities and inputs.

However, the continuity of the clinic/laboratory developed by Russ can be accounted for only by the continuous financial support by Anheuser-Busch. Probably one-fourth to one-third of the support required to maintain the various groups headed by Russ came from Anheuser-Busch.

Furthermore, Anheuser-Busch supported heavily the intellectual and physical migration of Russ and his principal associates from the Operations Research group at the Case Institute to the Statistics and Operations Research Department at the University of Pennsylvania that permitted Russ to take over a preexisting Management Science

Center in 1964. The support continued when a new Management and Behavioral Science Center was created that led in 1969 to the creation of the Busch Center at the University of Pennsylvania. And when in 1971–73, Russ left the Operations Research Department and established the Social Systems Science graduate program, the support and relationship continued with renewed vigor. It continues to this day. When Russ retired as Professor Emeritus in 1986, a large part of his group left the University of Pennsylvania with him and established the Institute for Interactive Management. Just recently, Russ accepted an appointment as a visiting professor in the newly endowed August A. Busch Chair of Management Science at Washington University in St. Louis.

The establishment of the Social Systems Science program at the University of Pennsylvania was a major new initiative in the organization and conduct of graduate education. This development by itself is worthy of a full-length review.

Conclusion

The fundamental factor in the success of the relationship has been the mutual respect that Russ and August A. Busch III have had for each other. The word "synergy" has been much overused and abused in the world of American business. However, it can be used properly to describe the impact of the relationship on the growth and development of both Russ and Anheuser-Busch.

Some new patterns of relationship between scientists and industry are now developing in the United States. Interestingly, these relationships involve scientists not only in university settings but also in Federal institutions, notably the National Institutes of Health. There is a growing, but by no means universal, belief that these arrangements will serve the interests of science as well as of the participants.

On this note, I return to the main purpose of this paper. There is a need to define new systems—new organizational forms and new ways of operating—within universities. The ivory tower continues to be a valid model but is not the only one. An in-depth study of Russ Ackoff's relationship with Anheuser-Busch and his other clients could help satisfy this need.

Note

1. Campbell Taggart, Inc. P.O. Box 660217, Dallas, Texas, 75266.

References

Ackoff, R. L. (1951). "The Methodology of Survey Research" (with Leon Pritzker). *International Journal of Opinion and Attitude Research* 5: 313–34.

———. (1953). *The Design of Social Research.* Chicago: University of Chicago Press.

———. (1957). *Introduction to Operations Research* (with C. W. Churchman and E. L. Arnoff). New York: John Wiley and Sons.

———. (1970). *A Concept of Corporate Planning.* New York: John Wiley and Sons.

———. (1972). *On Purposeful Systems* (with F. E. Emery). Chicago: Aldine-Atherton.

———. (1974). *Redesigning the Future.* New York: John Wiley and Sons.

———. (1975). "Advertising Research at Anheuser-Busch, Inc. (1963–68)" (with James R. Emshoff). *Sloan Management Review* 16 (no. 2): 1–15.

———. (1975). "Advertising Research at Anheuser-Busch, Inc. (1968–74): (with James R. Emshoff). *Sloan Management Review* 16 (no. 3): 1–16.

———. (1978). *The Art of Problem Solving.* New York: John Wiley and Sons.

———. (1981a). *Creating the Corporate Future.* New York: John Wiley and Sons.

———. (1981b). *On Purposeful Systems* (with F. E. Emery). Seaside, Calif.: Intersystems.

———. (1984). "The Revitalization of Alcoa's Tennessee Operations." *National Product Review* (Summer).

———. (1988). "Redesigning the Future: C. W. Churchman." *Systems Practice* 1: 351–56.

Rao, A. G. (1970). *Quantitative Theories in Advertising.* New York: John Wiley and Sons.

Singer, E. A., Jr. (1959). *Experience and Reflection.* Edited by C. W. Churchman. Philadelphia: University of Pennsylvania Press.

Section II
Pragmatism and
Progress: Foundations

The intellectual roots of Russell Ackoff's work can be traced to a distinctly American tradition. He is a product of the pragmatic tradition in philosophy, in particular, a branch of thought that can be traced directly to William James. It was from a student and assistant of James, Edgar Arthur Singer, Jr., that Ackoff was first exposed to what philosophy can and should be. These early studies as an undergraduate and graduate student at the University of Pennsylvania provided the framework that he has devoted his career to developing and improving.

There are certain elements of this tradition that distinguish Ackoff from other systems scientists and philosophers. Through the teaching of Singer, Ackoff became firm in the conviction that the philosopher and scientist should not have the job of simply reflecting upon the world. Instead, he should be working in the world, taking an active part in shaping its destiny. In other words, Ackoff's approach to systems is not to be viewed as a philosophy *of* action, but an application of philosophy *in* action. In using knowledge to change the world, the philosopher also assumes the moral consequences of his or her ideas and actions.

From Ackoff's point of view, then, philosophy becomes an applied discipline. In his own work he has chosen to apply philosophical and scientific methods to the study of social systems, large-scale organizations where human beings play the critical role in their success or failure. He has worked with numerous public and private corporate entities from this pragmatic perspective.

The papers in this section give deeper insight into Ackoff's intellectual roots and trace their subsequent development. Those contributing to this discussion are in a unique position to do so being students and teachers in the intellectual family tree going back to James. First, C. West Churchman, also a student of Singer and Ackoff's mentor and collaborator during his early years, discusses the overall impact of Singer on both his and Ackoff's early work. A later student of Churchman's, Richard O. Mason, discusses the contribution pragmatism has made to systems thinking and practice. In particular, he assesses Singer's notion of progress, of building a future that is better than the past, and its effect on the practitioner. Thomas A. Cowan, a mentor of Churchman and a self-proclaimed "tormentor" of Ackoff, discusses Ackoff's distinct view of the future that emerges from the concept of progress. Finally, Raúl Carvajal, who has studied and worked closely with Ackoff, traces the evolution of his career through a review article. He provides the reader with a detailed annotated bibliography that illuminates how Ackoff's scholarly work is intertwined with his interventions in social systems.

Chapter 3
Analysis of Concepts

C. West Churchman

This paper is an account of how Russ Ackoff and I met and worked together in the 1940s and 1950s, as well as a brief account at the end on how I now react to this earlier work. Of course, this latter part is based on my own opinions, not Russ's, nor do I feel certain that the earlier account is "accurate" historically, since to be in the middle of history does not provide evidence that one's own account will stand the test of other people's reports.

To begin the story, I believe I should go back several decades before I met Russ, to the teachings of an extraordinary professor in the Philosophy Department at the University of Pennsylvania in Philadelphia. His name was Edgar Arthur Singer, Jr. In my opinion, his writings belong among the great contributions to philosophy, not only in America but the world as well. Singer became interested in philosophy after he had worked in engineering and physics and did postdoctoral work at Harvard under William James. He went far beyond James's philosophical analysis of pragmatism, a fact that, I think, is evidenced by a 1900 letter from James to Fullerton, then head of the Philosophy Department at the University of Pennsylvania, recommending the young Singer to become an instructor at Penn. James stated that Singer was one of his best students and that he had placed Singer in charge of one of his advanced seminars.

Singer, around 1900, did go to Penn and taught a course in the "Philosophy of Nature." I have been to the archives at Penn, but in those days the catalogue contained no description of the course contents. Apparently, the Philosophy Department thought that students would easily find out what the course was about, or if they didn't, they shouldn't take the course at all.

I did discover from the old catalogues that around 1920 Singer began a graduate course called "Analysis of Concepts." This course became the basis of Russ's and my lifetime work in the philosophy of systems. Strangely, perhaps, I seem to have the only fairly complete set of notes on the course because there are none in the archives and I don't know how else I should search for additional ones. So I use this opportunity to give a description of it and how it fits into the work that Russ and I did later on. I will place the complete notes (including doodles and side comments to Betty Flower, who shared the experience) in the Penn Archives. My notes begin with 1937, so that Singer had had quite a time to develop the course over the decade and a half since its beginning. By that time, it was a three-year cycle.

The main points of the course were these: (1) what constitutes science of our day, (2) what are the basic concepts of science, (3) how can we use these concepts to increase human knowledge, (4) what is the basic (ethical) value of science, and (5) how can we give an account of progress in science, and especially the aesthetics of human behavior.

Singer began his story with what he called the "dialectic of the schools." He did this by describing the history of epistemology, or the theory of science. It was convenient for him to begin with the seventeenth century, because that was the century when philosophers like Descartes and Locke decided to wipe out dogmatism and begin again from a fresh start, to ask where human knowledge comes from and how it is justified. They did not agree, and their disagreement became two great "schools" of the theory of science.

I can do no better in my description of these two schools than to quote directly from my notes of Singer's course.

> *Rationalist Thesis:* To a sufficiently logical intellect it is possible to establish a law [of nature] without prior knowledge of fact. To no intellect is it possible to establish a fact without prior knowledge of law.

To explain this thesis, one should understand that a "law" of nature is a generalization, e.g., the Keplerian laws of planetary motion, Galileo's law of a freely falling body (constant acceleration), or Newton's law of gravitation. A fact is a statement about the condition (e.g., mass or velocity) of a body at a certain moment of time or place or of its color, size, etc.

Adherents to the rationalist thesis were philosophers like Descartes, Spinoza, and especially Leibniz. Geographically, they lived on the continent of Europe.

The contrasting thesis (antithesis?) was the

> *Empiricist Thesis:* To a sufficiently immediate observer it is possible to establish a fact without prior knowledge of law. To no observer is it possible to establish a law without prior knowledge of fact.

For Singer, the central question of the empiricist thesis was the meaning of "sufficiently immediate" in the thesis statement. John Locke, in his *Essay Concerning Human Understanding*, tried to explain the meaning of the phrase. For him, certain qualities of human experience are simple; others are complex. If I say, "This object appears to me to be red," there is no way I can break down the experience into components, whereas if I say, "This object weighs three pounds," I must give finer details as to how I make such a judgment.

Adherents to the empiricist thesis were Locke, Berkeley, and especially Hume, who pointed out its strong skeptical inferences (e.g., the future, according to the thesis, can never become a "fact," since one can hardly have a "sufficiently immediate" observation of it). But for Singer it was highly questionable whether one could have an immediate observation of anything.

He was not the first to raise this question if "immediate" means "without any presupposition." To explain this historical point, we the students were introduced to another level of philosophical speculation, that of Kant in his *Critique of Pure Reason*.

Critical Thesis: To a sufficiently complete reflection it is possible to establish *some* laws (those which Kant called the *a priori*) without prior knowledge of fact.

To no reflection is it possible to establish *all* laws (including the *a posteriori*) without prior knowledge of fact.

To sufficiently immediate observation it is possible to establish *some* facts (the purely subjective) without prior knowledge of law. To no observer is it possible to establish all facts (including the objective) without prior knowledge of law.

I should point out that none of the philosophers mentioned above ever stated their thesis in the form Singer gave it. Singer's main interest was metrology, the theory of measurement, where the relation between the specific ("fact") and the general ("law") is crucial.

But now we were asked whether these three theses exhausted the possibilities. We also had reached a stage of thinking where criticism appeared to answer the most serious problems of rationalism and empiricism. In criticism, laws gain their validity if they are used to establish facts, and facts become valid to the extent that their validity is partially based on laws and partially on observation. Hume's skepticism disappears because we cannot establish a present fact without presupposing laws that hold into the future.

Everything's going so well, what else can there be? The response is in the form of an uneasiness about the language of these three theses, which uses the word "established." All the theses imply that science is the gradual accumulation of facts and laws, of answers to meaningful questions anyone who wants to can ask.

But suppose I want to go buy a table that will fit into a nook in the living room. I ask "how wide and deep is the nook?" I get a yardstick. It tells me 3 feet, 4¼ inches is the width. Exactly? Well, no. Just about. Are you sure? Well, measure it again. Now it's more like 3 feet, 4⅓ inches. Which is right? The average of the two? Can I ever tell exactly? How important is it to be exact? Suppose all questions of fact have this same character? Surely they do not, for if I ask you what color sweater I am wearing, you reply "green." But exactly what shade of green? You can rudely reply "forget it!" But the same issue has come up for color as arose for length. In addition to responding to a question of fact, we also must respond to a question of exactitude. In the case of the table's width I could have responded "not very wide," but this response would not have helped very much once I got to the furniture store.

It has always been astonishing to me that no other philosopher of Singer's day, or before, ever reflected that a question of fact (or law) required a response to the question of exactitude. For example, if I do use a yardstick, how exact is it? I have seen yardsticks that are quite inexact. How about the observer? There are plenty of people who do not know how to use a yardstick. And so on.

For Singer, and for his many students, another thesis is therefore required, which he called the

> *Experimentalist Thesis:* To no science is it possible to answer any questions of fact so long as any question of law remains unanswered.
>
> To no science is it possible to answer any question of law so long as any question of fact remains unanswered.

The thesis could perhaps be stated in a more dramatic fashion: "The whole of science could be viewed as an attempt to answer one question of fact or law exactly."

In most sciences, exactitude can be measured. In Singer's day this was done by calculating a "probable error," and today by a "confidence interval." In this paper, I am not going to discuss the methods and problems of exactitude, since I and others have already done so. See, for example, *Theory of Experimental Inference* (1948). Nor am I interested in defending the thesis despite the fact that most philosophers—including positivists—either disagree with it or never thought about it. But none of them ever practiced metrology and, hence, never knew the importance of calibration and exactitude in studying the facts of nature.

What I do want to explore is the fantastic implication of the revised version of the experimentalist thesis. If it does take "all of science" to try to answer one fact exactly, then what is "all of science"?

This question became the chief topic of Singer's course on the *Analysis of Concepts*. "All of science" consists of all the basic and derived concepts that can be used to formulate both the questions of fact and law. If one or more basic concepts are omitted, then the progress toward the (unattainable) ideal of exactitude will be forever blocked. For example, suppose we were to say that all questions about human minds are nonsense and that there is no concept of mind. Then we could say nothing meaningful about the observer's mind. But we know, to a degree, that observers do influence the readings that are taken in the attempt to respond to a question of fact. I spent a large part of my intellectual life in applied metrology and found that observers make their readings in significantly and often seriously different ways. Hence, "mind" is a crucial concept for the enterprise of science. But what does it mean?

When Singer began his work on meaning, there were several theories around. Some were reductionist, like Bridgman's operationalism. Some assumed, as had Plato and later Euclid, that the concepts were "in the mind" at birth. Singer decided to accept another rather old theory, that meaning resided in the history of the concept. Specifically, I think, he borrowed an idea from Auguste Comte (1798–1857) who, among other things, set about to classify the sciences. I am not sure that this is an historical "fact," but Singer did follow Comte's principle, namely, that science proceeds in the order of decreasing generality and increasing complexity. So Singer, like Comte, was looking for an exploratory route that would lead him to the land of "all science." He went far beyond Comte on his route because Comte ended his travels in sociology (the design of an ideal society) whereas Singer ended in aesthetics.

But the beginning was clear in both cases. Comte called it "mathematics," but Singer who was really close to Aristotle called it "logic." Among Aristotle's extant writings is the *Analytica Priora*, an account of propositions that are true in the most general sense. For example, consider the proposition "if all the members of class *a* belong to class *b*, and all the members of *b* belong to class *c*, then all the members of *a* belong to *c*." ("Barbara" in classical logic: A(ab) A(bc) implies A(ac).) This proposition is true no matter what the classes *a*, *b*, and *c* represent. Logic, according to Singer, is a science the propositions of which are true for all possible meanings of the terms. I will be coming back to logic at the end of this paper with the suspicion that it is not at all the most general science and is in fact quite complex.

Back to the exploratory trail. Add number to the concepts of logic, which are basically classes and propositions, and we get arithmetic. Singer was never interested in whether number could be defined by logical concepts, or was a "new" concept, a matter that occupied a great deal of attention on the part of his contemporaries, Russell and Whitehead, in *Principia Mathematica*. Here Singer's intuition surpassed that of his contemporaries; the whole question is now irrelevant. The magic of the theory of whole numbers (integers) lies in mathematical induction (if a proposition about numbers $S(x)$ holds for the number 0 or 1, and also if $S(x)$ holds for any number n, it must hold for $n + 1$, then it holds for all numbers). Peano, around 1900, showed how the familiar propositions of addition, subtraction, multiplication, and division follow (with some additional minor assumptions) from the axiom of mathematical induction. I agree with Poincaré and other mathematicians that this is part of the magic of arithmetic, wherever it comes from.

In his course, Singer proceeded to geometry, kinematics, mechanics, and physics-chemistry. Now the world of laws and facts was opening up. Then, much to the surprise of many of us, he introduced "functional" classes. Up to this point, we had been thinking about "morphological" concepts—space, time, and especially the extensions of these into mechanics and physics. Objects obeyed deterministic laws of motion and interaction. If one knew properties like mass, space, and time, one could predict their future, provided other bodies surrounding them were known to have similar properties. As had many physical scientists before, these descriptions constituted all there was to say about "all science." Then Singer introduced a rather obvious class, namely, time-keepers. What is their common morphological structure? Consider a clock, a sundial, a celestial body, or a chemical process of some kind. All can be used for the function of telling time, yet they have no common morphology. Functional classes abound in a world of technology. The laws and facts of functional classes often are expressed in terms of effectiveness in accomplishing certain purposes.

It would require a book or two to describe how Singer carefully defined functional classes and their facts and laws; the interested reader can find a good account in Ackoff and Emery's *On Purposeful Systems* (1981). Singer himself was primarily interested in these classes in order to take the next major step in his route through "all science," namely to analyze the concept of living beings (biology). The attempts to define life go way back in history and occupied a great deal of Singer's attention. In fact, he was still in the midst of his own attempt near the end of his life; see his *Experience and Reflection,* edited by C. W. Churchman (1959). Singer did consider both psychological and sociological concepts that lie beyond the concept of life, as well as the concepts of ethics and aesthetics.

I had a great interest in all of this, especially after I had finished my Ph.D. thesis in symbolic modal logic in 1938. In that year I began teaching a course in modern philosophy at Penn. "Modern," to the Penn Philosophy Department, meant Descartes through Kant, roughly the seventeenth and eighteenth centuries. The manner in which I taught it was largely influenced by Singer's dialectic of the schools, as well as by Henry Bradford Smith's marvelous technique of first making the students into rationalists, then converting them to becoming empiricists, and finally converting them to being criticists.

After I had taught the course a couple of times, a young architecture student enrolled, an unusual event at that time. He (Russ) had one elective in his senior year, and a good friend of his in architecture urged him to take the course. Russ too became "converted"—to philosophy and Singer's version of it. We quickly became friends, and at the end of the course I was urging him to continue his philosophical studies toward a Ph.D. I and others told him about Singer's Analysis of Concepts course, and he and I agreed that the topic would make a marvelous Ph.D. thesis. The architecture department was, of course, outraged by the whole idea but had no way of stopping him.

World War II came along, and Russ went off to the South Pacific while I became a mathematician-statistician at the Frankford Arsenal. But we kept in touch during the war and began outlining the thesis. We decided that our major effort would be devoted to the concepts of psychology and sociology, as well as ethics. We would include Singer's work in logic, arithmetic, etc., but our chief contribution would be on the concepts of the human personality, but of the individual and of the group. I have been using the word "we" in this account, because our relation was not one of the typical thesis supervisor and the candidate but rather of collaboration much like the collaboration of two faculty members. To shorten a long story, the result was a book-length thesis called *Psychologistics* and was presented as a collaborative thesis (which was permissable, at least at that time, at Penn).

We continued our collaboration long after the thesis was completed and worked together on such matters as consumer interest, methodology, and operations research. For the purpose of this article, I should mention that one of our projects was what we called "rounding the circle." This meant, to us, that the Singerian (or Comtean) route turns on itself so that we go from ethics-aesthetics into logic.

The idea that the route of "all science" could be circular did not occur, I think, to Comte, and I do not recall that Singer ever mentioned it. There are suggestions of it in C. S. Peirce, with the point that logic, and especially the "laws" of logic, are social norms, so that the study of logic is a branch of sociology. There are the beginnings of a paradox in this statement, since the "logy" of sociology is based on some sort of logic.

However, I am more interested in the consequences as far as the structure of logic is concerned when logic emerges from social sciences, ethics, and aesthetics. Is it the same logic, for example, that was used to begin the journey through "all science"? I don't remember whether we paid much attention to this question some forty years ago, but I will end this paper by arguing that the emergent logic is quite different from the beginning logic.

I need to discuss one concept that was not included in *Psychologistics,* although it is central in the trilogy of sociology-ethics-aesthetics, and that is "opportunity cost." The concept appears in economics and is central in planning. From the point of view of economics, it means the opportunity cost a decision maker incurs when he or she makes a choice and thereby gives up all other choices. It is usually assumed that the opportunity cost is the value to the decision maker of the best choice he or she gives up. Its ethical meaning is the injustice committed by making a choice and thereby hurting or neglecting people who might have been served by another choice that was given up. Its aesthetic meaning is awesome; in the drama of life we are all cutting off other lives we could have led had we made other choices. Decision making consists of murder after murder of our lost opportunities; the tragedy of freedom consists of our lost opportunities.

Back to logic. It is customary in planning to assume that an organization is made up of parts and subparts. Can we also assume that the parts and subparts are the same as Aristotle's or Boole's classes? Can we assume, for example, that if subpart a belongs to part b, and b is a subpart of c, then a is a subpart of c? It seems almost obvious that this assumption is true, and most planners make it. But in planning we are interested in how the parts and subparts are managed, and management means making decisions. How should the manager of a subpart choose the actions of the subpart? When the manager chooses an action, he or she incurs an opportunity cost. How should this cost be estimated? Let's say the manager wants to purchase a piece of equipment. In doing so, he or she pays a certain number of dollars from the department's budget. The lost opportunity is not just the opportunities the department has to give up, but the whole organization. If some other part has a more desperate need, the manager is not justified in spending the money. Hence, the rational manager of a part has to make a decision about the use of money by the whole organization. (Of course, I am talking about the ideal organization; I am well aware that expenditures in most real organizations are based on politics and not on reason.) The argument given above leads us to say that the part, if rationally managed, must plan for the whole organization and, hence, is not a "part" in the sense of being a member of a class. Class logic in the emergent logic should not be based on the "laws" of the beginning logic.

In fact, part-whole is an inadequate labeling for the rational management of an organization, even though such things as organization charts are frequently used. Many organizations are finding that they must expand their boundaries because interconnections are becoming more and more important. This realization is a kind of explosion. But there is also an implosion, as the so-called part requires the attention of the whole. All this argument might be regarded as a logical defense of "interactive planning" which Russ and others have developed.

No one as yet has formulated the principles of the emergent class logic. We will continue to subdivide organizations into parts, and we will continue to see hierarchies in organizations. But from a rational point of view, these perceptions are illusions, probably very costly illusions.

When we turn our attention to the propositional calculus, and to Aristotle's "laws," the same lessons emerge. We are told by Aristotle that one cannot (should not?) state that A and non-A can both be true. Who, or what government or agency, passed this law? The emergent logic wants to know where, in the journey through "all of science," the authority of the law is to be found. Indeed, Singer, in an article called "Mechanism, Vitalism, Naturalism," had demonstrated that nature could be viewed as completely deterministic and also teleological (where choice is possible). This apparently is a case where A and non-A are both true. Similarly, the geometers of this and the last century wondered whether space obeys Euclidean laws or non-Euclidean, as Einstein wondered whether kinematics and mechanics were Newtonian or non-Newtonian. In each case the response is both. Perhaps in many cases, without knowing it, we have created a new logic of propositions, a logic where the "laws" are open to our own choices, depending on where we are in our decision making. No carpenter or engineer can assume non-Euclidean geometry, no accountant non-Euclidean arithmetic, yet the speculators on the nature of space and number can.

And, of course, the new inventors of arithmetic, those who design computer software, can invent fantastic modern versions of it. In a sense, applied mechanics precedes arithmetic in the area mislabeled "artificial intelligence."

What will happen to ethics in the second round? What is an emergent ethics? Eric Jantsch (1980) suggested that it might be based on evolutionary theory, on a kind of "self organizing" principle, based on Prigogine's work on nonequilibrium systems. I would be more inclined to say that the emergent ethics might be based on the emergent logic, that actions and policies can be both moral and immoral. But that speculation, which is certainly *not* relativism, must be the subject of another paper.

What have I been trying to say in this paper? Certainly not what Russ would regard as very important. But he is not a logician, and I am. What happens to "logic" is, to me, an important issue when one tries to plan. What is the "logic" of planning? Certainly not what Aristotle, and later Boole, Russell, Whitehead, or any contributor to the *Journal of Symbolic Logic* claims. We, as planners, have entered an age of non-Aristotelian, non-Boolean, logic: *not* what can logic, including the class and proposition calculus (and mathematical programming), tell about how planning should be conducted, but rather how should logic be reconstructed to become an aid to planning?

References

Ackoff, R. L., and Emery, F. E. (1981). *On Purposeful Systems*. Seaside, Calif.: Intersystems.

Churchman, C. West. (1948). *Theory of Experimental Inference*. New York: Macmillan.

Jantsch, Eric. (1980). *The Self-Organizing Universe*. New York: Pergamon Press.

Singer, E. A. (1946). "Mechanism, Vitalism, Naturalism." *Philosophy of Science* 13.

———. (1959). *Experience and Reflection*. Edited by C. W. Churchman. Philadelphia: University of Pennsylvania Press.

Chapter 4
The Apostle of Progress

Richard O. Mason

"Philosophers don't bake bread," goes an adage that riles the pragmatist who is likely to counter with, "Bake a loaf of bread and you provide a meal. Teach someone how to bake, and this learning will last a lifetime. Guidance for living a life is clearly a task for the philosopher, and if he or she is to provide sound advice, there had better be a little bread baked occasionally too."

The pragmatist's retort has not been very popular during the last half of the twentieth century. Logical positivism, existentialism, Buddhism, and Zen have been the darlings of the philosophical community. Today, however, we quite desperately need the kind of guidance philosophers, at least since Plato, have provided.

The "global village" is upon us. Telecommunications and television make events happening half a globe away available in our homes within seconds. A complex financial structure means that loan defaults in Brazil or Mexico could bring panic to Americans and ripple their effects through international currency and multinational corporations throughout the world. Nuclear weapons stand poised to destroy us all; just one Poseidon missile possesses more explosive power than all the bombs dropped during World War II. Computers now are capable of replacing our jobs, perhaps our minds. Genetics and bioengineering techniques promise to be expanded more during the next decade than throughout the history of humanity. With this comes the threat of replicating, perhaps replacing, *homo sapiens.*

How are we to think about these contemporary problems? One philosopher, Edgar Arthur Singer, Jr., I argue, provides insights for these and other problems of our "postindustrial," "ideational" age.

It is ironic that Singer would become the philosopher of a modern technological informational age, for in person, he was more a man of the past. A dinner with the Singers, I am told, was a very stiff affair. The meals were served in a formal Victorian manner. There was no small talk, no gossip, and certainly no breaking out the brandy and cigars after dinner for a few jokes and stories. And his classes were conducted in the same manner. Students were expected to read their philosophy in the original, and this meant translating from Greek, German, French, and whatever other language might be required for a scholarly inquiry into the topic at hand. One was expected to come to class prepared and to recite in depth when called on.

This formality of presence, however, belies a vitality of mind. Singer was a student of William James, who regarded him as "the best all-round man for philosophic business whom we have had among our students in the thirty years during which I have given instruction in philosophy here" at Harvard University. James admired in Singer the completeness with which he dealt with all facets of philosophy, and they shared a concern for humanity and the pragmatic conditions under which people must make a life for themselves. They both sought progress. Singer recalls:

> And most of us who in our youth sat at William James' feet were in full sympathy with the master when we heard him say in one of his lectures, "Let the orientalists and pessimists say what they will, the thing of deepest significance in life does seem to be *progress*, or that strange union of reality with ideal novelty which it continues from one moment to another to present." (1948, pp. 8–9)

He was to make this his life's work.

Singer viewed progress as a visionary might, not as an historian. Progress is going some of the "toilsome way toward the conquest we dream of" (1923b, p. 89). It is closing the gap between where you are and where you desire to be which is not necessarily how far you have traveled from whence you started. His measure of performance is clear. *"The measure of man's cooperation with man in the conquest of nature measures progress"* (1923b, p. 89).

This statement summarizes Singer's values. "Cooperation" is the operative word in this description of progress, for Singer's concept of cooperation is quite inclusive. "Conquest," I believe, is used in the classical sense of its Latin roots *com* and *quaerere*, which denote "getting what one seeks." As I will discuss later, the accent is on acquiring the knowledge necessary to achieve one's goals, not on exploiting nature.

A progressive is one who has sought to live life by these values. It is life's highest calling. How and why the progressive's life is to be lived is the task of Singer's philosophy. It begins with a metaphysical assumption about people and their place in the universe.

People's Place in the Universe

Pretend with me for the moment that you are a spaceship and that you are flying through universal space. This space is comprised of an infinite number of infinitesimal points—"atoms," if you please. These points are linked together in an inexorable cause and effect chain that clicks along like a giant machine. Thus the totality of the universe in which you travel is mechanistic and deterministic.

You, however, as a spaceship are comprised of a group of points. This group consists of more than one point and less than the totality, and it has a discernable, logical integration and coherence to it. You and others can identify this entity as a "spaceship." In systems terms, you qua spaceship are a *whole* which in turn is comprised of parts. As a whole you may be more than the sum of your parts, more, for example, than just a collection of a heart, kidneys, arms, legs, and nervous system. This something more that you possess is a necessary condition of Singer's concept of life.

There is something that keeps propelling you as a group of points through space. Singer called this the "pulse," indeed he referred to it as "the pulse of life." This pulse travels in a manner similar to the way a radio signal is transmitted through the atmosphere in the form of a wave. The signal is comprised of elements of the atmosphere, yet it is very distinguishable from it. And so, a radio signal uses the medium of the atmosphere to reach its ultimate destination while at the same time passing freely through it.

You, as a spaceship in the universe, have these same properties. You are a group of points. The group is of the nature of a pulse, and the pulse is defined by its purpose, that is, it is teleological. This means that to some extent you are the captain of your own spaceship, that you make choices, and that you have a free will.

Are these choices without limit? No, but this is partly a function of your mind. If, as I guide my spaceship, I can accomplish my purpose in n situations or "states of the world" the universe may present me with, then n defines the limits of my choice and the capacity of my mind. Suppose someone else can respond effectively in $n + 1$ situations. That person then has a broader capacity of mind and hence is better equipped to deal with the world than I am. Furthermore, if in the course of my travels the world can face me with m situations, then my "requisite variety" for success, to use Ross Ashby's term, is that I possess a repertoire of at least m responses.

It is worthwhile to note here that Singer with this conceptualization has broken through one of philosophy's classic impasses. The universe is mechanistic, yet the individual has a mind and a free will. The two coexist in the same world. There are some things in the universe that function as Aristotle contended. You and I think using concepts. We can reason and we can have intentions and purposes. At the same time, everything in the universe is mechanical, as Democritus contended, and has an independent structure to it. By continuing to use the spaceship metaphor, I hope to show some of the marvelous things that flow from this synthetic concept of purposeful man in a mechanistic universe.

The Definition of Mind

One question that naturally flows from this theory of humanity is "How do we know that minds exist?" Singer's answer was that there must be a "fellow man," that is, another spaceship to observe the behavior of one spaceship. Suppose another spaceship reports that it has traveled 10,000 miles. That is his "idea" about the distance between two points in space. It takes another observing mind to contrast this measurement, compare it with past measurements, check it for probable error, and to adjust it for constant error and bias. No meaning can be attached to this reading unless it can be reflected upon in this manner. It takes two minds to make one mind, that is, *"every experiencing mind presupposes a reflective mind"* (1959, p. 68).

The notion that it takes both an experiencing mind and a reflective mind to establish "facts" is fundamental to Singer's philosophy and the restlessness it projects. We shall return to it again. For now, let us be content to establish that as a spaceship we can experience the outside world through sensation, but we can only turn these experiences into facts by means of reflection, either our own at a later point in time or that of another spaceship. It is this reflective spaceship which ascertains that one spaceship is capable of responding to n situations and another to $n + 1$ situations. Therefore, it is the reflective mind that establishes the faculty of mind.

Ideals

What purposes propel your spaceship through time? A minimal but primary one is "self-preservation." Self-preservation is the ability to adjust and to adapt to the various mechanical situations in the universe.

As a purpose, self-preservation is an "ideal," an end that may be approached increasingly but never fully attained. Ideals, as we will see, are central. They are the destinations in infinity to which each spaceship is directed.

Singer, like Abraham Maslow, believed that there is a hierarchy of needs. The lower needs are for air, water, food, sex, and sleep, as revealed in the couplet: "I ate, drank, slept / and then I ate, drank, and slept again" (1924, p. 70). They must be pursued in order to achieve the good life. Then, although Singer was never as explicit as Maslow about the levels, a person could pursue safety, security, love, belongingness, esteem, and self-actualization. Success for Singer, just as it was for Aristotle, consisted in living a complete, contented, happy life lived in accordance with virtue and attended by an adequate supply of external goods.

Here, however, Singer parts company with the thinkers who have gone before and after him. First, he notes that one eats in order to eat, drink, sleep, and so on again. That is, every individual goal is related to every other goal. Second, individuals pursuing contentment may make radically different choices in what they eat and drink and in general how they conduct their affairs in order to achieve the good life. In modern systems terms, there is an "equifinality" in the pursuit of contentment. Third, and by far the most important, Singer argued that it is not the end—contentment or happiness—which is really desired. Rather it is the *capability* of achieving a set of ends that is desired. Thus, what one really needs is "power." The lesson "learned from a thousand fairy god-mothers" is this: "With only one wish to be had, choose rather the power to get whatever you may come to want than the pleasure of having any dearest thing in the world" (1923b, p. 145).

This is one of the reasons I find the spaceship metaphor so apt. Whenever we leave on a trip what we really want and what we actually have control over is the repertoire of responses at our command that may be used to deal with any of the situations we may encounter en route to our destination. In short, our spaceship needs power. The ideal to be pursued is omnipotence. This is not the acquisitive, materialistic power found in Machiavelli's *The Prince* with the deceitfulness or duplicity it implies. It is rather more in the spirit of Aristotle's notion of virtue:

> Virtue, then, is a state of character concerned with choice, lying in a mean, i.e., the mean relative to us, this being determined by a rational principle, and by that principle by which the man of practical wisdom would determine it. (Book II, Chapter 6, pp. 1106–7)

Singer (1979), however, probes much deeper into the meaning of power and the enabling conditions it implies. These enabling conditions are, in Churchman's words:

1. a richness of means at his disposal—that is, "plenty;"

2. an awareness of the appropriate means to select—that is "knowledge;" and

3. a desire for goals that are consistent with the goals of others—that is "cooperation." (p. 137)

Let us look at each of these factors in turn.

Plenty

In order for a spaceship to progress toward its destination it must have resources. It must have fuel, water, spare parts, etc. The same is true for human beings. In order to live a contented life they must have food, clothing, shelter, money, and all of the other tangible things necessary to achieve a full life. Although he does not say so explicitly, there are indications that a society which has haves and have-nots would be immoral in Singer's view. If an individual does not have the "basic kit" of resources to move toward his or her goals and these resources are available, then the society is unjust, especially in the distributive sense that John Rawls was to develop several decades later. I believe Rawls's notion that economic differences between the haves and the "have-mores" should be justified in terms of the benefits accruing to the least advantaged person would have appealed to Singer because Singer believed deeply that each person required adequate resources in order to live and to pursue the good life.

Knowledge

The need for knowledge is closely tied to Singer's concept of mind. As our spaceship encounters situations, it must respond. As we have seen, the more situations it can successfully respond to and still pursue its purpose, the greater its faculty of mind, and accordingly, the more knowledge it requires. Knowledge has to do with the efficiency of choice, that is, with the ability to relate means to ends so that the most efficient means is selected for achieving one's purpose. Knowledge is the product of science, education, and information systems. It is the information and command center for our spaceship. The design of this information and command center, this ongoing inquiring system, is central to Singer's philosophy. Let me summarize it briefly.

Since the universe in its totality is mechanistic, it is amenable to systematic inquiry. The purpose of science is to collect data and to construct laws that reflect the nature of the universe qua machine. Once a mind knows the nature of this external machine, that is, once it has *reconstructed* its nature, then it also knows how to relate means to ends in order to achieve its purposes.

So far, this looks like a purely analytic task. Science need only continue in a constant series of data collection, theory building, and hypothesis testing, and it will eventually converge on a deterministic truth. This is not so, Singer contends, and his argument contains one of the great insights in modern philosophical thought. The argument flows from his concept of mind although he arrives at it from a detailed examination of the process of measurement.

Let us begin with his conclusion: Truth is an *ideal.* Science can successively approximate it, but science can never fully attain truth. Every empirical measurement then is at best an approximation of the "true" value. Why is that so?

Recall our earlier report that a spaceship had traveled 10,000 miles. Let us probe that reading as Singer might have. This reading was taken by an individual in a certain location, using his own senses and an instrument calibrated to some standard in the context of an environment of changing temperature, humidity, barometric pressure, gravity, stress, light, atmospheric conditions, and an infinity of other conditions.

In the first place, this is just one single observation. It takes another mind to repeat this observation and to check it. And still another mind to check that one. And so on in an infinite regress. Our final reading then, must be the "average" of the observations made. The appropriate statement is that the distance should be taken to be $(10,000 \pm \lambda)$. Lambda (λ) represents the "probable error" in the reading, and it can never be zero. Progress in science is made by adding more controls and more precision so that the number of significant digits in the reading can be increased. The process is infinite. The probable error can be decreased but never eliminated.

Probable error, however, is only one source of error. The distance is $(10,000 \text{ miles} \pm \lambda)$ only *if* the temperature is known, the humidity is known, the barometric pressure is known, and an indefinite number of other conditions are known. If these conditions are not controlled, then there is also a "constant error" or a bias. How might constant error be reduced? Again for an answer we must appeal to another mind. This second mind sets up "standard conditions" that may be used to compare the observations and to adjust them, if necessary. But this too is fraught with difficulties as Singer recounts:

First, they are said to be "arbitrary," which does not mean that they are unmotivated and capricious, but only that they result from a choice. Second, the choice is social, not individual, and constitutes the "universe of discourse" within which the individual judgment is meaningful and true. Third, this choice selects from among several alternative accounts of Nature, each of which presents Nature as a thoroughly determinate process. Finally, no categorical account of Nature, i.e., no image of Nature "in the concrete," can be given which does not embody a series of such choices. (1924, p. 204)

How is progress to be made in the face of this complication of constant error? Singer has an answer. Each mind, each discipline, each point of view operates within its own "universe of discourse" as Augustus de Morgan described it. In order to reduce constant error one must expand the universe of discourse. This is done by an operation called "sweeping-in." The sweeping-in process brings as many variables, laws, and theories as possible to bear on the observation for adjusting it toward its "true value." This means bringing all disciplines—logic, arithmetic, geometry, kinematics, mechanics, physics, biology, psychology, sociology, and ethics—into the universe of discourse. Only by sweeping in an infinite number of perspectives can we hope to eliminate constant error.

Psychology and sociology, it turns out, are fundamental yet they are often ignored in the sweeping-in process. It was William James who in the *Will to Believe* first pointed out that the choices each scientist makes in the conduct of his research have a permanent influence on the results of his inquiry. Singer, in turn, dissected the process of science to show how this was so. Bessel's discovery of the "personal equation," that is, his finding that different observers viewing the same astronomic event arrived at systematically different readings, signaled the first warning that science was indeed a human process. West Churchman's discovery of an "organizational equation" among different units performing metallurgical tests was another decisive piece. Then came Ian Mitroff's study of lunar scientists, *The Subjective Side of Science*. In this study, he showed that participating Apollo project scientists evolved complex psychological, social, and political processes to deal with the data they wrung from the moon rocks. Each of these episodes only serves to make Singer's point: Science is a product of mind. Its "truths" can only be approximated in the limit. In order to make progress toward that limit, one must sweep in all relevant points of view.

In today's pluralist society, Singer's point takes on more force. There are many cultures, many different traditions, many unique psychological styles. If we are to make progress in knowledge, world knowledge, that is, it is imperative that these perspectives be swept into the inquiry process as well.

Another remarkable insight flows from this view of science. Because science can only approximate truth in the limit, it can never irrefutably identify a cause. Since a cause is both a necessary and sufficient condition for an effect to occur, a cause can only reside in the totality of the external universe. Any individual mind can never totally grasp a cause-and-effect relationship. What a mind can grasp, however, is a producer/product relationship. A producer is a necessary but not sufficient condition for a product to occur, just as an acorn is necessary but clearly not sufficient for an oak to grow. Water, soil, protest from squirrels, and a myriad of other things must happen to yield an oak. Sufficiency, therefore, resides in the unattainable totality of the world at large.

The process of production is statistical, however. Science can, and does, establish the *probability* with which a producer yields a specific product. Just as with elementary observations, these probabilities can be estimated with increasing precision—precision in the sense of adding more significant decimal points to the measurement. Since, however, "cause" is an ideal, just as "truth" is, a probability of 1.0 may never be fully attained. It can be approached, however, as the sweeping-in process eliminates probable and constant error.

All this may seem very disquieting for those who, as John Dewey put it, "quest for certainty." What now, pray tell, becomes our criteria for validity? Singer's answer harkens back to his mentor, William James. Science offers us imperatives, not declaratives; it serves up hypotheses, not absolutes. Its statements are really predictions. What they predict is the outcome of possible actions. Consequently, scientific statements should be "put to the test," that is, tested empirically or experimentally. If a statement "works out satisfactorily," that is, if the predicted actions result, then we "cut one more notch" in its "belt" and accept it, pragmatically, until disconfirming evidence appears. This is the deep sense in which "works out satisfactorily" is a criterion for a contingent truth, arrived at by a careful examination of the limits of science. This is not the shallower, more popular, sometimes flippant sense connoted by "If it works, it must be true."

One more implication of the pragmatic criterion of truth needs mentioning. I will return to this point later because it permeates Singer's philosophy. The point is this: "works out satisfactorily" implies the presence of a *worker*. Put otherwise, to bake bread, there must be a baker. Someone must provide the energy and attention necessary to carry out the experiment and must bear the brunt of the experience. There must be an adventuresome spirit among those who seek pragmatic truth. With this goes responsibility and courage. As we will see, a Singerian must also be a "hero."

So far, we have seen to it that our spaceship has an adequate stash of supplies and it has an information command and control system geared to steer it effectively through the vicissitudes of space. Resources and knowledge alone, however, are not enough. One must also have cooperation.

Cooperation

The worst thing that can happen to a spaceship en route to its destination is to crash into another spaceship. Even a well-equipped spaceship can be thwarted in pursuing its goals if during the course of its travels it runs into conflict with other ships pursuing their own goals. As the population of the world gets larger, and as we become more closely linked by politics, economics, and communications, the chances of conflict increase dramatically. In order for each of us to complete our journey, we must learn to cooperate.

Two premises underly the need for cooperation: (1) "every desirous being who wants anything must wish it were more in his power than it is (currently) to get the thing he wants" and (2) "any help a man may look for in fulfillment of this wish must come from man" (1948, p. 20). Thus, in order to achieve my goals, I need the contributions of others, both in terms of the resources they may provide me and the knowledge they introduce into the sweeping-in process. Furthermore, they must remove any barriers they place in the way of the pursuit of my goals.

Now, this may sound very self-serving and egotistic. In Singer's deft hands, however, this need for self-interest unfolds into one of the most compelling calls for social morality ever issued. It stems from his analysis of human beings' relationship to their fellow humans. Let us consider four genre:

1. Him- or herself
2. Contemporaries
3. Forerunners
4. Future generations

One's obligation to oneself is fairly straightforward. One should continue to pursue knowledge, both for oneself and for others. And that occasional unique person, should he or she have the insight or the inclination, "must help himself to any new science humanity can come by" (1948, p. 21).

The strong interdependence among people comes out when we consider relationships with contemporaries. Each person has resources, knowledge, and a path-clearing capacity that may help others. Other philosophers have noted that interdependence with one another gave rise to moral obligations. Jeremy Bentham saw it in terms of a pain and pleasure calculus. Immanuel Kant saw it in terms of a "kingdom of ends" held together by a set of universal laws, or categorical imperatives, as he called them, that each would will for one another. The unfortunate practical result of Kant's prescription, however, is a group linked together by the lowest common denominator of moral value.

Singer too, wanted a "kingdom of ends," but his prescription allows for each person to pursue his or her own ends. We should work toward a progressive community. Communities, Philip Slater reminds us in *Earthwalk* (1974), are different from networks. A network is a mere linkage among people that couples them together around a shared aspect of reality. Scientists, accountants, and the National Rifle Association are linked together in networks. Communities, on the other hand, are comprised of many different people with diverse backgrounds who share their whole lives with one another. Communities are comprised of old people, young people, rich people, poor people, smart people, dumb people, people with different careers, people with different experiences, and most of all, people with different worldviews. The members of communities have a free will and should be able to pursue their own goals. Singer binds the progressive community together with a single law that may be summarized as follows: Each individual should pursue his or her omnipotence in such a way that it furthers the capability of other members of the community to pursue their omnipotence.

This might be called the *mutually enabling* maxim. Few if any communities live by it. So how is it to be actualized? Singer's prescription is practical. The progressive should start at home and then, in ever increasing circles, bring in his or her city, state, company, nation, and finally the world. This will take a long time, perhaps centuries, but the effort is worth it. The reason is that there is something in it, in terms of self-development for the person who does it. It may be, perhaps should be, supplemented with altruism, charity, and love, but fundamentally, mutual enabling is a business deal. Both parties must profit.

Where does this leave those who have gone before us and those who are as yet unborn?

Piety is a matter of choice. We should certainly acknowledge the wisdom and the resources that were pasted onto us by our forebearers.

We must understand, as Jung especially would admonish us, the extended, though mostly unconscious, link that has bound together *Homo sapiens* for the 40,000 years we have existed on earth. Yet we must also challenge the assumption passed on to us in the form of dictum, ritual, and habit. In short, the contributions of people of the past should be evaluated in terms of their contributions to an ongoing progressive community.

We must also pass on the norms of the progressive community to future generations. Here, I extend Singer's argument somewhat. It is conceivable that we could create a progressive community today, one that is just and fair and in which each person is mutually enabling the others to achieve their goals. Indeed, it might be a community of abundance. Yet in order to achieve this abundance, we may, for example, be disposing nuclear waste or depleting natural resources in a way that will prohibit future generations from ever becoming a progressive society. We may create roadblocks so terrible and leave resources and knowledge so inadequate that there is no way that they can exercise their free will, nor is there any way in which they can pursue their fundamental goal of self-preservation. No one has a right to rob a future generation of its opportunity to participate in a progressive community, and this moral obligation goes beyond that of our natural instinct to give love and charity to our children.

Singer's cry for cooperation is vital for today's world. As the world's population gets larger, as technology advances in scope and sophistication, as pollution hovers over us, as military buildups threaten us and as poverty surrounds us, we need a concept of humanity and its place in the universe that will divert us from potential disaster. Each of us, qua spaceship, moves in an ever-tighter and more crowded galaxy. Singer created an ideal that serves to guide us. It is this: every person as well as his or her contemporaries, forebearers, and offspring, must become part of a progressive *civilization*.

So now we have adequate supplies, reliable knowledge, good allies, and a clear path to sail on. That's all we need. Or is it? No! It's too routine, too pat, too dull and boring. In its predictability the pulse of life grows dimmer and dimmer and dimmer. The free will is bridled. Something more is needed.

Art and Inspiration

In order to make progress, the will must have an energy source, and it must be free to define itself and its direction. It must be capable of what John Gardner calls "self-renewal." Self-renewal—that is, the free choice of new ideals to pursue—requires inspiration, motivation, and psychic energy in order to add amplitude to the pulse of life. Where is this source of inspiration to come from? Singer's answer was from art, especially the fine arts.

Art is not synonymous with beauty. Although some art is indeed beautiful, other art is simply hideous. To be art it need only create a feeling response in the beholder. Drawing on Singer's ideas, art might be defined as follows: any object or event introduced into a society and which is essentially irrelevant to the purposes it is currently pursuing.

Because it is not functional, at least to the beholder at the time it is experienced, art, as the saying goes, "disturbs" whereas science "comforts." It is the capacity to disturb us, to reawaken us and to reconsider our purposes that makes art vital to progress.

As Singer saw it, "art is (1) a messenger of discontent, yet, (2) no teacher of new ideals, but rather (3) an inspiration to each it touches, himself to turn creator of a world-more-ideal" (1923b, p. 42). It is important to note that art is disturbing and inspiring but *that it does not tell the beholder what to do*. It provides no answers, only questions. It is the responsibility of the beholder to deal with the feelings art evokes.

Singer hoped that the beholder would become the creator of new ideals and thereby would reenergize the drive for progress. He also sketched out a psychology through which this might happen. Upon perceiving it, there is first a physical response to art. Psychologists call this "arousal." The arousal is evaluated in terms of what Jung called the "feeling function," and from these feelings pour out emotions—fear, joy, anger, love, hate, etc. A piece of art normally generates more than one emotion, and these emotions are often conflicting. The matrix of emotions one experiences at a point in time creates a composite known as a *mood*. Russ Ackoff and Fred Emery (1972) define "mood" as follows: "A mood is a relatively short-lived feeling that includes everything or most things experienced during that period" (p. 105). As Singer had learned from William James, a mood also forms a predisposition to deal with the world in a certain way.

Duke Ellington understood this well when he wrote the jazz classic, "Mood Indigo." A lost lover, a life of despair makes "that feelin' go stealin' down to your shoes," while the slow blues rhythm seeps into your body. Melancholy creeps in. For a moment you reexperience not just your own sadness but also, atavistically, the blues of those who have gone before you. The mood is one of gloom and resignation. The condition is repose. The inclination is to stay where you are.

The mood that most interested Singer, however, was the one which encouraged a person to change, to move on, to redirect his or her course. It is the *heroic* mood, a mood often initiated by the feelings reflected in the saying, "Some people look at what is there and ask, 'Why?' Others look at what is not there and ask, 'Why not?'" For the hero, "Why not?" is such a compelling question that he feels the need to break with his past, to leave the comforts of home and to embark on an unchartered journey. The destination is not clear, but the beckoning is strong. There is a sense of excitement. The pulse of life pounds harder, and the hero ventures forth into the unknown.

The complete journey of the hero, as Joseph Campbell relates it in *The Hero with a Thousand Faces* (1956), includes wandering around, confronting challenges from unfriendly sources, and experiencing, as did Alice in Wonderland, the awesomeness of a new reality. And then there is the bounty. Some heroes never find it. Some such as Dorothy in the *Wizard of Oz* discover that it was really what she had at home all along. Some, having left destitution behind, come upon an enchanted land and they stay. Some, however, and these are the great stories of the ages, find the Golden Fleece or the Golden Goose, and they seek to bring it back to the community from whence they came. This is the most perilous part of the entire journey. It is the problem of reentry. The hero has changed, the community may have changed, and the bounty—be it an idea, a technology, or a new vision—is essentially alien to the intended host. The hero is likely to suffer ridicule and rejection. But the hero must persevere because he or she represents the hope of progress.

Two essential ingredients of civilization flow from the heroic mood. One is the moral spirit; the other is leadership. The moral spirit emerges whenever feelings of indignity well up within a person and must find expression. "That is wrong!" comes the cry, and with it the morally outraged begins on a hero's journey. The past is left behind, and a new social order is sought.

Leadership takes much the same form. The leader has a vision of a new social order, and the leader, as initial hero, implores others to join his or her on this quest, to become heroes themselves. This is both the art and the responsibility of leadership.

"The foxes are ruining the vineyards," proclaims the prophet, a saying that Talmudic scholars have interpreted as meaning, "Our leaders are looking over their shoulders, managing to the past and not leading us toward the future." Or "Our leaders are not heroes; we are not progressing."

The heroic mood is central to Singer's philosophy. It is the driving force that keeps pushing for progress. A spaceship's resources may be sufficient, its knowledge adequate, its community supportive. But it still needs to redirect, reenergize, and recommit itself if it is to continue to progress toward its ideals. Furthermore, and this is the central message of this paper, it is the responsibility of the philosopher to see to it that the tools of progress are fully integrated. The economist is concerned with resources and means. The scientist is concerned with knowledge. The politician or organization theorist is concerned with cooperation. The artist, the moralist, and the visionary are concerned with questioning one's prevailing ideals. Each individual must access these sources, as Singer indicates in his book, *In Search of a Way of Life* (1948). But it is the philosopher who must show the way. The philosopher must both bake bread and educate in the process of baking. This is Singer's legacy for us all.

From those who have taken up his call, the contributions have been substantial. Let us look at a few items on the record.

The Record

Among the following calls philosophers have accepted in the Singerian tradition are:

- They have worked with labor unions in Detroit to help them secure better working conditions.
- They calibrated and rationalized the method of inspecting primers during World War II to help protect infantry soldiers from misfires.
- They founded the first program in operations research so that private and public organizations could apply the scientific method to their problems.
- They helped a railroad improve its billing.
- They helped a brewery manage its affairs.
- They have brought philosophical analysis to the law and brought the law to many who were legally deprived.
- They have helped space scientists understand the micro-legal community that arises in confined societies.
- They helped apply the first artificial intelligence "expert system" to analytic organic chemistry.
- They have worked with a beach town to help people of different socioeconomic groups communicate better and form a community.
- They have worked with drug companies, computer companies, banks, and automobile companies, among others, to help them plan and strategize.

- They have worked with almost every federal agency—NASA, the Census Bureau, Fish and Wildlife, Energy, Forest Service, Health, Education, and Defense, to mention a few—to help bring values and rationality to public policy.
- They have helped bring food to the elderly in California.
- They have helped bring governance to people in Mantua.
- One even gave his life on the plains of Africa to help a forgotten people in their search for a way of life.

While they baked this bread they philosophized. They wrote books, published papers, gave lectures, and taught students in a flurry that would have surprised the little old-fashioned man from Philadelphia. And through his spirit, they have progressed. The theories and concepts, experiments and studies, theorems and methods developed by workers in the Singerian tradition reach far beyond the notions he gave us. Students of Singerians continue the work throughout the world. This is the philosopher's life.

> No life can be better calculated than this to let him who lives it know the best and worst as he goes. . . . And that is all; one thinks these things out as best one can, and that is all. (1948, p. 90)

References

Ackoff, R. L. (1953). *The Design of Social Research*. Chicago: University of Chicago Press.

———. (1962). *Scientific Method: Optimizing Applied Research Decisions*. New York: John Wiley and Sons.

———. (1968). "Toward an Idealized University." *Management Science* 15 (B): 121–31.

———. (1970). *A Concept of Corporate Planning*. New York: John Wiley and Sons.

———. (1972). *On Purposeful Systems* (with Fred E. Emery). Chicago: Aldene-Atherton.

———. (1974). *Redesigning the Future*. New York: John Wiley and Sons.

———. (1978). *The Art of Problem Solving*, New York: John Wiley and Sons.

Campbell, J. (1956). *The Hero with a Thousand Faces*. New York: Meridian Books.

Churchman, C. W. (1948a). "Statistics, Pragmatics and Induction," *Philosophy of Science* 15: 249–68.

———. (1948b). *Theory of Experimental Inference*. New York: The Macmillan Co.

———. (1959). *Measurement: Definition and Theories*. (with P. Ratoosh, Editor) New York: John Wiley and Sons.

———. (1961). *Prediction and Optimal Decision*. Englewood Cliffs, N.J.: Prentice-Hall.

———. (1968a). *Challenge to Reason*. New York: McGraw-Hill.

———. (1968b). *The Systems Approach*. New York: Delacorte Press.

———. (1971). *The Design of Inquiring Systems*. New York: Basic Books.

———. (1976). *World Models—A Dialogue*. Amsterdam: North Holland American Elsevier.

———. (1979). *The Systems Approach and Its Enemies*. New York: Basic Books.

———. (1982). *Thought and Wisdom*. Seaside, Calif.: Intersystems Publications.

Churchman, C. W. and R. L. Ackoff. (1946). *Psychologistics* (mimeographed). Philadelphia: University of Pennsylvania Press.

———. (1950). *Methods of Inquiry*. St. Louis: Educational Publishers.

———. (1955). "Operational Accounting and Operations Research." *The Journal of Accountancy* 99: 33–39.

———. (1957). *Introduction to Operations Research* (with E. Leonard Arnoff). New York: John Wiley and Sons.

Cowan, T. A. (1951a). "A Postulate for Experimental Jurisprudence." *Philosophy of Science* 18 (no. 1; January): 1–15.

———. (1951b). "The Relation of Law to Experimental Social Science." *University of Pennsylvania Law Review*, 99: 484–502.

———. (1963). "Decision Theory in Law, Science and Technology." *Science* 7 (June): 1065–75.

———. (1965). "The Legal Structure of a Confined Microsociety—A Report on the Case of Penthouse II and III." With various authors. Internal Working Paper No. 34, Social Sciences project, Space Sciences Laboratory, University of California, Berkeley (August).

———. (1972). "Paradoxes of Science Administration." *Science* (September): 956–66.

Dewey, J. (1929a). *Experience and Nature*. Chicago: Open Court.

———. (1929b). *The Quest for Certainty*. New York: Macmillan.

James, W. (1890). *The Principles of Psychology*. 2 vols. New York: Henry Holt and Co.

———. (1894) [1979]. *The Will to Believe, and Other Essays in Popular Philosophy*. Reprint. Cambridge: Harvard University Press.

———. (1902). *The Varieties of Religious Experience: A Study in Human Nature*. New York: Longmans, Green and Co.

———. (1907) [1975]. *Pragmatism: A New Name for Some Old Ways of Thinking*. Reprint. Cambridge: Harvard University Press.

———. (1909) [1975]. *The Meaning of Truth. A Sequel to Pragmatism*. Reprint. Cambridge: Harvard University Press.

Mason, R. (1981a). *Challenging Strategic Planning Assumptions* (with Ian I. Mitroff). New York: John Wiley and Sons.

———. (1981b). *Measurement for Management Decisions*. Reading, Mass.: Addison-Wesley.

Mitroff, I. I. (1974). *The Subjective Side of Science*. Amsterdam: Elsevier.

———. (1978). *Methodological Approaches to Social Science* (with Ralph H. Kilmann). San Francisco: Jossey-Bass.

———. (1981). *Creating a Dialectical Social Science* (with Richard O. Mason). Amsterdam: Reidel.

———. (1983). *The 1980 Census: Policymaking Amid Turbulence* (with Richard O. Mason and Vincent P. Barabba). Lexington: Lexington Books.

Singer, E. A. Jr. (1923a). *Modern Thinkers and Present Day Problems*. New York: Henry Holt and Co.

———. (1923b). *On the Contented Life*. New York: Henry Holt and Co.

———. (1924). *Mind as Behavior, and Studies in Empirical Idealism.* Columbus, Ohio: R. G. Adams and Co.

———. (1948). *In Search of a Way of Life.* New York: Columbia University Press.

———. (1959). *Experience and Reflection.* Edited by C. West Churchman. Philadelphia: University of Pennsylvania Press.

Slater, P. (1974). *Earthwalk.* Garden City, N.Y.: Anchor Press/Doubleday.

Chapter 5
A Present of the Future

Thomas A. Cowan

Russ Ackoff has made us a present of the future. Not the future of
the professional futurologists or the econometricians and other crys-
tal gazers who purport to know what fate the years ahead have in
store for us.

Russ's future is occurring right now—while you are reading this
paper. No need to predict it, though there is every reason to examine
it and to make up your mind about what to do with it. We could put
the matter quite neatly by venturing to suggest that Russ has the radical notion that all time is present time. And although he does not
exploit the idea, I am sure that he would accept the dictum of Henry
Bradford Smith (West Churchman's teacher of logic) that "the past is
just as plastic as the future." Hence, past, present, and future are
right here and just now. Seize it, and make something of it. Thus, Russ.

The implications of the position are, of course, both formidable
and venerable. It took many centuries to make out of Heraclitus's
omnipresent flux the great body of learning we now think we possess
on the differences between past, present, and future. This conventional learning is so deep that most of us think we no longer possess
the past and that only a perfected science will enable us to come into
possession of our future.

How this monstrous limitation on human ingenuity came to be so
widely accepted is a very tangled tale. That science, which is supposed
to be indefinitely perfectible and therefore is always "in error," should
be the sole custodian of our reliance on predictability in the future is
quite ironic. What if predictability were only one of the many criteria
by which science judges the worth of its efforts? What if science takes
its own attempts at prediction (statistical control) as nothing that seriously constrains scientific creativity? What, finally, if science were to

admit that what it is doing is remaking Nature? [The way in which Hannah Arendt described its behavior as it appears to a disinterested observer?] Then, if scientists of the hardest-headed variety (physicists, for example) were to admit that what they are doing is remaking Nature, a scientist of a different sort, such as Russell Ackoff, might feel that he or she is well within the best scientific tradition by offering to "re-create" this, that, or another form of organization. Indeed, under the aegis of a relativized conception of time, the past, present, and future are strictly relative conceptions, and the notion of prediction loses all forced association with the future. In this state of affairs, relativized prediction had better change its name. Russ calls it (and its other attendant conditions) an act of creation, and then, in order to sweep in the relativized past, he simply speaks of re-creation (pun intended).

A Philosopher's Philosopher

The ancient mythology of the relation between science and philosophy had philosophy as the Magic Tree, which as it matured, dropped off the separate and separated sciences. One spoke of Natural Philosophy, or the philosophy of Nature—what is now known as astronomy, kinematics, mechanics, physics, and chemistry. There was Political Philosophy, Economic Philosophy, and other more or less organized-ologies (logics). Then the myth degenerated wholly in a welter of diverse philosophies, now called worldviews, and many popular uses of the term "philosophy" by which we are supposed to assume that the speaker has given some thought to his or her discourse however trivial the subject matter.

Philosophers sat in the Magic Tree and watched the sciences mature under their careful tutelage. Of course, this top-down account of philosophy had its counter-image. The ancient Sophists were the Greek representatives of the teaching that philosophy rose from the bottom up. Out of use and wont, the agora and the streets emerged the philosophy that the pros thought they had invented.

Academic philosophy is quite a recent thing. It is usual to imagine that Kant started the business, but in examining this claim, it is necessary to remember that Kant was a scientist and that he had scant respect for those he called "professional thinkers." Still, Kant did give the profession of philosophizing a mighty push forward, and Hegel perfected the game. After Hegel, it seemed that philosophy could develop only from the top down.

Charles Peirce didn't agree. The little *Collegiate* dictionary calls him an "Am. physicist, math., and logician." It doesn't even mention that he also was a philosopher. William James did not agree, nor did Edgar Arthur Singer, Jr., who was heard by his students to say that no one should attempt to be merely a philosopher. To give philosophy substance, one should have a trade of some kind. The implication was that philosophy emerged out of life practice. Jürgen Habermas, leader of the European intellectual avant-garde and inheritor of the Frankfurt School enterprise, disavows being a philosopher, though all the while he is making tons of it. His position is that everyone (doctor, lawyer, and Indian chief) can and should supply philosophy with its authentic materials.

Russ and other students of Singer adopted this view of how philosophy is created. In addition to his prior training in architecture, he pursued the subjects of statistics and operations research as specialist.

Off and on, I've heard Russ claim that he was a philosopher, and just as often, perhaps oftener, I've heard him claim that he wasn't. This contradiction is very easily resolved. After trying it for a while, Russ gave up academic philosophy and devoted himself to making the materials out of which philosophy emerges. This is why, at the heading of this section, I call him a philosopher's philosopher. From social systems sciences, which is largely a result of his inspiration, a good deal of philosophy is churning up.

What is Philosophy à la Russ Ackoff?

The best Greek tradition believed that philosophy arises out of awe and wonder. Hannah Arendt chided Plato in the *Republic* for first saying that philosophy's origin is indeed awe and wonder and then devoting his efforts to making philosophers kings.

A while back, I said to Russ "I'm writing a piece for your festschrift. What do you want to know?" His instant reply was "What's it all about?" This short reply groans with the weight of the whole history of philosophy. Take its words separately.

- "What" engaged not only the ancient Greeks but fascinated medieval philosophers studying *quidditas* ("whatness"), and two millennia of the philosopher's "essences" bear testimony to the lasting (perennial?) quality of that question *what*—a question that is also a thing. James Joyce called it "radiance" in order to show how serious a matter the question-thing is for the artist. It is the shining world itself.
- "Is" is existence. Are there still any existentialists around?
- "It" is the universal designator for each and every object in the universe. Hegel's phenomenology dealt with "it" as "this." The phenomenology is still being debated in avant-garde circles.

· "All": James Joyce is best on this favorite philosophical tidbit and puts the "all" question in straightforward philosophical jargon that answers all questions about "all."

> Wherebejubers in the pancosmic urge the allimmanence of that which Itself is Itself Alone (hear, O hear Caller Errin!) exteriorises on this ourherenow plane in disunited solod, likeward and gushious bodies (science, say!) perilwhitened passionpanting pugnoplangent intuitions of reunited selfdom . . . in the higherdimissional selfless Allself. (*Finnegans Wake* 394.32 et seq.)

Apparently, all the elements of the solid, liquid, and gaseous world lead back in the higher dimensions of philosophy to this precious selfless allself of our own selves. We have Joyce's word for it.

Finally, we come to the real stumbler, "About." Here, I have nothing to say except that I have nothing to say. I do not know what about is about.

In any event, I do think that so many of the technical questions of philosophy in Russ's five-word summation of its deepest problems is first-rate evidence that he is a genuine philosopher whatever else he may think he is, and if you haven't anything to do in the near future, you may well spend some of your time in awe and wonderment at how Russ manages so skillfully to give us a present of it.

Chapter 6
OR, MS, Systems Science, and Russell Ackoff: The Development of Two Paradigms

Raúl Carvajal

In this essay I will trace the development of OR, MS, and Systems Science from 1946 through 1978, as reflected in the publications of Russell L. Ackoff (see Appendix). Five stages of operations research (OR) development are distinguished by emergence, expansion of frontiers, institutionalization, controversy, and separation. The latter stages of OR coincide with the early stages in the development of Systems Science: initial ideas, accumulation of deviants, expansion within OR, and formal launching of Systems Science.

This analysis not only demonstrates Russell Ackoff's particularly relevant role in the emergence and development of the OR and Systems Science paradigms but also attempts to design a general framework for evaluating the impact of a single individual on a science or a body of knowledge. This work falls into the area of the history of science, so much of which is dominated by purely narrative unstructured accounts of the influence of great minds on the course of development of the individual sciences. It should also be of interest for the general subject known as the sociology of knowledge, or sociology of science.

General Framework

To evaluate the impact of a person on a system one must:

- View the evaluation process as a play within a play. The first play refers to the inquiry, and the second one, to the acts of the person and context in which they occur.
- Select the roles and evaluate the person's performance in terms of the roles. A role has an implicit model for behavior that provides

criteria for evaluation. A role implies norms and values, relevant stakeholders and social structure, valid means of influence, and a diffusion process.

• Describe the context, stage, or area and field where the "play" is performed. The same situation can be described in several ways. Objectivity requires an explicit description of the situation.

• Examine the quality of the "dialogue with the situation," meaning the player's understanding of the culture of the system and particular situation in which he or she is involved. A good dialogue implies a comprehension of the free space in which one can negotiate, move, or innovate.

Three general criteria for evaluation are (1) the degree of congruency between the role actually performed and the one expected, (2) the quality of dialogue with the situation, and (3) the creation of a myth-institution. This last point may be the most significant criterion. A paradigm, ideal, or myth changes the way in which people frame their experiences, thinking, and acting. In order to grow and develop, a paradigm requires an institution that nurtures and diffuses it.

Russell Ackoff can be seen through different roles: scientist, educator, consultant, adviser, planner, social reformer, or social philosopher (Carvajal 1983). In this chapter, Ackoff is viewed as a scientist whose principal publications are related to the development of OR and Social Systems Science. The analysis takes as a point of departure a model of the development of a paradigm that has been extensively used in the sociology of science.

Development of an Area

The development of a scientific specialization may be conceptualized as a process with four phases (Figure 6.1). During the first phase, interesting discoveries are made, which become models (paradigms) for future work and which attract scientists to the emerging field. In the second phase, a few highly productive scientists set up priorities for research and hire and train students who become their collaborators (coworkers). These scientists maintain informal communications with other colleagues in the emerging specialty. Their activity produces a period of exponential growth in publications and new results in the field. In the third phase, the research groups proliferate and the specialty wins institutional recognition as an established field. In phase four, the initial ideas are wearing out or have to be strenuously defended because of anomalies which the paradigm is unable to

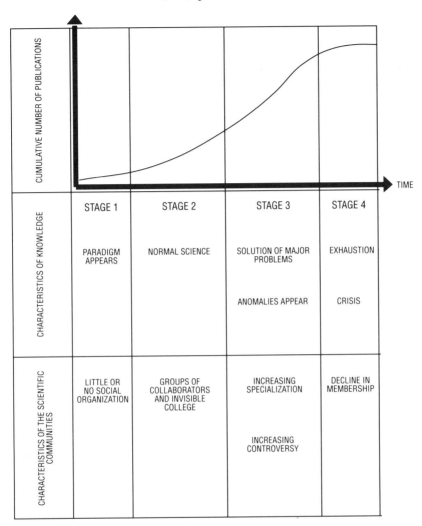

Figure 6.1. Development of a scientific area. From Diana Crane, *Invisible Colleges* (Chicago: University of Chicago Press, 1972; reprinted courtesy of the University of Chicago Press).

explain. This causes fewer scientists to enter, and some scientists to abandon the field. There is a gradual decrease in publications as well as in membership of the field. Those who remain in the area become increasingly specialized, as the possibilities for research are reduced. Theoretical controversies may generate factions. Finally, the appearance of a new paradigm gives rise to new growth (Carvajal and Lomnitz 1981).

Analysis of the Principal Publications of Russell Ackoff between 1946 and 1978

The development of the OR and the Systems Science paradigm is seen through the analysis of 164 publications: 161 in the period 1946–78 and three in 1979–81. The works are classified in eleven themes in Table 6.1.

Russell Ackoff's multifaceted career is revealed through his varied and prolific publications. Even though the major portion of his publications are on Operations Research and Systems Science, other themes were particularly influential in his development (Figure 6.2). The publications can naturally be divided into two groups of themes:

1. Formative and Lateral Themes: architecture, philosophy, methodology, information, marketing, and behavioral and conflict research.
2. Operations Research and Systems Science.

Formative and Lateral Themes

Architecture

Ackoff received a B.A. in architecture in 1941. The two articles in this area are related to philosophy and were published in 1947 and 1949 (5, 14). (Numbers in parentheses refer to the bibliography of Ackoff's publications presented in the appendix; italicized numbers refer to books.)

Philosophy

The main production in philosophy was from 1946 to 1949. In 1947, Ackoff got a Ph.D. in philosophy of science. Of the nine works in this period: two were related to architecture (5, 14), four in philosophy of science (6, 11, 12, 16), and three in philosophy (1, 2, 15).

Ethics (6, 12) and aesthetics (14) appear again later in works dealing with value judgments (91), the social responsibilities of a researcher (116, 138), and social needs and quality of life (112, 145). These themes were integrated into his conception of idealized planning and development. The problems of definition and measurement within

TABLE 6.1. Thematic Classification of the Principal
Publications of Russell Ackoff.

Theme	Number of Publications*
Architecture	2
Philosophy, philosophy of science	14
Methodology, scientific method, measurement, definition	16
Information and control	8
Dissemination of scientific information	5
Marketing	8
Behavioral research	9
Conflict research	7
Statistics	7
Operations research, management sciences	67
Planning, Systems Science	34

*Some works are classified in several themes.

the philosophy of science were developed at a greater length in his works on methodology.

Methodology, Scientific Method, Definition and Measurement

Three periods of activity can be distinguished. In the first period, 1947 to 1950, there are seven works related to the scientific method, methods of inquiry, and definition and measurement (3, 4, 7, 8, 9, 10, 17). Three of the five works were coauthored with C. West Churchman. The definition and measurement of behavioral variables (personality, belief, opinion, attitude) and values appeared throughout these works.

The second period, 1952 to 1954, includes three publications (23, 28, 34).

In the third period, 1961 to 1963, four works were very likely influenced by OR and statistics (78, 81, 83, 86). In 1972 appeared one of the most integrated works in this area coauthored with Fred Emery (127).

Information

Between 1954 and 1957, five works were produced mainly on the relationship of OR and information and control (32, 37, 48, 53, 65). In the period from 1965 to 1967, the dependence on OR was reduced

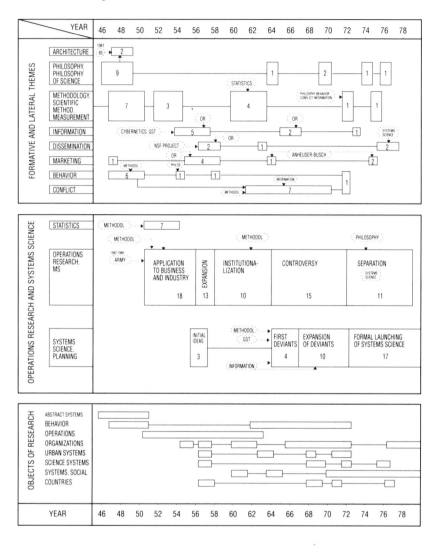

Figure 6.2. Analysis by theme of the principal publications of Ackoff. The numbers in squares indicate the quantity of works.

(94). This included an article critical of the ongoing trend in management information systems (102). In 1973 appeared a work critical of computer education (132).

As a result of a study made on behalf of the National Science Foundation, three works on the dissemination and use of scientific information were produced between 1957 and 1963 (63, 70, 84). Enriched by the concept of idealization, these works led in 1976 and 1977 to the SCATT (Scientific Communications and Technology Transfer) project.

Marketing

Interest in marketing can be traced as early as 1947 (4). Between 1955 and 1964, five works were produced (41, 45, 54, 69, 90). Work done at Anheuser-Busch between 1963 and 1964 was published in 1975 (140, 144).

Behavioral and Conflict Research

Between 1947 and 1954, there were seven publications on measuring psychological characteristics and values: personality, belief, opinion, attitude, and consumer interest (3, 4, 7, 8, 10, 18, 34). This work was partially integrated in 1958 in a behavioral theory of communication (68).

Works on conflict research were produced between 1962 and 1970 (83, 86, 92, 100, 101, 109, 115). The works on behavioral and conflict research were integrated in 1972 in the book *On Purposeful Systems* (127).

Operations Research and Systems Science

Operations Research, Statistics, and Management Science

Between 1951 and 1979, Ackoff published sixty-six articles in OR and MS, and seven in statistics. Five stages can be distinguished based on the orientation of the works.

1. *Emergence of the paradigm* (1951 to 1955): Certainly Russell Ackoff's Army career (1942–46) influenced his early work in this area. Since OR was initially developed for military use, civilian applications provided an open field for expansion. From 1951 to 1954, seven works on statistics were produced: two related to OR and five to methodology, survey research, and experimental design (19, 21, 24, 25, 30, 33, 36). This period influenced the later work on methodology. From 1951 to 1955, there were eighteen works in OR (20, 22, 24, 26, 27, 29, 31, 32, 35–40, 42–44, 46). Some of these works focused on the use of OR in business and industry (22, 29, 40), operational accounting (38), the use of statistics in OR (24, 36), and production

scheduling (27, 31, 39). The only expansion theme for OR was information (32).

2. *Expansion of Frontiers and Reflections on OR* (1956 to 1957): In the thirteen works produced in this stage (48, 49, 51–53, 55, 57–59, 61, 62, 64, 65), several new themes were proposed for expanding OR: data processing (48), planning (52, 61), control and decision making (53, 65), and urban services (64). A reflection process on the effectiveness of OR started by surveys (44, 49) and a comparison with other countries (59). An article and a book dealing with the institutionalization of OR appeared at this time (57, 58).

3. *Institutionalization, Further Expansion, and Initial Controversy* (1958 to 1963): In this stage ten works can be included (66, 70, 71, 73, 74, 77, 78, 80, 82, 85). Several articles and two books dealt with the institutionalization of OR (71, 77, 78, 80, 85). The expansion of OR to new areas continued in this stage, e.g., the study of the dissemination of scientific information (70). An early influence may have come from general systems theory, especially in those works related to information and systems. It may be reflected in the paper "Games, Decisions, and Organizations" (73). The expansion that brought a negative reaction was "Operations Research and National Planning" (66). The concept of planning was difficult to assimilate in OR. There were also some critical works dealing with unsuccessful case studies and unsolved problems in OR (74, 82). In these articles one can see the beginning of the controversy with traditional OR.

4. *Open Controversy, and Further Intention of Expansion of the OR Frontiers* (1964 to 1971): Fifteen works are found in this stage (89, 90, 93, 95–97, 103, 104, 106, 108, 114, 118, 120, 121, 125c). The works on the institutionalization of OR continue, including the book *Fundamentals of Operations Research* (104, 106). There are more critical works stating the limitations of OR (89, 96, 114, 120, 121).

The intention of expanding OR to new frontiers also continued, especially in relation to planning, urban systems, and management systems (93, 95, 108). There was an intent to expand the subject matter beyond the traditional ones included in OR (103, 125).

5. *Separation* (1972 to present): There are eleven works from 1972 to 1979 (125b, 130, 135, 138, 141, 142, 148–50, 160, 161). In the first two stages there was an effort to expand OR to new areas and broader subject matters. This effort started a controversy that grew in the fourth stage. At the end of the fourth stage, Ackoff made a strong stand to change the direction of MS. This effort is clearly illustrated in his "Open Letter to TIMS Members" (125b). Ackoff, when nominated as candidate for President of TIMS, chose to run on a platform rather than personality. He proposed to change the name of

The Institute of Management Sciences to the Institute of Systems Sciences.

> The terms "management science" and "operations research" are used interchangeably by most, and many of us who are members of both societies see no significant difference between them. For this reason I long sought their merger, but recently gave up any hope of accomplishing it.
>
> I have formulated an alternative to merger that I now prefer. It is presented here briefly as my "platform."
>
> Up until approximately World War II, science, in keeping with the reductionist philosophy and analytical mode of thought that dominated it, was preoccupied with decomposing everything including itself. It divided itself continuously into smaller and smaller disciplines. The disciplines were bounded by fine lines that were drawn with great care. A discipline-oriented loyalty ethic developed and scientists showed little interest in what was happening in even their neighboring disciplines.
>
> Since World War II, science, in keeping with an emerging holistic philosophy and synthesizing mode of thought, has been preoccupied with putting its parts back together again in systems-oriented interdisciplines. In the last few decades we have witnessed the development of operations research, the management sciences, cybernetics, the communications sciences, the policy sciences, the behavioral sciences, systems analysis, systems engineering, information systems, general systems, and many other interdisciplinary systems sciences. These interdisciplines are not preoccupied with drawing and maintaining boundaries, but with crossing them and, if anything, maximizing overlap. Most of those who identify with any one of these interdisciplines participate freely in, and identify with, one or more of the others. Such spill-overs have been fruitful for the development of each field taken separately and for the development of the systems sciences taken collectively.
>
> This synthesizing process can and should be facilitated by the creation of a society that provides a meeting ground for all systems-oriented science-based interdisciplines; a society in which thinking and discussion can flow freely across evanescent boundaries and thus facilitate generalization of every aspect of the basic and applied systems sciences.
>
> For this reason I propose *that TIMS transforms itself into the Institute of Systems Sciences.*

The platform was a clear statement of what "systems science" was to become in the future: a new paradigm (130, 142, 161). As has been shown in sociology of science, a change of paradigm entails a break with traditions. It cannot be accomplished by the same people who are immersed in the old paradigm. Even though it was a courageous move on Ackoff's part, it did not have a chance of succeeding.

> A memorandum to you of April 20, 1972, from Peter V. Norden and Sidney W. Hess on Change of Slate for TIMS 1972 Election stated, Russell L. Ackoff, nominated as a candidate for the Office of President Elect of TIMS for the 1972–73 term . . . has withdrawn his candidacy for personal

reasons. This is not true. But I can understand the reasons for explaining my withdrawal in this way. It puts the matter to rest. I withdrew because the officers of TIMS would not permit circulation of my platform for office with the ballot. (125b)

After 1972, criticism of OR and MS grew openly stronger (138, 141, 148, 149, 150, 160). Nevertheless, he always kept his hope of redirecting OR toward a more fruitful development. After a vigorous critique, "The Future of OR Is Past," he proposed again systems science as a solution in "Resurrecting the Future of OR" (160, 161).

In 1974 the article on OR for the *Encyclopaedia Britannica* appeared as the last work toward the institutionalization of OR (135). This article was written and published as a University of Pennsylvania report in 1970.

Planning and Systems Science

The initial mention of planning was made in 1956 and 1957 in three articles (50, 52, 61).

Accumulation of Deviants (1964–66): Systems Science was first named in 1964 in an article that appeared in *General Systems:* "General Systems Theory and Systems Research: Contrasting Conceptions of Systems Science" (88). Planning continued in 1964 as an expansion theme of OR (93) but received a separate treatment in 1965: "The Meaning of Strategic Planning" (98).

Expansion of Deviants (1967–71): The formal transition from OR to systems sciences most probably started in 1967. The ten works produced between 1968 and 1971 set a new direction. Some of these works were still based in OR but dealt with larger systems (103, 108, 119, 125). Planning and idealization were present in some works (105, 110, 120, 124). Planning was a common concept in economics at a national macro level. Application of planning to corporations was an expansion of the concept (113, 117).

The year 1972 can be taken as the formal launching of social systems sciences. Between 1972 and 1978, there were seventeen works, the main core in systems science (125a, 128, 130, 133, 134, 136, 139, 142, 143, 156, 159, 161). Two works dealt with urban services and developing countries (129, 151). Organizations and corporations were named in two works (154, 162). Even though until 1971 planning was a dominating concept in systems, after 1972, planning was embedded as a problem-solving instrument within Systems Science.

General Comments and Conclusions

General Comments on Ackoff's Main Publications

An analysis of the principal publications of Russell Ackoff shows several themes and influences.

Philosophy and philosophy of science had a definite influence in methodology and scientific method as well as planning and Systems Science. Methodology, scientific method, measurement, and definition influenced most areas: statistics, operations research, planning and Systems Science, behavioral research, and conflict research.

Ackoff continuously tried to expand the frontiers of OR, since the first works in 1951. At first, the expansion was from military to industrial and business applications. Then the expansion touched themes or objects of research that were more difficult or impossible to assimilate within OR. An unsuccessful effort to expand OR in terms of systems science led to the proposal of changing TIMS to the Institute of Systems Sciences. After this trial, the separation from OR was imminent.

Initial ideas of planning and systems science appeared fifteen years before the formal launching of systems science in 1972. The coexistence period of systems science and OR lasted eight years, from 1964 to 1971. Some works dealing with the emerging systems science appeared during this period (Churchman 1968 and 1971, Checkland 1971, Emery 1969, Jenkins 1969). Information and control may have been initially influenced by cybernetics but later were related to OR and integrated into systems science. A National Science Foundation project in 1957 lead to the SCATT project in 1976.

Interest in marketing was present since 1947. It may have been influenced by the work on methodology, OR, and statistics. The Anheuser-Busch project helped sustain interest in this theme through these years. Behavioral research was present at the outset as an application of methodology and scientific method. It led to two integrative works: one on a behavioral theory of communication in 1958 and the comprehensive work *On Purposeful Systems* in 1972. This work together with the conflict research influenced planning and systems science.

Object of Research

The object of study evolved from abstract systems and behavior to concrete systems. Operations were of key interest from 1952 to 1959. From 1955 the object of research became more and more complex, from organizations to urban systems, scientific and educational systems, and social systems (see Figure 6.2).

Abstract philosophical systems were the main object of research during the years when philosophy was the dominating theme, 1946–51 (1, 2, 6, 9, 11, 12, 15–17). Abstract mathematical systems were also an object of research (19, 21, 25).

Behavior was an object of research as an application of the research on measurement beginning in 1947 (3, 4, 7, 8, 10). In later years, the study of behavioral variables, such as choice behavior, conflict, cooperation, values, and collective behavior, continued (83, 86, 92, 100, 101, 109, 115).

Operations as a part of an organization was an object of research mainly during the first three stages of OR (20, 22, 26, 27, 29, 31, 35, 37–39, 40, 42, 44, 49, 57–59, 74, 77, 80, 85). Marketing, as one type of operation, was also an object of research (41, 45, 54, 69, 90, 140, 144).

Between 1954 and 1959, there was some mention about *organizations and corporations* (32, 52). Organizations in a general system theory context were treated between 1959 and 1961, e.g., "Games, Decisions, and Organizations" and "Systems, Organizations, and Interdisciplinary Research" (73, 76, 79). After 1965, organizations and corporations appeared related to planning and conflict research (101, 105, 113, 117, 126, 149, 154, 162).

Between 1957 and 1969, *urban services and systems* was an expansion theme of OR: "Applications of OR to Improved Utilization of Motor Power," "Planning, OR, and Metropolitan Systems," and "Strategies for OR in Urban Metropolitan Planning" (64, 93, 108). In 1963, urban services was an object of research in relation to methodology in the article "Toward Quantitative Evaluation of Urban Services" (87). Between 1970 and 1972, urban systems were treated in relation to planning and systems: "A Black Ghetto's Research on a University," "Possible and Likely Futures of Urban Transportation," and "A Systems Approach to the Problems of Solid Waste and Litter" (119, 123, 129).

Scientific and educational systems as an object of study appeared first in 1957 in "Report on a Study of Scientific Communication for the National Science Foundation" (63). It was an expansion theme of OR in 1968 in "OR and National Science Policy." Both appeared in a later period in relation to planning and systems science: "Toward Strategic Planning of Education," "Educational Systems," and the SCATT project (110, 131, 147, 152).

Systems appeared in 1960, influenced by general systems theory: "Systems, Organizations, and Interdisciplinary Research," "General Systems Theory and Systems Research," "Contrasting Conceptions of Systems Science" (76, 79, 88). As a specific object of study it appeared in 1970 related to Systems Science and planning (122, 124, 125a, 127, 128, 130, 133, 134, 136, 137, 139, 142, 143, 148, 156, 161).

Countries, an expansion theme of OR, began in 1956: "OR and National Planning" (61). Between 1968 and 1971, this theme continued to be developed in relation to OR: "OR and National Science Policy," "The Role of Research in Underdeveloped Countries," "Institutional Functions and Societal Needs," and "OR and Developing Countries" (103, 107, 112, 125). A reference to planning was made in 1977 in "National Development Planning Revisited" (151).

Countries, as an object of research, are likely to be too complex for OR and systems science. The initial controversy began within OR in 1956 with the paper "OR and National Planning," and continued to develop at a later time as seen in "Some Observations and Reflections on Mexican Development" (unpublished draft in 1976), "National Development Planning Revisited" (151), and "Some Further Reflections on Mexico" (Social Systems Sciences Paper published in 1980). Even though these works brought some criticism, they did not trigger a major reaction.

OR and Systems Science Paradigm Development

The "conscious" history of OR can be located between 1937 and 1945 in the military sector. Its rapid postwar development began with the applications to business and industry. The evolution of OR and Systems Science can be followed through the works of Russell Ackoff (Tables 6.2 and 6.3).

In the emergence phase, 1951 to 1955, the publications were directed toward the diffusion of OR and its applications to business and industry. Most of the expansion themes led to the development of OR. The main object of research was operations. The main coauthors in this phase were J. E. Townsend and C. West Churchman.

The expansion phase of OR is characterized by some works on the institutionalization of OR, proliferation of expansion themes, and some surveys and comparisons that may have started a reflection process. The expansion themes started to lead toward Systems Science. Among the objects of research that appeared in this phase were organizations, urban systems, and nation. The principal coauthors were C. West Churchman, E. L. Arnoff, and M. W. Sasieni. This phase coincides with the initial ideas in Systems Science development, when the planning theme appeared, as illustrated by Ackoff's article written with Walter G. Glover (50).

The institutionalization phase of OR, 1958 to 1963, saw continued expansion and some initial criticism. The themes continued leading

TABLE 6.2. OR Development in Ackoff's Works.

	Emergence of OR (1951–55)	Expansion of frontiers (1956–57)	Institutionalization (1958–63)	Controversy (1964–71)	Separation (1972–79)
Characteristics					
	Application of OR to business and industry	Institutionalization; expansion; reflection (surveys, comparisons)	Institutionalization; expansion; early criticism	Institutionalization; expansion; controversy	Institutionalization; criticism Systems Science
Expansion themes leading toward:					
OR	Survey research; experimental design; operational accounting; scheduling; inventory	Data processing			
OR and SS		Information	Information; decision making	Dissemination of scientific information; decision making	
SS		Control; planning	Planning	Science policy; planning	
Expansion objects of research leading toward:					
OR	Operations in business and industry				
OR and SS		Organizations; urban services	Organizations		
SS		Nations	Nations	Urban systems; science systems; social systems; developing countries	

TABLE 6.3. Development of Systems Science in Ackoff's Works.

Characteristics	Initial ideas (1956–57)	Accumulation of deviant themes (1964–66)	Expansion of deviant themes (1967–71)	Formal launching of Systems Science (1972–present)
	Planning theme appears	Planning works increase; Systems Science theme appears	Expansion of planning to larger and more complex objects; Systems Science continues to grow	Systems Science is formally launched; planning is embedded as a tool of systems science
Origin of influence themes				
OR	Information; decision making; control; planning	Systems theory; planning	Decision making; control; science policy; planning	
GST		Systems Science		
Other	Planning			
Work in Systems Science		Strategic planning	Idealization; planning; strategic planning	Systems science; idealization; humanization; planning; dissemination of scientific information
Origin of influence on objects of research				
OR	Organizations; urban services; nations	Urban systems	Organizations; science system; urban systems; developing countries	Urban systems; systems; social systems; organizations
GST		Systems		
Other			Educational systems	
Work in Systems Science			Social systems	

toward OR and systems science. The objects of research included organizations and nations. The main coauthors in this phase were E. L. Arnoff and B. H. P. Rivett.

From 1964 to 1971, during the controversial phase, one sees a proliferation of critical works. The expansion themes were leading mainly toward systems science. The objects of research were difficult to tackle within OR, they were proper themes of systems science: urban systems, scientific and educational systems, social systems, and developing countries. Among the principal coauthors were M. W. Sasieni and Britton Harris. This phase coincides with the phases of accumulation and expansion of deviant themes in Systems Science development. In the accumulation of deviants phase, the planning works continued and systems science appeared. Themes from OR and general systems theory (GST) appeared: planning, systems theory, Systems Science, and strategic planning. Objects of research such as urban systems and social systems, came from OR and GST.

From 1967 to 1971, during the expansion of deviants phase of Systems Science, idealization and strategic planning themes continued growing together with other themes that were linked to OR: decision making, control, and science policy. The objects of research were larger and more complex systems. The main coauthors in this phase were Britton Harris and S. S. Sengupta.

The separation phase of OR, after 1972, was characterized by a predominance of publications critical of OR. It marked the formal launching of systems science. Planning was embedded as a tool of systems science. The themes were characteristic of systems sciences as well as the objects of research. The analysis of the cumulative publications of Russell Ackoff shows the coincidence between the controversial phase in OR with the initiation of the new systems science paradigm (Figure 6.3).

Conclusion

The work of Ackoff illustrates the development of OR and the emergence of Systems Science. It is likely that four branches started from OR between 1971 and 1972:

1. Systems Science.
2. Practical applications (Interfaces started in 1971).
3. Mathematical orientation (The Mathematical Programming Society was founded in 1971).
4. "Normal" Operations Research.

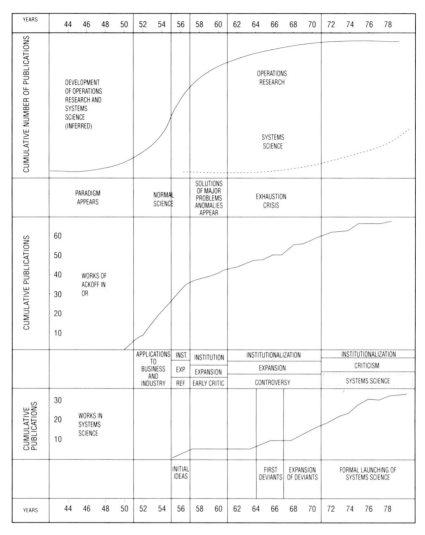

Figure 6.3. Development of OR and Systems Science derived from Ackoff's works.

In "The Impact of a Social Systems Scientist on a Country" (Carvajal 1983) it is stated that an evaluation process can be viewed as a play within a play. The selection of the role under which a person is seen conditions a great deal of the outcome. Imbedded in each role are criteria for evaluation that define the relevant stakeholders, diffusion process, social structure, and means of influence. A strong criterion of evaluation of impact is the degree of participation of a person in the development of a myth-institution. A paradigm, ideal, or myth powerful enough to change the way in which people frame their experiences, think, and act requires an institution that nurtures and diffuses it.

As a scientist Ackoff fullfils this criterion for impact. He played a key role in creating both paradigms and the institutions that supported the social systems science paradigm: the Social Systems Science Department of the Wharton School of Business and the Busch Center at the University of Pennsylvania.

References

Carvajal, R. (1983). "The Impact of a Social Systems Scientist on a Country." *Omega* 11 (6): 559–65.

Carvajal, R., and L. Lomnitz (1981). "El Desarrollo Científico de México: ¿Es posible multiplicarlo con los mismos recursos?" *Ciencia y Desarrollo* 7 (37).

Checkland, P. B. (1971). "A Systems Map of the Universe." *Journal of Systems Engineering* 2 (2).

Churchman, C. W. (1968). *The Systems Approach.* New York: Dell Publishing Co.
———. (1971). *The Design of Inquiring Systems.* New York: Basic Books.

Crane, D. (1972). *Invisible Colleges* (Chicago and London: University of Chicago Press.)

Emery, F. E. (ed.) (1969). *Systems Thinking.* Harmondsworth, Middlesex: Penguin.

Jenkins, G. M. (1969). "The Systems Approach." *Journal of Systems Engineering* 1 (1).

Appendix:
Principal Publications of Russell L. Ackoff

Asterisks indicate works co-authored with C. West Churchman.

1. "Towards an Interpretation of Contemporary Philosophy." *Philosophy of Science* 13 (1946): 131–36.
2. "Varieties of Unification." *Philosophy of Science* 13 (1946): 287–300.
3. "Towards an Experimental Measure of Personality." *Psychological Review* 54 (1947): 41–51.
4. *Measurement of Consumer Interest.* Ed. with C. W. Churchman and M. Wax. Philadelphia: University of Pennsylvania Press, 1947.
5. "Mr. Rieser on Architecture." *Philosophical Review* 56 (1947): 690–94.
6. "Ethics and Science." *Philosophy of Science* 14 (1947): 269–71.

7. *Psychologistics* (mimeographed). Philadelphia, University of Pennsylvania Faculty Research Fund, 1947.*

8. "An Experimental Definition of Personality." *Philosophy of Science* 14 (1947): 304–32.*

9. "Scientific Method." *American Peoples' Encyclopedia*, 1948.*

10. "Definitional Models for Belief, Opinion, and Attitude." *International Journal of Opinion and Attitude Research* 2 (1948): 151–68.

11. "Discussions: Symposium on Contributions of Social Science to Physical Sciences." *Philosophy of Science* 15 (1948): 116–17.

12. "On a Science of Ethics." *Philosophy and Phenomenological Research* 9 (1949): 663–72.

13. "The Missing Link—A Post-Mortem." *International Journal of Opinion and Attitude Research* 2 (1948–49): 489–93.

14. "Aesthetics of 20th Century Architecture." *1948 Convention Seminars*, American Institute of Architects, 1949, pp. 4–11.

15. "The Democratization of Philosophy." *Science and Society*, 13 (1949): 327–39.*

16. "An Educational Program in the Philosophy of Science." *Philosophy of Science* 16 (1949): 154–57.

17. *Methods of Inquiry*. St. Louis: Educational Publishers, 1950.*

18. "Purposive Behavior and Cybernetics." *Social Forces* 29 (1950): 32–39.*

19. "The Methodology of Survey Research." With Leon Pritzker. *International Journal of Opinion and Attitude Research* 5 (1951): 313–34.

20. "Principles of Operations Research." *Proceedings of the First Seminar in Operations Research*. Cleveland: Case Institute of Technology, 1951, pp. 8–16.

21. "Methodology and Mathematical Statistics and Their Applications in Research." *Proceedings of the Second Annual Conference on Industrial Research*. New York: Kings Crown Press, 1951, pp. 78–93.

22. "Operations Research in Business and Industry." *Industrial Quality Control* 8 (1952): 41ff.

23. "Scientific Method and Social Science—East and West." *Scientific Monthly* 75 (1952): 144–60, and in *Soviet Science*. Ed. R. C. Christman, AAAS, 1952, pp. 48–56.

24. "Some New Statistical Techniques Applicable to Operations Research." *Journal of the Operations Research Society of America*, 1 (1952): 10–17.

25. "The Design of Research and Experiments: Some Introductory Remarks." *Ergonetics* 1 (1952): 7–10.

26. "Operations Research." *Cleveland Engineering* 46 (1953): 21–27.

27. "Production Scheduling: A Case Study." *Proceedings of the Conference on Operations Research in Marketing.* Cleveland: Case Institute of Technology, 1953, pp. 31–39.

28. *The Design of Social Research,* Chicago: University of Chicago Press, 1953.

29. "Operations Research: A New Tool for Industrial Research." *Industrial Laboratories* (Nov. 1953): 64–67.

30. "Introduction to the Concept of the Designed Experiment." *Research Operations in Industry.* Ed. D. B. Hertz. New York: Kings Crown Press, 1953, pp. 295–302.

31. "Production Scheduling." *Proceedings of Operations Research Conference by Society for Advancement of Management.* New York: Society for Advancement of Management, 1954.

32. "Information for Overall Company Planning through Operations Research." *Seminar of Operations Research, Railway and Systems Procedures Association,* 1954, pp. 69–83.

33. "A Multidisciplinary Analysis of Estimating: A Methodologist's Approach." *The Journal of Industrial Engineering* 3 (1954): 11–12.

34. "An Approximate Measure of Value." *Journal of the Operations Research Society of America* 2 (1954): 172–80.

35. "Production and Inventory Control in a Chemical Process, II." *Proceedings of the Conference on OR in Production and Inventory Control.* Cleveland: Case Institute of Technology, 1954, pp. 13–22.

36. "Statistics in Operations Research and Operations Research in Statistics." *Operations Research for Management.* Ed. J. F. McCloskey and F. N. Trefethen. Baltimore: The Johns Hopkins Press, 1954, pp. 117–33.

37. "Operations Research for Control." With J. E. Townsend. *Chemical and Engineering News* 32 (1954): 2–22.

38. "Operational Accounting and Operations Research." *The Journal of Accountancy* 99 (1955): 53–59.*

39. "Production Scheduling: An Operations Research Case Study." *Advanced Management* 20 (1955): 21–28.

40. "Operations Research in Business and Industry: A Report to Management." *Proceedings: The Institute on Operations Research for Business and Industry.* Los Angeles: University of California, 1955, pp. 36–42.

41. "Allocation of Sales Effort" and "Summary." *Proceedings of the Conference on "What Is Operations Research Accomplishing in Industry?"* Cleveland: Case Institute of Technology, 1955, pp. 23–30 and 93–99.

42. "Production and Inventory Control in a Chemical Process." *Journal of the Operations Research Society of America* 3 (1955): 319–38.
43. "Comments on Operations Research." *The Journal of Marketing* 20 (1955): 47–48.
44. "A Survey of Operations Research in Industry." *Proceedings: Operations Research Conference*. New York: Society for Advancement of Management, 1955, pp. 52–61.
45. "Determining Optimum Allocation of Sales Effort," ibid., pp. 74–81.
46. "Automatic Management: A Forecast and Its Educational Implications." *Management Science* 2 (1955): 55–60.
47. "Automation of Production and Management." *American Petroleum Institute, Division of Refining* 35 (1955): 192–96.
48. "Operations Research—Its Relationship to Data Processing." *Proceedings: Automatic Data Processing Conference*. Cambridge: Harvard University, 1956, pp. 161–75.
49. "A Survey of Applications of O.R." *Case Studies in Operations Research—A Cross Section of Business and Industry*. Cleveland: Case Institute of Technology, 1956, pp. 9–17.
50. "Five Year Planning for an Integrated Operation." With Walter G. Glover, ibid., pp. 38–47.
51. "The Development of Operations Research as a Science." *Operations Research* 4 (1956): 265–95.
52. "Operations Research in Organizational Planning: A Case Study." *Proceedings of the Seventh Annual National Conference, American Institute of Industrial Engineers*, Columbus, Ohio, 1956.
53. "The Role of Recorded Information in the Decision-Making Process: Operational Research Approach." *Documentation in Action*. Ed. by J. H. Shera, Allen Kent, and J. W. Perry. New York: Reinhold Publishing Co., 1956, pp. 253–56.
54. "Allocation of Sales Effort in the Lamp Division of the General Electric Company." With Clark Waid and D. F. Clark. *Operations Research* 4 (1956): 629–47.
55. "OPSEARCH—What It Is—How It Is Conducted—What It Will Do." *Chemical Engineering Progress* 53 (1957): 41–71.
56. "Role de la Statistique dans la Recherche Opérationnelle et de la Recherche Opérationnelle dans la Statistique," *Introduction à la Recherche Opérationelle* (trans. no. 25). Paris: Dunod, 1957, pp. 33–47.
57. "The Fundamentals of Operations Research." *Proceedings: 1956 Annual Operations Research Conference*. New York: Society for Advancement of Management, 1957, pp. 1–11.

58. *Introduction to Operations Research.* With C. W. Churchman and E. L. Arnoff. New York: Wiley, 1957.

59. "A Comparison of Operational Research in the U.S.A. and in Great Britain." *Operational Research Quarterly* 8 (1957): 88–100.

60. "All Related Areas Probed in Search for Answers to Industry Problems." *New York Herald Tribune,* Engineer's News Supplement, July 1957, p. 2.

61. "Operations Research and National Planning." *Operations Research* 5 (1957): 457–68.

62. "The Basic Limitations of George S. Odiorne in Operations Research." *Journal of Industrial Engineering* 9 (1958): 530–31.

63. "Report on a Study of Scientific Communication for the National Science Foundation." *Information Systems in Documentation.* Ed. by J. H. Shera, Allen Kent, and J. W. Perry. New York: Interscience, 1957, pp. 66–74.

64. "Applications of Operations Research to Improved Utilization of Motor Power." With M. W. Sasieni. *Proceedings, Railway Systems and Procedures Association: Improved Motor Power Utilization.* Washington, D. C., 1957, pp. 25–31.

65. "The Concept and Exercise of Control in O.R." *Proceedings of the First International Conference on Operational Research.* Operations Research Society of America, 1957, pp. 26–43.

66. "On Hitch's Dissent on Operations Research on Operations Research and National Planning." *Operations Research* 6 (1958): 121–24.

67. "Discussion." *Proceedings of the Conference on Research and Development and Its impact on the Economy.* Washington, D.C.: National Science Foundation, NSF-58-36, 1958, pp. 69–74.

68. "Towards a Behavioral Theory of Communication." *Management Science* 4 (1958): 218–34.

69. "How Techniques of Mathematical Analysis Have Been Used to Determine Advertising Budgets and Strategy." With J.D.C. Tittle. *Proceedings: Fourth Annual Conference on "How Can Advertising Be Better Evaluated in Today's Economy."* New York: Advertising Research Foundation. 1958, pp. 19–23.

70. "An Operations Research Study of the Dissemination of Scientific Information." With Michael Halbert. *International Conference on Scientific Information.* Washington, D.C.: National Academy of Science, National Research Council, 1958, pp. 87–120.

71. "Historia del Grupo de Investigación Operativa del Case Institute of Technology." With E. L. Arnoff. *Boletin Ibero-Americano de Cultura Tecnia* 2 (1959): 25–41.

72. "A Report on Some Organizational Experiments." With D. F. Clark. *Operations Research* 7 (1959): 279–93.
73. "Games, Decisions, and Organizations." *General Systems* 4 (1959): 145–50.
74. "Unsuccessful Case Studies and Why." *Operations Research* 8 (1960): 259–62.
75. "An Addendum to General Heiman's Remarks." *Management Technology* 1 (1960): 26–29.
76. "Systems, Organizations, and Interdisciplinary Research." *General Systems* 5 (1960): 1–8.
77. *Progress in Operations Research I.* New York: Wiley, 1961.
78. "Some Methodological Aspects of Operations Research." *Proceedings of the Second International Conference on Operations Research.* London: English Universities Press, 1960, pp. 3–5.
79. "Systems, Organizations, and Interdisciplinary Research." *Systems Research and Design.* Ed. by D. P. Eckman. New York: Wiley, 1961, pp. 26–42.
80. Operational Research and Engineering." *The Indian and Eastern Engineer* (November 1962): 97–99.
81. *Scientific Method: Optimizing Applied Research Decisions.* With collaboration of J. S. Minas and S. K. Gupta. New York: Wiley, 1962.
82. "Some Unsolved Problems in Solving Problems." *Operational Research Quarterly* 13 (1962): 1–11.
83. "A Definitional Note on Cooperation, Conflict, and Competition." *Erhvervsokonomisk Tidsskrift* 4 (1962): 312–15.
84. "The Dissemination and Use of Recorded Scientific Information." With M. W. Martin. *Management Science* 9 (1963): 322–36.
85. *A Manager's Guide to Operations Research.* With B.H.P. Rivett. New York: Wiley, 1963.
86. "The Definition and Measurement of Cooperation, Conflict, Exploitation, and Competition." *Proceedings: U.S. Army Operations Research Symposium,* Part 1. Durham, N.C.: Army Research Office, 1963.
87. "Toward Quantitative Evaluation of Urban Services." *Public Expenditure Decisions in the Urban Community.* Ed. by H. G. Shaller. Washington, D.C.: Resources for the Future, 1963, pp. 91–117.
88. "General Systems Theory and Systems Research: Contrasting Conceptions of Systems Science." *General Systems* 9 (1964): 117–21.
89. "Beyond Optimization." *Opsearch* 1 (1964): 5–11.
90. "Some Observations on Marketing and Operations Research in

the United States." *Proceedings of the Third International Conference on Operations Research.* London: English Universities Press, 1964, pp. 171–78.

91. "Individual and Collective Value Judgments." With J. S. Minas. *Human Judgments and Optimality.* Ed. by M. W. Shelly II and G. L. Bryan. New York: Wiley, 1964, pp. 351–59.

92. "Conflict, Cooperation, Competition, and Cupid." *Essays on Econometrics and Planning.* Ed. by C. R. Rao. Oxford: Pergamon, 1964, pp. 7–18.

93. "Planning, Operations Research, and Metropolitan Systems." With Britton Harris. *Proceedings of 1964 Annual Conference.* Washington, D.C.: American Institute of Planners, 1964, pp. 92–96.

94. "Informational Requirements of Industrial Research and Development Management." With S. S. Sengupta. *Information System Sciences.* Ed. by J. Spiegel and D. Walker. Washington, D.C.: Spartan Books, 1965, pp. 133–39.

95. "Systems Theory from an Operations Research Point of View." With S. S. Sengupta. *General Systems* 10 (1965): 43–48, and *IEEE Transactions on Systems Science and Cybernetics* 1 (1965): 43–48.

96. "Rounding out the Management Sciences." *Columbia Journal of World Business* 1 (1966): 33–36.

97. "The Use of Simulation as a Pedagogical Device." With J. C. Porter, M. W. Sasieni and Eli Marks. *Management Science* 12 (1966): B170–79.

98. "The Meaning of Strategic Planning." *The McKinsey Quarterly* Summer (1966): 48–61.

99. "Specialized Versus Generalized Models in Research Budgeting." *Research Program Effectiveness.* Ed. by M. C. Youitzetal. New York: Gordon and Breach, 1966, pp. 169–85.

100. "Toward a Theory of the Dynamics of Conflict." With R. L. Sisson. *Conflict Resolution and World Education.* Ed. by Stuart Mudd. The Hague: Junk, 1966, pp. 125–42.

101. "Structural Conflicts within Organizations." *Operational Research and the Social Sciences.* Ed. by J. R. Lawrence. London: Tavistock Publications, 1966, pp. 420–38.

102. "Management Misinformation Systems." *Management Science* 14 (1967): B147–56.

103. "Operational Research and National Science Policy" and "Discussion." *Decision Making in National Science Policy.* Ed. by A. deReuck, M. Goldsmith, et al. London: Ciba Foundation, 1968, pp. 84–98.

104. *Fundamentals of Operations Research.* With M. W. Sasieni. New York: Wiley, 1968.
105. "Toward an Idealized University." *Management Science* 15 (1968): 121–31.
106. "Operations Research." *International Encyclopedia of the Social Sciences,* vol. 2. New York: Macmillan and The Free Press, 1968, pp. 290–94.
107. "The Role of Research in Underdeveloped Countries." *Operations Research* 16 (1968): 717–26.
108. "Strategies for Operations Research in Urban Metropolitan Planning." With Britton Harris. *Proceedings of the Fourth International Conference on Operational Research.* Ed. by D. B. Hertz and J. Melese. New York: Wiley-Interscience, 1966 (appeared 1969), pp. 471–80.
109. "Prediction, Explanation, and Control of Conflict." With J. R. Emshoff. *Peace Research Society, Papers XII, Cambridge Conference.* Peace Research Society, 1968, pp. 109–15.
110. "Toward Strategic Planning of Education." *Efficiency of Resource Allocation in Education.* Paris: OECD, 1969, pp. 339–80.
111. "In Conclusion: Some Beginnings." With Stafford Beer. *Progress in Operations Research: Relations Between Operations Research and the Computer, III.* Ed. by J. S. Aronofsky. New York: Wiley, 1969, pp. 423–49.
112. "Institutional Functions and Societal Needs." *Perspectives in Planning.* Ed. by Erich Jantsch. Paris: OECD, 1969, pp. 495–500.
113. *A Concept of Corporate Planning.* New York: Wiley, 1970.
114. "The Evolution of Management Systems." *Canadian Operational Research Society Journal* 8 (1970): 1–13.
115. "Explanatory Models of Interactive Choice Behavior." With J. R. Emshoff. *Conflict Resolution* 14 (1970): 77–89.
116. "On the Ambiguity of the Researcher and the Researched." *The Place of Research in Social Choice.* London: Tavistock Institute of Human Relations, 1970, pp. 19–32.
117. "Beering and Branching through Corporate Planning." *Proceedings of the Fifth International Conference of Operational Research.* Ed. by John Lawrence. London: Tavistock Publications, 1970, pp. 21–30.
118. "Some Ideas on Education in the Management Sciences." *Management Science* 17 (1970): B2–4.
119. "A Black Ghetto's Research on a University." *Operations Research* 18 (1970): 761–71.

120. *The Management of Change and How It Changes Management.* Lancaster, England: University of Lancaster, 1970.
121. "Frontiers of Management Science." *The Bulletin of the Institute of Management Sciences* 1 (1971): 19–24.
122. "Toward a System of Systems Concepts." *Management Science* 17 (1971): 661–71.
123. "Possible and Likely Futures of Urban Transportation." With Francisco Sagasti. *Socio-Economic Planning Science* 5 (1971): 413–28.
124. "Planning for Social Systems." *The Prison Journal* 51 (1971): 33–42.
125a. "A Note on Systems Science." *Interfaces* 2 (no. 4, 1972).
125b. "Open Letter to TIMS Members." *Interfaces* 2 (no. 4, 1972).
125c. "Operational Research and Developing Countries: The Control of Organized Systems and of the Decisions that Control Them." *Interregional Seminar on the Use of Modern Management Techniques in the Public Administration of Developing Countries,* vol. 2. New York: United Nations, 1971, pp. 58–85.
126. "A Revolution in Organizational Concepts." *Naval War College Review* 24 (1972): 4–14.
127. *On Purposeful Systems.* With F. E. Emery. Chicago: Aldine-Atherton, 1972.
128. "On Ideal Seeking Systems." With F. E. Emery. *General Systems* 17 (1972): 17–24.
129. "A Systems Approach to the Problems of Solid Waste and Litter." With John R. Hall, Jr. *Journal Environmental Systems* 2 (December, 1972): 351–64.
130. "Science in the Systems Age: Beyond IE, OR, and MS." *Operations Research* 21 (no. 3, May-June 1973).
131. "Educational Systems." *Operational Research '72.* Ed. by M. Ross. New York: North-Holland Publishing Co., American Elsevier. 1973, pp. 587–98.
132. "Computer Obstructed Education." *Data Base,* 5 (Winter 1973): 108–14.
133. "Planning In The Systems Age." *Sankhya: The Indian Journal of Statistics,* Series B, 35 (part 2, 1973).
134. "Beyond Problem Solving." *Decision Sciences* 5 (April, 1974): x–xv.
135. "Operations Research." *Encyclopaedia Britannica,* 15th ed. 13 (1974): 594–602.
136. *Redesigning the Future.* New York: Wiley, 1974.
137. *Systems and Management Annual* (editor and contributor). New York: Petrocelli Books, 1974.

138. "The Social Responsibility of Operational Research." *Operational Research Quarterly* 25 (1974): 361–71.
139. "The Systems Revolution." *The Journal of the Society for Long Range Planning* 7 (no. 6, December 1974): 2–20.
140. "Advertising Research at Anheuser-Busch, Inc. (1963–68)." With James R. Emshoff. *Sloan Management Review* 16 (Winter 1975): 1–15.
141. "A Reply to Keith Chesterton, Robert Goodsman, Jonathan Rosenhead and Colin Thunhurst." *Operational Research Quarterly* 26 (March, 1975): 96–99.
142. "Humanizing Management and the Management Sciences." *Proceedings—XX International Meeting, The Institute of Management Sciences.* Ed. by E. Shlifer. Jerusalem: Jerusalem Academic Press, 1975, pp. 1–8.
143. "The Second Industrial Revolution." Alban Institute Publication, Washington, D.C., 1975.
144. "Advertising Research at Anheuser-Busch, Inc. (1968–74)." With James R. Emshoff. *Sloan Management Review* 16 (no. 3, Spring 1975): 1–16.
145. "Does Quality of Life Have to be Quantified?" *General Systems* 20 (1975): 213–19; also in *Operational Research Quarterly* 27 (1976): 289–304.
146. "What is the Possibility of Convergence, Divergence, or Synthesis of Methodology between the Social Sciences and the Natural Sciences?" *The Centrality of Science and Absolute Values,* vol. 1. Tarrytown, N.Y.: The International Cultural Foundation, Inc., 1975, pp. 65–70 and 311–18.
147. *Designing a National Scientific and Technological Communications System: The SCATT Report.* With Thomas Cowan, Peter Davis, Martin Elton, James C. Emery, Marybeth Meditz, and Wladimir Sachs. Philadelphia: University of Pennsylvania Press, 1976.
148. "The Aging of a Young Profession: Operations Research." *Presidential Lectures 1975–76,* University of Pennsylvania, 1976.
149. "The Corporate Rain Dance." *The Wharton Magazine* 1 (Winter 1977): 36–41.
150. "Optimization + Objectivity = Opt Out." *European Journal of Operational Research* 1 (January 1977): 1–7.
151. "National Development Planning Revisited." *Operations Research* 25 (March–April 1977): 207–18.
152. "SCATT, Libraries, Relevance and Redundancy." With W. M. Sachs and M. L. Meditz. *International Forum on Information and Documentation* 2 (July 1977): 8–13.

153. "A Fishy Story." *The Wharton Magazine* 2 (Winter 1978): 17.
154. "Towards Flexible Organizations: A Multidimensional Design." *Omega* 5 (no. 6, 1977).
155. "A Story of Ups and Downs." *The Wharton Magazine* 2 (Spring 1978): 18.
156. "On Growth and Development of Social Systems." *The Zucker Lectures, 1975–77.* Hamilton, Ontario: McMaster University Publications, 1977, pp. 49–71.
157. "Looking Forward and Backward at Education in the Management Sciences." *TIMS/ORSA Bulletin* 5 (May 13, 1978): 10–11.
158. "Ackoff's Fables: It Hurts to Bend a Little." *The Wharton Magazine* 2 (Summer 1978): 66.
159. *The Art of Problem Solving.* New York: Wiley, 1978.
160. "The Future of OR Is Past." *J. Opl. Res. Soc.* 30 (no. 2, 1979): 96–104.
161. "Resurrecting the Future of OR." *J. Opl. Res. Soc.* 30 (no. 3, 1979): 189–99.
162. *Creating the Corporate Future.* New York: Wiley, 1981.

Section III
Systems Thinkers and
Systems Applications

One concept central to the work of Ackoff and many of his colleagues is experimentation. Only by application and controlled evaluation of ideas and methods can their relevance—or irrelevance—be understood. Because of the pragmatic nature of this approach, many of its developments and modifications have come as a direct consequence of interventions in social systems.

A second process in the development of the systems approach is what Singer called "sweeping-in." All branches of knowledge become the domains of the systems thinker, who is free to adopt methods and ideas from various sciences or disciplines. In the practice of systems planning and management these "borrowed" ideas are often tested in the experimental mode.

Those working with social systems are continually learning from each other. Most have come from diverse disciplinary backgrounds and have worked within a variety of organizational settings. Differences in orientation and context have fueled constructive debate within the systems community and perpetuated the dynamic development of its theoretical framework.

The readings in this section are representative of how systems thinkers have incorporated Ackoff's ideas in their own work. The contributors are colleagues of long-standing. They are in a position to judge the strengths, weaknesses, and potential of ideas based on long-term professional relationships.

The first article by John Friend discusses Ackoff's involvement with the operational research (OR) group at the Tavistock Institute of Human Relations in London. He describes the role that OR played in the development of the Tavistock approach to planning by providing examples of how this technical approach proves inadequate in public management settings where decision making is highly political.

Rolfe Tomlinson then provides another perspective on the contributions of operational research to the development of systems practice. He examines the roles that OR professionals play in organizational settings. The differences in orientation between external consultants and the in-house staff are discussed. Tomlinson concludes that those who are part of the organization are in a better position to contribute to its long-range planning.

The third article is also contributed by a Tavistock associate. Eric Trist brings another social science perspective to their collaboration. He critiques the work of the Hungarian psychiatrist Andras Angyal in terms of its contributions to systems theory. Emphasizing the individual's dependence on his or his social and biological environment, Angyal was among the first to move from mechanistic to contextual models of human behavior. However, his work was lost in the wake of cybernetics and general systems theory. Trist goes on to discuss how the concept of teleology developed by Ackoff with another Tavistock associate, Fred Emery, in *On Purposeful Systems* both complements and completes Angyal's model.

Not only has the systems perspective enriched psychological theory, but psychological theory has also contributed to understanding individual behavior within social systems. Both Donald Schon and Erik Johnsen emphasize the importance of studying managerial behavior for those who are attempting to understand and intervene in organizational settings. They also discuss the relevance of various psychological models. Johnsen outlines a general model of managerial behavior. Schon presents his specific model of the reflective practitioner and discusses its implications for managerial education.

Individual behavior is but one aspect in organizational settings of interest to the systems scientist. The process by which organizations are managed is a major area of inquiry. The pragmatic concept of progress is at the core of Ackoff's notion of interactive planning. Several contributors critique this view of planning and control. In their article, Jamshid Gharajedaghi and Ali Geranmayeh provide an overview of the interactive approach. Others focus on specific aspects of the process. Aron Katsenelinboigen discusses goal setting and argues that it is critical to understanding Ackoff's concepts of planning and purposeful systems. Stafford Beer brings a cybernetician's point of view to the discussion. From this perspective, he reevaluates Ackoff's concepts of "fable," "mess," and "idealized design." Paul Broholm discusses the implications of technological innovation for control within organizational structures. He uses the revolution in microcomputers to provide examples. Finally, William Evan discusses corporate democracy using the concept of stakeholder, which Ackoff was among the first to propose as an alternative to the more traditional, narrow notion of stockholder.

Chapter 7
Planning Concepts, Planning Contexts
John Friend

For many years now, I have been harboring a vague sense of puzzlement over the influence of Russ Ackoff on my working life. The paradox I would like to explore—and perhaps even attempt to dissolve—is that I can't think of scarcely anyone who has had such a powerful influence as Russ over the way in which my own work in the field of planning has evolved, yet the paradigm of planning that I and others have developed working from a Tavistock base seems quite different in emphasis to that which Russ has made his own.

I have never fully understood why this should have come about. I am sure that Russ would be the last person to suggest that everyone who becomes exposed to his thinking should seek to follow the same path; each of us, he would probably say, can have different stylistic objectives to pursue. But I hope that by exploring the differences in this paper I can learn something of value to my own practice, and furthermore that this learning can be of some relevance to others who are struggling to address the challenges of planning in a complex and uncertain world.

At a superficial level, I can begin by identifying phrases and concepts that seem to point to some of the more obvious similarities and differences between the Ackoff paradigm of planning and that of planning as a process of strategic choice which grew out of the work of Neil Jessop, myself, and others in Britain. The ideas that come to the fore in both paradigms are those of adaptiveness in planning; of continuity in process; and of an interactive, participatory approach. The aspects of the Ackoff approach that I have always found difficult to embrace are those with a more holistic flavor—the emphasis on idealized design of purposeful systems, on designing a desirable future and inventing ways of bringing it about. Instead, I tend to talk, less ambitiously, about planning as a means of managing uncertainty and about ways of making incremental progress over time. Recently, indeed, I have found it useful to float in discussion the idea of planning as responsible scheming—a concept that does not seem to fit at all comfortably with the emphasis on idealization which is the hallmark of the Ackoff style.

Yet I recognize that I myself have always been something of an idealizer; I like pursuing visions of a desirable future, and I feel most motivated when I can share that sense of a preferred future with others. Indeed, the story of the Institute for Operational Research (IOR), the unit of the Tavistock Institute I joined over two decades ago, has been one of a group of people working in pursuit of an ideal in the face of obstacles and constraints that seem to have combined to test the chosen ideal almost to the point of destruction. So, in looking for possible explorations for the differences that seem to have developed between the Ackoff and the IOR paradigms of planning, I find myself reexamining the *experiences* that have led to the development in Britain of the strategic choice approach rather than to contrasts of personal style alone.

I would not be so presumptuous as to try making systematic comparisons between the experiences that have molded my own approach to planning and those that have molded the approaches of other people—least of all Russ Ackoff, who began working in the planning field at least a decade before I did and who has built up his international influence and reputation from a base in a country other than my own. What I can do, however, is to run through the story of my own involvement in the fields of operational research, planning, and public policy in a way that brings out as clearly as possible the profound influence of Russ Ackoff on the directions of my own work at certain critical points during the last twenty-eight years. And this, I believe, will lead me toward plausible planning concepts—an explanation that focuses on the differences in planning *contexts*—and in contexts of engagement between planners and scientists—within which the respective paradigms developed and took root.

For me, the story begins in January 1958, not far from the ice-choked shores of Lake Erie. I was twenty-seven at the time, and it was my first visit to the United States. The opportunity arose because I had been employed for two years in what was rather grandiloquently called the Operational Research Branch of British Overseas Airways Corporation (BOAC)—the predecessor of British Airways on its intercontinental routes. I did not really consider myself an operational researcher at the time—more of a mathematical statistician who enjoyed doing applied work in organizations—though I had been doing work on queuing at airports and had recently joined the Operational Research Society.

My employers had by this time come to the view—to my subsequent gratitude—that it was time I went to an introductory course in operational research. There were two main possibilities at that time: a two-week course at Birmingham University in England and a course of similar duration at the then Case Institute of Technology in Cleveland, Ohio. To most British employers, there would have been no realistic alternative to Birmingham, but BOAC was in the happy position of being able to ignore the transportation element in the comparison. And so I found myself spending a fortnight in Cleveland, being introduced firsthand to the combined wisdom of Churchman, Ackoff, and Arnoff—joint authors of what was then seen as the leading text on OR methods (Churchman et al. 1957).

Here, I was exposed for the first time—and indeed virtually the last time—to such staple OR techniques as linear programming. More importantly, I was exposed to the thinking of Ackoff and Churchman on the organizational life. Their voices were persuasive, and when I returned to Britain, I felt that suddenly OR made sense, as something philosophically distinct from the discipline of applied statistics which had hitherto seemed to offer the most obvious career path for me to pursue.

Shortly after this experience, I moved to Wales to become OR team leader in a medium-sized group of companies in the plastics industry. I had little direct contact with Russ Ackoff during the next five years, though I remember feeling pleased when I heard he would be coming to Britain to spend a sabbatical year at Birmingham University. Then I recall listening to him addressing a meeting of the Operational Research Society—perhaps it was at a national conference—and putting over the convincing message that the future expansion of OR in Britain called for the establishment of enough university chairs to establish a critical mass of teaching and research.

Those days seem distant now, and Russ himself has since been as vigorous as anyone in condemning the influence of conventional academic paradigms on the development of OR practice both in the United States and the United Kingdom (Ackoff 1979a). What I was less aware of in 1961–62 was the rapport that was beginning to develop between Russ Ackoff and leading social scientists of the Tavistock Institute of Human Relations in London—prominent among them Eric Trist and Fred Emery, both of whom were to be acknowledged by Russ as significant influences on his ideas about participative planning. Eric Trist has told me since that his seminal contacts with Churchman and Ackoff were made during a conference of the

Institute of Management Science in Paris. From this beginning there grew exploratory contacts between the Tavistock Institute and the Operational Research Society in Britain which, in 1963, were to lead to the formation within the Tavistock matrix of an Institute for Operational Research. The new IOR was conceived as a base for fundamental research in OR with bold and pioneering aims that included extending its range of applications to address broader policy issues through a closer integration with the social sciences.

In a preface written a few years later to a booklet reporting on IOR's first four years (Jessop et al. 1967), Ackoff writes:

> More often than not it is the small things that one has done that bring the largest satisfactions. Such is the case relative to my role as a marriage broker in bringing Tavistock and the Operational Research Society together. I wish I could take credit for their offspring, the IOR.

This piece of brokerage may have been a small thing to Russ, but it was to affect my life profoundly. For in 1964 I became one of the first wave of OR scientists recruited by IOR's first director, Neil Jessop, and I was to remain an employee of the Tavistock Institute right up to the time of writing this twenty-two years later. Over this time, I have learned to live with a sense of continuing excitement and challenge—albeit accompanied, paradoxically, by a greater sense of insecurity than I had experienced in any of the much briefer spells of employment I had had in more conventional organizations during the preceding decade.

My introduction to planning processes came very abruptly. On the day I joined IOR, I found myself working on a four-year research project boldly entitled "Policy Research for Local Government: The Development of a Planning Process." Neil Jessop had managed to attract quite a substantial grant from the Nuffield Foundation for an interdisciplinary study of strategic decision making in city government, with the city council of Coventry in the English Midlands acting as willing hosts. My team colleagues were Neil Jessop, part-time director of the project; Hugh Murray, a social psychologist who had been closely involved in the seminal Tavistock studies of sociotechnical systems in coal mining; and Paul Spencer, a social anthropologist who had recently returned from spending two years with a branch of the Masai people in Kenya.

On my second day in Coventry, I recall sitting beside Hugh Murray as an observer in a meeting of the city council's Policy Advisory Committee—grasping for some understanding of who was who, what they were arguing about, and what possible relevance OR might have to what was going on. There were to be many more such experiences in the months and years to come, for we were encouraged to attend not only the formal meetings of the various committees and the full council but also more informal meetings in departmental offices and—more surprisingly—the private caucus meetings of both the opposing political groups (Labour being in control and the Conservatives in opposition at that time). The leading politicians and officers always seemed ready to talk to us outside the meetings about what was happening, regarding us as unbiased observers of the struggles in which they were enmeshed—though this was a position we found it increasingly difficult to sustain as time went on. From Paul Spencer in particular, I gradually learned much about the skills of listening and interpreting and the discipline of writing field notes to record our impressions of process with a view to subsequent reflection and discussion within the team.

But it all seemed a long way from OR, and from the beginning I felt a deep-seated urge—not shared by Paul Spencer—to establish my credentials as a management scientist by offering something to the decision makers in Coventry that could help them in some way. Neil Jessop seemed to share my concern, and in the early months of the project I found myself beginning to develop an idealized design for a model of a city as a system—an experimental device through which to simulate and aggregate the individual decisions of citizens in relation to residential location, employment, travel to work, schooling, and other aspects of their lives. The idea was that the model would reflect the types of relationships to be found within a real city, while simplifying them quite drastically. In talking to people in Coventry, we described this proposed model as a "town-like thing," bearing the same kind of relationship to the city itself as a matchstick picture of a man to a living human being but bringing a capacity to offer at least a few useful insights into how the real thing works. The spatial structure of the city would be represented through a hexagonal grid—this being the most original feature of the proposed model. A computer would be used to follow the effects of local government decisions, though we insisted that this was to be a purely an exploratory model in which number-crunching would be strenuously avoided.

The city fathers listened with politeness but no noticeable enthusiasm to these ideas. And this is where Russ Ackoff enters the story again; for he had agreed to act as one of a small panel of advisers to the project and happened to be paying a visit to London around this time. I presented our state of thinking about the town-like thing; he sat and puffed his pipe then, after what seemed a long silence, came out with one of the devastating critical judgments for which he has become well known. He told us that far greater resources than ours were being poured into urban modeling in the States, that there was already scepticism about what they could achieve, and that we in Coventry had a different kind of opportunity to seize. On this, he had a few illustrative suggestions to make; as I recall, they related to examples of major shifts in patterns of urban living, such as the trend in the States toward mobile homes, toward which adaptive planning would be required.

Neil and I came away from this meeting feeling somewhat numbed—and neither of us could see clear ways of building on Russ's suggestions at the time. What was, in retrospect, of crucial importance to our project was the severity of the jolt we received through Russ's trenchant criticism of our tentative ideas on urban simulation modeling. His views were forcibly enough put to dislodge us from our proposed path at a stage before any serious investment in modeling and computer programming had been made. As an OR scientist, I was thrown back into the uncomfortable position of seeing no clear way in which my skills could be of immediate use to people. But, as I now realize, the intervention from Russ at this critical juncture bought us time—time to learn more about what OR and social science could achieve together when presented with a rare opportunity to engage with some complex planning realities over a prolonged period and to tune in to the concerns and behaviors of those influential people whose business it was to deal with them.

After this turning point, other crises followed. As we struggled to find alternative planning paradigms, there were crises of relationships within the team; crises of relationships with our hosts on the city council; crises of confidence as to whether we could have anything useful to contribute at all. Once, when encouraged to offer some impartial advice on interdepartmental coordination, we found ourselves being sucked deeper and deeper into the tangled politics of city government against our will, and we found we had to draw deeply on our somewhat underdeveloped political skills, if only to find ways of disengaging with dignity. It was at roughly the two-thirds point of our four-year project that Neil Jessop concluded that we should henceforth concentrate all our efforts on the production of a good written product, rather than the ambition to act as agents of change in Coventry itself. For action-oriented operational researchers such as Neil and myself, it was a harsh decision but, in retrospect, a wise one. From then on we were to focus our energies on the drafting of a book, called *Local Government and Strategic Choice*, a book that was to become the springboard of all IOR's subsequent work in the public planning field (Friend and Jessop 1977).

During this period of writing, we felt that at last our alternative paradigm of planning was beginning to cohere. It was a paradigm that emphasized process rather than system and took a modest enough view of planning as an activity directed toward the conscious management of uncertainty through time. The most basic and distinctive feature of the paradigm was one that could be represented in the form of a simple diagram, with a circle in the center representing any current decision problem where difficulty was being experienced in deciding what to do. Around this circle are ranged three categories of uncertainty, all pulling in different directions—uncertainties about the working environment (UE), uncertainties about appropriate value judgments (UV), and uncertainties about intentions in related areas of decision (UR). Building on this basic picture, we went on to develop dynamic models of decision processes—or planning processes, for we saw no clear boundary between the two—in which commitments are built up incrementally and the choice of route through a complex organizational and procedural terrain is seen to depend critically on judgments about which areas of uncertainty seem most important and on what resources—financial, technical, political, or whatever—should be invested in response.

Now, almost two decades later, that paradigm has demonstrated its usefulness in practice in quite a range of fields beyond that of local government, and my associates and I have had the satisfaction of building up plenty of experience in applying the approach in a change agent role. The style that has developed is one in which we work interactively with groups of decision makers and planners, using plenty of large sheets of paper around the walls of the room with which to help them map out the structure of interconnected decisions and the uncertainties they face.

Reflecting now on this approach to planning and its origins in the Coventry project, I can distinguish four main strands in the work of that project upon which it drew. First, I in my OR role spent a lot of time in the middle stages of the project trying to analyze the structures of assumptions underlying some of the technical documents prepared by the city planners, presenting recommendations on such matters as the optimum size of the city's central shopping zone and the choice of a preferred design for Coventry's future road network. Then Paul Spencer, as a social scientist, carried out a penetrating analysis of the political structure of decision making in the city council, demonstrating, among other things, the various opportunities for steering difficult issues through different procedural channels—formal and informal, bureaucratic, coordinative, and representative. I was able to help him in casting some of the salient points of this analysis in flowchart form. So these were the first two strands of our work, both of which helped us bring together the technical and the political aspects of planning in Coventry in the same decision-centered frame.

But there were two more strands of our experience that we were able to bring into this picture as well. One was the experience of observing what was going on around us all the time within the various departmental, committee, and caucus meetings—in particular, the sometimes dramatic clashes over controversial issues where, faced with an impasse over how to proceed, different individuals would offer contrasting prescriptions for progress. Typically, some people would call for "more research" (responding as we saw it to UE), while others would call first for "clearer policies" (UV), and others again would call for a "broader view" of the current issue alongside other related issues (responding to UR and tending to push the process in the direction of a more comprehensive planning agenda). Meanwhile, we saw similar clashes being acted out on the stage of the city itself, with all its multitude of interests and representative groups. Controversies highlighted in the local press, campaigns by pressure groups, the annual political drama of the local elections, all of these provided a backdrop against which we were gradually able to develop our alternative paradigm of planning as a continuous process of strategic choice.

The paradigm was one we could claim, with some conviction, to be *sociotechnical,* in the well-established Tavistock tradition. Yet it is revealing to contrast it with the more holistic paradigm of planning that was envisaged at the time the original proposal for the Coventry project was submitted to the Nuffield Foundation. In that, the potential for synthesis between the OR and social science approaches was envisaged at a more ambitious systems level. It was argued that OR offered a means of modeling a city as a system, while the social science input to the team would allow the city council's organization to be viewed as a form of sociotechnical system, which should be designed to match the rich patterns of interactions to be found within the city itself.

Yet what provided the bridge between the OR and social science perspectives on the project was not so much this systems perspective as the prolonged exposure of Paul Spencer and myself to the comparative minutiae of day-to-day decision making on difficult, messy issues. Whereas the more holistic paradigms of systems thinking conjure up the saying about the danger of failing to see the woods for the trees, the experience for us was one of tramping around the forest at ground level, gradually building up a picture of the social ecology around us and the dynamic forces at work. But I would not wish to push the metaphor too far, because I believe biological analogies can be dangerous when applied to social structures. In Christopher Alexander's terms (1966), a city is not a tree, but neither is it a natural forest in which balances are maintained from generation to generation through mechanisms that have evolved slowly in a genetically determined process of natural selection. City government and planning are much more experimental than that.

But I want to return now to Russ Ackoff and his involvement with IOR in the period immediately after the Coventry project came to an end. The period was a traumatic one, for Neil Jessop died only two days after *Local Government and Strategic Choice* was first published in 1969. We knew he had been suffering from a long-standing illness, yet his death came suddenly and as a great shock to those of us who had known him well. Then, the following year, *A Concept of Corporate Planning* appeared (Ackoff 1970), with a dedication to Neil Jessop—whose death, in Russ's words, would have been untimely whenever it had occurred.

A comparison of the two books, as products of different bodies of experience, provides one starting point in exploring the similarities and differences between the Ackoff paradigm of planning and the IOR paradigm. In the case of the Ackoff book, the base of experience comes through as one of advising many industrial corporations, large and small, on the development of their central planning processes over a period of almost twenty years. There are places in the two books where the challenges to orthodox management, OR, and planning wisdom seem to follow quite similar lines, but other places where the recommended paradigms clearly diverge.

Much of the book by Neil Jessop and myself was concerned with extracting generalizations from the single rich source of experience we found in the Coventry project—and it must remain highly doubtful whether we would have had the confidence to attempt this task had it not been for Russ's brief intervention near the start of the project when we were preparing to embark on a more orthodox OR modeling course. Of the four sections of our book, the first two are descriptive and analytical while the two that follow launch into speculation about appropriate planning methods and then appropriate planning organization with the aid of stories about decision making in a fictitious town. It may be significant that our ideas about corporate planning and control structures for local government were to prove less durable than those about appropriate planning methods—appearing as they did at a time just when other ideas about corporate management were beginning to become fashionable in British governmental circles.

Indeed, most of the subsequent work of myself and my colleagues on the organization of planning processes has been set in intercorporate, rather than purely corporate, contexts—contexts where structures and working arrangements may have to be negotiated in an incremental way because there is no central point of authority at which a sense of unified design can be brought into play (Friend et al. 1974). So the work has moved on in an adaptive spirit—underlining the point that a comparison of paradigms on the basis of books published many years ago must be an exercise of only limited value, not the least when both paradigms have continued to evolve.

In Russ's case, it is now possible to see that *A Concept of Corporate Planning* reflected primarily those parts of his extensive experience where he was acting as adviser to central decision makers in corporations, whereas *Redesigning the Future*, appearing four years later (Ackoff 1974), covers a broader canvas of societal concern. Indeed, Russ's readiness to work experimentally outside the conventional corporate framework comes through clearly in a paper entitled "On the Ambiguity of the Researcher and the Researched," which he presented in late 1969 at a symposium arranged by the Tavistock Institute in London to commemorate the work of Neil Jessop (Ackoff 1969). Here Russ, invited specially for the occasion, reported on work with a community group in Philadelphia, where the University of Pennsylvania set out to do no more than make resources available to community leaders to use in whatever ways they felt appropriate. His role here was a far cry from that of expert adviser to the large and powerful corporation; the philosophy may have remained holistic in some sense, but the view of the life within the forest was not one obtained solely from the windows of an aircraft flying by overhead, any more than was our own view of Coventry and its city council.

Between the time of the Jessop symposium in London in 1969 and that of the surprise birthday party for Russ in Philadelphia in 1984, my own encounters with Russ have been brief. I recall a symposium on paradigms of long-range planning at a chateau outside Paris in 1974; a discussion conference on OR hosted by three universities in Sussex in 1980; a conference on OR and systems convened by the British OR Society at Henley Management Centre in 1983. Because of my preoccupation with other things in the late 1970s, I missed the drama of Russ's powerful critique of the decline of OR on both sides of the Atlantic, presented at the OR Society's York conference in 1978, though I was aware that his two papers, "The Future of OR Is Past" and "Resurrecting the Future of OR" (Ackoff 1979a and 1979b) set up a vigorous debate in Briain for years to come.

In my roles then as chairman of IOR's management committee and of its successor within the Tavistock Institute, the Centre for Organisational and Operational Research (COOR), I wrote to Russ at intervals to keep him in touch with developments and invariably received supportive and encouraging replies. From contacts with others at Penn during that period, I picked up a sense of organizational ferment at the Wharton School which seemed to have close parallels to the ferment I was experiencing all around me in Tavistock. However, reading about the genesis of Penn's Social Systems Sciences (S^3) program, I think I can see some of the contextual differences more clearly as well. For Tavistock has always existed and has adapted to its environment outside the structural framework of a university, with its rules, standards, and successive cohorts of students as an axis of continuity around which a desirable future can be conceived and designed. I recognize in saying this that the negotiation of research and consulting projects in the open market is a continuing preoccupation for the staff of the Wharton School—more so than in the case of most academic centers—but for Tavistock it is a condition of survival in a very immediate sense.

I could perhaps pursue this line of argument a little further— possibly by developing an anthropological metaphor, for I see the Tavistock Institute as in some ways based on a hunter-gatherer culture with little fixed territory to cultivate and till from year to year. But I do not think this would take me very far toward an understanding of differences in planning paradigms. For I appreciate that a diversity of linkages with different clienteles has been as much a feature of Russ Ackoff's work in planning as of my own—probably more so, when the range from national governments to industrial corporations to deprived urban communities is surveyed.

What may however be significant is that most of my work since the time of the Coventry project has involved working in the spaces between organizations, usually at a relatively local level of decision making where the configurations of stakeholders and relationships can become far from easy to disentangle—not the least because some of the more powerful organizational stakeholders have complex structures of internal and external accountability that extend far beyond the arena to which I may have secured local access. There are strategies for working gradually outward into wider arenas, but in my experience, the further one goes the more one finds that the stakeholders have other games to play—other subjects on which they would wish to focus their attention.

This point may not explain, in any historical sense, why I usually find myself in a typical project focusing on currently perceived decisions and uncertainties, rather than on issues dealing with the design of idealized futures. But I do find myself wondering how far a more future-oriented paradigm could work for me. I can imagine clearly enough how it might have been introduced into the Coventry project, working in the context of a single corporate organization with the future of the city around them as something on which all the decision makers could set their sights. But at the time, we were far from being confident enough in our methodology, or in our team identity, to have contemplated such a course—except in the simplistic terms of the "town-like thing" to which we almost became committed. Yet even had we been able to emulate the Ackoff style in the Coventry project, I suspect I would still have had difficulty in adapting it to many of the planning contexts in which I have subsequently worked.

Nor do I think this is entirely a matter of stylistic preferences or personal traits. What I believe I would find highly problematic in many contexts of local interorganizational working is the selection of any agreed *axis* along which the task of designing a desirable future could have been directed. In the process of drafting this paper, I find myself starting to think of the problem as one of selecting a vector in *n*-dimensional space—a space filled with swirling eddies and currents that could make any such selection hazardous in the extreme.

Yet I recognize the powerful appeal of the idealized design paradigm in planning, both in theory and as a guide to practice, so I am thrown back into speculation about the contextual factors that might influence a choice between a future-designing paradigm and the uncertainty-managing paradigm with which I have come to feel more at ease; a paradigm in which issues of guiding values and preferred futures are treated as sources of uncertainty to be explored and managed adaptively alongside others, while maintaining a primary focus on the decisions to be managed in the here and now.

This essay follows the publication of a new guide to the strategic choice approach, entitled *Planning under Pressure* (Friend and Hickling 1986). My coauthor Allen Hickling worked closely alongside me during the 1970s in developing the approach as a practical aid to the making of complex decisions and has since become deeply involved in consulting to governmental bodies on major policy problems, especially in the Netherlands. He too came under the influence of Russ Ackoff at a formative stage in his career, while studying at Penn for his masters' degrees in Architecture and City Planning in the late 1960s. Even though Allen and I embrace the same philosophy of planning and have shared many project experiences, we both recognize that we have different stylistic traits and preferences. So I find myself trying to imagine the ways in which any of us—Russ, Allen, myself, or various other people I know who are not afraid to walk into a messy problem situation or problematique—might act when first introduced to a new set of stakeholders and first begin to engage with their concerns.

My hunch is that there would be a more rapid convergence on the same critical areas of debate—somewhere between present urgencies and future aspirations—than a comparison of what published paradigms would lead an observer to expect. It is, of course, another matter to find ways of putting such a proposition to an empirical test. But I believe that there is a lot to be learned even from more modest attempts to reflect on experiences, on contexts, on personal and other influences—which is all I can realistically aspire to do in a paper such as this.

Concepts of planning that aspire to match the challenges of a turbulent and complex world can never perhaps be seen as more than bold steps along a difficult and hazardous road. I believe that Russ can claim credit enough for having designed and demonstrated so effectively the paradigm of adaptive planning which has become associated with his name. If my paper serves no other purpose, I hope it will indicate the credit he can also claim for having played a seminal role in creating the conditions in which another radical paradigm could take root, drawing on different experiences in another country. For a plurality of paradigms can only enrich the pool of ideas on which future innovators in planning theory and practice can draw, and the opportunity to compare, to contrast, and to synthesize is theirs.

References

Ackoff, R. L. (1969). "On the Ambiguity of the Researcher and the Researched." In *The Place of Research in Social Choice: A Symposium Dedicated to the Memory of William Neil Jessop*. London: Tavistock Institute of Human Relations.

———. (1970). *A Concept of Corporate Planning*. New York: Wiley.

———. (1974). *Redesigning the Future*. New York: Wiley.

———. (1979a). "The Future of Operational Research Is Past." *Journal of the Operational Research Society* 30: 92–104.

———. (1979b). "Resurrecting the Future of Operational Research." *Journal of the Operational Research Society* 30: 189–99.

Alexander, C. (1966). "A City Is Not a Tree." *Design* (February 1966).

Churchman, C. W., R. L. Ackoff, and E. L. Arnoff. (1957). *Introduction to Operations Research*. New York: Wiley.

Friend, J. K., and W. N. Jessop. (1977). *Local Government and Strategic Choice: An Operational Research Approach to the Processes of Public Planning*. 2nd ed. Oxford: Pergamon (first edition, London: Tavistock Publications, 1969).

Friend, J. K., J. M. Power, and C. J. L. Yewlett. (1974). *Public Planning: the Inter-Corporate Dimension*. London: Tavistock Publications.

Friend, J. K., and D. A. Hickling. (1986). *Planning under Pressure: The Strategic Choice Approach*. Oxford: Pergamon.

Jessop, W. N., et al. (1967). *Institute for Operational Research: The First Four Years 1963–1967*. London: Tavistock Institute of Human Relations.

Chapter 8
OR in Organizations

Rolfe Tomlinson

Introduction

One of the great virtues of Russ Ackoff is that he challenges his fellow practitioners and researchers to think about themselves and their work. Few follow him slavishly, but most absorb his ideas and transmute them into their own gold. This paper is a result of that process. As I listened at the birthday celebrations to the commentary on Russ's life work and heard what most of his friends and disciples had done and were doing, one thing began to stand out—practically none of them were "organization men," running advisory, analytical teams actually undertaking operations research (OR) or social systems science on a professional basis within an organization. There were many consultants (from universities and elsewhere) and plenty of clients but few pupils or disciples working in-house. This meant that none were engaged by what, in my experience, is the most effective form of operational research or social systems science, namely, in-house teams. Such an apparent contradiction surely needs an explanation.

Many in-house OR teams have failed in the past for reasons that have been abundantly exposed in Ackoff's papers in the OR/Management Science (MS) literature over the past twenty years. (But so have many managers and consultants failed.) Equally, many OR teams have been successful on a continuing basis, growing and developing with the organization it serves. Yet the literature on the methodology of OR, which is at last showing signs of growing to a serious maturity, follows the same pattern. It assumes, with few exceptions, that the analyst will operate as an outsider coming in to help, rather than acting as part of the internal criticizing, self-regulating activity of the organization itself. The continuity implied by this role is at the heart of an in-house team's success and gives a commitment to the organization it serves which is different in kind to the commitment of the consulting team.

It is not surprising that the methodological literature shows this bias, since it is largely written by academics and consultants. It is, perhaps, more surprising that the authors appear to be unaware that there are two sides to be considered. A full discussion of the issue merits a book rather than a short chapter, but it seems worth stating here a broad outline of the case for claiming that an in-house group is an effective, perhaps even the most effective, means of providing analytical support to an organization's endeavor to improve its performance—and that in doing so it performs a function which is different in kind, and thus complementary, to the consultant's function.

A Personal Odyssey

Since I have imputed that there is a bias in the methodological literature, stemming from the limited personal experience of the writers, it seems wise to establish my own bias, based, as it is, on my own personal experience.

My first industrial experience was as a consulting statistician within the Scientific Department of the British National Coal Board, concerned both with the development of general sampling and analytical procedures for headquarters clients and assistance in the design and analysis of experiments for clients in coalfield laboratories. Although I was a member of the Scientific Department's staff, my role was, in fact, close to the classical one of "independent" consultant. I was seen by the staff as a technical expert brought in to give advice on clearly defined problems. The actual decisions taken were none of my concern. In fact, since I worked in this position for nearly ten years, I was able to transcend the limitations of this position in a number of respects. Thus, I got to know most of the senior scientists who might act as my clients on a personal basis, and on that basis I would often be consulted on matters lying outside my technical expertise.

In one or two areas where I had a major part to play in developing and testing new procedures, I was given administrative responsibility and even negotiated on behalf of the board at national and international meetings. Nevertheless, my role, as I perceived it and as it was perceived by others, was very clear. I responded to requests for work relevant to my technical skill, i.e., to analyze data, establish successful procedures to design experiments, etc. My program of work consisted of a number of separate, mostly unrelated, projects coming from different clients within the organization.

I then moved to become second in command of the board's operational research team, which at that time consisted of about thirty professional staff. At first, I did not see much difference in the role that I fulfilled, other than the fact that I had much greater supervisory responsibilities for staff. At the time, I claimed the main difference was that, instead of advising advisers, I was directly advising decision makers. Even that, however, was a matter of degree rather than kind, since the scientists, despite their advisory role, were seeking my advice in order to make decisions about their work. In any case, I had always been conscious of the need in practice to be willing to go beyond the rigid limits set by the statistical analysis in order to meet the real requirements of those who were seeking advice. It was only later, when I had been director of OR for some time, that I began to realize that there had been a much more fundamental change in the nature of the work that I was doing.

This can best be understood by saying that my task went far beyond the need to ensure that management requests for assistance were met expeditiously and with full professional competence. As a senior manager on the board's staff, reporting at board level, it was my responsibility to ensure that the team's work was directed toward the most important and profitable targets, i.e., those which would be most advantageous to the board's interests in the long run. Increasingly, I found myself delegating responsibility for quality control to my deputy, whilst I concentrated on the more strategic issues. We also found that, in order to be fully effective with the various managerial groupings, we needed to establish small full-time teams working with each individual group and that these teams also had to start thinking in the same terms, i.e., they needed to think constructively about the problems facing their managerial group in order that they might undertake work that would be of maximum benefit to the organization. To use an Ackovian phrase, we had become proactive, not reactive, in our work. We had many advantages that made this possible. We reported at board level, were independent of other departments, had built up our reputation over many years, and were well-accepted by clients spread through every geographical and functional area of the board. The teams, working on a continuous basis for a particular management grouping, were clearly viewed by the managers as "us" rather than "them." The difference was, in fact, a major difference in culture.

After nearly twenty years with the Coal Board's OR team, I was seconded to the International Institute of Applied Systems Analysis (IIASA), a research institute supported by seventeen countries (including both the United States and the Soviet Union), to lead an international interdisciplinary team in the field of management and technology. The cultural contrast could not have been greater. Not only was the institute in an "outsider" position, but our clients, who were scientists and scientific committees from the member countries, were themselves "outsiders" (in the sense that they were not themselves decision makers wanting work done and would not in general be personally making use of the institute's output).

Our colleagues at the institute were highly intelligent, concerned, and full of exciting ideas, and the issues addressed were of mindstretching importance. But the output was too often irrelevant because of a lack of dialogue between the analysts and those responsible for the policy issues that the research was intended to serve. Many members of the staff at IIASA were concerned about this situation, and as a consequence, a good deal of important methodological research has been carried out. The experience certainly gave me a reinforced belief that effective policy analysis could only be carried out if there was a continuing dialogue between the client and the analyst.

Finally, I have come to an innovative and growing management school at the University of Warwick, where I have recently taken particular responsibility for an institute that houses all the school's fulltime research workers. We have thus set out to avoid the traditional university trap, whereby research workers only talk to those within their own narrow disciplinary confines. Thus, not only do we undertake a number of interdisciplinary research projects, but we also set out to achieve synergy between the disciplinary research teams as they learn how their research topics overlap. As I observe and encourage the work of these researchers, I find myself conscious of the need for corresponding groups of people within organizations who can pick up the ideas and methods being developed so that they can be effectively absorbed into wider practice. It is clear that the personal advocacy of a single consultant or researcher, selling his or her own personal expertise, is quite insufficient on its own. Going back to my own experience, it is clear that the existence of an in-house team, who sees as their task to scan what is happening in the outside world and to retrieve what is of value for their own organization, is a most powerful advantage.

The Distinctive Features of an In-House Analytical Team

In this section we shall move from the anecdotal discussion of some of the characteristics of in-house teams to a more detailed analysis, which will show that the differences between in-house and consulting teams are not simply differences of degree but rather in kind. We are not talking about two alternative ways of doing the same thing. I argue that in-house and consultancy teams have, in fact, quite different roles. This will enable us, in the final section of the chapter, to discuss in ideal terms what the role of the in-house team should be.

The main differences between in-house and consultancy teams may be discussed in three categories relating to:

1. The team's observational base.
2. Its management relationships.
3. Its objectives.

At first sight, the observational base of the in-house team might be thought to be identical to the consulting group's. When a particular project is proposed, a series of meetings take place with staff at various levels, files and existing data sources are examined, relevant information is extracted, and new information is requested. In order to do this, the investigator has to obtain an understanding of the real issues involved in order to ensure that relevant data is obtained. He or she also needs a clear idea of how any information collected would be used, together with the ability to set the value of additional information against the cost of collection. Information obtained in this way is used to sharpen the problem, analyze it, and test alternative solutions before developing an implementation scheme.

The question that the in-house team would ask is whether that is enough. They could point to the very strong movement in the social sciences at present which claims that the only way to understand what is happening in an organization, and therefore to understand the ways in which change can be managed, is through longitudinal studies. In these studies the behavior and interaction of all the actors (relevant to a particular decision stream) is studied over a period of time, leading up to the time when the actual decisions have to be made.

There is no way by which the external consulting group can achieve this knowledge and understanding. In the first place, it can only tackle the past on a historical basis, which is a doubtful substitute for on-the-spot observation. In the second place, collection of such material is usually too time-consuming to be allowed within the normal consultancy project. The in-house team, on the other hand, if it is properly attuned, is unconsciously undertaking this longitudinal study all the time. By undertaking many studies over a period of time in most parts of the organization, a unique understanding can be obtained. The skilled leader of any such in-house team is constantly observing the interactions between senior members of staff that may lead to changes in policy, which would thus affect the kind of work the team can undertake as well as the way in which its results can be absorbed in the mainstream of the organization. In many cases, this broad continuing observational basis can be critical in identifying hidden assumptions, in explaining behavior, and in anticipating future occurrences.

Of course, there are dangers in this continual process of observation. For one thing, the accustomed observer can only too easily see what he or she expects to see and be blind to changes occurring outside the limited area which is the focus of attention. We shall return to this issue later on.

A second way in which this broader observational base can be of major importance to the analyst is in the way it enriches his or her understanding of "process." It is still inadequately recognized in the literature that an understanding of the processes (both formal and informal) by which an organization survives, controls, and develops is essential if the advisory analytical team is to be effective. These processes include both the formal procedures for planning and control, which are set out in the organizational manuals, but also the informal processes by which ideas are developed and opinions formed and hardened. Without such an understanding, the recommendations of an investigating team are likely to be made either too early or too late or by a route that does not lead to a consideration of the ideas by the right people at the right time. It is a truism that in order to understand these processes they have to be observed in person. Even the formal processes, as actually carried out, usually differ significantly from what is laid down in the procedural manuals. Furthermore, although something of the informal procedures can usually be gleaned from discussion with interested parties, those descriptions are usually based on an inadequate knowledge of the reality and a misleading belief concerning causality. There is no substitute for ongoing observation.

A further advantage of the continuing internal observation base is that it makes anticipation possible and more reliable. This is as important in the negative sense of anticipating what will happen if nothing is changed, as it is in the positive sense of anticipating the consequences of a proposed change. The positive aspect of anticipation is clearly important, and some skill at it is obviously necessary for all consultancy, but even here, the in-house consultant has certain advantages. His or her continuing observation base will have made it possible to observe the actual results of previous implementations and to identify the causes for departures from target. Even more, the continuing presence of that same observation base, while implementation is taking place and afterward, provides a much greater assurance that the implementation will be successful. Difficulties that might arise from small departures from the assumptions implied in the proposed solution can quickly be identified rather than waiting for them to become major issues.

But the negative aspect of anticipation is perhaps the most important difference between the in-house group and consultancy. It is in the nature of events that the observer can often see trends and patterns that the person involved in the process cannot. The continuing observer of the organizational process can often identify problems arising and thus anticipate decisions that may have to be taken before the actors themselves become aware of them, certainly before they realize that they may need help. By anticipation of "what is going to happen unless," the in-house team can often prepare to provide the assistance and help required by the staff in the organization themselves in advance of the request. This, indeed, is often the only way in which an OR team can help with crises. Since the very nature of a crisis is that it demands a quick response, an OR study often cannot be completed within the time span between the crisis becoming apparent and the necessity for an answer. If, however, the crisis has been anticipated, the preliminary work can be done and the OR team can help in time. But such anticipation can only be the result of the broader continuing observation base that the in-house team possesses.

The third way in which the in-house team's broader observation base gives an advantage in kind is in understanding the "culture" of the organization. Culture still tends to be discussed in the methodological literature as an unavoidable evil that distorts the message the analyst tries to give and leads to irrational responses from the managers and decision makers in the organization. We are now beginning to realize that such an attitude is both unreal and irresponsible.

All organizations have their culture molded by history, custom, fashion, and the whims and beliefs of those holding power within the organization (and in modern organizations this power is as likely to lie outside the management grouping as within it). The organizational culture carries with it a set of assumptions about relationships and motivation within the organization, as well as beliefs about the external environment that may not relate to the reality. The culture is both one of the most important and most difficult aspects of organizational life to identify, partly because we still do not have an adequate language for its description and classification. Culture may not only affect the processes that lead to a decision being taken, but perhaps more importantly, culture is likely to determine whether a proposal enters the decision making process at all.

Culture influences the roles that people play and the importance given to the various roles; it determines the way in which new ideas are absorbed and the way in which new staff are recruited. If you ask cultural anthropologists to lay out a simple set of questions that will define an organization's culture, they will tell you that it cannot be done. On the contrary, they will say that, if you understand cultural theory, a careful analysis over a period of time inevitably reveals the culture and enables you to anticipate future patterns of behavior. Again, it is only possible to do this with the broad continuing observation base of a group living and working within an organization.

Although many of the advantages mentioned above could be gained by a suitably trained individual, they are most effectively secured within a group. The danger of relying solely on in-house observers is that they can so absorb the organizational culture as to become incapable of making any accurate observations in certain areas, since they will always do this within the cultural assumptions of the organization. The "professional" in-house group undertaking investigational work of this kind can avoid this trap, if it so organizes itself. Accurate observation requires that observers need frequent checking with periodical reference to some absolute reference point. This can only effectively be done by cross-checking between members of the team and by reference to some more absolute criteria, either maintained by the team itself or from the world outside.

The second way in which the in-house group is different in kind from the consultancy team is in its relationships. Again the difference here is not apparent at first. Any investigational team has to make itself acceptable to its client group. This acceptability may be based on professional respect, rather than personal liking, but it needs to be a good working relationship. If, on the other hand, there is positive dislike between client and analyst, it is unlikely that the latter will be able to complete an effective investigation.

The question of relationships for an in-house group is altogether deeper and more complex than this, stemming from the fact that the relationship is not a short-term one but rather one that existed before the project was undertaken and will continue after it has been completed. Even if the manager concerned has not had previous experience with the in-house consulting group, he or she will almost certainly have found out a great deal about it from the grapevine and, of course, vice versa. Equally, the fact that the in-house team does not disappear at the end of the investigation but is available for consultation afterward strongly affects the relationship. The fact that the analysts are still around to collect praise and/or blame and to consult, and are prepared to take some continuing personal responsibility to ensure the success of what they have done, is a major lure in forging continuing relationships. Much of this can be summarized in that an in-house group is not simply there, it belongs. This means that it is tacitly assumed by the staff concerned that the in-house group is "on their side," that they are there to help and not simply to make a quick killing.

To reinforce what was said in the previous paragraph, we have to remember that the relationship between the in-house group and the organization being served is multilayered, i.e., connections exist at more than one level in the two systems. This is particularly important in hierarchical organizations where points of disagreement at the operating level can be hammered out and clarified in discussion at a higher level, represented both by the in-house group and the management hierarchy. In the National Coal Board environment, I routinely met each area director and director general on an annual basis, and my senior staff would be meeting with their deputies more frequently. This multilayered approach, on a continuous basis, greatly simplified the identification of suitable projects and made the resolution of difficulties possible as a matter of course rather than as a matter of crisis.

It should not be necessary to emphasize in a paper like this that the question of relationships is vital to the success of any investigational study directed toward organizational change, and we need to recognize that the outcome of these studies will almost invariably be a change in individual behavior patterns. These changes do not take place simply because of the presentation of a logical argument, they require discussion, understanding, and eventually a personal commitment by the staff concerned that the recommended path is the one to be chosen. The creation of such change involves a continual interchange between those who have to be responsible for the continued process that is being investigated and those responsible for the investigation. Success at that interchange depends critically on relationships.

Finally, we come to a third main difference in kind, which relates to the objective of the group itself. The prime objective of the external consultant group must be the success of that group. Different groups may measure success in different ways. Clearly, financial survival is important and profits inevitably enter into the calculations, but given those requirements, some groups will be more concerned with influence or developing personal interests or simply using the consultancy as an aid to research. In all cases, however, the interests of the group are paramount. This does not necessarily work against the client's interests. Success can only be achieved through establishing a reputation, and this comes from client satisfaction.

The people in charge of in-house groups have, however, a totally different primary objective, even though they too cannot achieve it without client satisfaction. Although the in-house leader's objective does not relate to the in-house groups themselves, it is to best serve the interests of the organizations of which they are a part. They are not at liberty (or should not be) to choose the most "interesting" work or, indeed, the work that shows the best short-term profits. They are in command of what must, in any organization, be a scarce resource (that of highly skilled investigators), and they have a duty to the organization to allocate those resources in the way that will most benefit the organization itself.

As I discussed in the previous section, I found when I was in charge of the National Coal Board's Operational Research Executive that a high proportion of my time was devoted to the question of identifying what were the best projects that we should be working on in order that the organization as a whole might benefit to the maximum extent. Clearly, the identification of the best projects depended on a number of factors, such as meeting the needs of senior managers, creating an interesting environment for my own staff and, indeed, making a profit (or the particular version of that universal requirement which we operated within the OR Executive). But the identification of the organization-centered objective created a difference in kind between the culture and methodology of our group and that of most external consultants. Basically, we were committed to the success of the Coal Board not just for the duration of a single project but as a major part of our existence. An acceptance that this was the case was a major factor in developing special relationships with the management concerned and in their willingness to allow us to obtain a variety of observational information.

It may be worth emphasizing these points by two examples. At one stage of our development, we started to undertake some consultancy work for the Department of Health and Social Security. Most of the early work was for the Supplies Department, looking at the traditional problems of stores organization, ordering procedures, etc. After we had been working with one management group for about twelve months, one of their staff turned round to our team leader and said that he could not understand our people—they behaved consistently as if they belonged to his organization. Needless to say, he meant the remark as praise, but it also expressed clearly his understanding of the different culture of our team from that of traditional consultants.

Even within the National Coal Board, the same picture emerged. From time to time we were asked to advise management on matters related to their use of the computer. At the time, the Computer Service had set out to organize themselves on a commercial basis, providing a service both to clients within the board and outside in an even-handed way. The board's management kept on coming to the OR staff for help on computer matters because, they said, they needed someone who would approach the problems from their point of view rather than from the point of view of selling an existing service. A purely market approach is not necessarily the cheapest or most efficient way to handle internal needs.

In discussing the potential advantages of one form of organization, one must not lose sight of the fact that, in practice, a team may not take advantage of their opportunities. It may not set out to make use of its broad observational base, it may not develop strong personal relationships, and it may never absorb and understand the organizational culture. That does not weaken the case any more than the fact that many external consultants do succeed in overcoming the disadvantages of their position by developing permanent relationships, as Russ Ackoff has done with Anheuser-Busch. Moreover, these advantages are not relevant to all kinds of problem—many of which require the shock of the concentrated attack provided by the outsider. As we have already said, our thesis is that the two groups, in-house and consultancy, have different functions.

Conclusion: Ideal Design

Our discussion so far has identified what appear to be real differences in the roles of in-house and consultancy groups. It has, however, been a group-centered discussion. Since the purpose of both kinds of team is to support and strengthen the management of organizations, this approach could be considered as inappropriate. On the contrary, an organization-centered approach is required. Comparisons should not be based on the way that the groups operate but in terms of the function that they fulfill for the organization. Viewed in this way, the role of the consultant is straightforward: it is to strengthen points of weakness or to replace gaps in the existing organizational system. The thesis of this paper is that the in-house group has a fundamentally different role, which is inherent to the organizational system. If this is so, its role can only be understood in relation to the functioning of the whole system. In order to obtain this understanding, we need to have a model of the system to relate to.

Many systems models of organizations could be used for this discussion, but the most convenient for the present purpose is Stafford Beer's "Brain of the Firm." Beer asserts that any viable system operates at five levels, which can be designated as follows:

Level 1: The board (policy and strategy).
Level 2: Regulatory center.
Level 3: Corporate management (coordination, objective setting, and control).
Level 4: Development directorate.
Level 5: Unit management.

In very simple terms Levels 1, 3, and 5 may be described as the "doers" and Levels 2 and 4 as the "thinkers." Essentially, the thinkers provide the sensing, analyzing, feedback, and trouble-shooting activities that enable the doers to exert the appropriate controls for the effective operation of the whole system.

The in-house team clearly comes somewhere within the "thinking" part. The fact that there is often great difficulty in deciding where to locate the OR team follows naturally from the fact that most organizations have not solved the problem of how to organize those thinking activities—indeed, they have not even studied the problem of organizational design in systems terms. A case can be argued that organization of the thinking activities is the most critical as well as the most difficult problem for organizations. It is a problem complicated by the fact that some key staff in the organization may have dual roles (e.g., some members of the board must be personally involved in the development directorate) and also by the fact that many of the thinking activities have semiroutine elements (e.g., data collection and dissemination or preparation of annual budgets), which may be classed as "doing." Indeed, it is for this reason, among others, that the Beer model is primarily used for the analysis of process and is a valuable precursor to organizational design, rather than as an embryonic organization chart. It describes necessary activities without in any way prescribing the organizational relationships of those who undertake those activities.

The reason that many organizations survive without giving this element of organization formal thought is that these functions are often perceived as necessary and picked up informally by groups or individuals, thus extending their formal activities. The danger of such a process is that the linkages between these functions are not managed, that no one is formally responsible for ensuring they are actually carried out, and that they are too often handled in a nonprofessional fashion. It is systems failures, based on inadequate design, that often lead to planning lapses.

It is sometimes said that the thinking functions are part of management and cannot be delegated. There is some truth in this but only some. Management must be involved in, and take the responsibility for, planning, objective setting, and control (to mention the three most obvious thinking functions), but there is no reason to believe that they cannot delegate, just as they do for doing activities. Indeed, since there is a wide range of professional skills involved, there is a need that they should. The methods of delegation may, however, be quite different, and this is a problem that in-house teams often have to solve.

We now have the basic elements for an ideal design of an in-house team. If one accepts that there is a need to design the functions in relation to the organizational system as a whole, then the role and function of the in-house team starts to fall into place. Indeed, it is easy to see that the special properties of the in-house team discussed in the previous sections are necessary elements of the thinking function; the match is ideal. The implication, therefore, is that most of the previous argumentation concerning OR teams has been wrong-headed. Those arguments started with an initial justification of the existence of the team—usually by reference to the "profitability" of individual projects—and then trying to find a location for it. We are now starting by looking at the organization and the functions that have to be carried out and find that a significant part of the thinker's role is what the more successful internal OR teams actually do. The role can be defined in those terms.

We cannot work out the consequences of this in the present paper. It is clear, however, that the new concept calls for a radical revision of ideas about the role of OR in an organization, not the least as to where its natural alliances and affinities are to be found. However, enough should have been said that there is a very distinctive role to be carried out, which is quite different from the role usually assumed when OR is discussed in the literature.

Chapter 9
Andras Angyal and Systems Thinking

Eric Trist

Andras Angyal was a Hungarian psychiatrist who settled in the United States in the late 1920s. After a sojourn at the Phipps Clinic, he became Research Director of the State Mental Hospital at Worcester, Massachusetts, but later went into private practice as a psychotherapist and became associated with Brandeis University. At the Phipps Clinic he came under the influence of Adolf Meyer who, more strongly than any other psychiatrist of that time, put forward the view that the individual had to be considered as a social, psychological, and biological whole. This tradition of dynamic holism was strengthened in Angyal's case by the influence of the early Gestalt psychologists and of Wilhelm Stern (1930) who had introduced a theory of personalism. Kurt Goldstein (1940), who approached neuropsychiatry from a Gestalt viewpoint, was an even stronger influence.

Angyal, however, took a further step than these writers by formulating dynamic holism not only in systems terms but explicitly in terms of a theory of open systems. While the general idea of a system being open to its environment may be traced back to von Bertalanffy (1932) or Kohler (1938)—and some may look for even earlier roots—no one before Angyal (1941) in his book *Foundations for a Science of Personality* (hereafter, FSP), which appeared in the early years of World War II, had stated the open systems concept in a way that showed its central relevance to the biological and social sciences as a whole.

Though within psychology both this book and his later posthumous volume on *Neurosis and Treatment* (Angyal 1966) exercised a considerable influence on the human potential movement, his contribution was passed by when the systems idea came to the forefront in the wake of cybernetics and information theory in the 1950s and 1960s. To remedy this neglect, Trist (1970) presented a brief overview of

Angyal's ideas in a special number of the *Revue française de sociologie* intended to introduce the systems viewpoint to French social scientists. Sachs (1976) developed these ideas further in a critical evaluation in which he extended Angyal's concept of "relation" on the basis of the work of Ackoff and Emery (1972) *On Purposeful Systems*. Very few writers have taken up any of Angyal's ideas at the social level of analysis. Emery (1967) would appear to be an exception in using Angyal's vertical, progression, and transverse dimensions and his notions of pressure, intrusion, and mutual invasion in order to develop a theory of maladaptive social defenses.

In this paper I will present certain of Angyal's ideas that seem to me to have retained their significance, describe my own use of them, and attempt to show how later developments, especially those made by Ackoff and Emery (1972), have corrected some aspects in which they are inadequate.

Organization, System, and System Connectedness

The need for a systems approach arises in Angyal's view when the world is regarded as consisting of a set of concrete objects. Each member of a set of concrete objects has being only as a substantive whole; otherwise, it would have no identity, no existence. Sooner or later, any empirical science has to cope with the members of this set in its own domain, whether as atoms, molecules, crystals, cells, brains, organisms, groups, or societies. Angyal is not, however, concerned with isomorphisms that may be found in this series, as general systems theory is, but rather with the fact that, while all concrete objects display organization, each class of such objects is differentiated from other classes by having its own organizing or systems principle. Like Vickers (1984), he thought that "human systems are different."

Wholeness is not simple but represents, in Angyal's phrase, a *unitas multiplex*—a system of interdependencies. It consists in complexity—which expresses organization. Organization is the primary datum when nature—physical, biological, or social—is considered as a set of concrete whole objects. It is organization—and organizations—one has to study if this is the perspective adopted. How far organizational forms may prove to be isomorphic has to be established empirically.

Organization refers to both structure and process, concepts that have created much confusion and, in terms of one of which, to the exclusion of the other, many theories have been developed. Angyal's writings suggest that a structure is a process and that a process has structure. This double character of organization as structure and process seems to me to be demonstrable on the psychological level by the responses to the artificial creation of random fields:

1. A random perceptual field may be created in the experimental laboratory, as in the classic Gestalt experiments with the "white fog" situation. A spontaneous differentiation then occurs between figure and ground.
2. A random association field may be created in the clinical "laboratory" of the psychoanalytic session. A structuring by unconscious processes then occurs with the patient's associations.
3. A random group field may be created in the social "laboratory" of the small-group situation. Leaderless groups proceed to establish social structures, however temporary.

The double character of organization as structure and process means that organizations are inherently self-regulating. Organization, the opposite of chaos (randomness), is temporally as well as spatially extended. In his view the organized object resists disorganization.

We must now ask how we may handle conceptually the type of problem arising from irreducible complexity, since this is what organization possesses. The "distinctive competence" of system theory is to offer a conceptual strategy for analyzing the irreducibly complex—namely, the phenomenon of organization. This means leaving the part in the whole and handling relations of interdependence. This requires its own logic and new forms of mathematics.

Traditional scientific method has been developed for the complementary purpose—the reduction of the complex to the simple—by abstracting the part from the whole and analyzing relations of dependence and independence. The logical and mathematical forms that have become classical have been concerned with functional relations.

If the concrete whole object is organized, then a system is a logical representation (or model) of its organization. What then is distinctive about system connectedness? Von Bertalanffy (1956) was content to say: "Systems are complexes of elements standing in interaction." Hall and Fagen (1956) became more precise but continued along the same line: "A system is a set of objects together with relationships between the objects and between their attributes." This, which is the usual definition, does not refer the parts back to the whole. It suggests all over again that the system equals the sum of its objects, relationships, and attributes. Summation, however, is *not* organization, but it is of little help simply to say that a system is more than the sum of its parts.

Angyal's definition allows the distinctive nature of the system problem to be grasped: "A system is a distribution of constituents with positional values in a dimensional domain." The logical model of a system cannot be directly constructed from the concept of functional relationship. Functional relationship is the key concept of the reductive approach. For a systems approach a different concept, such as that of positional value, is required which expresses arrangement and compels reference of the parts back to the whole. The value of parts is what they do for the whole. Their function is its maintenance. Only a whole maintained in this way can relate to an environment. To make possible relations with an environment is the function of the whole. Angyal is, of course, concerned with living systems.

Only, however, through certain properties (relevant attributes) can parts fill the required system positions. This allows relational thinking to be redeployed in the context of positional thinking. The old strategy can be used to reinforce rather than to extinguish the new strategy. Similarly, the new strategy can be brought in when a limit has been reached through the old. At least this is my interpretation. Otherwise, the two approaches would be in contradiction under all conditions. Complementary use would be impossible. The position taken here is that they can be used in the order determined by the problem. A psychologist familiar with the Rorschach inkblot test will recognize this complementarity: the "location" responses represent positional values, and the "determinants," relevant attributes such as form, color, shading, or ascribed movement.

Codetermination by relevant attributes varies between systems. It is greater in more complex systems that achieve greater "economy" by using more of the properties of the parts. This increases their range of responsiveness. They are able to deal with greater variation from their environments. Codetermination is greater in more open systems, as is the holistic reference of positions.

Angyal was the first writer to make a distinction between system connectedness and functional relations and between positional values and relevant attributes. This was a major advance. As the preceding account has shown, however, he limited the concept of systems to entities that could be regarded as bounded wholes. Such entities are inherently hierarchical as the parts are subordinate to the whole. Whether such a restriction is justified will be discussed in a later section of this chapter. For the present, we shall follow Angyal's usage.

System and Environment

Differences between systems can, in fact, only be settled by considering the relation of a system to its environment. Little progress was made in understanding system-environment relations until the distinction was drawn between open and closed systems. If this is now commonplace and if systems in various degrees and in various ways open to their environments are now taken as the general case, while systems closed to their environments are taken as the special case, it must not be forgotten how radical a development this represented.

Conceptually, the distinction between open and closed systems had been adumbrated by von Bertalanffy as early as 1932, but it took a number of years before equations were found and experiments carried out in sufficient number to make this concept operational in various branches of the biological sciences. Its reference back to physics itself was made operational by the earlier work of Prigogine (1947) on the thermodynamics of irreversible processes. There was, however, little reference to psychology and the social sciences. The advent of information theory concentrated attention, for rather too long, on communications systems based on electronic machines, though this served to show how many "organic" and goal-seeking properties a machine could possess.

A system is usually regarded as closed if no components enter or leave it, open if there is import and export. It became generally recognized that physics and chemistry were traditionally concerned with processes in closed reaction systems leading to equilibrium states with maximum entropy—in accordance with the second law of thermodynamics—and that living systems could not be modeled in these terms. They required the concept of the open system with changing components that could attain a time-independent steady state in which work could be done and with which maximum rather than minimum energy was associated. The organism earned a living by making a net profit in the value of its imports over its exports, a process called negative entropy by von Bertalanffy (1950).

Once the property of "negentropy" became established other properties could follow, such as capacity for growth and "equifinality." Greater closure of part systems could permit greater openness of the whole so that more complex systems could establish ranges of adaptability far greater than simpler systems. They could extend into wider and richer environments and at the same time absorb the increased uncertainty and variance. The capacity to encode and decode information became critical. On this depended regulation through negative feedback, so that directions could be taken or held, or avoided or discontinued.[1] Otherwise, no "terms of reference" could be set, no missions undertaken. The organism being incomplete—a necessary consequence of being open—had actively to establish and maintain environmental conditions—a domain—which permitted its continued existence. Open system theory began to characterize environmental context and to conceptualize the interdependence between system and environment.

The above brief account summarizes ideas in good currency in systems thinking in the mid-1950s. Angyal had, however, anticipated most of them in an earlier language. On page 21 of his 1941 book is a diagram that opens the "closed circle of life." On one side, the circle is open for "intake" from the environment and its "assimilation" and "transformation" by the organism; on the other, it is open for "production." The exchanges in both directions are described on the physical, psychological, and sociocultural levels. His argument is against what he called the "immanence hypothesis."

In conceptualizing the interdependence between system and environment, Angyal made a novel contribution by making this interdependence his starting point. Instead of taking two terms "system" and "environment," which he must then relate in interactionist terms, he starts with one, the "universe," which includes them both. This he calls the "biosphere." For Angyal (1941), life takes place in the biosphere rather than inside the organism (or organization):

> I propose to call the realm in which the biological total process takes place the "biosphere", that is, the realm or sphere of life. The biosphere includes both the individual and the environment, not as interacting parts, not as constituents which have independent existence, but as aspects of a single reality which can be separated only by abstraction. (p. 106)

His treatment of the abstraction process is basic and merits quotation at length:

> The biosphere, although an undivided unit, still is not structureless. It is differentiated along various dimensions. In the biosphere two definite directions can be distinguished: autonomous determination or environmental government. These two directions do not exist independently but only within the biospheric happenings, in other words, as components of the biological total process. Both directions extend to the very limit of the biosphere. At one pole of the biological total process, the autonomous determination is the most potent one, and it extends to the opposite pole in the way of a gradient of decrease. At the other pole the heteronomous factor is the prevailing one which extends as a gradient of decrease toward the opposite pole. The two trends are like two currents of opposing direction, inseparably united in the total dynamics of the biosphere.
>
> According to the dominance of one or the other determinant the biosphere is roughly differentiated into two fields. Those factors which are prevalently under autonomous government constitute the organism or self or subject, while the factors which are prevalently under heteronomous government form the objects or the environment. The words "subject" and "object" express very aptly the difference which I have in mind. "Subject" is that factor which governs, "subjects", the raw environment. "Object"

means that which is "thrown before" the subject, but also that which opposes, offers resistance, i.e., "*objects*" to the subject's influences. It is the non-system–determined, heteronomous factor. The differentiation of the biosphere into subject and object is the basic organization of the biosphere and forms the foundation for further structuralizations.

The single factors have no fixed position in the biosphere. Processes which, at a given moment, stand prevalently under environmental government may at the next moment come under prevalently organismic government.

Strictly speaking, one cannot generalize and state to what extent a given type of biological occurrence is organismically or environmentally governed. The exact value of this ratio can be determined only in specific instances. There is, in other words, a continuous flux between the two poles of the biosphere. (FSP, pp. 101–102)

When a new unit of analysis such as this is introduced, one may expect a major conceptual shift to follow, as with the transition from closed to open systems with which it is congruent. The shift this time is in "root metaphor"—in Pepper's (1950) use of this term—from "mechanism" to "contextualism." This alters the approach to causality from that of "linear causal trains" to "field determination." This parallels the change from functional relations to system connectedness. This does not mean that the concept of causality in the traditional sense is no longer useful; simply that it may now be seen as a special case in a more general theory of contextual determination—as with the concepts of closed systems and functional relation.

Angyal's approach to behavior as consisting of biospheric events is compatible with Lewin's assertion (1935) that

$$B = f(P, E)$$

or that behavior (B) is a function of personality (P) and environment (E). But to treat behavior in his manner as jointly determined by autonomous (a) and heteronomous (h) factors has the form

$$B = f\left(\frac{a_1}{h_1}, \frac{a_2}{h_2}, \ldots\right)$$

which more clearly states the problem of the coupling of correlative but independent systems. The values of the ratio a/h can vary through time and context for any given system. Moreover, as Angyal is at pains to point out, the value of a relative to h increases in complex living systems that expand into their environment and to some extent fill it with their products. People, for example, have come to live largely in an environment of their own making.

Angyal's views on the joint determination of the life process by the organism and the environment foreshadow those of Singer (1947) on coproduction and of Sommerhoff (1950) on directive correlation. As discussed later, these writers took a step regarding the teleological question which Angyal was unable to take. Meanwhile, it may be noted that Angyal's view of the total "biological process" as life-expanding depended on his assigning a positive function to catabolism rather than merely the negative function (the disposal of matter and energy as wastes), which conventional biology assigned to it. More than the simple opposite of anabolism, the primary function of catabolism was for him the mobilization of the assimilated resources of the organism for "production," i.e., adaptive behavior in the environment at the physical, psychological, and sociocultural levels. He contrasts his view with that of Freud who based his idea of a death instinct on the analogy of catabolism as simple breakdown—a definition consistent with the immanence hypothesis.

In the terms of Ackoff and Emery (1972), Angyal treats the organism as a functional rather than a morphological class. As his whole account of organism-environment relations shows, this has major implications for where boundaries are placed. This problem increases in importance as the psychological and social levels are reached as distinct from the physiological level, but the treatment in terms of functional class holds for all levels.

Models Abstracting in the Direction of the Subject and Object Poles

A new orientation may be gained if some of the main theoretical schemes that have been used in psychology and the social sciences are considered as abstractions in the direction of what Angyal called the subject or object poles of the biospheric process. Models abstracted in the direction of the subject pole regard all events as being exclusively determined by processes internal to the target system. This is equally the case whether the target system is, at one extreme, an individual or, at the other, a society. In models abstracted in the direction of the object pole, the individual (or group) is reduced to a limit (a boundary condition) to permit examination of the environmental characteristics. However, the individual has to be retained at least as a "point region" (Lewin 1935), since it is, after all, his or her environment that is being examined, a field affected by his or her attributes and composed of objects affecting, and relevant to, the individual. The environment, when abstracted, can be treated as seen by the subject whose environment it is or by an external observer. This makes no difference to the direction of the abstraction being that of the object pole in Angyal's sense.

The models made from the subject pole are of two main types called by Dahrendorf (1967) "harmony models" and "conflict models." Harmony models are constructed to explain stability; conflict models, to explain change.

Examples of theories concerned with harmony dynamics abound in classical Gestalt psychology—the law of Pragnanz, closure, good continuation, etc. Later Gestalt-derived theories such as dissonance reduction, balance theory, and cognitive consistency are also harmony models. In all of them stabilization is presented as a self-organizing process. The structural-functional approach in sociology is no less a harmony model, particularly as developed in social anthropology by Radcliffe-Brown and his followers. Counterpoint is added to simple harmony in that Durkheim from the beginning considered social cohesion as resulting from the division of labor. Nevertheless, the intent is to show that a society as a whole maintains itself as a going concern through the compatibility of its parts.

Turning now to models concerned with conflict dynamics, we may illustrate from the work of writers as different as Marx and Freud. Marx postulated that internal contradictions in class relations would lead to the replacement of one form of society by another. But this was an immanent process inherent in the dialectic. Freud postulated a primary ambivalence in unconscious object-relations derivable from a dualistic instinct system, which he regarded as the psychological representative of the processes of anabolism and catabolism. Though this led to a positive concept of an id as well as an ego, the underlying premise is again that of immanent conflict.

However dynamic, these theories are based on closed system equilibrium models. Consequently, they cannot relate concepts of harmony and conflict. Stability and change remain incompatible states. A steady state as distinct from an equilibrium is characterized by the simultaneous presence of stability and change. Open system theory, as foreshadowed by Agnyal, can include harmony and conflict in the same model. It would expect them to coexist. If environment and organism each have their own causal texture while interpenetrating and belonging to each other, incompatibilities as well as compatibilities will arise in each system, and heteronomous and autonomous processes will both be present.

Among models based on the object pole, two perspectives may be distinguished—the projective and the introjective. In the projective perspective the environment is treated as external to the individual (or group), and in the introjective perspective it is treated as internal. Claude Bernard introduced the idea of an internal environment into physiology; Freud introduced it to psychology. As Angyal has pointed out, what is to be regarded as organismic and what environmental cannot be decided morphologically but according to which system is in control.

An example of the projective perspective is Lewin's field theory (1935)—the person in his or her life space (or the group in its life space). Of interest now become the valences of objects, regions of locomotion, barriers, and the permeability of boundaries. Such contentless dynamics has its own advantages but needs supplementing by a scheme such as the "action frame of reference" of Parsons (1949). The actor is now placed in a situation the content of which is defined in terms of a given social structure and culture.

An example of the introjective perspective is object-relations theory in psychoanalysis. Since Freud introduced the idea of the superego as a system of internalized figures existing in the person but largely outside the ego, psychoanalysts, such as Melanie Klein (1948) and Fairbairn (1952), have greatly extended the idea of an "internal society" invested with unconscious phantasy. An extension of this perspective is the personality-culture approach in which the culture of a society is viewed as internalized by the individual, though not passively carried but actively shaped by him or her (Kluckholn and Murray 1948).

If the difficulty of reconciling harmony and conflict models is that of relating stability and change, the difficulty of reconciling the projective and introjective perspectives is that of relating to each other the external and internal worlds. For Angyal, the traditional difficulties arise only because of the dualism inherent in any conceptual scheme that begins by separating the organism and the environment—thus closing off one from the other. By assuming that life is a function of a total biospheric process, Angyal can regard perception in any of its sensory modalities as a medium regulating the transactions between autonomous and heteronomous aspects. Like any medium, the perceptual apparatus has a degree of error, but in people its outstanding feature is *symbolic representation*, which creates the "psychological level." In so doing it allows a new economy because only a part of the total object or state of affairs needs to be represented. It also increases the scope for communication between system and environment, since this no longer needs to be actual.

Angyal considers the function of the psychological level in system terms as follows:

The individual and the environment can now meet on the symbolic, representative ground of psychological functions. . . . In the psychological realm life takes place, not through the interaction of the concrete individual with a concrete environment—which is only tangential—but by the interaction of symbols representing the individual and the environment. (FSP, p. 77)

Symbolism raises system openness to an altogether new level.

The problem of relating theories of stability to theories of change and of the subjective to the objective perspectives has continued to haunt psychology and the social sciences. Burrell and Morgan (1981) maintain that the four historical viewpoints in sociology constitute separate paradigms which only make sense in terms of their own premises. While each has its own truth-value, transparadigmatic traffic is not possible. An open systems framework such as Angyal began to develop shows them to be complementary rather than contradictory and boundary crossing to be required rather than infeasible.

We can now see more fully the implications of Freud's concept of the ego as an intervening organization between organismic and environmental processes. This concept, unlike his instinct theory, belongs to open systems thinking. The ego coheres and integrates the individual while containing and regulating his or her conflicts. Its growth is the stuff of environmental exchanges (internal and external), its repertoire the degree of flexibility, and its direction the delineation of identity.

The ego does work (consciously and unconsciously), and it is the work process that relates the organism to the environment. This process consists of activities undertaken in the interests of adaptive survival, sometimes successfully, sometimes unsuccessfully, pursued. Once the mediating function of work in this wider sense is realized, the same conceptual scheme can be transferred from the individual to the group—to the "work group" in Bion's (1961) sense. This permits the examination of a very wide set of human activities in one frame of reference. It allows the inclusion of the technical component whether as person-carried skills or their extension in artifacts. Sociotechnical systems are work systems. Work is the key transaction (behavior) which, by relating an operating individual or group to its environment, allows it to maintain the steady state. Individuals and groups develop "cultures" as mediating instruments that make possible the satisfaction of their needs in their environments.

The necessity of satisfying needs in an environment raises the question of individuals and groups being purposeful systems in the sense of Ackoff and Emery (1972) rather than in the traditional

Aristotelian sense. This will be discussed in the next section. Meanwhile, we may note that Glazer (1984) makes his case for looking at systems in terms of "outcomes" with special reference to Angyal's views on system connectedness.

Autonomy and Homonomy

Angyal asserts that the human life process is characterized by what he calls a trend toward autonomy. The organism has to establish itself in terms of its own intrinsic pattern and in so doing attempts to extend its control over its heteronomous environment. It has to lay claim to, enlarge, and protect its own space. Drives and traits of competitiveness, aggressiveness, individualism, mastery, and acquisitiveness all derive from the trend toward autonomy that establishes the independence value of the individual.

The trend toward autonomy is balanced by an opposite and complementary trend he calls "homonomy." This concerns the ways in which individuals relate to the larger world of which they are a part rather than relating this world to their own needs. The others to whom they relate and to varying degrees surrender may include a loved one, family, a social group, an organization, society, or, at the farthest limit, the cosmos. In developing relations with others, individuals establish their interdependence value which is as deeply necessary as their independence value. In his second book, Angyal (1966) greatly extends his treatment of homonomy, going so far as to say that the individual can achieve personal identity only through and by recognition of the other. He felt his earlier account had been misunderstood, largely because the values deriving from homonomy have been underemphasized in Western industrial societies whereas those deriving from autonomy have been overemphasized. He is at pains to show that aesthetic as well as religious experiences are expressive of the homonomous trend, a point since elaborated by Emery (1977).

In *Neurosis and Treatment* Angyal summarizes as follows:

> Far from being irreconcilable opposites the autonomous and the homonomous trends can be viewed as part aspects of one trend or perhaps as one trend functioning in two directions—downward and upward. To put it abstractly, the human being behaves as if he were a whole of an intermediate order, comparable to the cardiovascular system or the central nervous system, each of which is a whole, an organization of many parts, but at the same time a part of the total physical organism. The human being is both a unifier, an organizer of his immediate personal world, and a participant in what he conceives to be the superordinate whole to which he belongs. His striving for mastery is embedded in his longing for participation. (p. 29)

These two trends, or opposite aspects of the same underlying trend, which can be contradictory under some conditions and complementary under others, are of fundamental importance to his general position. They constitute a novel characterization of the human condition at the level of abstraction he has chosen as his idiom. Yet in FSP (p. 52), he says that these trends are not explanatory principles but generalized descriptions of "the way according to which the life process takes place."

His reason for insisting on this distinction becomes clear later when he goes on to say that they are directional but not teleological. The concept of purpose obviously created insurmountable difficulties for him.

Nevertheless, in discussing the means-end dimension of personality, he introduces the concept of goals. This puts him in the position of maintaining that a purposeful subsystem can exist in a nonpurposeful total system. He attempts to correct this anomaly by saying that the direction selects the goal—goals for him being specific and subordinate to direction, which is general at the level of the basic trends, which are psychophysically neutral. He felt it necessary even at the cost of inconsistency and self-contradiction to avoid the accusation that his main position was teleological.

Teleology was anathema in the scientific world of the 1940s and the stranglehold of the ateleological position has only gradually loosened since that time. That a man otherwise so in advance of his times should have avoided the teleological issue in the way he did exemplifies the force of the prevailing paradigm.

Except for some very early work of Singer (1924), the search for a conceptual framework that would allow the inclusion of teleology in a language acceptable to science had scarcely begun when Angyal was writing FSP. This was well before the arrival of what Ackoff (1974) has called the "Systems Age." Apart from the contributions of cybernetics and information theory, those of Churchman and Ackoff (1950), Singer (1953) and Churchman (1961) opened up a path that might have been attractive to Angyal had he known of their work. A rigorous treatment of the teleological issue became available only after his death when the publication of *On Purposeful Systems* (Ackoff and Emery 1972) repunctuated the field.

In my 1970 paper I had rested content with his notion of direction as a halfway house between an ateleological and a teleological position. Nor did I see any contradiction between talking about goals in their usual place in a psychology of motivation and denying purposefulness to the organism as a whole which represented the total biological process with which Angyal was so concerned.

Even with this realization it took me some time before I could pinpoint a difficulty I still had with Angyal's account of the symbolic function of consciousness (in all its modalities from perceiving to thinking) as contributing the distinctive attribute of humankind. If elementary acts of perception are regarded as having a symbolic component it would be difficult to regard them as species-specific for humans. It would be necessary to identify certain kinds of symbolization that are distinctively human. This led me back to the distinctions made by Ackoff and Emery not only between goal-seeking and purposeful systems but among purposeful systems the special class that they termed "ideal-seeking" and which they regarded as constituting the specifically human attribute.

My position now is that the capacity for ideal-seeking behavior is related to the capacity for conceptual thinking. This latter is a function of the frontal lobes that are uniquely developed in *Homo sapiens*. If these connections hold good, one would expect conceptual thinking to be severely restricted in patients with diffuse frontal lobe damage. A theory that this would be so was put forward by Goldstein (1934 and 1940) and referred to as "reduction to the concrete." The results obtained by Trist and Trist (1943) and Semeonoff and Trist (1958), among other experimental work, supported this theory. When given simple sorting tests, such patients could not pick out common shapes if the objects were differently colored or common colors if the objects had different shapes. Even if they managed to sort by similarity in one way they could not shift to sorting by it in another. They could not conceive of alternatives. This requires the ability to abstract from the concrete, and it was this capability that had been impaired. The capability to abstract gives humans the capability of conceiving of possible worlds.

To think of possible worlds is also necessary for thinking about the future which was a capacity also impaired in these patients, as was will. They became distracted when changes were made in their situation, could not sustain courses of action, and experienced what Goldstein called "catastrophic anxiety."

Some four decades before the futures movement and the reconceptualization of planning as a process began to attract serious attention in the social sciences, J.B.S. Haldane (1924) published a short book called *Possible Worlds*. This contained the germ of much that was to come, but neither the conceptual nor the empirical work on which this has been founded had yet been done. It may now with considerable confidence be asserted that the capacity to envisage possible worlds and to choose among them is a necessary condition for ideal-seeking behavior and that this in turn depends on symbolization at the level of conceptual thinking. This, as Angyal points out, has intuitive, affective, and conative as well as strictly cognitive aspects.

Now that these clarifications have been made on the conceptual level, it has become possible to devise methodologies that will consciously utilize and develop a person's capacity for ideal-seeking behavior. Among those that have been tried with considerable success under a variety of empirical conditions are idealized design (Ackoff 1981, Ackoff et al. 1984) and search conferences (Emery and Emery 1978, Williams 1982).

Couplings and Networks

Angyal thought of systems as holistic, and his primary concern was to elucidate the distinctive nature of part-whole relations. Nevertheless, it may be asked whether all interrelated entities are holistic in the strict sense that he defined them. This question raises issues that Angyal did not address, such as the tightness or looseness of coupling among system constituents and whether entities may be interconnected without being parts of a whole.

The systems with which Angyal is concerned are what would now be referred to as tightly coupled systems. The body is his constant analogue in which the parts have no independent existence of their own, and by extension, he treats the psychological level of the psychobiological individual in the same way. At the social level, however, as Ackoff and Emery (1972) point out, an organization or group is composed of parts (individuals) which are themselves purposeful systems and have their own independence value. Social systems have a higher degree of openness than the psychobiological systems on which Angyal focused.

Ackoff (1974) introduces a classification of organizations that makes distinctions between what he calls "nodality" and "geneity." At one extreme is the uninodal homogeneous organization, then the uninodal but heterogeneous organization, next the multinodal homogeneous organizations, and finally multinodal heterogeneous organizations. This series proceeds in the direction of tight to loose couplings. Ackoff refers to multinodal heterogeneous organizations as communities in which the whole serves the interests of the member parts. The members are interrelated in many respects and therefore generate a large system to regulate these relations on their behalf, but this larger whole has no legitimate purpose independent of them, whereas in a uninodal homogeneous organization, such as in a conventional bureaucracy, the parts serve the purpose of the whole (though these parts [roles] include only parts of the individuals concerned). The same holds true in a more loosely coupled sense in a divisionalized corporation which is a uninodal heterogeneous organization. Multinodality introduces the notion of heterarchy as distinct from hierarchy (Schwartz and Ogilvy 1979). With heterarchy we begin to enter the type of organizational space in which part-whole relations in the sense discussed by Angyal no longer hold. It would therefore seem necessary to regard his holistic systems as a special class within a more generic category of systems.

Moreover, since the discovery of the hologram an entirely new concept of organization has arisen in which the whole is contained in the parts. Pribram (1971) has taken this up in neurophysiology as affording a new principle in terms of which the brain, the most complex organization at the biological level, needs to be considered. A number of social scientists have been exploring its relevance to forms of self-regulating organization which appear to be necessary once certain thresholds of complexity are passed. The holographic principle would appear to indicate a new system class which constitutes a figure-ground reversal of that with which Angyal was concerned.

In recent years, the concept of network has come to the fore. It must be asked whether networks fall within the general category of systems or whether they constitute another genus. They are not discussed at all by Angyal.

The concept of network, like the concept of system, has a long history in psychology and the social sciences. In social psychology it was introduced by Moreno (1934) and referred to sociometric choices among individuals requiring the aid of others in critical situations such as escaping from a reform school. In the Regimental Nomination Experiment in World War II, I introduced a network approach myself to increase the flow of candidates to the War Office Selection Boards when a dearth raised fear that the army in Britain could not officer itself (Trist 1985). In social anthropology Barnes (1954) showed the pivotal role of networks in connecting the work and social life of a Norwegian fishing community. Bott (1957) in her book *Family and Social Network* generated a whole literature with regard to the wider social conditions that fashioned kinship relations. Since then interdisciplinary studies in communication have taken over the term with many meanings. The verb "to network" and the term "networking" have become fashionable in innovative groups on the social periphery and those concerned with the implications of high technology. Elaborate mathematical formulation has now developed around these terms in the academic literature.

In its core meaning a network refers to a set of relations between individuals that is unbounded and nonhierarchical. The usage can be extended to groups and organizations wherever suitable referents can be found. By contrast, the term "system," especially as defined by Angyal, refers to a bounded whole which is hierarchical in that there are at least two levels—that of the whole and that of the parts which are subordinate to it.

The members of a network do not necessarily all know each other. They need not all be actually interrelated, though potentially they may be. The membership is not stable or complete; it may grow or decline. Some of the members may form nodes, and in turn, nodes may form groups or even organizations. Networks may be postulated as having a complementary function to bounded groups and organizations and to have a special role in processes of innovation and change.

Their members are, however, related by some form of common tie whatever this may be—a value, an affinity, a goal, an idea, or a kindred. For this reason the set of relationships they compose or evolve seems to have something "systemic" about it. Having initially thought of networks as nonsystems, I have come to think of them as a class of systems, the opposite of the tightly coupled holistic systems discussed by Angyal. The loosely coupled systems described by Ackoff would occupy intervening positions.[2]

Mathematically, the concepts of system and network may be derived from the same theorem in topology (Rescher 1979). Such a connection is also mentioned by Wilson (1975).[3]

Fields

If networks may be included within a generic class of systems, may fields also be so included? My own inclination is not to include them but to reserve the term "field" for one way among others of characterizing a system's environment. Every system has an environment in which, as Angyal says, heteronomous rather than autonomous factors predominate. My suggestion is to use the term "system" when attention is directed to the subject pole and the term "field" when attention is directed to the object pole. Though his thinking suggests the distinction, note that Angyal continues to use the two terms interchangeably. Once he had made his critical *a/h* distinction, he was not much interested in the analysis of the environment as such.

While system centers on the subject organization, field centers on the environment in which the subject organization is embedded and which it partially creates. Systems may be regarded as generating, or being affected by, fields rather than as being fields in themselves. In conjunction with other systems they produce directive correlations in the system-environment relationship (the universe or biospheric process in Angyal's sense) which coproduce event-clusters that have field qualities. These directive correlations may be short-, middle-, or long-range and refer to the past and future as well as the present (Sommerhoff 1950). They are temporal Gestalten (Emery 1967).

In Angyal's view, systems are primarily structural: their qualitative attributes are secondary. Fields reverse this order: qualitative attributes that suffuse them as wholes are primary; their structural properties are secondary. The two perspectives are complementary.

While systems may be characterized as holistic, tightly or loosely coupled, or network-like, fields may be characterized by the undifferentiated qualities that suffuse them as wholes. They may be strong or weak in power, greater than or less than as regard to magnitude, quasi-permanent or short-lived, densely or sparsely populated, and of varying texture, stability, degree of obstructedness, conflict, motion, etc. Lewin (1951) has described how as he approached the "region" of the battlefront in World War I, the whole landscape changed in his perception from its ordinary everyday character into "a war landscape." Social climate and group atmosphere are undifferentiated field properties to which he later refers. The alternating unconscious patterns that Bion (1961) found in the emotional life of groups have field properties.

In introducing the idea of causal texture, Emery and Trist (1965) postulated four kinds of qualitatively distinct fields in the contextual environment: the placid-random, the placid-clustered, the disturbed-reactive, and the turbulent. Requirements for adaptation differ in these four fields and become precarious under conditions of turbulence.

The system-states that produce fields, or have field effects, are those that are action-directed, whether the action be actual or potential. This action emphasis characterized the language of field theory as originally developed by Lewin—force fields, power fields, paths of locomotion, barriers, regions of free movement, etc. Later, he approached the problem of change as the unfreezing of an existing steady state and its refreezing at a new level. The language of field theory is transtopological because of the action component. Lewin tried out a concept of hodological space to remedy this but met mathematical objections. Graph theory has since been tried, but its relevance has proved limited. Ordinal treatment of multidimensional qualitative descriptors is usually the most that can be done with the present state of knowledge in approaching measurement of field properties—at any rate, at the human level.

Churchman and Emery (1966) have postulated a duality in organizations:

Any organization, in tying together individuals whose properties are partly determined by their relations to a multiplicity of diffent organizations, creates for itself a statistical aggregate that has properties of its own—an internal environment with field properties.

Their statement on the dual characteristic of human organizations as structured role-sets and as statistical aggregates of persons exemplifies my distinction between systems and fields, the need to retain two terms and their complementarity. Emery has since shown that, as "ground" phenomena, social aggregates accompany wider social systems even at the level of a society into which they may intrude unexpectedly, either destructively or constructively, as maladaptive defenses or as emergent transformative processes (Emery and Trist 1973, Emery 1977).

Emery and Emery (1976) have further introduced the idea of "the extended social field" to explain the influence of individuals, groups, organizations, events, values, and ideas existing beyond the immediate life space of a given individual:

> The network or mesh of interlocking directive correlations implicates the individual's behaviour, as well as his fate, in events taking place outside his immediate psychological life space. A husband, even while at work or travelling in distant places, is in some ways still implicated in the daily home setting of his wife and the school setting of the children. He is also implicated in conditions existing well back in the past (the past of others as well as himself) as these have created or failed to create present opportunities. Similarly the future becomes immediately relevant as one acts to set in motion chains of joint action that may or may not converge or diverge in the future. . . . The extended social field . . . [reaches] to the horizon of possible human action. . . . The goals served by the extended field seem to be nothing less than the survival of the population of that kind of individual system of which it is composed within the range of conditions that confront them.

To cope adaptively with social fields, social systems have to develop an appropriate response-capability (Trist 1980). Beer (1979) has posed the question: what is a viable system? One answer would be a system that can survive the field effects that it and other systems create in its environment.

The increasing turbulence present in the current world environment has drawn attention to the incapacity of existing social institutions to produce the response-capability necessary for human survival. A new response capability leading to both personal and social transformation seems to be required. This will need to be based on the primacy of symbiotic and collaborative, as compared with individualistic and competitive, relations (Perlmutter and Trist 1986).

Angyal (1966) foreshadowed this shift in values by his emphasis on homonomy which he strengthened in his posthumous book—published when a substantial increase in social turbulence was already beginning to be apparent and, as a result of the stresses induced, the new form of negativistic hysteria he identified was becoming epidemic.

Notes

1. At this early period the role of positive feedback (Maruyama 1963) and of order through fluctuations (Prigogine 1976) in morphogenesis had not been recognized.
2. An alternative treatment is offered by Carvajal (1983, 1985), who relates networks to systems through a concept of "systemic networks" which is linked to an overall concept of "systemic net-fields."
3. I am indebted to Dr. Stuart Albert of the School of Management, University of Minnesota, for drawing my attention to these references.

References

Ackoff, R. L. (1974). *Redesigning the Future.* New York: Wiley.
———. (1981). *Creating the Corporate Future.* New York: Wiley.
Ackoff, R. L., and F. E. Emery. (1972). *On Purposeful Systems.* Chicago: Aldine Atherton.
Ackoff, R. L., E. V. Finnel, and J. Gharajedaghi. (1984). *A Guide to Controlling Your Corporate Future.* New York: Wiley.
Angyal, A. (1941). *Foundations for a Science of Personality.* Cambridge: Harvard University Press.
———. (1966). *Neurosis and Treatment.* New York: Wiley.
Barnes, J. A. (1954). "Class and Committees in a Norwegian Island Parish." *Human Relations* 7: 39–58.
Beer, S. (1976). *The Heart of Enterprise.* New York: Wiley.
Bertalanffy, L. von. (1932). *Theoretische Biologie.* Berlin: Gebruder Borntrager.
———. (1950). "The Theory of Open Systems in Physics and Biology." *Science* 3: 23–29.
———. (1956). "The Theory of Open Systems." *General Systems Yearbook.* Washington, D.C.: Society for General Systems Research.
Bion, W. R. (1961). *Experiences in Groups.* London: Tavistock Publications.
Bott, E. (1957). *Family and Social Network.* London: Tavistock Publications.
Burrell, G., and G. Morgan. (1981). *Sociological Paradigms and Organizational Analysis.* London: Heinemann.
Carvajal, R. (1983). "Systemic-Netfields. Part I: The Systems Paradigm Crisis." *Human Relations* 36: 227–46.
———. (1985). "Systemic-Netfields. Part II: The Emergence of New Frames." *Human Relations* 39: 857–75.
Churchman, C. W. (1961). *Prediction and Optimal Decision: Philosophical Issues of a Science of Values.* Englewood Cliffs, N.J.: Prentice-Hall.
Churchman, C. W., and R. L. Ackoff. (1950). "Purposive Behavior and Cybernetics." *Social Forces* 29: 32–39.

Churchman, C. W., and F. E. Emery. (1966). "Three Approaches to the Study of Organization." In T. Lawrence (ed.): *Operational Research and the Social Sciences*. London: Tavistock Publications.

Dahrendorf, R. (1967). "Die Funktion Sozialer Konflikte." *Pjade aus Utopia*. Munich: Piper.

Emery, F. E. (1967). "The Next Thirty Years: Concepts, Methods and Anticipations." *Human Relations* 20: 199–237.

———. (1977). *Futures We Are In*. The Hague: Martinus Nijhoff,.

Emery, F. E., and M. Emery. (1976). *A Choice of Futures*. The Hague: Martinus Nijhoff.

Emery, F. E., and E. L. Trist. (1965). "The Causal Texture of Organizational Environments." *Human Relations* 18: 21–31.

———. (1973). *Towards a Social Ecology*. London: Plenum.

Emery, M., and F. E. Emery. (1978). "Searching: For New Directions, in New Ways . . . for New Times." In J. W. Sutherland (ed.): *Management Handbook for Public Administrators*. New York: Van Nostrand Reinhold.

Fairbairn, W.R.D. (1952). *Psychoanalytic Studies of the Personality*. London: Tavistock Publications.

Glazer, S. (1984). "Once More Unto the System." *Human Relations* 37: 473–90.

Goldstein, K. (1934). *Der Aufhau des Organismus*. The Hague: Martinus Nijhoff.

———. (1940). *Human Nature in the Light of Psychopathology*. Cambridge: Harvard University Press.

Haldane, J.B.S. (1924). *Possible Worlds*. London: Routledge and Kegan Paul.

Hall, A., and R. Fagan. (1956). "The Definition of a System." *General Systems Yearbook*. Washington, D.C.: Society for General Systems Research.

Klein, M. (1948). *Contributions to Psycho-analysis*. London: Hogarth Press.

Kluckhohn, C., and H. Murray. (eds.). (1948). *Personality in Nature, Society and Culture*. New York: Alfred Knopf.

Kohler, W. (1938). *The Place of Value in the World of Fact*. New York: Liveright.

Lewin, K. (1935). *A Dynamic Theory of Personality*. New York: Macmillan.

———. (1951). *Field Theory in the Social Sciences*. Ed. D. Cartwright. New York: Harper.

Maruyama, M. (1963). "The Second Cybernetics." *American Scientist* 51: 164–79.

Moreno, J. (1934). *Who Shall Survive?* New York: Beacon House.

Parsons, T. (1949). *The Structure of Social Action*. New York: Free Press.

Pepper, S. C. (1950). *World Hypotheses*. Berkeley: University of California Press.

Perlmutter, H. V., and E. L. Trist. (1986). "Paradigms for Societal Transition." *Human Relations* 39: 1–27.

Pribram, K. (1971). *Languages of the Brain*. Englewood Cliffs, N.J.: Prentice-Hall.

Prigogine, I. (1947). *Étude thermodynamique des phénomènes irréversibles*. Paris: Dunod.

———. (1976). "Order Through Fluctuation: Self-Organization and Social System." In E. Jantsch and C. H. Waddington (eds.): *Evolution and Consciousness: Human Systems in Transition*. Reading, Mass.: Addison-Wesley.

Rescher, N. (1979). *Cognitive Systematization*. Tatowa, N.J.: Rowan and Littlefield.

Sachs, W. M. (1976). "Toward Formal Foundations of Teleological Science." *General Systems* 21: 146–53.

Schwartz, P., and J. Ogilvy. (1979). *The Emerging Paradigm.* Stanford, Calif.: S.R.I.

Semeonoff, B., and E. L. Trist. (1958). *Diagnostic Performance Tests.* London: Tavistock Publications.

Singer, E. A. (1924). *Mind As Behavior.* Columbus, Ohio: R. G. Adams.

———. (1947). "Mechanism, Vitalism, Naturalism." *Philosophy of Science* 13: 81–89.

———. (1953). *Experience and Reflection.* Ed. C. W. Churchman. Philadelphia: University of Pennsylvania Press.

Sommerhoff, G. (1950). *Analytical Biology.* London: Oxford University Press.

Stern, W. (1930). *Studien zur Personurssenschaft: Personalistick als Wissenschaft.* Leipzig: Barth.

Trist, E. L. (1970). "Organisation et Système." *Revue française de Sociologie* 11–12, No. Spéc. Analyse de Systèmes en Sciences Sociales, 123–39.

———. (1980). "Environment and System-Response Capability." *Futures* 12(2): 113–27.

———. (1985). "Working with Bion in the Forties: The Group Decade." In M. Pines (ed.): *Bion and Group Psychotherapy.* London: Routledge and Kegan Paul.

Trist, E. L., and V. Trist. (1943). "Discussion on the Quality of Mental Test Performance in Intellectual Deterioration." *Proceedings of the Royal Society of Medicine* 36: 243–49.

Vickers, G. (1968). *Value Systems and Social Process.* New York: Basic Books.

———. (1984). *Human Systems Are Different.* New York: Harper and Row.

Williams, T. A. (1982). *Learning to Manage Our Futures.* New York: Wiley.

Wilson, C. (1975). *Socio-Biology.* Cambridge: Harvard University Press.

Chapter 10
A Theory of Management

Erik Johnsen

The Roots of Management Theory

Individual Work Roles and the Work Role of Executives

It has become customary to describe individual behavior in terms of roles, such as family and work roles. This can also be done for executives. In Figure 10.1 the properties of executive behavior are described by three interacting subsets. The first is the executive's professional behavior. Although employed as an economist, engineer, or lawyer, he or she may combine knowledge from several disciplines in performing the job. The second subset describes the executive's personal job-relevant properties, i.e., properties which are not "purely" professional. The third subset contains properties defining the executive's management behavior. I argue that the core of this is different from professional and personal performance in the job.

Theories of management have been developed based upon either professional or personal behavior or possibly combinations of these.

Profession-Based Theories

At the beginning of this century, one had to become a *professional* in order to manage. It was necessary for the manager to show other people how they should perform. Later on, the general professional was replaced by the *expert*. Perhaps the firm needed a production oriented manager, a sales oriented manager, a finance oriented manager, etc. The board could ask the expert to take the general manager position. Today, a common view is that top executives should know something about production and sales as a necessary, but not nearly sufficient, professional knowledge. You must be able to speak the

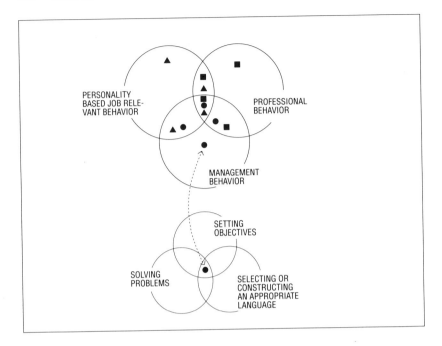

Figure 10.1.

language of the firm if you want to participate in the managerial process. This language will often be based upon professional disciplines, especially in smaller firms.

The usual worldview in practice is to look upon the firm as an *economic* system, as a *technical* system, as an *information* system, as a system of *judicial* agreements, and as an *organizational* system of tasks, responsibilities, and influence. Professionally based management is characterized by the fact that you are legitimized by professional skills and insight. This is another way to state that you are able to manage because of the abilities you have gained by adopting a specific view of the world and commanding a specific language created by one or several scientific disciplines.

The study of executives trying to manage based upon professional theories has created three main types of management theories:

- Those based upon the decision languages.
- Those based upon the behavioral languages.
- Those based upon the systems languages.

Managerial economics and operations research are typical examples of the broader discipline of decision theory. The behavioral languages contain a complex of disciplines, such as psychology, sociology, organizational theory, political science, and theories of value. These languages are developed in disciplines having their own way of looking upon managerial behavior. The systems languages enable us to have an overview and insight at the same time. Examples are computer programs, organization charts, information flow, money flow, physical flows, and organizational manuals. A spin-off of the systems view is to look upon the firm as a closed, open, or open dynamic system.

Theories of management based upon professional disciplines give us ammunition to formulate and solve problems. They have given us a wide variety of detailed methods for the formulation and solution of real management problems.

Person-Based Theories

Most management theories take their starting point in properties defining the personality of the manager or the team of managers. One could talk about specific personal traits and of properties relevant for the specific job.

There has been a tendency to look upon three subsets of properties:

- Those related to the personality.
- Those related to the person's social abilities.
- Those relating to abilities to adapt according to the situation.

As far as *personality* traits are concerned, we have been faced with theories producing a desired psychological profile. "Big man theories," on the one hand, and psychoanalytical archetypes, on the other hand, have tried to tell us the truth of what management is. We have theories based upon the authority-democracy axis and others related to the laissez-faire–conscious management axis. Specific properties as creativity, entrepreneurship, and political abilities have always been popular. Nevertheless, we do not as yet know which minimal specific personal properties are necessary in order to perform managerial tasks.

The specific theories related to a person's *social* behavior are many. One of them is that management activity is group-based; the group is the brick of the organization's management building. The group is also the battlefield of the power struggle, although the formal leader's legitimate power may be based upon sources outside the system.

Three special dimensions have been treated in the literature. One is process orientation versus task orientation. The second is the function of the (leader's) group according to authoritarian versus democratic relations between the group members. The third dimension is active participation in all aspects of the group process versus giving and taking orders from a single group member. These theories concentrate their attention on the social nature of the management process. The management process is realized in a milieu in which people interact actively.

The third set of theories take the environment as their starting point. Related to each new *situation* a manager or a group leader should perform new behavior dependent upon the situation. This means that executives should enable themselves to differentiate their behavior. It is necessary to be conscious about objectives; it is necessary to enable oneself to structure the situation and fight it by management tools. The demand for flexibility may cause role conflicts, frustration, and stress for the executive.

Management Theories

Management theories up to now constitute two subsets with some common elements. Theories based upon professional disciplines provide us with languages in which people who want to manage can communicate about problems experienced. At the same time, they provide methods and techniques for general and special problem solving.

The personality theories produce a varied picture. Dominant personal traits may include cognitive, motivational, and emotional properties as well as cognitive and emotional motives and personal values (preferences, ethics, and morale).

Group theories stress managerial behavior as a social phenomenon. Managerial behavior is accomplished together with others. Situational (contingency) theories focus on people performing various managerial roles and how these roles should be executed in a different way according to the situation and according to one's own personality. They also state that people should enable themselves to realize new cooperative relations with new people.

Invariable Dimensions Constituting Management Behavior

People are considered in their work roles, and their behavior is based upon professional education as well as genuine and adapted personal traits. People may function as individuals, as members of a group, or in one or several organizational roles. But what is *management behavior* and this complicated know-how called a professional executive?

Management behavior unites three types of specific behavior. It is the *amalgamation* of setting objectives, solving problems, and constructing an appropriate language together with relevant others (Figure 10.2). These three dimensions—setting objectives, solving problems, and constructing an appropriate language—are considered invariable dimensions in a theory describing management behavior.

Management behavior is defined differently for managers and executives. Management behavior is the sort of behavior these people desire to perform when they claim that they manage. We now have empirical evidence for the fact that people generally consider these three types of behavior as—at least—a necessary combination for management performance.

In order to provide sufficient properties for an operational definition of management behavior, we now assign further properties to the three invariable dimensions. These properties are simply subsets of some (not all) of the elements described above.

Setting Objectives

It seems likely that every firm and public institution must formulate three minimum sets of objectives. The first set is related to the life of the organization that is considered to be managed in a relative stable environment. The objectives of this *operations control situation* are

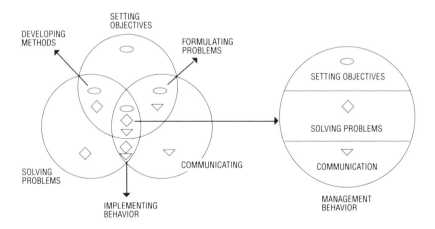

Figure 10.2.

normally a multiobjective formulation with measures of efficiency, social well-being, etc. Second, the environment is changing all the time demanding changes in the organization's structure and/or function. Specific objectives are related to this *adaptation process*. The third set of objectives are related to a situation not yet existing. These strategic objectives are related to the organization's *development process*. In practice we always work with development, adaptation, and operations control at the same time. One may, however, concentrate on attaining the objectives in one situation at a time. Normally, operations control activities are considered as a subset of adaptation activities, which is considered as a subset of development activities.

Organizing Problem-Solving Behavior

Problem solving in the management situation is not a cookbook thing. Management problems are problems; therefore, they require basic human problem-solving activity:

- Analyzing/synthesizing problem-solving behavior.
- Interactive problem-solving behavior.
- Search-learning behavior.

In practice, we always perform a search-learning behavior of some sort. One may, however, concentrate on interaction and/or analysis/synthesis. Usually, the cognitive problem-solving behavior is considered as a subset of interactive behavior, which is a subset per se of a general search-learning process.

Selecting or Constructing an Appropriate Language to Communicate

The disciplines upon which managerial education is based can be grouped into:

- Decision languages.
- Behavioral languages.
- Systems languages.

You always need a "systems view," but you may temporarily select a behavior language or a decisions point of view. Normally, decision theory is considered as a subset of behavioral theories, which in turn, are often considered as a subset of a general systems theory. At least systems theory can systematize, by definition, other theories.

The three invariable dimensions have now been assigned three properties each. These properties are claimed to include elements in the classical theories of management based upon professional disciplines as well as job-related personal abilities. They also include objective setting as a discipline. This total universe is depicted in Figures 10.3. and 10.4. The properties are placed on the axis according to increasing complexity.

The Theory of Management Behavior

Based on Figures 10.3 and 10.4, we can now describe management behavior. A *manager's role* is defined as the behavior performed when one "fills out" an element constituted by one objective-setting property, one problem-solving property, and one language property. A *manager profile* is a set of manager roles. The *management process* is a set of manager profiles. The manager role is to be "filled out" by the individual, given his or her professional and job-related personal traits. The point is that managers should be conscious of when they perform management behavior and when they perform some other job-related behavior. Every individual may be assigned several manager roles to perform. This profile may shift according to new interpersonal agreements of how to share (and develop) the roles in a total management process.

The contents of the roles will not be discussed here. It should only be said that there is a wide empirical evidence that people "see the light" when they are confronted with the marked differences in management behavior related to the operational control situation, the adaptation situation, and the development situation.

A theory of management should live up to the demands stated in philosophy of science as far as "theory" is concerned. Such demands include, for example, that a theory should be based upon a relative, invariable *structure* consisting of a few properties—so many, however, that there is enough of *variety* in the theory to delineate all practical situations. Also the demand for a *test criterion* should be satisfied together with the claim that the theory should have a built-in self-developing mechanism. In our case, the test criterion has been applicability.

As far as the demand for *self-development* is concerned, new accumulated knowledge can be added to the firm's own theory of management, which may be built in the way described. At the present stage in theory development, we must allow for overlapping subsets of elements. We must also allow for reversibility.

As far as *ethics* is concerned, the present theory is based on these assumptions:

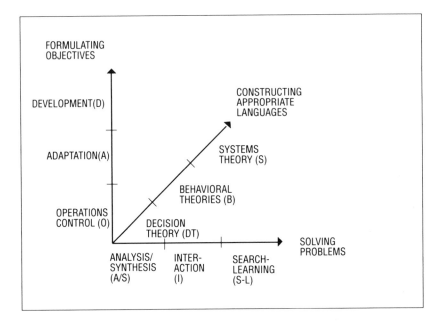

Figure 10.3.

- Management behavior is looked upon as a natural subset of normal human behavior.
- Everybody performs management behavior in his or her job, but the intensity and extent is very different.
- It is desirable to establish a better current management behavior for the individual and for each natural entity of individuals.
- "Better" is looked upon as an interactional phenomenon, the social process in a person-machine-management system.
- Since management is based upon interaction (cooperation) and since everybody performs management, everybody is a manager as well as managed.

We could have chosen another paradigm, chosen other premises, e.g., political values. Other constructors of theories may, however, contribute to the development of the theory of management through a dialogue built upon other presuppositions. Hopefully, it is possible to form a theory for the management process in an organization. The principles set forth should be applied by firms who wish to improve their management process. A local theory based upon a local culture is a necessary tool in a management development process.

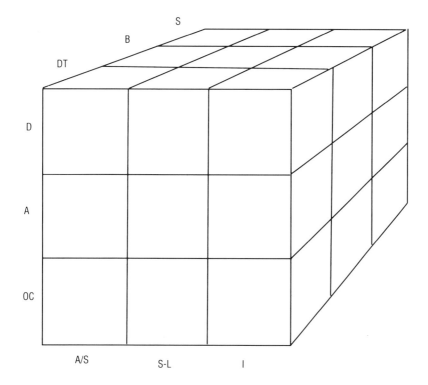

Figure 10.4.

Russell L. Ackoff

Russ Ackoff has given us languages to communicate, decision theory, behavioral theories, and systems theory. He has taught us analytical, interactive, and experimental methods. He has made us conscious of the importance of stating objectives for the present and especially for the future. His rich production has provided us with elements giving us a position from which we can formulate the theory of management.

Reference

Johnsen E. (1975). *Teorien om ledelse*. Copenhagen: Nyt Nordisk Forlag. Dedicated to Russell L. Ackoff.

Chapter 11
Educating for Reflection-in-Action

Donald A. Schon

What Reflection-in-Action Is and Why It's Important

On March 28, 1979, operators at the nuclear power plant at Three Mile Island were experiencing an uneventful shift in their windowless control room where, unable to see inside the plant, they operate remotely, trusting in their instruments, meters, and switches. Within the four-foot thick concrete safety containment, there is the 100-ton uranium fuel core, the furnace in which nuclear reactions create heat. Water pumping in the primary loop through the fuel core collects this heat and transfers it to water pumping around the secondary loop, the non-nuclear side, where water is turned into steam to drive a turbine and an electric generator.[1]

These were the events that occurred in the first few seconds of what became known as the accident at Three Mile Island, according to the operators' account:

The alarms started sounding, and I looked up to see what was wrong.
The pumps tripped in the secondary loop (shut themselves down automatically stopping the circulation).
Pressure rises in the primary loop (as normal).
The PORV (pressure relief value in the primary loop) opens automatically, to relieve the pressure.
The back-up pumps kicked on in the secondary loop as they should, to restart the circulation.
The reactor scrams (shuts itself down, stopping the nuclear reactions in the fuel core).
The pressure falls.
The PORV closes shut, automatically; the PORV light goes out, indicating that the PORV is shut.

This is the apparent situation, four seconds into the accident. What the operators did not know at this point was that (1) the backup pumps in the secondary loop were isolated from the rest of the system by a valve that had been mistakenly closed during a maintenance check and so were pumping with nothing to pump, and (2) the PORV hadn't closed since it was stuck open. The PORV light going out was misinformation due to an electrical malfunction. Through the open PORV, steam from the primary cooling quarter was gushing out. This was a loss of coolant accident (LOCA) and was extremely dangerous because, even though there is no nuclear reaction, the coolant water must cover the core. If the core is uncovered, the exposed radioactive fuel will heat spontaneously, and, with nothing to cool it, at about four or five thousand degrees it will melt, i.e., become a molten mass and start dissolving itself out of the plant: a meltdown.

At this point the operators' misunderstanding of the situation was perhaps unavoidable. All the signals available to them gave them a false picture of the situation. But then:

Alarms started sounding with a hundred or more warning lights, "like a Christmas tree."

The emergency injection water came in on the primary loop (designed to come on when a LOCA occurs), but it has come on so many times, by mistake, when there has been no LOCA, that this time the operators are not concerned.

Then "water level in the primary is rising too fast, and it's not clear why; while at the same time, the pressure is going down."

Operators say, "This is weird. . . . We've never seen anything like it. We couldn't figure it out."

Their response: "Cut the injection of emergency water—we didn't need it." Faced with the "weird" combination of rising water level readings and falling pressure readings, they respond only to the first—do exactly what they shouldn't do, cutting the compensating water—heading for meltdown.

Later, an operator checking the system finds the closed cut-off valves on the backup pumps and opens them up. Later still, an operator coming in on a new shift, discovers that the PORV has been stuck open and closes it. But nobody stops to ask how much water had been lost by that time (the answer: about 3,000 gallons).

Thereafter, there is a series of "crazy" readings:

The primary pumps begin to cavitate, and are shut down.

The "hot-leg pipes"—coming out of the core—had temperature readings "way off the scale at the high end."

Radioactivity readings in the dome were at 10,000 rems.
Core temperature was read at 2,400 degrees.
There was a sudden spike of pressure in the containment, a spray
   came on, and there was a thud in the control room.

All of these were read as minor malfunctions, small deviations from
the norm. The 2,400 degree reading was interpreted as a faulty ther-
mocouple. The thud was interpreted as a "ventilator damper changing mode" (it was actually an explosion of hydrogen gas, produced by
the disintegrating core). The 10,000 rem reading was dismissed with,
"The readings must be wrong." All these data were assimilated to a
view of minor malfunction: perhaps a breach of a steamline, steam
bubbles in the primary.
   Not until twelve hours into the accident did one key manager insist,
despite the disagreement of others in the plant, that "future actions
will be based on the assumption that the core has been uncovered and
the fuel is severely damaged."
   Why did it take so long for this to happen? One operator said, "Nobody knew for sure. You don't want to believe this. When you start
seeing 3,000 to 4,000 degrees in the core, you think that you are uncovered. You think meltdown. You don't want to believe this." And
you stick with the first diagnosis, the view that minimizes the problem.
   What was *not* happening:

Anomalous data would produce uncertainty and confusion, and the
   operators would *stay with* their confusion,
The prevailing diagnosis of the situation would be questioned.
Earlier readings and interpretations would be revised and checked,
   and new data would be sought.
Operators would produce alternative theories of what was going on
   and alternative settings of the problem they were facing.

   In short, what was not happening was *reflection-in-action* by the operators on their strategies of action, assumptions, and ways of framing
the problem. Why it was not happening is another story. A full explanation would include:

The operators' reliance on their procedure manuals. (As one of them
   said, "We were riffling through the procedures to find one that fit
   the situation.")
The definition of the operators' roles in terms of specialized tasks.
The design of training for those roles in terms of compliance with
   procedures. (As one commentator later said, ruefully, "Not a single

man panicked, not a single man violated his training. Sure, with
hindsight, we all wish their training had been different.")
There was an unwillingness of the operators to take responsibility for
trying to make sense of the whole situation for themselves.

Yet, if we assume that it is impossible to design a fail-safe automatic
system for a nuclear power plant—a system that would successfully
predict *all* possible contingencies and build in automatic responses to
them—then an essential condition for the safe operation of such a
plant is that the operators be adept at reflection-in-action. (When I
discussed this case with a group of engineering graduate students at
MIT, it was interesting that *none* of them believed in the possibility of
predicting accurately ahead of time all possible contingencies, yet
several of them maintained that a fully automatic system was the
solution.)

Let me generalize this idea of reflection-in-action. The process can
be understood as a series of "moments."

To begin with, the starting condition of reflection-in-action is the
repertoire of routinized responses that skillful practitioners bring to
their practice. This is what I call the practitioner's *knowing-in-action*. It
can be seen as consisting of strategies of action, understanding of
phenomena, ways of framing problematic situations encountered in
day-to-day experience. It is acquired through training or on-the-job
experience. It is usually tacit, and it is delivered spontaneously, without conscious deliberation. It works, in the sense of yielding intended
consequences, as long as practice situations fall within the boundaries
of the normal and routine. It is a dynamic know*ing* process, rather
than a static body of know*ledge,* in the sense that it takes the form of
continuing detection and correction of error, online fine-tuning, all
within the framework of a relatively unchanging system of understanding. A process of continual adjustment in the service of maintaining a sense of constancy. As Gregory Bateson put it, "The more
things are the same, the more change [to keep them the same]."

Sometimes, however, there are *surprises.* These take the form of
unanticipated events that do not fit existing understanding, i.e., fall
outside the categories of knowing-in-action. They are anomalous, and
if they are noticed, they yield uncertainty—meaning not merely that
one cannot predict for sure what will happen but that, at least for a
time, one cannot make sense of the situation.

Often, such surprises appear as *unique* events—things one has
never seen before and may never see again (as the operator said, "This
was weird, we'd never seen anything like it"). Often, they are associated

with conflicting values, conflicting ways of framing the problematic situation, or even conflicting paradigms of practice. These are tensions or contradictions in what Geoffrey Vickers called the appreciative system of the practitioner.

Together, uncertainty, uniqueness, and value conflict make up what I call the *indeterminate zones of practice*. In these zones, competence takes on a new meaning. There is a demand for reflection, thought turning to the surprising phenomena and, at the same time, back on itself to the spontaneous knowing-in-action that triggered surprise. It is as though the practitioner asked himself or herself, "What *is* this?" and at the same time, "How have I been *thinking* about this?" (like the anonymous manager at Three Mile Island who surfaced and questioned the assumptions on which everyone had been operating).

Such reflection must be at least in some degree conscious. It converts tacit knowing-in-action to explicit knowledge for action. It must take place in the *action-present*—the period of time in which thinking can still make a difference to the outcomes of action. It has a *critical* function, questioning and challenging the assumptional basis of action, and a *restructuring* function, reshaping strategies, the understanding of phenomena, and ways of framing problems.

Thinking gives rise to *experimenting*—but to a particular kind of experimenting, unique to practice, like and unlike the experience of laboratory science. It occurs on-the-spot in the practice situation. It consists in actions that function in three ways, to *test* new understandings ("That thud may have been exploding hydrogen in the containment"), to *explore* new phenomena ("What else looks odd here?"), and to *affirm or negate the moves* by which the practitioner tries to change things for the better ("How can we get this under control?").

On-the-spot experiment may "work," in the sense that you get what you intend and/or like what you get, or it may yield further surprises, pleasant or unpleasant. In these instances, we can think of the inquirer moving in the situation and the situation *"talking back"* to the inquirer, triggering a reframing of the problem, a reunderstanding of what is going on. The entire process then has the quality of a *reflective "conversation with the situation."*

These are examples of reflection-in-action drawn from other domains of professional practice:

• A *banker*'s judgment of credit risks: Sometimes all the customer's numbers look right but to an experienced banker something still "feels wrong." The banker then experiments on-the-spot to test his intuitive feeling about the situation. Note that, in such a case, reflection begins with attention to the *feeling*, which is treated as information. The banker asks, "What am I picking up that causes me to feel this?"

• A *physician* who, recognizing that 85% of the cases that come into his office are not in the book, responds to unique, anomalous configurations of symptoms by inventing and testing a new diagnosis.

• A *market researcher* who is attentive to the market's response to a new product introduction. She listens to what the market is telling her, by its behavior, about the meaning of the product, sometimes recasting it away from initial product definition toward the unanticipated uses the market has discovered (as in the case of Scotch Tape).

• Similarly, *planners* who detect the unanticipated meanings planned interventions have for those affected by them. They may construe these deviations from intentions not as "failure" but as a sign that they have misunderstood the problem they were trying to solve (as in the case of housing allowances).

• *Managers* who study a failure to perform, like a plant that fails to deliver products on time. As managers explore the situation with their colleagues, they may unearth a normal *Rashomon* of conflicting views of the problem. They may also seek to mobilize staff in a continuing inquiry which is at once exploratory, testing understandings of the situation, and aimed at fixing it. Note that, in such a case, the managers' reflection-in-action entails organizational inquiry that may result in a critically important kind of *organizational learning*.

In all such cases, the notion of reflection-in-action goes a long way toward describing what we mean when we speak of a practitioner's *artistry*. It is a capacity to combine reflection and action, on-the-spot, often under stress—to examine understandings and appreciations while the train is running, in the midst of performance. It is artistry, in this sense, that enables some individuals to be competent in situations that do not fit the preconceived categories of technique, theory, or rule of thumb, that make up the corpus of "professional knowledge." In the indeterminate zones of practice, some practitioners are sometimes able to make sense of uncertain, confusing situations and to test the sense they make.

Their reflection-in-action is not at war with the instrumental problem solving that we are used to associating with professional competence. Rather, reflection-in-action on the problematic situation at hand may convert "messes" into the well-formed problems to which research-based techniques can be applied. Competent practice, as we are increasingly coming to see, demands a *marriage* of problem setting and problem solving.

Unfortunately, the professional schools are largely based on an *epistemology of practice*, which leaves no room for reflection-in-action—an epistemology of practice built into the modern research university, taken on by the professions as part of the diabolitical bargain in which their schools are permitted to enter the universities. In this bargain, formulated by Thorstein Veblen in the early years of this century,[2] it was the business of the university to produce new, research-based knowledge which the professions would apply to the instrumental problems of practice. From the professions, their problems; from the university, its knowledge. Professional competence is then construed as the application of theories and techniques derived from university-based research to the selection of means for achieving the clear, fixed ends of practice.

This now-traditional epistemology of practice, sometimes called technical rationality, is built into the institutions of the professional schools. It is built into what Edgar Schein[3] has called the "normative professional curriculum": first teach them the relevant basic science, then the relevant applied science, then give them a practicum in which to practice applying that science to the everyday problems of practice. (Although this practicum is usually problematic and double-edged—seeming to the students and instructors involved in it to entail a very different kind of knowing and learning, closer to the artistry I have just described.) And the traditional epistemology of practice is also built into the institutionalized *division of research from practice*, a division that has entrained an increasing divergence of research from practice. These epistemological commitments are built into the institutions of the professions, whether individuals espouse them or not.

These arrangements have contributed to a *dilemma of rigor or relevance*. Practitioners, students, and educators are faced with a terrible choice. In the topography of practice, they must either remain on the high hard ground where they can function according to the canons of technical rationality, applying research-based theory and technique to a narrow range of well-formed problems—often problems of limited scope and importance—or they can descend to the swampy terrain below where the most important problems lie, but where they cannot be rigorous in any sense they know how to describe.

All of this I have set out in another paper[4] and, along with it, a proposal that we turn the problem of professional knowledge on its head. I have proposed that we ask not how research-based knowledge can be *applied* to practice but what kind of knowing is already built into what practitioners do when they show themselves to be competent in the indeterminate zones of practice—a quest that leads, I think, to a focus on the artistry that I have talked about as reflection-in-action.

How Do We Learn to Become Adept at Reflection-in-Action?

Here, I wish to pose a new set of questions:

- How is it that some people learn to become adept at reflection-in-action? How is artistry acquired?
- If those who acquire it are sometimes helped to do so by others—others whose role is less than that of teachers imparting knowledge than that of coaches guiding and prodding performers toward greater competences—then how does that help work?
- What is the character of the knowing that good coaches sometimes display in what they do? What is the nature of coaching artistry?

In order to think about these questions, we must look not to the normative formal curricula of the professional schools but to other traditions of education for performance—traditions that deviate from the formal professional norms. I mean,

The *studio* where artists, architects, and other aspiring designers learn to make things, including representations of things to be built.
The musical *conservatory,* where performers, conductors, and composers learn their trades.
Traditions of *athletic training,* where coaches help athletes to improve performance.
The deviant tradition of *the case method,* as it has evolved at the Harvard Business School and elsewhere, by imitation and adaptation.
Apprenticeships of all kinds, in the crafts, in industry, office, and clinic.
Perhaps also in the *informal underside* of some of the professional schools—what students sometimes do for one another, for example, or what goes on in the problematic practicum that does not fit the norms of the formal curriculum.

I shall take only a few examples from these sources to suggest what answers to our questions might look like. I shall begin with the architectural studio, partly because I happen to have spent some years studying it—and partly because architecture is a bimodal practice, part art, part profession, a throwback to traditions of education that antedate the modern research university (a fact that helps to account for architecture's universal marginality in the university context).

I have been struck by a kind of student reaction that seems to be endemic in the first-year design studios. In one studio, headed by a studio master called Quist, fully half the group find it difficult or impossible to grasp what Quist meant by "thinking architecturally."[5] Judith, one of the students, has a jury of her work in which a critic tells her, "Unless you can begin to think of the problem architecturally . . . you aren't going to find any way to proceed." And Judith says, in a later interview, "I began to realize that my approach wasn't architectural at all."

In yet another studio, the studio master says of a student, "Lauda is the hardest guy to deal with. Intelligent, articulate, comes up with something that works, but architecturally it's horrible . . . he has not internalized some of the covert things. . . . He is bright but totally unvisual . . . I wouldn't know what to do with him." And Lauda, bewildered by the demand that he perform according to standards that he finds alien and mysterious, says, "I think at times [the teacher] assumed a greater awareness than I had. . . . My standards were far surpassed . . . [I want] to go out and learn first. I want to know what it is we are arguing about."

And elsewhere a student who has not been singled out by his teachers as a problem makes this poignant observation:

> What we have is a very Kafkaesque situation where you really don't know where you are, and you have no basis for evaluation. You hang on the inflection of the tone of voice in your critic to discover if something is really wrong.

So I have noticed that students in the first-year studios develop a sense of confusion and mystery. Initially, the student does not and cannot understand what designing means. He or she finds the artistry of "thinking and doing like an architect" to be elusive, obscure, alien, and mysterious. Conversely, the studio master realizes that the students do not initially understand the essential things and cannot be *told* those things at the outset because the fundamental concepts of designing can be grasped only in the context of the doing—only through the experience of designing. Further, at least some studio masters, like Lauda's, believe that, even in the experience of designing, some of the essential things must remain covert; one cannot explain them, the student must somehow internalize them.

In this sense, the design studio shares in a general paradox attendant on the teaching and learning of any really new competence or understanding for students seek to learn things whose meaning and importance they cannot grasp ahead of time. They are caught in the paradox Plato has described in his dialogue, *The Meno*. Here, just as

Socrates induces him to admit that he hasn't got the least idea what virtue is, Meno bursts out with the question:

> But how will you look for something when you don't in the least know what it is? How on earth are you going to set up something you don't know as the object of your search? To put in another way, even if you come right up against it, how will you know what you have found is the thing you didn't know?[6]

Students do not yet know what they need to know, yet they know they need to look for it. Their instructor cannot tell them what they need to know, even if he or she has words for it, because the students would not understand.

Students are expected to find out for themselves, to learn by doing. The studio seems to rest on the assumption that it is only in this way that they can learn. Though others may be able to help them, they can only do so as they begin to understand for themselves the process they do not yet understand. And although instructors may help, the student is ultimately responsible. In a fundamental sense, students are expected to educate themselves in designing.

Or as my friend, Tom Cowan, has put it,

> I like old Carl Gustav Jung best on education. You know that unlike Freud for whom psychoanalysis is a branch of the healing arts, Jung always insisted that it is a propaedeutic, a branch of education. For him, education is what one does to and for one's self. Hence the universal irrelevance of all systems of education. . . . This view forced me to distinguish education from training: Education—the self-learning process. Training—what others make you do. . . . What are educational systems (so-called) *really* doing? For example, law school, I discovered, primarily trains students to listen. . . . Law school *trains* people to think and talk the way the rest of the profession does. What is its educational function then? To drive you mad with its incessant drill to educate yourself. The process appears terribly wasteful, yet some do get educated. If the teacher had a big stick and hit you over the head every time you tried to get him to educate you, the thing would be done in less than a semester. It seems to me that this is the Zen method of education, so of course, I can't claim to have invented it.[7]

In the context of the studio, there is a double paradox: on the one hand, students cannot initially understand what they need to learn; on the other hand, they can only learn it by educating themselves, and they can only educate themselves by beginning to do it. This places students in a predicament. They are expected to plunge into the studio, trying from the very outset to do what they do not yet know how to do, in order to get the sort of experience that will help them learn what "designing" means.

In this predicament, it is as though the teacher said:

> I can tell you that there is something you need to know, and I can tell you that with my help you can probably learn it. But I cannot tell you what it is in a way that you can now understand. You must be willing, therefore, to undergo certain experiences as I direct you to undergo them so that I can learn what it is you need to know and what I mean by the words I use. Then and only then can you make an informed choice about whether you wish to learn this new competence. If you are unwilling to step into this new experience without knowing ahead of time what it will be like, then I cannot help you. You must trust me.

Students are asked to enter into a kind of contract in which the teacher agrees to be open to challenge and defend a position and in which they, in turn, must be willing to *suspend their disbelief,* in order to try out the teacher's suggestion.

What makes this a predicament for students is that they are likely to feel that this commitment entails high costs. They must give up for a time the sense of confidence, competence, and control that goes with what they already know how to do. They must enter into a relationship of dependence on their instructor ("trust me"). At the same time, dependence also goes the other way: the instructor cannot do his or her job unless the students choose to take responsibility for educating themselves.

This contractual relationship and mutual dependence can be complicated by the *defensiveness* of either party—triggered, in both cases, by a sense of vulnerability. The instructor can begin to mystify his or her expertise. Students can make their resistance into an ideology. Defensiveness can make the learning predicament, inherent in the situation, into a *learning bind*—a situation of reciprocal misunderstanding that becomes self-sealing. When this happens, neither party can break through to understand the other or to make himself or herself understood; each new intervention simply makes the situation worse.

From this perspective, we can see a coach's artistry as consisting in the competent performance of a three-fold task:

1. Making multiple sense of the phenomena.
2. Giving the student a reason.
3. Reducing defensiveness.

First, the coach has to understand the substantive stuff of the situation in a special way. He or she must be able to see it in *multiple* ways, in order for there to be a *range* of acceptable responses, and must not believe in the magic of "one right answer" (a myth students often hold in their hearts). The coach must also not fall into the relativistic, soft-hearted view that "any answer is good."

Second, the coach must become interested in psyching out students' understanding of the subject, as revealed by what they say and do. To illustrate, in a session of what has come to be called the Teacher Project—a program of in-service education for elementary school teachers conducted by Jeanne Bamberger and Eleanor Duckworth[8]—a group of teachers watched a videotape of two boys seated at a table, separated from one another by a screen. One boy had in front of him a pattern made of blocks. The other was to use similar blocks to build the same pattern following the first boy's instructions. After the first few instructions, the boys lost touch with one another, although neither of them was aware of the fact. The teachers saw the situation as a "communication problem." The second boy seemed to them to be "unable to follow instructions" while the first seemed "orderly and clear," with "well-developed verbal skills." One of the seminar leaders pointed out, however, that she had heard the first boy tell the second to take a green square, although there were no green squares (all the squares were orange, and only the triangles were green). This misleading instruction had been the starting point for the second boy's troubles. He had put a green triangle where the first boy's pattern required an orange square. From then on, all the instructions had been ambiguous, unbeknownst to the boys.

When the teachers watched the videotape again, checking on this observation, they were astonished. The whole situation now seemed upside down. They could see exactly why the second boy had made the moves that got him in difficulty. He no longer seemed dull but had, in fact, followed instructions and had actually been remarkably inventive in his efforts to reconcile later instructions with the pattern before him. One of the teachers then said of the seminar leader's remark, "She gave the kid a reason"—a phrase that became a slogan for the group's later attempts to find sense in behavior they may have initially judged as stupid or stubborn.

A teacher who tries to find a reason for a child's behavior makes teaching into a kind of online research. He or she must not only invent interpretations that make sense of a child's behavior but also test this sense by on-the-spot experiments that are, at the same time, teaching interventions.

This is what Tolstoy (who compressed a teaching career into a fallow period between the writing of *The Cossacks* and *War and Peace*) says about teaching reading:

Every individual must, in order to acquire the art of reading in the shortest possible time, be taught quite apart from any other, and therefore there must be a separate method for each. That which forms an insuperable difficulty to one does not in the least keep back another, and vice versa. One pupil has a good memory, and it is easier for him to memorize the syllables than to comprehend the vowellessness of the consonants; another reflects calmly and will comprehend a most rational sound method; another has a fine instinct, and he grasps the law of word combination by reading whole words at a time.

The best teacher will be he who has at his tongue's end the explanation of what it is that is bothering the pupil. These explanations give the teacher the knowledge of the greatest possible number of methods, the ability of inventing new methods and, above all, not a blind adherence to one method but the conviction that all methods are one-sided, and that the best method would be the one which would answer best to all the possible difficulties incurred by a pupil, that is, not a method but an art and talent.[9]

Finally, while entertaining multiple views of the subject to the learned, exploring the student's understanding and difficulties, and experimenting with methods matched to this particular pupil, a good coach must bring to his or her interaction with the student a way of acting that reduces the likelihood of triggering defensiveness and learning binds.

I would like to give two examples of what seem to me to be elegant instances of coaching artistry—competent performances of the threefold coaching task.

The first comes from a design studio in Israel. The studio master, Danny, has assigned the problem of designing a field school—a training school located in a rural setting. One student, Elena, came in with what she subsequently described as a "school solution." (Nobody had asked her to do this; it was what she had tacitly assumed the situation called for.) Danny described it as an arrangement of banana-shaped buildings in a field, a kind of motel. He asked her whether she *liked* what she had done. She said, no, she didn't, but she thought it was what would be called for in the studio. He asked her what she would *like* such a school to be. The question took her by surprise. It had not occurred to her that what she liked would matter. After some thought, she said she would like the field school to be "hidden," she would like it to be "one with nature," and she would like it to stimulate social activity. With a few quick sketches, Danny showed her several different ways in which she might consider producing the qualities she liked. She went home and, over a two-week period of intense immersion, came up with a series of lively, evocative drawings in which, indeed, she had found ways of "hiding" the school in its natural setting and constructing arrangements conducive to social interaction.

In the workshop I conducted, where Danny gave this example, the student was present. Although the event had occurred eight years earlier, she had kept all her drawings and remembered every detail of the interaction.

The second example I've drawn from is a master class in violin. Dorothy DeLay of the Julliard School (famous now as Itzhak Perlman's coach) sat listening to a series of performances by gifted young performers. Each student had prepared a piece and each performed it in turn, uninterruptedly, sometimes for as long as twenty minutes, while Miss DeLay sat impassively, listening. After each student played, she would say something like, "That was wonderful, sugar," and then would do something quite particular to *that* performer. Sometimes, her comments would have to do with intonation (she kept an electronic tuning fork for cases such as this), the technical details of fingering or bowing, or (in the case of a German student who listed precariously to one side) with posture.

The only time she talked about specifically *musical* issues was to a young Chilean woman who had played with outstanding musicality—not a virtuoso stint but the first movement of a Brahms sonata. Dorothy asked the student to play what she felt to be the main themes of the movement. The student obliged by playing first one, then another. The third one, Dorothy observed, seemed to be not a new theme but a variation of the first. She asked then whether there wasn't something "transitional." The student found it, played it, and agreed that it was, indeed, a third theme. Dorothy asked her, then, how she would describe the qualities of these themes. The student thought for a moment, then offered the opinion that the first was "lively," the second "stormy," the third, "reflective." Dorothy said, "Suppose we wanted to accentuate the liveliness of the first, how would we do it?" She put her head in her hands, thinking about the problem. Then she said, "There's an upbeat that goes to a resting place, ta-dum. Perhaps you could really *spring* off of it, and land on the next—ta-*dum*." The student tried it, produced the effect, and liked it. Then, "How about the third, how would you make it really 'reflective'?" The student seemed puzzled, then proposed a fingering and bowing that gave a very gentle performance. Dorothy said, "Yes, you could do that. Or you could also *restrict* the bowing," and she mimed what she meant. The student tried it. Yes, that would work, too. "Which do you think you'll use?" Dorothy asked. The student seemed puzzled again. "I'm not sure, I'll have to think about it." Dorothy sat back, obviously pleased.

I'm struck by several features common to both of these examples. First, both coaches asked their students to reflect on their feelings about what they are doing. In both cases, they made it legitimate for the student to like or dislike something, and in both they invited the student to reflect on and describe the qualities of what was liked. Then, these descriptions were taken as the materials of a problem: how to *produce* what was liked? This was taken as a problem for the student *and* instructor. Both parties stood, as it were, in front of the same problem. Suggestions were made as to ways in which the described qualities might be produced. The coach seemed to be inviting the student to join her in the process of experimentation—indeed, if anything was being taught by demonstration, not by description, it was the idea of practice as experimentation. And the relationship that had been constructed was not that of performer and critic but that of a partnership in the setting and experimental solving of a problem.

Let me attempt, finally, to bring this discussion to bear on an example of teaching by the case method. I have read one of C. Roland Christensen's cases about case teaching, "The Section Just Took Over." [10] In this case, a marketing problem, which has to do with the distribution of a contraceptive drug in a third world country, gives rise to a debate. The debate is triggered by one student's, Kay's, protest:

> Here is this huge drug company, restricted in its own country from distributing the pill without careful medical supervision, pushing wholesale distribution of a hazardous drug to illiterates under the guise of doing them a favor.

To which another student answers, "I didn't come here to learn what I missed in Sunday School." The resulting "explosion" continues for many minutes until Professor Webster steps in to rescue his lesson plan.

The question posed by the case seemed to include two questions:

a question of *control:* are they learning if I'm not teaching them? And if I should at some point reassert control, how should I do so and when?

a question of *boundaries of relevance:* What's relevant to allow into the discussion? What should be excluded as irrelevant? Is it my responsibility to police this boundary?

What Professor Webster actually does, as the case tells it, is to let the class go for some time (perhaps to let off steam because he's uncertain what to do?) and then to rule the question of social ethics out of bounds, unsuitable for discussion in a marketing class. He takes the discussion back to the main question of the case: how (not whether) the company should distribute the product?

The immediate consequence of this action is that the class becomes subdued but compliant, and "no further social-ethical issues
are brought up in his marketing course that semester." Students
might infer that social-ethical considerations are not a legitimate part
of marketing, that the question of *how* best to distribute a product is
divorced from the question of *whether* to distribute it, and perhaps
also that what's appropriately "in" or "out" of bounds is a matter of
authority with which one should comply if one wants to get along.
The second-order lessons may lodge as firmly in the students' minds
as the more directly intended lessons about methods of distribution.

Suppose, however, that the professor had wanted to enlarge the
debate, or at least had not wanted simply to rule ethics out of bounds
but rather had wanted to draw on the energy it had unleashed. How
might he have gone about it?

The problematic situation, it seems to me, would include these
elements:

How can he join and guide the discussion without suppressing it or
   wholly taking over? In short, how could he increase the likelihood
   of sharing control with his class?
How can he recognize the legitimacy of the ethical issues raised, if he
   wishes to, without accepting at face value the assumptions underlying either Kay's position or her opponent's?
How should he frame inquiry into these issues in such a way as to
   decompartmentalize the "ethical" from the "marketing" questions
   of the case?

These are elements of the problematic situation that call for the
professor's reflection-in-action. Indeed, he would have gone a long
way, it seems to me, if he succeeds, on his feet and under stress, in
making them clear to himself.

What he might actually say would depend, I think, on whether he
believed the social-ethical issue was a legitimate subject of class discussion. If he thought it was, he might say something like:

> I think the debate Kay has triggered is important not only because it's about
> a critical social issue but also because it can and should influence how we
> think about the marketing problem. Let's take a look, however, at the as-
> sumptions each of the parties to the debate has been making. To begin
> with, those who think Kay's question is out of bounds . . .

Or, if he were less sure about the legitimacy of the issue for class
discussion:

Some of you have said we should be discussing the issue; others, that we shouldn't. I feel that we shouldn't be ignoring an aspect of the case that has so powerfully involved us, but also that we shouldn't consider it in isolation from the marketing dimensions of the case. Let's look at the question of method of distribution. How would we look at it if we left the ethical issue aside? And how might we look at it differently if we took that issue into account?

In either case, the professor would be trying to make on-the-spot sense of the unexpected fervor of the debate. He would be surfacing, at least for himself, and perhaps also for the class, the dilemmas the debate has created for him. And he would be inviting the class to explore these dilemmas, which means exploring their own assumptions.

Implications for Education for Reflective Practice

Those who learn the artistry of a new practice face the epistemological paradox of needing to educate themselves in something when they don't yet know what it is they need to learn. And they therefore face the psychological predicament of having to take a plunge into *doing* without yet knowing what it is they are doing.

Those who would help them must possess an artistry of their own—a coach's artistry similar to the artistry they want to help others acquire. It is a threefold capacity for reflection-in-action which centers on the task of figuring out how *what* is to be learned can best be linked to a student's present understanding and difficulties. It requires:

Multiple representations of the substantive knowledge and know-how and a capacity to shift easily from one representation to another.
An ability to function as on-the-spot researcher into the student's understanding of the subject, "giving the kid reason."
Having on the tip of the tongue, or inventing, a method suited to this particular student,
Keeping alive the question, "What are they making of this?"

And all of this must be done in such a way as to avoid being responsible for triggering the students' defense.

Coaching artistry flourishes in a setting conducive to it, by which I mean not only a physical setting (studio loft or U-shaped seminar room) and an organizational setting (including a structure of time, procedure, and reward) but also a cultural tradition. The building of such a tradition serves to punctuate the otherwise amorphous and unlimited doing in which students and coaches need to be engaged, to give a more or less predictable framework to the interactions of students with one another and with their coach (perhaps even to help with the daunting problem of making it possible really to listen to individuals in a class of eighty students), and to institutionalize expectations about performance, demonstration, imitation, and criticism.

Such a setting is what I mean by a *reflective practicum*. It exists already, in greater or lesser degree, in some studios, master classes, clinics, perhaps even in some institutions for case-teaching. Beyond these existing examples, the effort to create a reflective practicum may be an appropriate strategy of reform in the professional schools. It would focus on the jugular—the practicum, problematic because it faces in two directions: the "professional knowledge" of the classroom and the "practical competence" of the field. It therefore bears a major share of the burden of the failings of the epistemology of practice that has tended to dominate the professional schools. It is a vulnerable and promising target.

A reflective practicum ought to be grounded in research, but in research of a sort appropriate to education for practice. I think it would include at least two components.

First, systematic reflection on the knowing-in-action built into competent practice, including the dilemmas and dead ends encountered there and what practitioners do with them as well as the attention paid to the ways in which the artistry of problem setting clears the ground for technical problem solving and how reflection-in-action mediates the uses of theory in practice. This would be a kind of aided reflection-in-action in which competent practitioners would be coresearchers. It might be mistaken for a particularly intensive form of continuing education.

Second, systematic reflection on coaching artistry of the sort represented by this colloquium.

These sorts of research can use and give rise to theory, as well as to heuristics and strategies of action. But in the indeterminate zones of practice—both inside and outside the professional school—these need to be *held* in a certain way: not as rules or formal models to be instituted in appropriate situations but as a *repertoire* of exemplars and ways of looking at situations. A set of themes around which to invent personal variations in the next situation. Otherwise, the knowledge derived from such research would become absurd, as Raymond Hainer has pointed out in his parable of the Clock[11]:

A Clock

An aunt of mine was a teacher of small children in a large city during the thirties. Her style of teaching was derived from deep springs of feelings about children. She was more their friend than their teacher, and she taught by entering their world.

In the period of the thirties no one could afford much in the way of teaching aids. They had a few things, but primarily they had blocks and orange crates which the children painted by way both of designing and of possessing. Someone had made the face and hands of a clock as an aid in learning to tell time. They had one expensive machine, a metronome; it, along with a pitch pipe, had been provided by the school to encourage music. The metronome was not supposed to be used by the children; it was delicate to adjust, and it was not a toy. But my aunt let the children employ it at times; she felt they were not going to hurt it on purpose, and if an accident happened, she would pay for having it repaired.

Even after many years, one incident remains particularly memorable. A small group was organizing orange crates and blocks as usual into this or that when someone set an orange crate on end and someone else placed another crate on end on top of the first—and someone placed the face of the clock on top—and someone else ran to get the metronome to put in the back. By a series of swift events the children "discovered" the Grandfather Clock. Did they have fun! For a few moments everyone was caught up in the experience of both discovering and being pleased by the object of their discovery.

The odd coincidence right in the middle of this event was that the principal entered the room to observe. He saw the appropriation of the expensive metronome—but most of all, he saw the joy of everyone's participation in the process of discovering the Grandfather Clock. Immediately he congratulated the teacher on her teaching skills and requested that she write up this exercise for him so that he could insert it into the general study program. He said that he felt every first grader in the city of Pittsburgh should experience the joy of making a Grandfather Clock, and he left the room.

For a moment the teacher was immobilized by a portentous vision of the mass recapitulation of the Grandfather Clock exercise all across the town. She imagined the Board of Education's year after year requisitioning a large quantity of orange crates, faces of clocks, and metronomes, and of teachers executing the exercise of planned spontaneous discovery.

Notes

1. This summary is drawn from the transcript of "Sixty Minutes to Meltdown," *Nova*, March 29, 1983.

2. Thorstein Veblen, *The Higher Learning in America* (New York: A. M. Kelley, 1965 [1918]).

3. Edgar Schein, *Professional Education* (New York: McGraw-Hill, 1973).

4. Donald A. Schon, "The Crisis of Professional Education and the Pursuit of an Epistemology of Practice," Research Paper, 75th Anniversary Series, Harvard Business School.

5. This example and others that follow are drawn from my "Learning a Language, Learning to Design." In *Architectural Education*, edited by W. Porter and M. Kilbridge (Cambridge: MIT Press, 1983).

6. Plato, *The Meno*, trans. W. K. C. Guthrie (Indianapolis: Bobbs-Merrill, 1971).

7. Thomas Cowan, the Wharton School, University of Pennsylvania; personal communication, 1985.

8. See Jeanne Bamberger and Eleanor Duckworth, *The Teacher Project: Report to the National Institute of Education* (Cambridge: MIT Press, 1982).

9. Leo Tolstoy, "On Teaching the Rudiments." In *Tolstoy on Education*, edited by Leo Wiener (Chicago: University of Chicago Press, 1967), pp. 58–59.

10. C. Roland Christensen, *Teaching by the Case Method* (Cambridge: Harvard University Press, 1983).

11. Raymond Hainer, "Rationalism, Pragmatism, and Existentialism," in *The Research Society*, edited by E. Glatt and M. Shelley.

Chapter 12
Performance Criteria as a Means of Social Integration

Jamshid Gharajedaghi and Ali Geranmayeh

In contrast to machines and organisms in which integration of the parts into a cohesive whole is a one-time proposition, for social systems, the problem of integration is a constant struggle and a continuous process. In seeking effective social integration, compatibility must be continuously re-created, first, between the different levels of purposeful systems (vertical) and, second, among purposeful members at the same level (horizontal). A third kind of compatibility should be included, a continuing concern for the interests of past and future stakeholders in a social system (diachronic). In this context, the dichotomy of individuality and collectivity poses a dilemma that cannot be resolved under current sets of assumptions and traditional concepts of organization.

As discussed extensively (Gharajedaghi and Ackoff 1984), there are three different ways of looking at organization: mechanistic, organismic, or as a social system. In the mechanistic view organizations are considered to be instruments of their owners, and efficiency, reliability, and predictability are the organization's main functions. A machine with passive, nondeviating parts is a metaphor for such systems.

The organismic view conceptualizes organizations as living systems with the parts as organs having essential functions but no purposes of their own. Environments are also seen as purposeless and passive providers of necessary inputs. Thus, exploitation of the parts and of the environment for the maintenance and growth of an unstable structure becomes the main preoccupation of the system.

The social systems view considers organizations as voluntary associations of purposeful members—systems that manifest a choice of both ends and means. The function of an organization, therefore, is to serve the purposes of its members by serving the purposes of its environment.

The presence of an element of choice places social systems in a class by itself. Lack of appreciation for the implications of the factor of choice in the behavior of members of social systems becomes the main source of the confusion and dilemmas encountered in organizations conceived of as mechanistic or organismic systems.

In the context of purposeful behavior, the relationship of an individual with the larger system of which he or she is a member is critical. Despite a desire for individuality and uniqueness, individuals also display a strong tendency toward conformity and a desire to identify with and to be members of groups of their choice.

To the extent that membership in a group is desired, the performance criteria by which the group evaluates the behavior of its members have a profound effect on the manner in which individuals conduct themselves. The degree of the influence, however, depends on the extent to which the performance criteria (1) represent collective choice, (2) are legitimized by the culture, and (3) are compatible with the performance criteria of the other groups of which the individual is a willing member.

In this paper we will deal with the concept of social integration by reflecting on the roles of performance criteria, performance measures, and incentive systems, and we propose a framework to synthesize these concerns in the design of performance centers.

Vertical Compatibility

As an open purposeful system an organization is part of a larger purposeful system, the nation. At the same time it has purposeful members, individuals, as its own parts. These create a hierarchy of purposeful systems on three distinct levels, which are so interconnected that it is inconceivable to find an optimal solution at one level independent of the other two (Ackoff and Emery 1981). So much so that effective integration of multilevel purposeful systems cannot be achieved without performance criteria that make the fulfillment of the needs and desires of a purposeful system dependent on fulfillment of the needs of the larger system of which it is a part and vice versa.

This means that the implicit sets of zero-sum assumptions ought to be challenged and a win/win environment created so that the struggle of individuals for their own gain is enhanced by the degree of contribution they make toward satisfying the needs of the higher system of which they are willing members. This would change the measure of success and relative advantage of various activities for the actors in favor of those activities that jointly optimize the trilevel objectives of multilevel purposeful systems.

If organizations are to serve their members as well as their containing whole, they must be able to dissolve any conflict among them. In contrast to solving or resolving, which is used whenever the conflict situation is conceived to be unidimensional (a zero-sum game), dissolving a conflict is to change the nature and/or the environment of the entity in which it is embedded in order to remove the conflict. This is a multidimensional conception of conflict characterizing a non–zero-sum situation.

This concept is based on the recognition that sets of opposing tendencies, usually treated as dichotomies, are in fact complementaries. They coexist and interact continuously so that the relationship between opposing pairs might be characterized as an "AND" rather than "OR" relationship.

For example, one of the prime functions of social systems, the production and distribution of wealth, is a constant source of conflict, which results in the dichotomies of collectivity and individuality, market economy and planned economy, and so on. However, production and distribution of wealth form a complementary pair. Without an effective production system there can never be an effective distribution system. To fail to note this important interdependency is to leave out the most important challenge of the problem. An obsession with distribution without a proper concern about production, will result in nothing but equitable distribution of poverty. This is not to undervalue the importance of an equitable distribution system but rather to emphasize its inseparable connection with production.

The answer is not compromise, but synthesis. This synthesis can be approached only when production and distribution of wealth happens at the same time. Consider the following simple exchange system:

ENVIRONMENT

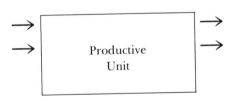

A productive unit consumes the scarce resources of its environment; in return it produces outputs (goods or services) that are supposed to partially fulfill the needs of that environment. The assumption is that the unit will survive as long as the total value of the outputs produced exceeds or matches the total value of the inputs it consumes. The pricing system determined by "dollar votes" is supposed to be a reliable and sufficient criterion for determining production and distribution priorities. This supposition might be tenable if (1) dollar votes were more equitably distributed and (2) end-prices were not manipulated. However, factors such as price control or government protection make the actual cost of service much higher than perceived. In other words, inputs are purchased from the environment at a lower price and outputs (measured by the classical accounting method) are made to look more valuable than they really are. Furthermore, despite the fact that creation of employment opportunity for all members of a social system is an effective means of simultaneous production and distribution of wealth, existing social calculus considers employment only as a cost, therefore, and not surprisingly, tries to minimize it.

To remedy the situation we need a new framework, one that will use employment on both sides of the equation, input as well as output. We also need a performance criteria that in addition to efficient production of wealth explicitly considers its proper distribution as a social service to be adequately rewarded.

The following scheme is a simplified version of an attempt to measure the actual costs and benefits of each major economic activity as perceived on the national level. It complements the productive strength of market economy by enhancing its allocation function. The model registers the needs of those members who lack the dollar vote to register their needs. It also explicitly values the distribution of wealth (salaries paid) as social service.

For simplicity, let us limit inputs to the two categories of (1) raw materials and (2) human resources and the outputs to the two corresponding categories of (1) finished goods produced and (2) employment opportunity created (this assumes that distribution of wealth is a social service). Assigning a "scarcity coefficient" to each set of inputs obtained from the environment, and "need coefficient" to each set of outputs (goods/services) yielded to the environment, we can compute the relative contribution of each major economic activity using Table 12.1.

This conception of social calculus, if it has embedded in it an explicit incentive system to reward activities with higher social contributions will result in a more effective vertical integration.

Suppose a certain productive unit produces bread with a contribution ratio of 2, but the low rate of return on investment of 8% (because of the weak purchasing power of the consuming class). On the

TABLE 12.1

Input Consumed

Raw material	A: Quantity(a) × Price(a) × Scarcity coefficient(a) = VC(a) B: Quantity(b) × Price(b) × Scarcity coefficient(b) = VC(b) C: Quantity(c) × Price(c) × Scarcity coefficient(c) = VC(c)

Human
  resources
  utilized
	Number of employees(I) × average training cost/
	  productive years × scarcity coefficient = VC(I)
	Number of employees(II) × average training cost/
	  productive years × scarcity coefficient = VC(II)
	Number of employees(III) × average training cost/
	  productive years × scarcity coefficient = VC(III)

Total value consumed	TVC

Output Produced

Goods produced	D: Quantity(d) × Price(d) × need coefficient(d) = VP(d) E: Quantity(e) × Price(e) × need coefficient(e) = VP(e) F: Quantity(f) × Price(f) × need coefficient(f) = VP(f)

Employment
  opportunity
  created
	Number of employees(I) × salary paid × NCE = VP(I)
	Number of employees(II) × salary paid(II) × NCE =
	  VP(II)
	Number of employees(III) × salary paid(III) × NCE =
	  VP(III)

Total value produced	TVP

Total value produced/total value consumed = Contribution ratio
Category (I) = highly specialized
Category (II) = skilled
Category (III) = unskilled
VC = value consumed
VP = value produced
NCE = need coefficient for creation of employment in the category

other hand, suppose another unit produces yoyos with a contribution ratio of 1, but the rate of return on investment of 18%. Then our incentive system ought to be able to change the relative rates of return on investment in favor of bread. An integrated and coordinated application of well-known tools such as (1) differentiated loan structure, (2) differentiated interest rate structure, and (3) differentiated tax structure will overcome the problem. Depending on the contribution ratios (computed from the previous table), a different loan/equity ratio, a different interest rate, and a different tax rate can be assigned to each major economic activity. This, as demonstrated by Table 12.2, will increase the rate of return on investment for bread to 18% and decrease that of yoyos to 10%. The advantage of such a scheme is that it will minimize the bureaucratic dangers associated with centralized planning while enhancing the strength of market economy by promoting a more equitable allocation and distribution system.

The method of determining scarcity and need coefficients is based on successive approximation utilizing interactive planning (Ackoff et al. 1984). The details of this process, although a critical aspect of this conception, is beyond the scope of the present paper. However, it is important to note that the initial raw coefficients, are revised and updated regularly and continuously in the light of further experiences.

Horizontal Compatibility

The development of major organizational theories is associated with increasing complexity and an emerging need for further differentiation. In response to requirements for specialization, the prime concern of every organizational theory is to define the criteria by which the whole is to be divided into functional parts. Most major organizational theories have implicitly assumed that the whole is nothing but the sum of its parts and have conveniently ignored the fact that

TABLE 12.2. Changing Relative Rate of Return on Investment Based on Contribution Ratio.

Product	Bread	Candy	Yoyo
Contribution ratio	2	1.5	1
Current return on investment	8%	12%	18%
Initial equity	$1,000,000	$1,000,000	$1,000,000
Equity/loan ratio	1/4	1/2	1/1
Total loan	$4,000,000	$2,000,000	$1,000,000
Interest rate	5%	9%	16%
Cost of loan	$200,000	$180,000	$160,000
Total capital employed	$5,000,000	$3,000,000	$2,000,000
Income	$400,000	$360,000	$360,000
(Income-cost of loan)	$200,000	$180,000	$200,000
Tax coefficient	10%	25%	50%
Net income after taxes	$180,000	$135,000	$100,000
Final return on investment	18%	13.5%	10%

effective differentiation requires incorporation of a mechanism that would integrate the differentiated parts into a cohesive whole. In this regard, the classical school of management, depends solely on the *unity of command* and the imperative of *no deviation*. At the opposite end, the neoclassical school, advocating decentralized structure, relies on the assumption that perfectly rational micro-decisions would automatically produce perfectly rational macro-conditions. More significantly, the assumption that criteria by which functional units are to be evaluated must be differentiated has led to the whole range of incompatible performance criteria embedded in the so-called cost center, revenue center, overhead center, and so on.

Consider, for example, a typical setup within a corporation. The performance criterion for manufacturing units is the minimization of production costs. That of the marketing units is to maximize sales. Intuitively, one would expect that the interaction between the two centers are complementary and would result in maximum efficiency. Unfortunately, this is not so. In fact, in most organizations the relationship between marketing and production is fraught with constant friction, and here lies the heart of this organizational problem.

The reason is that this design violates a basic systemic principle. Optimization of each of the parts of a system in isolation will not lead to optimization of the system as a whole. The two objectives of cost minimization and revenue maximization, taken independently, lead to a basic contradiction within the system. In order to maximize sales, marketing will have to respond to market demands for a variety of products, change of delivery schedules on short notice, customized features, and so on. Minimization of cost of production, on the other hand, is achieved through standardization of the production process, reduction in the number of products, regularization of the production schedules, and similar measures. Thus, the basic contradiction emerges: marketing can comply with its performance criteria only at the cost of manufacturing and vice versa.

Ironically, the only reason that this setup works in present-day organizations to the extent that it does is that the performance criteria are not taken seriously. (This is the major advantage of systems with purposeful parts over mechanistic and organismic systems. Such incompatibility could never be tolerated in a mechanistic system.)

The usual solution that most corporations adopt for this problem is one of compromise. The higher-level authority over both centers determines which set of criteria should dominate the other at any particular time. The dominance, of course, would oscillate between manufacturing and marketing in order to keep a sense of balance.

A totally different approach to this problem is to attempt to create compatibility of performance criteria rather than seek a compromise between incompatible sets. One way to achieve this is to change the performance criteria for marketing and for manufacturing so that they would both try to maximize the *difference* between cost and revenue. This concept can be operationalized in a profit center design where the relationship between marketing and manufacturing is based on *exchange,* much like that of a customer and a supplier. Both units are now expected to be value-adding operations.

Consider the difference in how the question of flexibility of delivery schedules is handled by the two designs. Flexibility is a value to some users for which they are willing to pay a certain premium. For a cost center, this premium has no value whatsoever. The only thing that is important to the cost center is that a change in production schedules will increase the cost. Since it is not concerned with revenues, the cost center will resist flexibility even when it results in positive net values to the corporation as a whole. Furthermore, since transfer of costs is based on average cost rather than marginal cost, there can be no distinction between users who demand flexibility (or various degrees of it) and those who do not; average cost is the same for both.

A profit center, on the other hand, examines each opportunity on a marginal cost versus marginal revenue basis. The price that the customer is willing to pay for the additional service is balanced against the marginal cost that the supplier will have to incur. While a cost center is instinctively resistant to any change of operations requested by marketing, a profit center looks forward to opportunities to increase its net contribution to the system.

Note that in a profit center design it may still be possible for one unit to benefit at the cost of another. But the critical difference is that a win/win situation is now a possibility. Both production and marketing can benefit from meeting customer demands, and more significantly, all units have the same performance criteria, which will insure their compatibility. Note that uniformity of performance criteria although desirable is not necessary, the important point is compatibility. That is to say, performance criteria must be designed in such a way that the success of one part does not imply failure of another.

Diachronic Compatibility

Concern for diachronic compatibility in a social system is concern for its continuity. Among stakeholders of an organization there are those who had been members of the system in the past and those who will be its members in the future. The argument for compatibility between the interest of past, present, and future members, especially on ethical grounds, is so rich that it is beyond the scope of the present paper; our concern here is more or less pragmatic.

It is not difficult to appreciate that a social system can succeed today, at the expense of its future, or suffer in the creation of a better future. It can also be demonstrated that past members of a social system can have a profound (negative or positive) influence in shaping its present. However, although a need for compatibility between the interest of present and future members is more or less appreciated, the same need for compatibility between the interest of present and past members is not readily recognized.

In some cultures, interests of past members continue to dominate the present, while in other cultures there is no concern for the interests of those who are gone—"out of sight, out of mind." Nevertheless, pragmatically, rejection of the interests of past members is as undesirable as acceptance of their dominance. The effectiveness of an organization, as a voluntary association of purposeful systems, depends on the degree of commitment of its members and on their sense of belonging. In this context, alienation is a serious obstruction to an organization's development. Odd as it may seem, incompatibility between the interests of past, present, and future members is one of the main sources of alienation of its present members. This is so because a constant threat to the long-term viability of the organization is a continuous coproducer of anxiety and insecurity among those members who identify with the future. But members identify themselves with the past as well. They can see the image of their own future in the fate of those who in the past had been effective members of the system and served it well. An undesirable and unfortunate image is a serious source of insecurity that is at the core of alienation, corruption, and lust for power. This is why concern for the interests of past members, minimally in the form of an acceptable retirement system, is essential. In this respect, the notion of gradual retirement, with all of its ramifications, should be considered more seriously than it has been.

Finally, the requirement for diachronic compatibility is based on the notion that a social system, unlike a biological system, is not necessarily subject to life cycles. The purpose of an organization is to serve its members by effectively serving its environment. This is a continuous and never-ending function. Unlike a product-based organization, which will necessarily experience a life cycle, a learning and adaptive social system continuously recreates itself to meet the requirements of an ever-changing environment and the changing desires of its members.

Performance Criteria, Measure of Performance, and Incentives

Thus far, we have discussed integration in social systems through creation of vertical, horizontal, and diachronic compatibility of performance criteria. These criteria, however, are always operationalized by *measures* of performance and reinforced by the *incentive* system. In this section, we will elaborate on the distinction among these and discuss the role that each plays in the behavior of the system.

Performance criteria are expressions of the value system governing the organization. They establish the framework for the evaluation of the performance of the system. With these criteria, a set of relevant variables can be identified by which success of the system is evaluated. Measures of performance are the link between this framework and the concrete experience of evaluation and reward. These are the indicators by which the members are directly affected. They should be measured along the set of variables identified by the criteria, but this is seldom the case, as we shall see.

The incentive system is a priority scheme that is superimposed on the measures of performance. It emphasizes certain measures and discounts others in order to produce the desired behavior. Incentive systems are often equated with explicit bonus programs and financial rewards. In reality, these are but a small part of such systems. The incentive system comprises all the various evaluations and inducements that affect the behavior of the members of the system: financial and nonfinancial; implicit or explicit; imposed by superiors, peers, and subordinates, and so on. Furthermore, the totality of this intricate system is seldom consciously designed. In fact, parts of it that are designed, such as bonus programs, do not usually lead to expected outcomes because other intervening factors that may lead to counterintuitive behaviors are disregarded.

In practice, the performance criteria are usually left vague, ambiguous, and unoperationalized. Even when their underlying concepts are relatively simple, such as minimization of costs in an organizational unit, they create complicated problems of measurement (how to allocate the overhead). In the interest of uniformity of measures across the various systems, be they organizational units or national economics, the traditional approach has been to settle for simple, intuitive, and conventional measures. The overriding concern has been with the accuracy of measures rather than with their relevance. Thus, performance measures are no longer justified by their relationship to the performance criteria. Instead, their justification is based on their simplicity, universal applicability, and conventionality. What seemed to be an innocent matter of convenience has changed the nature of performance measures for such things as navigational instruments to ends and objectives in and of themselves. Since we cannot measure what we want, we pretend to want what we can measure.

The irony of the situation is that the more accurate the measurement of the wrong performance criteria, the faster the road to disaster. The right criteria inaccurately measured, is much safer than the wrong criteria accurately measured. Let us explore the practical implications of this argument by means of two examples at the corporate and national levels.

In the case of a corporation, the usual practice of allocating overhead expenses to various operating units provides examples of unintended consequences of simple measures of performance. Despite the fact that overhead constitutes a major portion of the costs of the operating units (often running as high as 40% of total costs), the criteria for allocation of this overhead are usually selected based on simplicity of measurement. Single factors (*at best, gross estimates of a fair share of common expenses*), such as the space occupied by a unit or the direct labor content of production, are among the most popular allocation criteria. Therefore, these variables naturally become the driving force for improvement of performance measures. The fact that the allocation rule was simply an accounting convenience and that these measures are at best *estimates* of a fair share of common expenses, is easily forgotten. Once the allocation criteria becomes a rule, its relationship to the generation of costs is, by default, assumed to be causal, as demonstrated by the following case.

Concerned with its cost disadvantage, a multinational manufacturing concern instructed its operating units to reduce their costs by 20%. The overhead costs in this company were allocated based on direct labor content of production. The rule was simply that overhead was equal to 300% of direct labor. The cost structure of the operating units were: raw material and energy 40%, direct labor 15%, overhead 45%. Although direct labor contributed the lowest proportion of cost to the production process, it was targeted for reduction—because of the allocation rule of overhead costs. The operating units' managers realized that a 5% reduction in their direct labor costs would achieve the 20% "savings" required (it would reduce the allocated overhead by an additional 15%). The only problem was that when they all chose this path the corporation suddenly found itself with unallocated overhead. Although the operating units showed the 20% reduction, the corporation had not realized more than 5% real reduction of costs. The immediate reaction was the conventional one. The rate of overhead allocation was increased from 300% to 450%! Only as a result of the outrage that this action produced (and the impossible implications that it had of having to further reduce the labor costs) did the corporation finally decide to examine its overhead costs. The number of employees at the headquarters was subsequently reduced from 850 to 130.

This situation is by no means atypical. Because of the prevalance of allocation rules based on labor, pressure is unduly shifted to direct labor and the knee-jerk reaction is to lay off productive employees. If the police department is facing deficits, policemen are the first to be fired. If schools are in financial trouble, the number of teachers is reduced. Reduction of operating units does not automatically reduce overhead, as management seems to assume. On the contrary, it will increase the burden of the remaining units until the whole system comes to a halt.

Recently, a large supermarket chain decided to close ten of its stores because the accounting system showed that they were not covering the allocated overhead. Since the overhead did not decline proportionately, and in this case not at all, the other stores had to offset a larger share of overhead, which then made more of them unprofitable. Therefore, the company gradually withdrew more stores from the market, blaming high labor costs for its decision. When the stores reopened after some unprecedented labor initiatives, a new contract emphasizing participation of labor in decision making and the establishment of a new subsidiary of the original corporation, there was no overhead allocated to the stores. Each store became responsible for its own operating budget, the balance of which was passed on to the corporation. The corporation, in turn, had to provide its services within the bounds of these surpluses. The extent of its services and the size of its bureaucracy thus reflected the needs of its operating units.

Perhaps the most dramatic instance of implications of performance measures is a recent experience at a chemical company. Overhead was allocated based on the square footage of the facilities. A talented plant manager devised a new production process in his plant that eliminated the need for four large buildings. The machinery was moved out and the buildings vacated for other uses. Soon after, the manager realized there was no reduction in his overhead charges. The accounting department explained to him that overhead was allocated based on the space available to the plant; it did not matter whether the buildings were used or not. The next day bulldozers were tearing down the buildings! The overhead charges and total costs of the plant were reduced accordingly. In the meantime the company had lost perhaps millions of valuable assets.

A similar situation exists at the national level. Development is widely regarded as an objective of the social system. Initial struggle with designing measures for this complex process led to the conclusion that it would be difficult to measure development directly. It was noticed, however, that there are certain correlates of development that could be easily measured. Rate of growth of per capita income became the conventional measure of development. This identification grew so strong in the following years that the two concepts became identical in the minds of most people. Societies around the world became preoccupied with increasing their per capita incomes. There was no longer a need to be concerned with development because of this simple substitution.

In the early 1970s an increase in oil prices produced instantly developed nations, according to the accepted measures. The shock that this produced resulted in some rethinking about the measures of development. However, the concept of correlates was so embedded in the concerned community that it was not questioned. The solution was merely to increase the number of correlates being measured. We now have a series of these indicators that substitute for development, such as per capita steel production, number of doctors per 1,000 population, and per capita consumption of fuel. It is not surprising, then, to find national development policies aimed at improving these measures, usually at incredible cost to the society at large.

Performance Center

Since the members of an organization are purposeful systems, their patterns of interaction cannot be predefined and therefore are not subject to a mechanistic concept of design. Actors (individually or in groups) by agreeing or disagreeing with each other on the compatibility of their ends, means, or both may at the same time cooperate with regard to one pair of tendencies, compete over others, and be in conflict with respect to different sets.

In the systems view, performance of the whole is not the sum of the performances of its parts but rather it is the product of their interaction. The proper management of this interaction defines the main role of a manager, a role that cannot be replaced, mechanized, or predefined. This is why the ultimate success of an organization depends on its management talent. However, proliferation of variety (Beer 1978) produced by highly differentiated functional structures presents a severe challenge to this critical management function. So much so that the law of diminishing returns is increasingly overtaking the advantages of economies of scale. In this context an organizational culture that promotes the cooperative type of interactions is the most important help a manager can have.

By rejecting unquestionable acceptance of zero-sum situations, the systems view of organization considers both lose/lose and win/win situations to be strong possibilities; therefore, the objective is to create an organizational setting that will improve the chances of win/win situations. Among the fundamental decisions to be made in the design of an organization is how authority and responsibility will be allocated. Any large organization contains smaller units each of which has a defined responsibility and a certain level of authority. More difficult than allocating authority and responsibility is building these into the design in proper combination. Too often, units that have the authority to make decisions in organizations have no responsibility for the consequences of those decisions. Conversely, units may be held responsible for situations over which they have no control. Both situations result in frustration and ineffectiveness.

A U T H O R I T Y	high authority low responsibility	high authority high responsibility
	low authority low responsibility	low authority high responsibility

RESPONSIBILITY

In organizations where the high-high quadrant is unknown or rare, the name of the game becomes avoidance of the low authority–high responsibility quadrant and jockeying for the high authority–low responsibility positions. These positions soon become competitive and relatively unattainable. Thus, most members of the organizations drift toward the low-low quadrant in preference to the only alternative, low authority–high responsibility. This results in an organizational culture of "just following orders" and "passing the buck," a bureaucratic culture ultimately with lose/lose results.

Traditionally, control in organizations is achieved through a hierarchical reporting relationship. In this approach, optimization of performance of the higher-level unit requires that the lower level's objectives be subordinated. For example, if a marketing unit requires low manufacturing costs, it can best assure this by direct control over manufacturing. Control, however, can be achieved in one other way: an exchange or interactive relationship. The model for this is the relationship between suppliers and consumers. Although consumers hold no authority to direct the supplier to produce a specific product, they exert considerable influence on the decision by placing orders for that product. Units within an organization can also relate to each other in an exchange relationship. However, for an exchange relationship to work, a vertical, horizontal, and diachronic compatibility between the performance criteria of different units must be assured. These, along with relevant performance measures and an appropriate incentive system are required for interactions among units to result in win/win situations.

As argued earlier, a pure profit center, although useful for providing horizontal compatibility, has serious shortcomings with regard to diachronic compatibility. There is the potential for profit centers to look to short-term results, to focus on the single objective of profit, and to disregard opportunities that might have short-term negative consequences for the center but that could provide significant long-term gains. The following concept of performance centers is intended to overcome this deficiency.

Effectiveness of a performance center is reflected not only by its efficiency (input-output ratios) but also its latency (future potential).

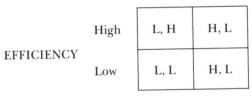

LATENCY

It is obvious that current performance of a system can be improved at the expense of its future (L,H), and vice versa (H,L). But it is not so obvious that a system can be a low performer today and be obstructing its future as well (L,L). More important, not only is there the possibility of a High, High situation, but it is a necessity.

The critical point of this conception is that the market value of a performance center, that is, the present value of its future earnings together with its present profit and loss performance, becomes an important measure of its performance. By accepting long-term responsibility for its viability, a performance center will become sensitive to the marketing consequences of its actions. Thus, a market orientation is developed and internalized. The necessary change of emphasis from products to markets will reduce the system's dependency on product life cycle and create an entrepreneurial culture, which will insure its continuity and enhance its diachronic compatibility.

A performance center, like a profit center, has profit-and-loss responsibility, so its concern is with adding value not minimizing cost or maximizing revenue. However, critical to the successful operation of a performance center is its ability to have partial control or influence over determining its (1) product mix, (2) pricing of outputs, (3) selection of sources of inputs, and (4) ability to retain part of its earnings for future development.

Finally, an incentive system is needed to encourage the search for win/win solutions by creating positive value to members as a result of cooperative strategies. An organizational unit or member should be rewarded not only for improvement in measure of performance but also for any contribution made to other units that improves their measures. An example of this is provided by the following scheme implemented in a professional firm. All members received 10% of their annually generated income if certain performance measures were met. This percentage, however, would be increased to 15% if other members of a group achieved their set objective and would even increase to 20% if all the units of the organization were able to meet their performance objectives.

Unfortunately, all this is easier said than done. The majority of present corporate citizens are too happy with their perceived sense of security, embedded in the low authority and low responsibility culture of bureaucratic corporations to permit any meaningful change in the system without the active support and commitment of its top level management. However, our previous experiences show that the concept can more easily be introduced in the formative stages of new corporations.

To summarize, we propose that the incompatibility of performance criteria among the units within an organization is the main source of the frustration and dilemmas encountered in most organizational settings. Proliferation of these incompatibilities, at least partially, explains the reason why the famous "invisible hand" has been converted to an "invisible kick."

Reflection on the nature and working mechanism of the "invisible hand" would reveal that it is the vertical, horizontal, and diachronic compatibility of performance criteria. Note that implicit in the notion of the invisible hand is a uniform performance criteria. Adam Smith assumed that all actors are profit centers. To conclude, the answer to the question of why the system is in such a mess now when it worked so well before is provided by Boulding's famous assertion, "the name of the devil is suboptimization" (Boulding 1968).

References

Ackoff, R. L., and F. E. Emery. (1981). *On Purposeful Systems.* Reprint. Seaside, Calif.: Intersystems Publications.

Ackoff, R. L., E. V. Finnel, and J. Gharajedaghi. (1984). *A Guide to Controlling Your Corporation's Future,* New York: Wiley.

Beer, S. (1978). *The Brain of the Firm.* New York: Wiley.

Boulding, K. (1968). *Beyond Economics: Essays on Society, Religion and Ethics.* Ann Arbor: University of Michigan Press.

Gharajedaghi, J., and R. L. Ackoff. (1984). *Mechanisms, Organisms and Social Systems,* New York: Wiley.

Chapter 13
Some Comments on R. Ackoff's Concept of Interactive Planning

Aron Katsenelinboigen

Closers

At the heart of Ackoff's approach to interactive planning lies the concept of *purposeful* systems that are capable of both generating their own goals and the means of reaching them through the course of their development. The concept of *purpose-goal* is a key one here and it dominates all stages of the planning process.

Goals, by playing the role of *"closers"*[1] for any given stage of the planning process, also help us in organizing and systematizing it. Furthermore, it needs to be pointed out that "closers" are not *"isolators"* and that each stage of the process influences the formation of closers for later stages. For example, a goal at one stage in the process can become a starting point for another part of the process further down the line.

This active, organizing feature of goals distinguishes them from another type of "closer" that, unwilled, appear passively at the end of the process and signify the exhaustion of its potential for change.[2]

This kind of goal-oriented planning differs sharply from methods that place the heaviest emphasis on the initial conditions that prevail at the beginning of the process and stress the extrapolation of past trends. A goal-oriented approach introduces into the planning process the idea of *designing* or *redesigning* the future (in case a previous

My comments on R. Ackoff's concept of interactive planning are based on the most part, on the ideas contained in his book *Creating the Corporate Future* (New York: Wiley, 1981). Unless otherwise indicated, I refer to a particular page number in the above-mentioned book.

This article was translated into English by my son Gregory and edited by A. Veresano. Many thanks to both of them.

design has already been accomplished) and contrasts with a passive repetition of the past through extrapolation.

The formation of stages and their goals in a multistage planning process can be studied from a variety of different perspectives, but a fundamental requirement that they all have to meet as far as goal formulation is concerned has to do with the fact that each goal must holistically reflect the entirety of the developmental process. In other words, the attainment of any particular goal should not effectively rule out a possibility of continued development. It is highly undesirable to reach a goal that, for example, turns out to be an isolated, suboptimal result. The attainment of such goals leaves us with a sense of Pyrrhic victory.

Ackoff has suggested that we should distinguish between three different types of categories: *ideals, objectives,* and *goals.*[3] Ackoff's classification of ends is two-dimensional; the first dimension deals with attainability of ends, and the second, with a program necessary for reaching them. From this classification it follows that ideals are not attainable at all; objectives, though attainable, do not present us with ready programs for realizing them; and goals are both attainable and lend themselves to programmatic realization.

In my opinion, there is also another way of looking at the problem of formulating ends and means for their realization in a multistage planning process. Initially, we do that on the basis of articles of faith. At later stages, it is largely the aesthetic criteria that are used to formulate ends and means, and it is only at the third stage of the planning process that scientific principles of performing the task come into their own.[4]

Idealization, in the sense that Ackoff talks about it, relates to the ends of the initial stage in the scheme just outlined above. Since a crucial function of this stage consists in setting a direction for an entire planning process we can call it the "*directional*" stage.

Objectives of the second stage are less remote than ideals and the means of reaching them are more visible. However, this should not be at all construed to imply that from our position in the present we know precisely how to create a program for attaining such objectives. Therefore, it is important that we create such initial conditions at the second stage that would be able to provide for the most efficacious development of the system in an unknown future. In other words, these initial conditions should be such as to make it possible to steer a future development of the system in a desirable direction. In practice, it means that the system should be able to induce the change of the environment in a desirable direction, to absorb unexpected positive contingencies and react in a proper manner to unexpected negative ones.

It is precisely the aesthetic criteria, associated as they are with incomplete structures that cover this particular set of initial conditions. A structure that measures up to the requirements we set for the conditions in question can be called a *potential*, and the process of its formation and movement toward ideals may be called *potentiating*. Since objectives and goals, as they are defined by Ackoff, can assume the role of conditions for future activities unanalyzed in a plan, they should, in principle, be able to satisfy the requirements of our definition of potential.

Finally, the third stage is characterized by having goals that can contribute in a well-perceived manner to the realization of higher-level ends, as well as by offering a real possibility of generating programs for reaching such goals. We should note that the third stage itself can have several substages with a goal of one of them being expressed in say, aggregate, probabilistic terms, and that of another, lower-order one, in terms of concrete parameters having a high degree of precision. Unfortunately, Ackoff has not specifically considered this separate phenomenon of goals that may emerge in the very process of program formulation.

The third stage, taken as a whole, can be called *programmatic*, for it is program-generation with which it is chiefly concerned. Possibly the term "planning" can be used to denote a certain metaconcept that fixes and synthesizes the above-mentioned processes of directing, potentiating, and programming.

Combination of Ends and Planning Types

Ackoff combines in one matrix the three different types of ends that he introduced with four types of planning. The fact that there are only three kinds of ends and four kinds of planning follows from Ackoff's assumption that the ends of the operational, tactical, and strategic types of planning are exogenous,[5] whereas in the case of normative planning, they are endogenous to it.

Before I proceed to analyze this matrix of end and planning types, I would like to make a few remarks that hopefully will make explicit the problem of temporal dimension in the process of planning. The very concepts of operational, tactical, strategic, and normative planning, though based primarily on differing methods of formulating ends and means, are not associated with any clear-cut time intervals. Although time parameters are correlated with planning methods, they also have their own specificity not tied to any one method in particular.

First of all, one never sees the problem of determining the time needed to achieve various ends explicitly formulated as a separate concern—it is assumed that these ends lie outside the program. It is additionally assumed that the ends are remote from us in time. Even when programming is feasible, it does not mean that we know the time required to achieve a certain end—time here is an unknown variable. All this is made even more complex by the non-markovian nature of social processes (i.e., the future depends not only on a state of the system at a given time, but also on its previous development). It follows that, in setting social ends, we cannot ignore the problem of the means that we are going to use in realizing them. We cannot, in other words, sidestep a consideration of those social processes that will attend our movement toward the desired ends.

For example, a society can have a mission to aspire to such a level of development that will guarantee each of its citizens, irrespective of social status and perturbations in the environment, a subsistence minimum of nutrition, clothing, shelter, medical care, education, etc. If we have come fairly close to realizing such an end, it can become, in Ackoff's terms—a "goal." When we then turn to the problem of generating a program, our task may be not to minimize the time needed to achieve that goal but to minimize the amount of "damage" that will have been incurred by society before this goal is realized. In this case, the time requirements for achieving the goal are unknown in formal terms; it is akin to dealing with an extremal problem possessing a variable upper limit of integration.

Moreover, even if we were to know how much time it takes to realize the entire program, we will still be faced with the problem of establishing temporal subperiods, be they homogeneous (i.e., given in exact same terms of aggregation level of concreteness) or not. In this case, too, time periods will be an unknown variable. The problem of determining exact quantitative values in the course of solving the general programming problem clearly depends on costs involved in evaluating the realization of the program, on one hand, and the possibility of effectively correcting the program after an evaluation has been done, on the other. It follows, therefore, that the greater the turbulence, i.e., the greater the instability present in the system and its environment, the ampler the opportunities for correcting the system's development and the cheaper the evaluation—the shorter the time periods into which the planning process ought to be broken.

In this regard, we may note that at the time of the original Soviet five-year plans, the basic time unit for major output series such as steel, oil, tractors, etc., was one day. The most important papers used to print figures for these series on *a daily basis*. In recent years, as the economy has become progressively more stable, the basic time unit for planning at the national level has been moved up to one month.

Thus, while using clearly time-laden terms to describe various planning methods, i.e., strategic, mid-term, tactical, and operational, it ought to be kept in mind that we are dealing here only with a correlation between these methods and planning intervals. It is quite conceivable that in a less turbulent environment, the methods of tactical planning may be stretched out to coincide with time periods equal to those that are presently associated with strategic planning. The practice of corporations indicates that, depending on the turbulence in the environment, the time intervals for strategic planning vary within the span from three to five years.

Now let us come back to the matrix of three end types and four planning types suggested by Ackoff. Readily conceding a value of such an approach, we may at the same time suggest another schemata in which exogenously-generated ends will represent only one case among many. It seems to me that we first can assign individual ends to each of the four planning methods and only afterward try and tackle the problem of whether these ends are generated endogenously by a given method or exogenously by a higher-level one. Such an approach would make it possible to establish explicit connections between the process of formulating ends and the two parts of the holistic principle suggested by Ackoff in reference to hierarchically organized systems: *coordination* and *integration*. The principle of coordination states that we cannot effectively plan the activities of a cell at any given level without regard to the activities of all other cells at the same level. The principle of integration claims that planning for any single level cannot be effective without consideration of other levels of the organization.

The principle of coordination, then, will be associated with ends generated by the cell itself; that of integration, with ends formulated exogenously at a higher level. In addition, we can assume that a given economic cell may be guided by more complex methods of end-generation: under the principle of integration, it may be offered an end expressed in *aggregate* terms; the process of disaggregation, in turn, will be carried out pursuant to the concept of coordination. For example, the center can pass down to an individual factory the plan for the exact number of leather shoes it has to produce. The concretization of that plan (i.e., determination of shoe sizes, styles, color, etc.) can be done directly through the interaction of the shoe factory and a wholesale organization.

Following up on my own suggestion concerning the principle of generating ends for each type of planning, I would like to use the term *targets* to describe "the final destination point" of operational type-planning.

On the Concept of Ideal

Ackoff's introduction of the concept of ideal into the planning process has signified a very important development in theoretical thought. On the face of it, the concept resembles communist and religious utopias that have been knocked down from their pedestals by the wrecking ball of scientific methods on which modern planning theory rests. The principal difference between ideal and utopia, however, lies in the fact that ideals are explicitly formulated as inherently unfulfillable: we can come infinitely close to them without ever quite reaching them. Ackoff's definition of ideals bears repeating here:

> *Ideals:* those ends that are believed to be unattainable but towards which we believe progress is possible during and after the period planned for.

In this regard, I would like to suggest that great successes in science are not confined to providing solutions to problems posed—they also accrue to those who can show that a certain problem does *not* have a solution. From this standpoint, nineteenth-century science differs significantly from that of the eighteenth century. The 1700s witnessed a whole series of great scientific discoveries and inventions that produced in some a powerful illusion that purposeful and deliberate coordination of all these discoveries and inventions could offer boundless opportunities for bettering the lot of mankind. The advent of the nineteenth century saw the appearance of monumental theoretical breakthroughs in the field of thermodynamics which proved the impossibility of creating a perpetual motion machine. Right then and there, the hopes of many inventors for ridding humanity of energy shortages were dashed. Instead of devoting their time and energy to finding that final, last idea which would make the creation of a perpetual motion machine a reality, scientists and inventors had to become meticulous sloggers striving for a gradual increase of the mechanical efficiency of engines.

The great nineteenth-century discoveries in the field of mathematics were to a considerable extent connected with impossibility theories. Thus, Evariste Galois proved that higher than fourth degree equations cannot have analytical solutions. Demonstrating that a proof of a certain problem *exists* prior to launching an investigation of the best method for solving it has, over the years, acquired a separate and considerable importance for mathematicians.

Needless to say, there were many outstanding discoveries in the nineteenth century that provided positive solutions to problems. In my preceding remarks, I only wanted to draw the reader's attention to the fact that scientists and scholars of that time began to attach to proofs of impossibility a much greater importance than was the case before.

Proof positive of the enduring interest in this new line of thought in our own century is furnished by, among other things, Gödel's famous theorem of impossibility. It should also be pointed out that along with natural sciences and mathematics, proofs of impossibility began to appear in the field of social sciences. I am here referring to a remarkable theorem of K. Arrow in which he proved that under certain circumstances there was no conceivable way for people to make general social welfare decisions in a way that could be considered democratic. Still, social sciences in general are characterized by the persistent and erroneous faith that ideals constitute attainable ends: the existence of strong Marxist schools in the West seems to support the proposition that the category of impossibility has not yet been firmly implanted in the works of social scientists. In all fairness, I must add that claims of impossibility should, doubtless, be handled with considerable care: there have been some cases when even great scientists have mistakenly held to the infeasibility of doing something that later proved to be quite doable, e.g., designing an operational aircraft. Moreover, in many instances, we can neither prove nor disprove whether something is accomplishable or not. In such cases, we have to accord equal weight to the rival claims of proponents and opponents of a certain course of action.

Still, my principal concern here is with a revolutionary role played by the concept of impossibility and an urgent need to see it further developed for application to the field of social science. What are the root causes that make for the unattainability of ideals? I think there are at least two of them. According to the first one, an ideal state is unreachable for the good and sufficient reason that it runs counter to the fundamental principles on which our world is based. Under this category of explanation fall such things as perpetual motion machines, communism, etc. If by communism we understand such a state in which all human needs will be satisfied, then its attainment is impossible, if for no other reason than the existence of a contradiction between a very strong desire that people have to live a long life and the potential of a boundless and unknown cosmos to threaten them with possible destruction.

The second reason, in my opinion, refers to those situations in which a theoretical possibility that an ideal state may be attained is vitiated by the real-life patterns of action characteristic of a given system. This can be illustrated, for example, by the so-called retrograde positions in chess. In those positions, the actual location of pieces on the board does not violate any of the existing chess rules, but if we were to retrace our steps in order to see what sequence of moves might have led to one of those positions, we would discover that as long as we stick only to legal moves, none of those "retrograde" situations can *ever* be recreated. It may be interesting from this perspective to look at the problem of disarmament. Theoretically, we can conceive a situation in which all weapons of mass destruction will be eliminated. However, the actual rules of the game, long accepted and used by the states, have prevented the realization of this ideal since the beginning of recorded history. This does not mean that an ideal state of global and complete disarmament cannot be reached; what it means is that so far it is unclear whether the operational methods of relations between nations can bring it about, and what new difficulties, e.g., an all-round enslavement of people by some global overlord, may follow the realization of such an ideal.

Being aware of the fact that ideals are unreachable has an enormous practical significance since it frees people from the illusion that all they need is just one last push that would culminate in the solution of age-old problems and reward them for countless years of suffering. Those who exploit and misrepresent ideals as real ends realizable by means of practical action bring terrible misery to people. It is worthwhile in this regard to recall the dangers inherent in the ideals of communism as a society blessed with universal abundance. If Western societies make use of the ideal of material plenty, they use it only as an ideal, without promising that it can be completely fulfilled, much less fulfilled within a definite period of time.

In this regard, I think it is an unfortunate misunderstanding that makes Ackoff write that the ideal of material plenty is shared by both the United States and the Soviet Union.

> Ideologies have less to do with ideals than with means for pursuing them. (The similarity of these two words is misleading.) For example, the ideological question involving who should own the means of production concerns the selection of a means for pursuing the ideal of plenty. Both nations accept this as an ideal. (p. 118)

Ideals and Their Realization

Ackoff has proposed a very original concept of "idealized design" which is meant to ensure both an operational role for the notion of ideal and provide a methodology for realizing ideals. But before I proceed to comment on this subject, I would like to take some time to put forward my own views on how the various stages and their attendant ends are generated within the process of idealized design. The original impetus for my own thoughts on this matter came from Ackoff's works in which he deals directly with the concept of idealized design, as well as from a number of his other works referred to below.

There is a strong correlation between the way people generate ideals for themselves and the way that, at any given time, they choose to answer the key questions of social development, namely, "What are the root causes of dissatisfaction among people?" and "Where does the means for overcoming this dissatisfaction lie?" Ackoff and Emery called attention to these two questions. On this basis, they develop an interesting typology according to which there are basically four different kinds of individuals: objective internalizers, subjective internalizers, objective externalizers, and subjective externalizers.[6]

It may be argued that people's ideals are to a certain extent related to this typology. Thus, one may suppose that subjective internalists will lean toward *nirvana* as their ideal, for they are entirely preoccupied with changing their inner world and see no possibility in the external environment to help them overcome their suffering. According to Buddhists, individuals cannot avoid suffering as long as they remain even in the smallest degree connected to the external world with its never-ending processes of creation and destruction. Subjective externalists may express their ideal in the following manner: *enjoy life* within the *constraints* embedded in a culture to which you belong and adapt to your environment. Such an ideal in life is rather characteristic of Jews who do not believe in the notion of the immortal soul which may come to reside in heaven. Objective internalists may choose for their ideal the concept of *paradise*. Believing that the environment is responsible for their lack of satisfaction, objective internalists do not strive to change it but instead create in their mind an ideal, the realization of which they associate with the fulfillment of all their wishes. Objective externalists are also inclined to blame the environment for their misfortunes and strongly tend toward the view that by changing the environment they will succeed in attaining happiness. Someone with this kind of attitude can be easily satisfied with an ideal of *communism*.

In the eyes of true believers, all these ideals undoubtedly appear as utopias. Still, we can meaningfully talk of them as ideals (in the strict sense of the word) on condition that we continue to interpret them not as realizable ends but merely as guideposts for choosing this or that road in life. There exists a whole spectrum of different states between the opposing poles of ideals, on one hand, and fairly concrete ends, on the other one, with the latter kind being suitable for use in more immediate, short-term actions. This last statement will become clearer as we proceed with our exposition. First of all, the spectrum that I have in mind should include the determination of a *mission*, i.e., of an end which, according to Ackoff, is theoretically attainable but only in a distant future. A mission is characterized by the pursuit of an end which is both very desirable and morally binding upon its seekers, e.g., the quest of the Holy Grail for a crusader (p. 107). If we are talking about the ideal of communism, then the mission of a country that espouses it would be to attain such a state in which each of its citizens is guaranteed a minimum subsistence level of nutrition, housing, clothing, medical care, etc., irrespective of his or her social position and fluctuations in the environment, that is, regardless of the given of the country's economic situation, environmental conditions, etc. The fulfillment of such an end can be classed among the historical achievements of humanity since, in a state like that, people, for the first time, will have a tangible guarantee of their material independence from both society and nature.

A hypothetical situation of this sort does not entail the elimination of *inequality* among people. The principle of equity is exactly the one that allows for a wide range of inequality beyond the guaranteed level of subsistence; moreover, under an equitable distribution, the minimum level is not necessarily provided free of charge. What is important is to guarantee all members of society an easy and *affordable* access to goods—distribution of goods free of charge being but one of many different allocation patterns. Although any mission may be theoretically attainable, it does not mean that its attainability is automatically ensured given our present level of knowledge of the necessary methods and resources for fulfilling the mission.

It will be of considerable interest, therefore, to introduce the concept of such a state, the attainment of which will bring us as close as possible to the point of fulfilling a mission, and one that provides for the complete realization of the system's technological possibilities regardless of the resources that the system happens to have available. This idea, as it relates to mathematical economics, is based upon the concept of the *turnpike* developed by John Von Neumann. The turnpike theorems have to do with the determination of those processes that make for the best possible utilization of given technologies irrespective of the initial conditions which, generally speaking, do not permit an immediate realization of these technologies. Moreover, the present-day notions in this field go as far as to concede that the technologies may be completely unrealizable. To deal with this rigorous assumption, certain meta-methods for completing the first-order technologies have been developed.

In the light of what I have said above, it seems to me that after the stages of formulating ideals and missions have been completed, we should bring into consideration yet another stage: *reaching the turnpike*. In this case, the term "turnpike" refers to a situation where the only limitations upon the speed of a car are imposed by the inherent constraints of the automobile's design and road conditions. No other external factor, e.g., the place of entrance or exit from the turnpike, or stoplights, has any effect on the fastest possible (or economically most efficient) speed of the automobile.

At different stages of the planning process, the notions of *ideal, mission*, and *turnpike* can all conceivably be brought under the roof of Ackoff's concept of idealized design. In point of fact, Ackoff has already done this but in a manner somewhat different from one adumbrated here. What are then, in Ackoff's view, the specific requirements that his concept of idealized design has to meet? First of all, it must be technologically feasible, that is, it should not involve any science fiction. Second, from the operational point of view, it must be viable, i.e., capable of economic survival once it is implemented. Third, it must provide for quick learning and adaptation on the part of the system. Another important characteristic of the idealized design has to do with its being completely independent of presently existing conditions.

It seems to me that this kind of design meets the requirements set above for the concept of turnpike. The design in question is not tantamount to an ideal for, unlike an ideal, it can, in principle, be realized. As to the concept of a mission, its role, apparently, lies more in generating distant yet realizable and mobilizing social goals, and not in pinpointing the technological means that can theoretically bring us to the fulfillment of these goals. Thus, readily admitting that Ackoff's concept of idealized design merits the highest acclaim I think that it can be further sharpened by explicitly breaking it down into the three distinct stages outlined above: *ideals, missions*, and *turnpikes*.

Constructivism and a Free Society

In the light of the preceding discussion, the reader may ask whether the practice of idealized design may not eventuate in totalitarianism, inasmuch as it involves a deliberate redesign by the leaders' imposing their will upon the helpless subjects as they strive to implement the plan passed down from on high. Ackoff's concept of idealized design is immune to this kind of charge. The process of design, in Ackoff's view, provides for a broad participation of many different groups of concerned parties. Along with this large-scale participation, it is the competence of various participants that determines the level of the hierarchy at which they are empowered to make decisions.

It is my understanding that Ackoff's shift of emphasis away from operations research and toward the development of Social Systems Sciences (S³) was connected precisely with his deep awareness of how vitally important it was to get large groups of plan implementers involved in the very process of formulating the plan. As distinct from the S³ approach, operations research methodology places the main emphasis on perfecting the traditional planning schemes, that is, on refining techniques of plan formulation by experts with its subsequent implementation by subordinates. Ackoff's democratically oriented approach to planning differs not only from the procedures of *representative* democracy, where the opinions of the rank and file are expressed by their representatives, but also from the patterns of *mobocracy,* which allows unqualified participants manipulated by autocrats to take part in making overall decisions that affect the entire system.

It seems to me, however, that in talking about the participation of the rank and file in the process of formulating the plan, Ackoff has neglected one rather important aspect of the problem. His primary concern is with the democratic issue, namely, with a number of participants that are involved in the mechanism of decision making and the way this mechanism is supposed to function. The other relevant aspects of the problem, i.e., a variety of opinions that the participants have and the best way of preserving and expanding this variety, has not received Ackoff's full attention. Of course, he very well understands that people have different conceptions of the most desirable path of development that a system should follow, be it a corporation or a country. Still, Ackoff seems to think that democratically organized *low*erarchy as opposed to *hi*erarchy with its top-heavy structure of decision making, is an effective vehicle for solving problems in a situation marked by a variety of opinions held by the participants in the system.

Furthermore, Ackoff maintains that a well-organized system of planning can, in theory at least, bring about an agreement between previously conflicting viewpoints.

> Consensus arises in idealized design because it focuses on ultimate values rather than on means for pursuing them. In general, people disagree less about ideals than about shorter-range goals and the means for obtaining them. For example, the constitutions of the United States and the Soviet

Union are surprisingly alike. Most of the disagreements between these two countries derive from their differences over means, not ultimate ends. (p. 118)

It seems to me, however, that differences between ideals or rather, utopias also in a large measure account for disagreements among people. The principal differences between world religions lie in the emphasis that they attach to various ideals. It is sufficient to compare the Christian ideal with the Buddhist one to see how dissimilar would be the patterns of life led by the people who espouse these ideals. The ideal of nirvana will tend to stimulate its devotees to renounce their material desires and the attendant striving for prosperity. The ideal of heaven, on the other hand, may be conducive to bringing about an increase of desire for material riches. Thus, the ideal of communism amounts, in effect, to a dream of heaven on earth. I do not want to oversimplify the situation and try to establish a rigid one-to-one correspondence between the ideals in question and the attitude of people toward a state of material abundance. One can give examples of Christian communities that give up any desire of accumulating riches and, conversely, of Buddhist communities that are actively engaged in material production. Still there is, I believe, a rather strong correlation between ideals and people's earthly patterns of desires.

A systemic approach to describing political structures, therefore, should rest on representing them as *multidimensional systems*. Pluralism, democracy, and openness are all examples of these different dimensions that should be interpreted as independent variables.

Pluralism refers primarily to a manifold of development programs, i.e., to a set of equally valued programs, along with the creation of conditions that are favorable to maintaining and expanding this manifold. Hence, the organizational problem of how to create such conditions that have to do with the establishment of *independent* organizations, e.g., parties, universities, and corporations, because without an organizational setting, groups of like-minded people usually find it quite impossible to develop and defend their point of view. To preserve and strengthen these organizations we need, along with the separation of powers, manifold sources of financial support: it is unlikely that a manifold can be maintained if there is only one source of financing. Pluralism further supposes the necessity for selecting during any given period of time a certain program.

Democracy is characterized first of all by the *number* of people who are involved in this mechanism of selection. Democracy and pluralism influence on each other and this influence can sometimes assume openly conflictual forms.

It seems to me that the key factor in the process of development belongs to the creation of a manifold that preserves a potential for choice in a changing environment. A mechanism of selecting a certain program should subsequently ensure the preservation and expansion of the manifold. The main course of historical development followed by the Western societies of today has been along the road of expanding pluralism, e.g., by increasing the plurality of political parties or their official publications. Gradually, as more and more people became competent and responsible, the number of participants involved in national decision making began to grow. Thus, such a classical example of a free society as Great Britain which had long allowed the coexistence of many parties, including those of Communists and anarchists, gave universal suffrage to adult males of the working class only in the 1870s, with women in Britain attaining the same right only in the 1920s. One possible reason for the instability of Latin American countries and societies similar to one that existed in Iran during the rule of the late Shah may be due to the narrowing of pluralism in the name of democracy. This usually takes the form of banning extremist parties including the communists, while at the same time allowing broad stratas of the population, often incompetent and irresponsible, to take part in electing their representatives to institutions of national governance.

The above-mentioned systemic dimension of *openness* is also of quite considerable importance. Let us, for example, take a look at Yugoslavia which has always occupied a rather special place within the communist block. On one hand, Yugoslavia, just like any other communist country, did not allow pluralism—it was a one-party state. Nor did it permit democracy—the Yugoslav people could not be said to exercise a meaningful choice of their government representatives as long as a name of only one candidate was entered into election slates. On the other hand, Yugoslavia was a fairly open country as far as the two-way movement of people, goods, and information was concerned. This openness was one of the main reasons of a relatively successful development of Yugoslavia in comparison with other communist countries.

What has been said above about pluralism, democracy, and openness at the national level can be applied to the analysis of the performance of corporations as well. It seems to me that corporations have not yet sufficiently developed internal pluralistic structures: neither the employees nor the corporate stockholders possess the vitally important independent organizations in which they can work out manifold plans and programs of the corporate future. True, stockholders do take part in democratically styled decision-making procedures—

but at the same time, they act as *atomized* individuals. They can only criticize the programs presented to them by corporate officers and find themselves in no position to counter these plans with their own programs, equally well thought-out and detailed. A good number of corporations are not sufficiently open either. Many corporate subdivisions are prevented from acquiring needed goods and services from the outside if these goods and services happen to be produced by the corporation itself.

Notes

1. B. Smith, *Poetic Closure* (Chicago: University of Chicago Press, 1968).
2. The approach to closers suggested here is similar to "teleonomic" and "teleomatic" concepts that have been proposed by E. Mayr. According to Mayr, teleonomic processes are those whose goals strongly impact on their program of development. Teleomatic processes, in turn, relate mainly to "inanimate objects which reach a certain terminal point as a result of physical laws." E. Mayr, *The Growth of Biological Thought* (Cambridge, Mass.: The Belnap Press, 1982), pp. 48–49.
3. The English language appears to be extremely well-endowed with the vocabulary for expressing different shades of such categories. Thus, along with ideals, objectives, and goals we also have purposes, aims, and targets. Possibly, all these categories can be brought together under the generic heading of "ends."
4. A. Katsenelinboigen, *Some New Trends in Systems Theory* (Seaside, Calif.: Intersystems Publications, 1984), pp. 19–34, 65–107.
5. For example, an end of tactical-type planning is generated and brought into it from the strategic level.
6. R. Ackoff and F. Emery. *On Purposeful Systems* (Chicago: Aldine-Atherton, 1972), pp. 117–18.

Chapter 14
On Suicidal Rabbits:
A Relativity of Systems

Stafford Beer

This paper hinges on three of Russell Ackoff's characteristic approaches: the use of fables, his acceptance of "messes" as distinct from well-formulated problems, and his concept of idealized planning. Current thoughts of the author, dealing respectively with recursive logic, the implementation of change, and the theory of democratic organization, are attached to these hinges, and between them express his own theme as to a relativity of systems.

Starting with Fables

"Ackoff's fables are fabulous": is this statement a tautology? Or should such a statement be reserved as a metasystemic comment of some kind? The fables I wish to recount are non-Ackovian in some such sense, because they concern an intergalactic alien scientist (called therefore Igas) who is a commentator upon fables of every kind—and especially those that we weave ourselves around experience to call "fact." Even so, Igas knows an Aesop or an Ackoff when he meets one and herewith doffs his hat.

One pleasant day in England, Igas was sitting on a grassy hill that sloped downward to a distant river. Halfway down the slope a hedge ran across the foreground, left to right. Igas, for cultural reasons of his own, thought of it as running right to left—a matter that need not detain us here. The rabbit, on the other hand, which was hopping along the hedge, moved (without dint of culture) left to right. Just below Igas, a gamekeeper lay face-downward in the grass. He had a gun. For many long, slow seconds, the muzzle of the gun (as Igas carefully observed) moved to the right, aimed below the hedge, some seconds of arc ahead of the wandering rabbit. "No wonder," Igas thought, "they call this man a gamekeeper. Although he is obviously prepared to fire his gun, he does his best to avoid the wandering rabbit." And yet, for all the gamekeeper's efforts to preserve wildlife, when the gun eventually went off, the rabbit quite perversely hopped straight into the bullet and lay dead. "Terrestrial rabbits," wrote Igas sadly in his fieldwork notes, "are suicidal."

That fable goes back maybe fifteen years, although it has not seen print before. The second that I want to relate is maybe twenty-five years' old and came out of a discussion with Grey Walter, whom I wish also to salute. He was an English neurophysiologist and electroencephalographer of high renown. He was also a cybernetician: the inventor of *machina speculatrix*, a mechanical tortoise. For Grey, Igas was a Martian—but we knew less of the inhospitality to life on Mars in those days than we do now.

Igas was living incognito in a typical household of our consumer-oriented world. He noticed that a small room in the house was set aside for the private use of individuals. That is to say that each person in the household made visits to this room alone. Once inside, each person locked the door. Igas, rendering himself invisible, was able to observe the strange and complicated ritual that ensued. The social anthropologist in Igas understood this to be a religious observance of some kind, and the liberal use of water as a libation on each occasion was wholly consistent with this conclusion. But Igas knew his cybernetics too. A regulatory system, even or especially one that involved a theocratic loop, must surely hold steady some critical variable: that would indicate its fundamental purpose. "Beyond the superstitious beliefs of these people," wrote Igas in his notebook, "is the unrecognized societary requirement to keep the water levels in their cisterns constant."

From the earliest days of the systems sciences it was clearly in mind that, as Heisenberg had taught us, the observer is part of the system. But having taken the lesson from so well-instrumented a science as physics, maybe our expectations of our observational tools were too high. Microscopes and telescopes perform extremely well-defined functions, and their optical limitations are thoroughly understood. In biology, however, the limitations of the perceptual apparatus introduce serious epistemological difficulties into any observing system. In the social sciences, the situation is even worse: the observer is an Igas—namely, someone laden with a self-imposed ideology masquerading as a corpus of scientific knowledge.

To observe the observing system requires a new level of logical recursion. What often seems to happen instead is that protagonists of various ideologies (positivists, structuralists, phenomenalists, and so on) abuse each others' *descriptions* of what is going on. It is like saying that Igas comes from the wrong galaxy and should not have been given a visa in the first place. One moral of these fables is that Igas is one of us too.

Should you wish to illumine the point that name-calling at one level of recursion cannot substitute for insight at the next, your fable is already written long ago. When Alice asked the White Knight what song he proposed to sing, he replied that the name of the song was called "Haddock's Eyes." Alice, of course, objected that this was a funny name for a song. The White Knight was kind enough to explain that it was *not* the name of the song, only that the name of the song was called this.

The *relativity of systems* has to do with both the state and the status of included observers. The state has to do with the perceptual competence of the observer in relation to the observations made. Not only do our eyes and ears fail to register frequencies beyond their threshold, but the limits of discrimination may be internal to the very structure of perception itself. For example, aural events less than a twentieth of a second apart cannot be distinguished; therefore, if recorded speech is broken up into units of this length and if each unit is actually *reversed,* we have a product that really "ought" to sound incomprehensible, but which in fact sounds perfectly all right. As to observational status, this has to do with the level of relative recursion from which the observation is made.

The two sections that follow, like this first section, hinge upon notable approaches developed by Russell Ackoff. All three, nonetheless, are concerned with the theme that they share in common: a relativity of systems.

The Amelioration of Messes

It is an extraordinary fact that Ackoff should more or less singlehandedly have secured acceptance into the technical vocabulary of management science so unusual a term as "mess." It is, after all, not a precisely definable word; rather it would seem to denote (fashionably enough) a fuzzy set. But practitioners, as distinct from theorists, know all too well how fuzzy their problem sets can be. They recognize in particular that were it possible in that context to generate well-formulated propositions about well-defined problems, their worries would be over. It is so often in the nature of the problem that it should defy satisfactory description. In that case how could anyone ever determine what would count as a solution?

One of the ways of treating a mess is to poke it with the stick of enquiry until it reacts, and then to reinforce behavior that answers to some criterion fixed at a next higher level of logical recursion. To this methodology belong the heuristic techniques: "hill-climbing," Box-Jenkins, and in general "evolutionary operation." Many of us have undertaken our share of these approaches. There is however an approach so radically different that it runs the risk of defying the whole psychology of change. It involves ignoring the mess as currently presented and redesigning the whole system from the first principles of its intensionality—from its teleology, if you prefer. The Ackovian methodology for doing this, based on idealized planning, is mentioned in the next section. It involves asking the question: how do we get from here to there? But I wish to consider the case where there is evidently no such feasible route. It is a situation that I have encountered a number of times, but one on which I have been entertaining some fresh thoughts.

The first encounter with the problem happened thirty-five years ago. I designed a totally original system for controlling production in a steelworks. There could be no means of gradual adaptation whereby the old arrangements would be replaced eventually by the new ones: there were simply no points of contact between the two methodologies. Moreover, there was the constraint (and it is common enough) that the new system did not yet enjoy any credibility. So the possibility of embarking on a retraining exercise for all the staff involved and then suddenly switching "on Monday morning" from system A to system B, which I have successfully used elsewhere, was excluded. There was no alternative but to create the second system separately from the first, and then to run it in parallel until agreement was reached that the new approach could take over and the original system be scrapped. Predictably enough, this strategy caused all manner of difficulties in staffing, office space utilization, and so on. But worst of all was the crucial question as to when the critical decision to change over had to be faced. As time progressed, the account of "reality" presented by the two systems steadily diverged; if the crucial decision were left too late, a proper judgment would be hard to make—and moreover, the new system would be badly placed to take over as the result of the discrepancies introduced during the interregnum.

When the problem was encountered on a truly massive scale twenty years later in Chile (Project Cybersyn), the circumstances were different. There were no existing means for controlling the social economy, so the newly invented ones had no methodological rival. But there certainly was an organizational entity in place, namely, a very large and heavily institutionalized bureaucracy, which had the expectation that whatever systems of management and social regulation would be adopted would be operated by it—after investigation and approval, of course. The Allende government was perfectly aware that it had no time for these maneuvers, and in any case, the reform of the bureaucracy itself was on the political menu. The project therefore proceeded almost independently of the establishment, and for a long time virtually in secret, its outputs being taken into use by ministers, their staffs, and agencies, together with the managements of the nationalized industries in whose aid the project was basically designed for service at plant level. The story has been told at length elsewhere (in particular in the second edition of my *Brain of the Firm* [Wiley, 1981]). The point here about the implementation of change, especially as compared with the previous example, is that the new system went into control as fast as it could be installed, there being no comparable system beyond bureaucratic monitoring of a market economy to declare defunct. Had the Allende government not been overthrown, however, the establishment reaction to the surreptitious introduction of these revolutionary techniques would doubtless have been difficult to handle. But it would have been impossible to evaluate the situation, as a management scientist would wish to do, independently of the political threat to bureaucratic survival that the political programmer posed and that Cybersyn undoubtedly facilitated.

The point of these two case stories, to which others could repetitively have been added, is that the implementation of massive change is difficult not only because of systemic inertia, managerial timidity, resistance to novelty, and other familiar scapegoats, actively four-legged as these may be. It is also difficult because of the perfectly genuine problem of how to make the switch—given all the goodwill in the world. This goodwill presupposes that the system designers, management, and trade unions are working together for the common good. Although the public believes that no two of these three are ever on speaking terms, a likelihood that steadily increases the more the mass media inform the public so, I have often experienced collaboration. This leads to the speculation that maybe it behooves the management scientist to come up with an approach to the implementation of change that actually takes account of the misgivings experienced by the other two sides—not only of the proposals, but of each other. (So much is purely ironical in the ears of Ackovian operations research people, let it be clear, but it may be quite shocking to a later and more academic generation.) Well, let us expect the goodwill that we ought to be able to engineer and then see if we can suggest another way to the problem under discussion.

The following is prompted by the recollection of conversations with the neurocybernetician (the late) Christopher Evans, who did much to further our understanding of the nature of sleep. He had an especially interesting theory as to the role of dreams. As is generally agreed, dreams occur during the relatively short bursts of REM sleep (that is, sleep characterized by random eye movements). Evans came to the conclusion that during REM sleep the brain goes off-line, in order to *rewrite its programs* on the strength of the day's experience. Surely this is a most appealing hypothesis. If the brain did not have a compiler capable of recasting its executive programs at several levels of logical recursion, why, the brain's data processing would be in as big a mess as that of the average corporation, which has so little to do that is at all comparable to cerebral activity. The question is: how can the brain perform this task without devastating routine operations? To take the three broadest levels of cerebral recursion, we cannot afford to fall down (old brain), to see double (midbrain), or to associate policemen and custard pies (cortex), just because the pink-jello computer is "swapping"—still less recompiling a compiler.

Suppose that Evans was right: the brain goes off-line during REM sleep. In case the idea offends any psychoanalytic susceptibilities as to the role of dreaming and gets in the way of what is being said here, there seems to be no conflict between the Freudian interpretation of dreams (should one wish to maintain it) and the recompilation of programs—although it has been argued that there is. In fact, it seems to be quite unsurprising that the detritus of images chopped up and churned about as they would be by reprogramming, should become the raw materials for dreaming displacements, symbols, and all the other impedimenta of the Freudian endopsychic censor. Be that as it may, we cannot dream ourselves into institutional change, but maybe we could handle it off-line.

The new thought, evidently, is midway between the heuristic that might well rewrite programs at the end of each day in order to maximize adaptational advantage (and without having any teleological ideal in mind), and a predetermined plan that is supposed to "get us from here to there" (without having much regard to the day-to-day exigencies of the situation, or of the need to learn on the way that the "ideal" has in fact changed). Thinking in principle as to how this could be done, we must invoke again a relativity of systems, and this time, explicitly for the amelioration of an Ackovian mess.

We should take the mess's control system off-line "every night"—or whatever is the appropriate operational analogue of that. Then we should implement a recompilation of the control system, in which two separate principles would necessarily operate, as they would have to do in the brain if Evans was right. The first principle would undertake a heuristic search of the day's operations and rewrite the control program so as to take advantage of the day's learning opportunity: that is to say, to reinforce success and to extinguish failure on the basis of a probabilistic model of effectiveness. The *criteria* of that operational effectiveness would be set at the next higher level of logical recursion, in accordance with an idealized plan. Now comes the tricky part, which is a species of second order learning. The *operation* of applying the plan criteria would now itself be subjected to a process of heuristic learning, the criteria for which would be set as the outcome of the next logical recursion of the idealized plan, and so on. The outcome ought to be that the "ultimate" plan would change daily, in order to converge asymptotically on some actually unrealizable ideal, and that operational effectiveness at each level of recursion in the criterion mode would seek an heuristic optimum.

There is no doubt whatever that this approach would be difficult to accomplish in a practical application, but two comments may be made that reflect the introductory arguments. It has always been my own teaching and practice to develop (at whatever expense in time and money) the deep logical infrastructure of a regulatory process. It is because of that approach that we were able to mount a real-time control system for the social economy of Chile in less than two years—only to be denounced by some in the Information Systems community who are unable to think in logical depth below the "massive data base" beloved of data processors. If we were to put in this kind of effort to other processes of institutional change, we might be able to accomplish them. I do not add "more effectively," please notice: this is not a matter of marginal differences. I mean, to accomplish them at all. Hence, the second comment. It is that if we had so profound an instrument of change, learned of the brain, we might the more readily convince our managerial and labor colleagues that what we recommend is not only right but actually feasible too.

Organizational Tensegrity

Now I turn to some current thinking based essentially on the Ackovian planning principle of idealized models. It arose because the appearance (it is not more than that) of my own model of the Viable System is hierarchical. Useless to protest, I have found, that Systems Two through Five are merely service functions of the embedded Viable System One: the higher structures *look* like "the boss," and it is difficult to explain the sense in which System Five reflects the operational reality—the only reality we have. Nonetheless, the lowest autonomic functions in the human body have representation in the cortex, and the leadership of a democracy supposedly embodies the will of the people.

To "idealize" this state of affairs we need a model that ubiquitously manifests the whole in each of its parts. The immediate choice lay in holography, since any piece of a broken holographic plate will regenerate the original image entirely. For some years I experimented with lasers and toyed with the mathematics of Denis Gabor. Only recently, while thinking about Buckminster Fuller in quite another context did I remember his dictum: "All systems are polyhedra." And nothing structural could be less hierarchical than a regular polyhedron—or, as he devised it, a geodesic dome.

There is another dictum of my own that says: Every system can be formally mapped onto any other system under some transformation. We might well postulate that a management team could be represented, together with its connectivity to other teams, at one of the nodes of a regular polyhedron. What Fuller discovered was that a polyhedral structure (such as a dome) may be held together by what he called "tensile integrity"—or tensegrity for short. Accordingly, he ran struts between the faces of his polyhedral domes in such a way that the whole gained its cohesive strength from the tension induced between the faces. This is structural synergy with a vengeance and something virtually impossible to analyze by orthodox engineering techniques. When I started to construct physical polyhedra with my own hands, it was truly a revelation to follow Bucky's route. An unwholesome mess of wooden doweling, panel pins, rubber bands, string and glue, strengthened with gratuitous contributions from skin and beard, quite suddenly transformed itself into a polyhedron so strong that I could actually stand on it. I wanted to explain how I came to set forth the next hypothesis by following through an Ackovian idealization procedure, and here it is.

Let us typify an organization as an icosahedron. Its twenty sides are triangles. It has thirty edges. Let each edge represent a person. Now an icosahedron gathers itself together in twelve nodes, each connecting five edges. If each node stands for a management team, there will be sixty team members. Since each edge (equals a person) has two ends, each of thirty people belongs to two teams, and no two people belong to the same two teams. Already it is apparent that not only do we have a complete democracy within our organizational globe, in that the twelve teams have identical structures, connectivities, and relative position, but we have a network that exhibits total closure. The setup is in logical terms self-referential. This does not of itself mean that it is a "closed" system in the von Bertalanffy sense (it may or may not be open to exotic inputs of either energy or information), only that it is absolutely and regularly cohesive. Moreover, it exhibits no global but only local or nodal hierarchy. This is a good start for a model of an idealized or perfect democracy.

Even so, the real power of the model is supposed to lie in its structural strength. It is tensegrity that holds up the geodesic dome; it is tensegrity that made it possible for me to stand on the physical model made out of bits and pieces. In a dome, the tensile members join the centers of adjacent triangular faces, providing a thick two-dimensional skin, and hence the necessary rigidity to maintain the overall shape. But in a theoretical structure of an organization with tensegrity, we can improve on a rigid skin by running tensile members straight through the central spaces that would be required to be open in an architectural artifact. Obviously this driving through the center of the organizational phase-space provides a binding cohesion of tremendous strength.

Then what could be the organizational correlate of the tensile member? According to this hypothesis, or perhaps rather idealized design, each member of a team becomes an appointed *critic* of another team, distant across the phase space. The idea is that the critic would not be accountable for the decisions of the management group to which he or she is appointed critic, but that he or she would offer constructive advice from two points of view: that of a relatively disinterested member of the total organization, and that of someone having detailed specialized knowledge of one other but unadjacent team. The tension induced across the icosahedral phase space in this way would be balanced by appointing a critic from the receiving team to another distant team—none other than that second team of which the original critic is also a member. Let me now translate the geometric model into a managerial statement, which may well be easier to follow.

AN ICOSAHEDRAL ORGANIZATION WITH TENSEGRITY
- There are thirty people, divided into twelve management teams.
- Each person belongs to two teams, which he calls his or her lefthand and righthand teams. Thus there are sixty team members. No person may belong to the same two teams as anyone else.
- Each person is appointed a critic of that team of which he or she is not a member, but of which a lefthand teammate is a member. The team to which he or she is thereby appointed a critic will appoint a critic to his or her righthand team.
- Similarly, each person becomes a critic in that team of which he or she is not a member, but of which a righthand teammate is a member. And that team will appoint a critic to his or her lefthand team.

• Since each person has two critical appointments, there are sixty critics spread with tensegrity over twelve teams. So each five-member team has five more quasi members who are critics as defined. This arrangement exhibits *requisite variety*, which is to say that it obeys Ashby's law. The critical team is called the "antithetical management group."

Then note: The idealized model predicts that an actual organization operating according to this protocol would exhibit not only "perfect democracy" in structural terms but tremendous cohesion. The title that heads this list would not need to be bandied about!

Obviously experiments need to be run in order to investigate the usefulness of this hypothesis and idealized model, and they are easy to envisage in terms of games whereby twelve independent teams would attempt to solve a variety of problems—to have their results compared with an equivalent organization based upon the principle of tensegrity working through the instrumentality specified.

It is necessary to add that if any "real" organization, as distinct from one that has been idealized in icosahedral metric, should not happen to have exactly twelve nodes, or should not happen to embody exactly five members per node, then we should seek the transformation under which the "real" organization matches the notional one.

Finally, it should be recorded that the very term "antithetical management" was the innovation, some decades ago, of Lord Shackleton (son of the explorer), when he set up critical managerial groups within one of Britain's major retailing businesses. These were not however based on the theoretical considerations advanced here.

Epilogue

I have enjoyed the friendship of Russell Ackoff for well-nigh thirty years. We have a convention between us that we rarely consult in advance about the content of our writings. And this is just as well, for we have a proneness to disagree about almost everything. Thus my friend is not in the least responsible for anything that is written here, though I hope that some of it will please him. For example, he will be thankful to be spared yet further discourse (despite a brief reference) on my Viable System Model. It is a topic of which I myself am heartily sick, but it was only last year that I tripped over a most efficacious technique for suppressing calls to lecture about it. At Preservation Hall in New Orleans, there is a modest entry charge, but once inside special requests are entertained by the venerable old jazzmen. The notice on the wall says: "Requests $1, Saints $5." Evidently, the jazzmen in their turn were tired of marching in. Using this model, I have also priced my "Saints" out of the market—none too soon. On the positive side, however, I hope that, for example, the architect in Russ will be attracted by the model of structural organization.

At the birthday party, I was the only delegate who lives in Wales. Hence, I came armed with a motto for the retiring man in Welsh: "Nid oes ar uffern ond eisiau ei threfnu." May it serve him well in his continuing lifework. The translation reads: "Hell only needs reorganizing."

Chapter 15
Personal Computers and the Shifting Control of Information in Corporations

Paul Broholm

The rapid proliferation of personal computers is a major trend now almost universally recognized. Equally important is the growth in computing power they represent. A typical personal computer purchased in 1985 had many times the computing power of a more expensive predecessor from 1981 or 1982. The United States Treasury estimates that the annual increment to America's base computing capability by 1988 will be approximately six times that at the beginning of 1985 (The Department of the Treasury 1985, pp. 1–2).

Among the less obvious consequences of the growth of personal computing have been important changes in the management and control of information in large corporations. It is important to realize that the "personal computer revolution" is fundamentally a revolution in the way people in organizations handle information. By far the greatest number of personal computers and the greatest computing power have been purchased by major corporations (MicroGuide 1985). The purpose of any computer is to manipulate or process information stored in electronic form, and corporations have a tremendous need for such processing.[1]

The changes in the management and control of information represent a major organizational challenge. To examine, and ultimately, to manage, these changes requires an adequate conceptual framework. Near the end of *On Purposeful Systems*, Ackoff and Emery (1972, p. 227) introduce the concepts of the "geneity" and "nodality" of organizations. Each concept refers to a scale. The extremes of the geneity scale are "homogeneous" organizations, in which the organization has greater control over its members than they have over it, and "heterogeneous" organizations, in which the members have greater control over the organization than it has over them. The extremes of the nodality scale are "uninodal" organizations, which are hierarchically structured, and "multinodal" organizations, which lack "higher authority" and thus require agreement between two or more autonomous decision makers. These concepts, only briefly discussed, are used to characterize entire organizations. For instance, Ackoff and Emery suggest that "corporations . . . tend to be dominantly uninodal and homogeneous" (p. 227). The concepts can also be applied to subsystems of an organization—in this case, information processing. In doing so, we may begin to evaluate their utility for understanding the process of change in a given subsystem of the organization, or in the organization as a whole.

To illustrate the changes in information processing we can begin with a look at corporate data bases. Those responsible for the computer repositories of these corporate statistics have usually been data processing managers. Historically, data were entered (or "input") into the data bases under carefully controlled circumstances. This control served to provide checks on data integrity and validity and to safeguard the overall system. Certain standard reports were generated as a matter of course from these data bases. Requests for new or special reports, or requests for changes in current reports would come to the data processing department, where the requests were evaluated for relative priority, and in light of data processing resources required and available. Tales of the conflicts created by this situation are legion. Data processing managers complained of scarce resources, both computing power and personnel, while departments complained of interminable delays if they were lucky enough to get what they requested. Computer resources were centrally controlled and managed. Access to those resources was indirect, and conflicting claims were resolved by a central authority.

Given the situation, it should not have been surprising when individuals and departments began acquiring their own processing power as soon as it appeared in an affordable form: personal computers. The general consensus is that personal computers entered organizations through the "back door," in an attempt to free users from dependence on data processing departments (cf. "Looking for Mr. Visicalc," 1984, pp. 2–5; Pournelle 1985, pp. 48–49). Personal computer users could create data bases better tailored to their needs and build extensive, sophisticated models at their desks at a fraction of the previous cost. New reports or analyses could be generated in far less time.

We can characterize the spread of personal computing as a shift from the "dominant" uninodal and homogeneous form of corporate organization toward the multinodal, heterogeneous ends of the scales. Personal computer users had no need to appeal to a higher, central authority to resolve competing data processing requests. The ranks of those involved in information processing changed, and the range of information processing broadened. The new members enjoyed greater control over their information processing activity than the formal information processing organization had over them. The benefit to individual, departmental, and ultimately, corporate productivity was tremendous.

But a new set of problems emerged. Personal computer models were less likely to be checked for validity—either of data or logic—than those on larger computers. As more important issues were analyzed on personal computers, more important mistakes were made. But reports generated on personal computers shared the same aura as other computer reports: they were likely to be accepted without question. With separate data bases in each department, coordination between departments became more of a problem, especially in the area of planning. In particular, new problems with the security of information arose.

Information is a corporate asset, and the information that is created, processed, stored, and transmitted with personal computers is no exception. The valuable nature of corporate information has been clear long before the advent of widespread computing capability, indeed before computers at all. While quantification of the value of any information remains elusive (especially problematic is the issue of how the value of information may change by restricting or promoting its dissemination), we can safely assert that corporations have information that is valuable and that corporations typically would suffer if some of this information were to be widely disclosed (cf. Merten et al. 1984). Therefore, corporations have a legitimate need to protect at least some of the information with which their members work.[2]

Computer-stored information is distinguished in several important interrelated ways that are of special concern for security. Such information is concentrated, often massively so. These concentrations often create a qualitative difference: a collection of information can be extremely valuable even though any single item is of relatively little value. The information is also "condensed"; that is, such concentrations are far more easily portable than previously. Further, the information is easy to change and easy to lose. Alterations to the stored data, either accidental or intentional, may not leave any detectable trace.

The background of electronic information security was clearly tied to the background of data processing: centrally controlled security measures for centrally controlled systems. "Access control" was the operative term; if access to the central system could be controlled, then the information would be secure. The measures of access control evolved with the computer systems. Some sort of physical control limiting entry to the computer room was among the earliest of security measures. As remote terminals and teleprocessing developed, it became infeasible to rely on physical control of every logical access point; someone at a terminal in the next state had as much access as someone at a terminal in the computer room. Logical controls were developed to keep pace with the changes. Passwords were imposed; in theory secret passwords identified the individual at a terminal even if she was in another state. More elaborate controls were added, so that even entry with a proper password only provided access to carefully delimited portions of the computer's total resources. The original physical controls, and passwords, authorization levels, and more elaborate logical controls were all administered by the data processing managers. The very few individuals with titles or job descriptions directly concerning information security were mainframe specialists with large computer concerns.

The advent of personal computers introduced a significant change in the distribution of computing power, but it did not, at first, occasion any particular concern about information security. Data processing managers were often oblivious, and sometimes close to contemptuous, of these small machines. More than one data processing manager offered an estimate of the number of personal computers in his or her organization that was low by one or two orders of magnitude. Personal computers were not part of the centrally controlled information processing system and therefore akin to calculators or electric typewriters as security concerns. The issue of personal computer information security never arose in the minds of those charged with overall information security, in large measure because personal computers had no access to the important information stored in the large computer data bases.

Inexorably, the computing power represented by personal computers grew. Personal computers answered many individual and departmental data processing needs, and central data processing budgets were growing less rapidly as a result. Ironically, as personal computer data analysis became more sophisticated, the users began requesting access to corporate data bases in order to transfer data to their own models for analysis. This growth, fed by increasing numbers and increasing power, soon made it impossible to ignore the reality of personal computers as a de facto part of the corporation's computing base. And as recognition of the computing power of personal computers grew, so did recognition of the potential security problems.

Personal computers often store information as, or more, valuable than that on the corporate mainframe. As an illustration, consider the personal computer used by a director of strategic planning. On it he or she evaluates acquisition and divestment scenarios, charts consolidated earnings projections, and so on. In many corporations, this information is more valuable than anything stored in the mainframe data bases. And where mainframe data is itself vital, key information may have been retrieved from the mainframe by the director of strategic planning and stored on his or her personal computer. Guarding the mainframe while such personal computers sit unnoticed is to construct a latter-day Maginot Line to maintain information security.

The illustration only suggests the scope of the problem. As the Department of the Treasury (1985) noted:

> The explosion in personal computer technology has led to cheaper, and more powerful machines, with increasingly sophisticated software and telecommunications peripherals. Access to a previously uncharted world of information systems is, for millions, only a few keystrokes away. As a result, familiar concepts—trespass, illegal entry, sabotage, theft, fraud— have taken a new electronic twist, and new protective measures are required. (p. 2)

Even isolated from the issue of telecommunications, personal computers present problems. Personal computers are often shared by people who would not wish to share their computer-stored information. Personal computers with hard disk drives capable of storing thousands of pages of information sit in open offices accessible to anyone who can throw a small power switch. And the very architecture of a personal computer is inimical to securing the information stored in it. It would cost more than the personal computer to provide physical security for it like that for a mainframe. With respect to the logical aspect of computer security, mainframe computer architecture—the design of the hardware and the system logic—supports security systems that divide the computer's resources and restrict access. Not so with personal computer architecture, where restarting the system takes less than a minute, and substituting one operating system for another is supremely easy with the barest knowledge.

We have noted the shift from the dominant uninodal and homogeneous form of organization in corporations toward a multinodal, heterogeneous organizational form in corporate information processing. This shift, driven by unmet information processing needs and made possible by the advent of the personal computer, undermined the extant approach to information security which was itself based on the earlier, uninodal, heterogeneous organization of information processing. While information processing had informally evolved, the management functions of information security had not.

The question facing corporate managers in the particular instance is how to respond. The available answers have implications for the larger issues of the management of information processing resources, and management in the organization as a whole.

One alternative is to remove much of the personal computer information security problem through an attempt to reimpose the central control on information processing. To some extent, this is occurring. Corporations are promulgating personal computer acquisition policies, publishing lists of "approved software," appointing "micro managers," and creating a hierarchical management structure to address the presence and implications of personal computers (cf. Petrofsky 1986). Such an attempt to rationalize diverse and decentralized activity is probably inevitable in a hierarchical organization. Recentralized control of information processing will not immediately end security problems because personal computers are still not well suited to the usual security measures. But with central control of information processing, the security problem would be relegated to its historically subordinate role.

But there are reasons to believe that the uninodal, homogeneous structure of information processing is a past that cannot be re-created. The low cost of the personal computer is an important factor. Where authorization procedures and centralized purchasing are instituted to establish controls, managers resort to leasing or other measures to obtain the resources they believe they need. The methods may change, but personal computers entered the corporate back door in response to unmet needs, and the attempt to create new, central information processing controls will create new frustrations that are likely to engender new circumventions. Information security cannot be centrally controlled when information processing is not.

An alternative to re-creating central controls is to acknowledge the shift in the organization of information processing and to make a parallel shift in order to meet the needs of information security. If we look for a moment at corporate information in the broadest sense, security has always been socially, rather than centrally, controlled. This is not to say that everyone knew everything but rather that many individuals had to exercise judgment about what to convey to whom, about what required access controls such as locks, and generally about how to maintain the security of corporate information. Electronic information systems are becoming decentralized in structure, and thus similar models of control for information security appear appropriate. In a multimodal, heterogeneous organization, control must reside in the system itself, expressed by the members. The shift must be from central to social system control. Each user of sensitive corporate information must act to preserve its security as a member of a system alert to information security concerns.

The issue becomes a problem of social—or more precisely, sociotechnical—management as the controls shift from the technical side of the system—that is, physical locks and logical barriers—to the social side—that is, administrative and social controls. Education becomes important, as the members of the system must become aware of the need for security, of the appropriate tools and measures for achieving security, and of what must be secured. Managers must begin to think not in terms of automatic controls but in terms of managing a social system, motivating its members to take on a new function.

The temptation to reassert the dominant form of corporate organization is clear: central controls are familiar and comforting. But such controls may work only in a centrally controlled (uninodal, homogeneous) system. However, the technology of personal computers is not friendly to central controls; thus it is unlikely that a centralized information processing system can be re-created. If that is the case, and if models of central control are inappropriate in heterogeneous, multinodal systems, then corporations must find and adopt different strategies for management and control.

Notes

1. The distinction between information and data should be noted here. According to Ackoff and Emery, data become information only as a part of some communication that "changes the recipient's probabilities of choice" (1972: 144). Strictly speaking, computer-stored data are data until they are retrieved, at which time they may become information. The nomenclature of the computer field, however, does not generally reflect a distinction between information and data. A choice for "*data* processing" or "*information* security" is often stylistic. In order not to attempt to impose order and divert attention from my focus, I use "information" as a general term here, and I employ generally accepted terminology (e.g., "data processing") where appropriate.

2. I use the qualifiers "legitimate" and "at least some" because certain information should not be concealed regardless of potential harm to the organization; for example, information on toxic wastes. It should also be noted that organizations have a legal obligation to secure certain information, such as personal data pertaining to employees, the disclosure of which would not in itself be harmful to the organization.

References

Ackoff, R. L., and F. E. Emery. (1972). *On Purposeful Systems*. New York: Aldine Atherton.

The Department of the Treasury. "The Security Effort: Focus on Electronic Funds Transfer." Draft Version. Washington, D.C., January 28, 1985.

"Looking for Mr. Visicalc: The Next Wave." *Electronic Mail and Micro Systems.* August 15, 1984, pp. 2–5.

Merten, A. G., P. Delaney, B. Pomerantz, and P. Kelley. (1984). "Putting Information Assets on the Balance Sheet." *Risk Management.* January, 1982. (Reprinted in *The Computer Security Handbook.* Northborough, Mass.: Computer Security Institute, pp. 9A-31–9A-34.)

"MicroGuide: Personal Computer Markets, 1984." International Data Corporation. Cited in "Personal Computers—Not for the Masses!" *Cahners Computer Comments.* February, 1985, p. 2.

Petrofsky, M. (1986). "Micro Managers Find Their Place in the Corporate Structure." *InfoWorld.* February 17, 1986, pp. 13–14.

Pournelle, J. (1985). "The EDP Manager's Blues." *Popular Computing.* August 1985, pp. 48–49.

Chapter 16
Democratizing the Corporation: A Stakeholder Perspective

William M. Evan

The British writer, E. M. Forster, in a 1939 essay entitled "What I Believe," sets forth a novel view of democracy: "two cheers for democracy: one because it admits variety and two because it permits criticism. Two cheers are quite enough: There is no occasion to give three" (Forster 1947, p. 70). Forster doesn't explain why he gives only two cheers for democracy, leaving the reader to conjecture that democracy lacks sufficient variety and criticism to satisfy his dedication to individualism. Nor does Forster refer anywhere in his essay to the role of the corporation in a capitalist democracy. If he had, my guess is that he would have given the corporation at most *one* cheer.

Political Democracy vs. Economic Democracy

To explain my surmise about Forster's view of the corporation, I turn now to the work of the distinguished economist, Arthur Okun. In his book *Equality and Efficiency,* Okun (1975) identifies an incongruency between the political and economic institutions of capitalist democracy. All citizens are guaranteed equal justice and equal political rights in what Okun calls the "domain of rights." On the other hand, economic institutions, which Okun refers to as the "domain of dollars," are based on voluntary exchanges in the marketplace and private ownership of productive assets. These institutional arrangements result in unequal distribution of income and wealth. Although Okun presents a vigorous argument for the superior efficiency of the market economy as compared with any socialist centrally planned economy, he is nevertheless troubled by the conflict between equality in the political realm and inequality in the economic realm. He claims that this

conflict involves an unavoidable tradeoff between equality and ineffi-
ciency. He sums up his thesis in the following provocative manner:

> A democratic capitalist society will keep searching for better ways of draw-
> ing the boundary lines between the domain of rights and the domain of
> dollars. And it can make progress. To be sure, it will never solve the prob-
> lem, for the conflict between equality and economic efficiency is inescap-
> able. In that sense, capitalism and democracy are really a most improbable
> mixture. Maybe that is why they need each other—to put some rationality
> into equality and some humanity into efficiency. (p. 120)

Okun's conclusion constitutes a profound formulation of the dilemma facing capitalist democracy. Like Forster, he too in effect gives
only two cheers for democracy.

When we now turn to the corporation itself as the dominant component of the economic institutions of democratic capitalism, the
clash between the values of equality and efficiency, or between the
"domain of rights" and the "domain of dollars," is quite pronounced.
Corporate managers, as the legal representatives of stockholders, exercise overwhelming power over the entire range of decision making,
including strategic planning, personnel, production, marketing, and
finance. Although incorporated as a citizen of one of the fifty democratically governed states in the union, the internal governance of the
corporation can scarcely be described as partaking of democracy. A
more accurate description is that a corporation is a self-perpetuating
oligarchy. Top executives and board members are carefully selected
and they, in turn, carefully select their successors. The idea of democratizing the governance of corporations, I suspect, would be dismissed
out of hand by most executives as impractical, irrelevant, and even
ridiculous for fear that it would jeopardize efficiency and also inter-
fere with their legal obligations to maximize the profits of stockholders.

Stakeholder Management and Redesigning the Corporation

Because the modern corporation has been the engine for industrial-
ization as well as the stimulus for promoting social welfare, it does
make sense to consider the question whether the corporation can be
redesigned as a democratic institution without impairing its efficiency
as a wealth-creating institution. My answer to this question, in a nut-
shell, is that the corporation can be democratized with the aid of a
theory of stakeholder management. But before I explain what I have
in mind, I would like to share with you an intriguing remark made to

me by a Chinese social scientist during my recent visit to the People's Republic of China:

> Americans have "big democracy," which we in China do not have. Americans can vote for their President. We can't vote for the Premier and the General Secretary of the Party. That is big democracy, but big democracy occurs only every four years, or every two years when you vote for Congressmen. But we in China have "small democracy," which American people do not have. In everyday life, Chinese people can participate in what happens to them on their jobs. My boss can't fire me or refuse to give me a raise in salary. This is something that can only be done by the relevant collective or organizational unit. So we in China have small democracy which Americans do not have because capitalism governs your enterprises.

Without considering here the relative merits of China's socialist democracy and America's capitalist democracy, I think you will agree that the Chinese social scientist has, in effect, raised a relevant question about the governance of the American corporation.

Existing provisions of corporate law as well as conventional wisdom dictate that corporate managers owe a responsibility only to stockholders. It is, however, the basic premise of the stakeholder theory of the firm that corporate managers also owe a responsibility to other constituencies that have a legitimate claim on the resources of the corporation. The philosophical rationale for this theory has been presented elsewhere (Evan and Freeman 1988). Here I shall focus on the political and pragmatic considerations.

Generalizing the position of stockholders who have a stake in the firm by virtue of ownership of stocks, bonds, and so on to other constituencies, the term "stakeholder" has been used to designate those constituents who significantly affect or are significantly affected by decisions and operations of the corporation. For present purposes, it is sufficient to identify six principal stakeholders, each of whom has a reciprocal relationship to the corporation:

- The owners
- The employees
- The customers
- The suppliers
- The local community
- Management.

Let us consider, in turn, the stakes of each of these six stakeholders in the corporation. The stakes of owners require little elaboration. By purchasing equity in the firm, owners enable the firm to operate with sufficient capital and to undertake plans for expansion of operations. In return, the corporation pays owners a dividend sufficient to motivate them to continue their investment in the corporation.

Employees have long, and sometimes vociferously, staked out their claims on the resources of the corporation. By investing their labor, employees produce the products or services of the corporation for sale in the marketplace. Without the loyalty and commitment of employees, the productive efficiency of the corporation would suffer. In return for their labor, employees expect wages, benefits, and job security. To retain the loyalty and commitment of employees, management seeks to develop compensation systems and benefit programs to reward them for their contribution to the firm.

Customers, who purchase the products or services of the corporation, are the lifeblood of the firm because they provide revenue essential for its operations and growth. Unless the corporation convinces its customers of its determination to meet their needs and expectations regarding price and quality, the corporation will not succeed in retaining their loyalty to its products or services.

Suppliers of raw materials or services to the corporation constitute yet another stakeholder. The supplier-corporation relationship is vital to the success of the firm. Suppliers can either enable the corporation to meet its contractual obligations or fail to do so, with dire consequences for corporate performance and its reputation. In turn, the corporation is a customer of the supplier and is therefore vital to the success and survival of the supplier. To the extent that the corporation adequately compensates suppliers for their faithful performance, suppliers will continue to contribute to the success of the corporation.

The local community in which the corporation establishes its facilities is yet another stakeholder. By providing the corporation with an infrastructure of transportation, communication, housing, and educational facilities for its employees as well as, occasionally, tax concessions, the corporation greatly benefits from its location in the community. In return for the provision of local services, the corporation is expected to be a good citizen. Among other things, this means that the firm cannot expose the community to unreasonable hazards in the form of air and water pollution or toxic wastes. And if the firm, because of unforeseen economic developments, must close its plant, it should provide the leaders of community with sufficient advance notice to make the transition as smooth as possible.

Finally, the last stakeholder is the management of the corporation. According to conventional wisdom, management is so closely identified with the interests of the owners that we would not normally think of them as a distinct stakeholder. Given the separation of ownership and control in the modern corporation, one would be inclined to treat management as part of the employee stakeholder group. However, within the framework of the stakeholder theory of the firm, it is essential to conceive of management as a separate stakeholder. The following four stakeholder functions of management can be identified:

1. To safeguard the stakes of each of the five other stakeholders.
2. To seek to balance the interests and claims of the five other stakeholders.
3. To resolve disputes among stakeholders.
4. To promote the well-being of the corporation itself.

To discharge these unique and demanding tasks, management has to perform its functions as a fiduciary and in accordance with professional ethical standards. To articulate a new conception of the role of management, I have used the term "fiduciary management" (Evan 1976, pp. 58–60). I would now like to say a word about each of the four challenging tasks of fiduciary management.

Instead of performing its fiduciary obligations only to stockholders, management operating in a corporation committed to the stakeholder theory of the firm would extend its fiduciary obligations to each of the other four stakeholders as well. Admittedly, the interests and claims of the five stakeholders do come into conflict with one another: Raising dividends leaves less profit after taxes for increases in wages and salaries for employees, for research and development to upgrade the quality of products for customers, for price adjustments for suppliers, and for promoting the welfare of the community. Balancing stakeholders' conflicting claims is a daunting challenge of fiduciary management.

In the course of attempting to balance the conflicting claims of stakeholders, disputes will unavoidably arise. When they do, fiduciary management ought to ensure that the stakeholders involved—through their representatives—are accorded due process rights (Evan 1976, pp. 55–56) in adjudicating their grievances at the level of the board of directors.

There is yet another crucial task of fiduciary management, and that is to protect and promote the long-term well-being of the corporation itself—or the corporate person, to use a legalism—as distinct from the five stakeholders. Unless fiduciary management attends to the long-term needs of the corporation by, for example, plowing back sufficient earnings for research and development, innovation, and growth, the future of the corporation may well be in jeopardy.

I suspect you will agree that these four tasks of fiduciary management are immensely challenging, and, furthermore, that few executives indeed are currently performing them.

Some Principles of Corporate Democracy

Now to return to the question of democracy and the corporation. The underlying presupposition of stakeholder management theory is that each stakeholder should be accorded "organizational citizenship" rights (Evan 1976, pp. 56–58). To effectuate stakeholder citizenship rights, a number of structural reforms in the corporation are required (Evan and Freeman 1988, pp. 104–5). First, the membership of the board of directors would have to represent each of the six principal stakeholders—quite different from the prevailing practice in selecting board members.

Second, the marketing department would appoint special personnel to undertake a continuing dialogue with samples of customers to insure that their needs and expectations are being met.

Third, the personnel department would appoint special personnel charged with the responsibility of organizing an "employee council" representing all employees in the firm who are not performing any managerial function. This council would provide a channel of communication to top management for the needs, expectations, and grievances of employees.

Fourth, a special department linking the functions of procurement, production, and law would organize a "supplier council" to ensure fair contractual treatment of suppliers, an adequate two-way channel of communication, and a grievance mechanism.

Finally, attached to the office of the president or the chief executive officer, a special department would be charged with maintaining cooperative relations with the local community via the appointment of a "local community council" consisting of key officials and representatives of major social groups.

Time and space do not permit drawing up an adequate blueprint for protecting the citizenship rights of each of the six stakeholders of the firm—a major omission being the need for fundamental revision of corporate law (Evan and Freeman 1988, p. 105). Besides, this is in large measure a subject for future systematic corporate experimentation rather than armchair theorizing. In designing such a system, adaptations of democratic political institutions to the demands of a business enterprise are required. As corporate executives experiment with alternative designs for building democracy into the decision-making structure of the corporation, they should bear in mind that a fundamental principle of democracy is the right to dissent. Conflicts will inevitably arise among all six stakeholders. In that event, each stakeholder group should be accorded the right to voice its claims and demands in the presence of the highest corporate tribunal, so to speak, namely, the board of directors.

Institutionalizing dissent—in the context of a pluralistic political framework—is the essence of democracy. This distinguishes it from any nondemocratic political system dominated by a single political party. As the internationally renowned sociologist, Ralf Dahrendorf, recently put it in a lecture at the University of Pennsylvania, "Democracy provides for continuing change without revolution. It has the capacity to adapt to environmental changes without traumatic ruptures."

By building in democratic institutions, with the help of stakeholder management theory, the corporation will enhance its capacity in the long-term to cope with environmental uncertainties in domestic as well as global markets.

Conclusion

This skeletal outline of corporate democracy, based on stakeholder management principles, should be distinguished from concepts of socialism or communism advocated by the Soviet Union, Eastern European countries, and China. Recent economic reforms in the Soviet Union and, particularly in China, that provide for the introduction of some elements of capitalism are an admission of the failure of the system of state ownership of the means of production and of a centrally planned economy—the foundational principles of a socialist economy.

Gorbachev's efforts at launching a program of perestroika and economic reconstruction, and China's experiments, since 1979, with decollectivization of agriculture and with the introduction of some elements of a market economy—including joint ventures with capitalist enterprises—constitute evidence of the failure of underlying principles of a socialist economy.

Perhaps the clearest acknowledgement of the shortcomings of socialism was recently articulated by Hu Sheng, President of the Chinese Academy of the Social Sciences:

> China's views on capitalism have undergone drastic changes during the past decade. We have come to realize that capitalism represents a fairly developed social stage in the whole process of human civilization, which, to a large extent, is still promoting the development of productivity.... But since socialism is in its primary stage at present, it has much to learn

from the capitalist system, such as the high work efficiency, large-scale production management skills and legal systems. (*China Daily*, May 7, 1988)

Yet another recent critique of China's socialism is even more telling:

State ownership, which has dominated China's economy over the past 30 years, has hindered not only the development of social productivity but also socialist democratic politics. Under state ownership, the country owns the means of production in the name of the whole society. This leads to a lack of direct ownership by members of the society in the means of production. So the system has lessened people's sense of being masters of their society. (*China Daily*, May 16, 1988)

These assertions represent a sophisticated acknowledgement of the superiority of capitalist democracy relative to China's socialist democracy. By democratizing the corporation, in accordance with the pluralistic theory of stakeholder management, capitalist democracy will be reinforced with a Jeffersonian grass-roots democratic foundation, so much so that critics—the likes of Forster, Okun, and others—may yet be moved to give democracy three cheers.

References

Dahrendorf, R. (1988). "Democracy without Opposition: In Search of Political Ideas," a lecture presented on April 18, 1988 at The University of Pennsylvania.

Evan, W. M. (1976). *Organization Theory.* New York: Wiley.

Evan, W. M., and R. E. Freeman. (1988). "A Stakeholder Theory of the Modern Corporation: Kantian Capitalism." In Tom L. Beauchamp and Norman E. Bowie (eds.): *Ethical Theory and Business*, 3rd ed. Englewood Cliffs, N.J.: Prentice-Hall.

Forster, E. M. (1947). *Two Cheers for Democracy.* New York: Harcourt, Brace and Company.

Okun, A. M. (1975). *Equality and Efficiency: The Big Tradeoff.* Washington, D.C.: The Brookings Institution.

Section IV
Decision Making and
Problem Solving:
Purposeful Action Within
Systems

A focus throughout Ackoff's work is the issue of describing and understanding how individuals and groups act to control and change social systems. From his early work concerning definition to the development of his choice model for decision making and his latest work in creativity and problem solving, Ackoff has relied upon formal methodology.

The notion that individuals and groups exhibit purposeful behavior and that this behavior can be described formally is central to the Singerian philosophy. The use of logical constructs and mathematical models allows the systems scientist to evaluate the possible outcomes of interventions and enable him or her to formulate and choose an "optimal" course of action under a given set of circumstances. Moreover, they provide a means by which he or she can measure and therefore monitor and evaluate the effects of each choice.

The contributors to this fourth section have been influenced by Ackoff's thinking on decision making and problem solving as purposeful behavior. Their work further explores the concepts of definition, decision, and creativity. Some work with the tools provided by mathematics and logic, others assess the adequacy of those tools, and some employ qualitative approaches that complement the quantitative.

Several colleagues present formal ways of viewing the processes practitioners utilize in managing social systems. Peter C. Fishburn discusses the notion of preference within the mathematics of decision theory. Thomas L. Saaty presents his own method of analyzing the hierarchic nature of priorities in decision making. Elsa Vergara Finnel describes a method for measuring creativity in problem solving and planning. Others discuss the limitations of formal analysis and present alternative approaches. Britton Harris discusses the dichotomy between the operations research paradigm and the rational action paradigm to professional procedures. K. Brian Haley illustrates how a number of problems that have almost identical definitions do not possess the same solutions. Ian I. Mitroff discusses the generation of different problem definitions as critical to understanding complex situations. Finally, Thomas N. Gilmore and Burton Cohen utilize the case study method to describe and evaluate the creative process used in the development of an innovative juvenile justice program.

Chapter 17
Inequalities in Decision Theory

Peter C. Fishburn

Introduction

About twenty-five years ago, in his course in scientific method at Case Tech, Russ Ackoff presented an example to show that exact measurements may not be needed to arrive at desired and definitive conclusions. The precise example Russ used escapes me today, but it went roughly as follows. Suppose each of two courses of action, C_1 and C_2, will lead to one of three consequences with relative values or utilities of V_1, V_2, and V_3. Suppose further that the probabilities of consequences, given either action, are known as follows:

	V_1	V_2	V_3	totals
C_1	0.29	0.35	0.36	1.00
C_2	0.12	0.51	0.37	1.00

Let $E(C_i)$ denote the expected utility of C_i. We would like to know which action has the larger expected utility. If only the ordering $V_1 > V_2 > V_3$ of the V_j is known without knowing more about the magnitude of V_2 relative to V_1 and V_3, then we can conclude that $E(C_1) > E(C_2)$ since

$$E(C_1) - E(C_2) = (0.17)V_1 - (0.16)V_2 - (0.01)V_3$$
$$= (0.17)[V_1 - V_2] + (0.01)[V_2 - V_3] > 0.$$

Note that the same conclusion cannot be reached if the probability matrix is changed to

	V_1	V_2	V_3	totals
C_1	0.29	0.35	0.36	1.00
C_2	0.12	0.68	0.20	1.00

for now the sign of $E(C_1) - E(C_2)$ will depend on more than just $V_1 > V_2 > V_3$ since

$$E(C_1) - E(C_2) = (0.17)[V_1 - V_2] - (0.16)[V_2 - V_3].$$

However, if it is known that V_2 is closer to V_3 than to V_1, i.e., $V_1 - V_2 > V_2 - V_3$, then again we can conclude that $E(C_1) > E(C_2)$ since

$$E(C_1) - E(C_2) = (0.17)[(V_1 - V_2) - (V_2 - V_3)] + (0.01)[V_2 - V_3] > 0.$$

Russ's subsequent text, *Scientific Method,* says a bit more about these things (1962, pp. 93–97).

To put it mildly, I was intrigued by his example. More accurately, and in retrospect, I must have been captivated since it led directly to my dissertation (1961) and a later book (1964), which in turn have influenced a substantial part of my research since that time. In the present paper, I would like to recount some of the pathways that Russ's teaching has led me down.

To set the stage, I list a few questions that were stimulated by his example and related topics in his course.

1. What is being presumed about the structure of decision that gives rise to expected-utility comparisons, and what is being assumed about the decision maker's preferences that makes such comparisons meaningful?
2. What types of measurement data on utilities and/or subjective probabilities are reasonable to expect in view of people's limited abilities to assess these things precisely?
3. How can such data be used most efficiently to compare alternative decisions or courses of action?
4. In view of limited discriminatory powers and vagueness in preference or relative-likelihood judgments, what can be said about formal models that incorporate these limitations?

The research on my dissertation and its subsequent book took me rather deeply into the first three questions, so I will say something about those in the next two sections. The emphasis there will be on questions 2 and 3. As regards the first question, I note only that it led into the strange, and for me wonderful, world of axiomatic theory, most noticeably the expected utility theory of von Neumann and Morgenstern (1944) and the subjective expected utility theory of Savage (1954). These are adopted as the underlying models for the next two sections (see Fishburn 1970 and 1982).

The fourth question in due time gave rise to a variety of axiomatic models that in part result from relaxations of one or more of the assumptions used by von Neumann and Morgenstern or by Savage. Some of this work is very new and is discussed in the sections on interval orders and nonlinear utility theory. The paper concludes with a recently proved correlational inequality for random processes. Viewed abstractly, this inequality may seem remote from where we started. However, it is very much in the spirit of Russ's example and his message of making the most of whatever is available.

Inequalities for Utilities and Probabilities

My early work (Fishburn 1961 and 1964) considered alternative data structures for utilities and probabilities, and described in detail expected-utility comparisons based on these structures. Two forms of the expected utility model will be used to illustrate this research. Here, and later, we shall use Abel's identity for summation by parts. It says that for all real numbers $a_1, \ldots, a_n, b_1, \ldots, b_n$,

$$\sum_{j=1}^{n} a_j b_j = \sum_{j=1}^{n-1} \left(\sum_{k=1}^{j} a_k \right) \left(b_j - b_{j+1} \right) + b_n \sum_{k=1}^{n} a_k.$$

The companion formula for integration by parts is

$$\int_a^b f(x)\,dg(x) = f(b)g(b) - f(a)g(a) - \int_a^b g(x)\,df(x),$$

which holds when the integrals are well defined for real valued functions f and g on the real interval $[a, b]$.

Suppose first that one of n consequences with different utilities V_1, $V_2, \ldots, V_n$ will follow from the decision taken. Let p_{ij} be the probability that act C_i will produce the jth consequence, with $p_i = (p_{i1}, \ldots, p_{in})$ and $\Sigma_j p_{ij} = 1$. The difference in the expected utilities of C_1 and C_2 is

$$E(C_1) - E(C_2) = \sum_{j=1}^{n} (p_{1j} - p_{2j})V_j.$$

Suppose the utilities of the consequences have been ranked, say, as $V_1 > V_2 > \ldots > V_n$. By Abel's identity,

$$E(C_1) - E(C_2) = \sum_{j=1}^{n-1} \left[\sum_{k=1}^{j} (p_{1k} - p_{2k}) \right] [V_j - V_{j+1}].$$

Hence, if nothing more than $V_1 > \ldots V_n$ is known about the V_j, then we can conclude that $E(C_1) > E(C_2)$ if, and only if,

$$p_1 \neq p_2 \quad \text{and} \quad \sum_{k=1}^{j} p_{1k} \geq \sum_{k=1}^{j} p_{2k} \quad \text{for} \quad j = 1, \ldots, n - 1.$$

What matters here is the comparison of the cumulatives of p_1 and p_2 according to the order of the V_j.

Suppose that, in addition to $V_1 > \ldots > V_n$, a ranking of adjacent differences $V_j - V_{j+1}$ is determined by comparing 50-50 lotteries. Assume this is

$$V_{\sigma(1)} - V_{\sigma(1)+1} > V_{\sigma(2)} - V_{\sigma(2)+1} > \ldots > V_{\sigma(n-1)} - V_{\sigma(n-1)+1},$$

where σ is a permutation on $\{1, \ldots, n - 1\}$. Then a second application of Abel's identity yields

$$E(C_1) - E(C_2) = \sum_{j=1}^{n-1} \left[\sum_{k=1}^{\sigma(j)} (p_{1k} - p_{2k}) \right] [V_{\sigma(j)} - V_{\sigma(j)+1}]$$

$$= \sum_{j=1}^{n-2} \left\{ \sum_{k=1}^{j} \left[\sum_{r=1}^{\sigma(k)} (p_{1r} - p_{2r}) \right] \right\}$$

$$\times \{ [V_{\sigma(j)} - V_{\sigma(j)+1}] - [V_{\sigma(j+1)} - V_{\sigma(j+1)+1}] \}$$

$$+ [V_{\sigma(n-1)} - V_{\sigma(n-1)+1}] \sum_{k=1}^{n-1} \left[\sum_{r=1}^{\sigma(k)} (p_{1r} - p_{2r}) \right].$$

Hence, given the additional data but nothing further, we can conclude that $E(C_1) > E(C_2)$ if, and only if,

$$p_1 \neq p_2 \quad \text{and} \quad \sum_{k=1}^{j} \sum_{r=1}^{\sigma(k)} p_{1r} \geq \sum_{k=1}^{j} \sum_{r=1}^{\sigma(k)} p_{2r} \quad \text{for} \quad j = 1, \ldots, n - 1.$$

So here we compare cumulatives of the first cumulatives reordered by σ.

The second model used to illustrate this approach is the states-of-the-world model from statistics. Assume now that there are n mutually exclusive and collectively exhaustive states. The decision maker is uncertain about which state will obtain (is the true state), and his or her decision will not alter the true state. Let P_j, with $\Sigma P_j = 1$, be the decision maker's subjective probability that state j is the true state. Also let u_{ij} denote the utility he or she derives from act C_i when state j obtains. Then

$$E(C_1) - E(C_2) = \sum_{j=1}^{n} (u_{1j} - u_{2j})P_j.$$

With our focus now on probability comparisons, suppose the P_j have been ranked, say as $P_1 \geq P_2 \geq \ldots \geq P_n$. Then since Abel's identity with $P_{n+1} = 0$ gives

$$E(C_1) - E(C_2) = \sum_{j=1}^{n} \left[\sum_{k=1}^{j} (u_{1k} - u_{2k}) \right] [P_j - P_{j+1}],$$

we can conclude that $E(C_1) \geq E(C_2)$ if

$$\sum_{k=1}^{j} u_{1k} \geq \sum_{k=1}^{j} u_{2k} \quad \text{for} \quad j = 1, \ldots, n.$$

If, in addition, the $P_j - P_{j+1}$ are ranked as

$$P_{\sigma(1)} - P_{\sigma(1)+1} > \ldots > P_{\sigma(n)} - P_{\sigma(n)+1},$$

where σ is a permutation on $\{1, \ldots, n\}$, then a second application of Abel's identity shows that $E(C_1) \geq E(C_2)$ if

$$\sum_{k=1}^{j} \sum_{r=1}^{\sigma(k)} u_{1r} \geq \sum_{k=1}^{j} \sum_{r=1}^{\sigma(k)} u_{2r} \quad \text{for} \quad j = 1, \ldots, n.$$

Thus, when we shift from utility to probability rankings, we encounter cumulatives of utilities rather than probabilities.

Stochastic Dominance

The preceding section illustrates a small part of a broad subject known as stochastic dominance (Bawa 1982, Whitmore and Findlay 1978) and majorization (Marshall and Olkin 1979). In the present section I shall describe recent developments in stochastic dominance that evolved rather naturally from my earlier work (Fishburn 1980a and 1980b).

Let $\mathcal{F}$ be the set of all right-continuous cumulative probability distribution functions $F, G, \ldots$ on the real line for which $F(0) = 0$ and $sup\ F(x) = 1$. If $F \in \mathcal{F}$ encodes the probabilities of a risky decision over a valued asset x with utility function u on $[0, \infty]$, then the expected utility of this decision is

$$u(F) = \int_{x=0}^{\infty} u(x)dF(x).$$

We are interested in comparing the expected utilities of different risky decisions under various assumptions about u.

For example, suppose that u is differentiable, increasing, and bounded above. Then integration by parts shows that

$$u(F) - u(G) = -\int_{x=0}^{\infty} [F(x) - G(x)]\, u'(x)dx$$

so that $u(F) > u(G)$ if F *first-degree stochastically dominates* G, i.e., if

$$F \neq G \quad \text{and} \quad F(x) \leqslant G(x) \quad \text{for all} \quad x \geqslant 0.$$

If it is assumed further that u increases at a decreasing rate, or is concave, then a second integration by parts gives

$$u(F) - u(G) = -\int_{x=0}^{\infty} u'(x)d \left[\int_{y=0}^{x} F(y)dy - \int_{y=0}^{x} G(y)dy \right]$$

$$= \int_{x=0}^{\infty} \left[\int_{y=0}^{x} F(y)dy - \int_{y=0}^{x} G(y)dy \right] u''(x)dx,$$

and, since $u'' < 0$ by concavity, we can conclude that $u(F) > u(G)$ if

$$F \neq G \quad \text{and} \quad \int_{y=0}^{x} F(y)dy \leqslant \int_{y=0}^{x} G(y)dy \quad \text{for all} \quad x \geqslant 0.$$

This expression says that F *second-degree stochastically dominates* G.

We now generalize to degree-α stochastic dominance for every $\alpha \geqslant 1$, rational or otherwise. For each $F \in \mathscr{F}$ and every $\alpha \geqslant 1$, let $F^\alpha(x)$ be the fractional integral defined by

$$F^\alpha(x) = \frac{1}{\Gamma(\alpha)} \int_{y=0}^{x} (x - y)^{\alpha-1}\, dF(y) \quad \text{for all} \quad x \geqslant 0,$$

where Γ is the gamma function. Nonstrict ($\geqslant_\alpha$) and strict ($>_\alpha$) stochastic dominance relations of degree α are defined on $\mathscr{F}$ by

$$F \geqslant_\alpha G \quad \text{if} \quad F^\alpha(x) \leqslant G^\alpha(x) \quad \text{for all} \quad x \geqslant 0,$$

$$F >_\alpha G \quad \text{if} \quad F \neq G \quad \text{and} \quad F \geqslant_\alpha G.$$

Since $>_\alpha$ differs from $\geqslant_\alpha$ only by the identity relation, we shall focus on $>_\alpha$.

It is easily seen that each $>_\alpha$ is an asymmetric partial order on $\mathscr{F}$. Moreover, as proved by Fishburn (1980a), if $\alpha < \beta$ then $>_\alpha$ is a proper subset of $>_\beta$, so that the later relation orders more pairs in $\mathscr{F}$. That paper also defines suitable classes U_α of utility function u on on $[0, \infty]$ so that, for all $\alpha \geqslant 1$ and all $F, G \in \mathscr{F}$,

$$F >_\alpha G \Leftrightarrow u(F) > u(G) \quad \text{for all} \quad u \in U_\alpha.$$

Classes U_1 and U_2 for first-degree and second-degree stochastic dominance are similar to the u (increasing, increasing and concave) mentioned above. More generally, all $u \in U_\alpha$ are increasing, bounded and continuously differentiable, $U_\beta \subset U_\alpha$ when $\alpha < \beta$, and, when $n \leqslant \alpha < n + 1$, the first n derivatives of $u \in U_\alpha$ exist, are continuous, and alternate in sign.

Two other features of these relations bear mentioning. First, there is a close relationship between $>_n$ for integral n and the first n moments of the distributions. Let $\mu_F^k = \int x^k \, dF(x)$ for $k \geqslant 1$, and assume that these moments are finite. Define $>_n^*$ lexicographically on moment sequences through order n by

$$(\mu_F^1, \ldots, \mu_F^n) >_n^* (\mu_G^1, \ldots, \mu_G^n) \quad \text{if} \quad \mu_F^k \neq \mu_G^k \quad \text{for some} \quad k \leqslant n$$

$$\text{and} \quad (-1)^{k-1} \mu_F^k > (-1)^{k-1} \mu_G^k \quad \text{for the smallest such } k.$$

It then follows (Fishburn 1980b) that $(\mu_F^1, \ldots, \mu_F^n) >_n^* (\mu_G^1, \ldots, \mu_G^n)$ whenever $F >_n G$.

Second, define the limit relation $>_\infty$ on $\mathscr{F}$ by

$$F >_\infty G \quad \text{if} \quad F >_n G \quad \text{for some} \quad n \in \{1, 2, \ldots\},$$

and suppose that F and G are simple distributions, i.e., each distributes the total mass of 1 over a finite set of points on the line. Then (Fishburn 1980a),

$$F >_\infty G \Leftrightarrow \int_{x=0}^\infty e^{-ax} \, dF(x) < \int_{x=0}^\infty e^{-ax} \, dG(x) \quad \text{for all} \quad a > 0,$$

so that the class of simple exponentials $u(x) = -e^{-ax}$ characterizes the limit relation in the manner indicated. Additional conditions are needed for this characterization when F and G are not simple.

Interval Orders

This section and the next comment on axiomatizations of preferences that emerged over time from questions 1, 2, and 4 in the introduction. This section considers only elementary preference comparisons with little explicit trace of risky or uncertain decisions. The latter are addressed in the next section.

Let $>$ denote an individual's binary preference relation on a non-empty finite set X. Read $x > y$ as "x is preferred to y." Also let $x \sim y$ mean that neither $x > y$ nor $y > x$. We assume that $>$ is asymmetric [$x > y \Rightarrow$ not $(y > x)$] and transitive [$x > y$ and $y > z \Rightarrow x > z$], so $(X, >)$ is an asymmetric partially ordered set with indifference relation $\sim$.

As pointed out by Luce (1956), among others, it is unreasonable in many situations to suppose that $\sim$ is transitive. For example, most people would be indifferent between x and $x + 1$ grains of sugar in their coffee for $x = 0, 1, \ldots$, yet not be indifferent between 0 and 2,000 grains. Similar limitations on discriminatory powers, or vagueness/uncertainty about one's own preferences, could lead to nontransitive indifference in other settings.

Guided by the concept of a just-noticeable-difference from psychology, Luce (1956) proposed the notion of a semiorder for such preference structures. A semiorder is described by a few simple axioms which were later shown (Scott and Suppes 1958) to be equivalent to the assertion that each x in X can be mapped into a closed real interval $I(x)$ of length 1 such that, for all $x, y \in X$,

$$x > y \Leftrightarrow I(x) > I(y),$$

where $I(x) > I(y)$ means that $a > b$ for all $a \in I(x)$ and all $b \in I(y)$. Thus, instead of mapping each x into a utility piont $u(x)$, the "utility range" for x is spread across a unit interval, with $x \sim y$ whenever $I(x) \cap I(y) \neq \emptyset$.

This was subsequently generalized (Fishburn 1970) to the notion of an interval order, which has the same representation as a semiorder except that no restriction is put on the lengths of the different $I(x)$. Thus, interval orders allow for nested hierarchies of intervals, and there can be a preference chain $x_1 > x_2 > \ldots > x_m$, with $m \geq 3$, and another $y \in X$ such that $y \sim x_i$ for every x_i in the chain. This would be the case if \$114 > \$113 > . . . > \$107 and each of these sure-thing amounts was indifferent to an even-chance gamble for either \$300 or \$0. Intervals for events on a time line provide another example of an interval order that is unlikely to be a semiorder.

In axiomatic terms, an *interval order* is an asymmetric partially or-dered set $(X, >)$ which satisfies the following condition for all $a, b, x, y \in X$:

$$(a > x, b > y) \rightarrow (a > y \quad \text{or} \quad b > x).$$

If, in addition,

$$(a > b > c) \rightarrow (a > x \quad \text{or} \quad x > c) \quad \text{for all} \quad a, b, c, x \in X,$$

then $(X, >)$ is a *semiorder*. Each type of order has a close relative in the graph-theory literature. They are respectively known as interval graphs (Gilmore and Hoffman 1964) and indifference graphs (Rob-erts 1969), or unit interval graphs (Golumbic 1980). When X is finite, $(X, \sim)$ is an *interval graph* if each $x \in X$ can be mapped into a closed real interval $I(x)$ such that, for all $x, y \in X$,

$$x \sim y \Leftrightarrow I(x) \cap I(y) \neq \emptyset.$$

If, in addition, all assigned intervals can be given the same length, then $(X, \sim)$ is an *indifference graph*.

A fairly complete account of interval orders, interval graphs, and related concepts is given in Fishburn (1985). This includes detailed characterizations and representations of various types of related sets, and considers several extremization problems that arise in connection with finite interval orders.

Nonlinear Utility Theory

My initial generalizations of the von Neumann–Morgenstern and Savage expected utility theories, which were motivated by the in-clusion of more-realistic preference structures in formal models, fo-cused on relaxing their assumptions of complete orders to partial orders. This allowed for nontransitive indifference but maintained the assumption of transitive strict preference. It also retained the core of their linearity or independence axioms, which are critical in deriving representations that use *expected* utilities. The types of representations obtained are briefly summarized by the "one-way" implications

$$p > q \rightarrow \int_x u(x)dp(x) > \int_x u(x)dq(x),$$

when p and q are probability measures on consequences, and

$$f > g \rightarrow \int_s u(f(s))dP(s) > \int_s u(g(s))dP(s),$$

when f and g are mappings from states into consequences. A detailed discussion of these and other ramifications of traditional expected utility appears in Fishburn (1982).

To illustrate the independence axiom that is fundamental for expected utility, let $\mathcal{P}$ be a set of probability measures on a consequence space, and assume that $\mathcal{P}$ is closed under convex linear combinations so that $\lambda p + (1 - \lambda)q$ is in $\mathcal{P}$ when $p, q \in \mathcal{P}$ and $0 \leqslant \lambda \leqslant 1$. A typical independence axiom asserts that, for all $p, q, r \in \mathcal{P}$ and all $0 < \lambda < 1$,

$$p > q \rightarrow \lambda p + (1 - \lambda)r > \lambda q + (1 - \lambda)r.$$

The main problem with this axiom, as shown by Allais (1953), Kahneman and Tversky (1979), and MacCrimmon and Larsson (1979), is that it is sometimes systematically and persistently violated by people's preferences. For example, if the measures are lotteries on monetary amounts that can be won or lost, and if p, q, and r are suitably chosen, then many people prefer $\lambda p + (1 - \lambda)r$ to $\lambda q + (1 - \lambda)r$ when λ is near 1, but have the opposite preference when λ is near 0.

Consequently, new theories that do not assume independence have emerged in the last few years (Chew 1983, Fishburn 1982b and 1983, Kahneman and Tversky 1979, Loomes and Sugden 1982, Machina 1982). Fishburn (1982b) and Loomes and Sugden (1982) also drop the assumption that strict preferences are transitive. I will say more about one of these since it illustrates the new trends and relates to our previous discussion (Fishburn 1982b).

SSB utility theory, so-called because it represents preferences on $\mathcal{P}$ by a skew-symmetric bilinear (SSB) functional ϕ on $\mathcal{P} \times \mathcal{P}$, is axiomatized in Fishburn (1982b). The crucial assumption that supports the bilinear form is a convexity axiom which says that if one measure p is preferred to (less preferred than, indifferent to) each of two other measures, then p will be preferred to (less preferred than, indifferent to) every convex linear combination of the other two. The axioms of

SSB theory imply that there is a real valued function ϕ on $\mathcal{P} \times \mathcal{P}$ that is skew-symmetric $[\phi(q, p) = -\phi(p, q)]$, linear separately in each argument, i.e.,

$$\phi(\lambda p + (1 - \lambda)q, r) = \lambda\phi(p, r) + (1 - \lambda)\phi(q, r)$$
$$\phi(r, \lambda p + (1 - \lambda)q) = \lambda\phi(r, p) + (1 - \lambda)\phi(r, q),$$

and satisfies

$$p > q \Leftrightarrow \phi(p, q) > 0, \quad \text{for all} \quad p, q \in \mathcal{P}.$$

Moreover, such a ϕ is unique up to multiplication by a positive constant. Additional assumptions (Fishburn 1982b and 1984) lead to the integral characterization

$$\phi(p, q) = \int_y \int_x \phi(x, y) \, dp(x)dq(y),$$

so that $\phi(p, q)$ is the expected value of $\phi(x, y)$ with respect to the product measure $p \times q$.

Although this theory is a radical departure from the von Neumann–Morgenstern theory, it supports many of the same conclusions, which can be illustrated in two ways.

Suppose first that Q is a nonempty finite subset of $\mathcal{P}$. Let $H(Q)$ be the convex hull of Q. Then, even though every measure in Q can be strictly less preferred than some other measure in Q, $H(Q)$ has a maximal element that is preferred or indifferent to everything else in $H(Q)$. This follows from von Neumann's minimax theorem, which yields

$$\max_{p \in H(Q)} \min_{q \in H(Q)} \phi(p, q) = \min_{q \in H(Q)} \max_{p \in H(Q)} \phi(p, q)$$
$$= \min_q \max_p [-\phi(q, p)]$$
$$= -\max_p \min_q \phi(p, q),$$

so that $\max_p \min_q \phi(p, q) = 0$. Hence $\phi(p*, q) \geq 0$ for some $p*$ and all q in $H(Q)$.

Our second illustration returns to stochastic dominance. As in section 3, let X be a real interval with preference increasing in x. Let $\mathcal{P}_0$ be the measures in $\mathcal{P}$ with finite supports, and for each $p \in \mathcal{P}_0$ let p^1 and p^2 denote its first two cumulatives. The first $(>_1)$ and second

$>_2$) degree stochastic dominance relations of $\mathcal{P}_0$ are defined as before:

$$p >_i q \quad \text{if} \quad p \neq q \quad \text{and} \quad p^i(x) \leq q^i(x) \quad \text{for all} \quad x.$$

For "utility" classes, let Φ_1 be the set of all skew-symmetric ϕ on $X \times X$ that have continuous derivatives through the second order and satisfy $\delta\phi(x, y)/\delta x > 0$ for all x and y. Also let Φ_2 consist of the functions in Φ_1 that have $\delta^2\phi(x, y)/\delta x^2 < 0$ everywhere. These classes correspond to U_1 and U_2 in the section on stochastic dominance.

We assume that ϕ on $\mathcal{P}_0 \times \mathcal{P}_0$ is defined from ϕ on $X \times X$ by bilinear extension:

$$\phi(p, q) = \sum_x \sum_y \phi(x, y)p(x)q(y).$$

It then follows that, for $i \in \{1, 2\}$ and all $p, q \in \mathcal{P}_0$,

$$p >_i q \Leftrightarrow \phi(p,q) > 0 \quad \text{for all} \quad \phi \in \Phi_i.$$

Abel's identity is used again to verify this. Suppose $x_1 < x_2 < \cdots < x_n$ are the points where $p(x) + q(x) > 0$, and let

$$p_i = p(x_i), \qquad p_i^1 = p^1(x_i) = \sum_{j \leq i} p_j, \qquad p_i^2 = p^2(x_i) = \int_{-\infty}^{x_i} p^1(y)\, dy;$$

$$q_i = q(x_i), \qquad q_i^1 = q^1(x_i), \qquad q_i^2 = q^2(x_i);$$

and $\phi_{ij} = \phi(x_i, x_j)$. Then, omitting some steps, we have

$$\phi(p, q) = \sum_{i=1}^{n} (p_i - q_i) \sum_{j=1}^{n} q_j \phi_{ij}$$

$$= \sum_{i=1}^{n-1} (q_i^1 - p_i^1) \sum_{j=1}^{n} q_j(\phi_{i+1\,j} - \phi_{ij})$$

$$= \sum_{i=1}^{n-2} (q_{i+1}^2 - p_{i+1}^2) \sum_{j=1}^{n} q_j \left\{ \frac{\phi_{i+1\,j} - \phi_{ij}}{x_{i+1} - x_i} - \frac{\phi_{i+2\,j} - \phi_{i+1\,j}}{x_{i+2} - x_{i+1}} \right\}$$

$$+ (q_n^2 - p_n^2) \sum_{j=1}^{n} q_j \left\{ \frac{\phi_{nj} - \phi_{n-1\,j}}{x_n - x_{n-1}} \right\}.$$

The middle expression shows that $\phi(p, q) > 0$ when $p >_1 q$ and $\phi \in \Phi_1$, and the final expression shows that $\phi(p, q) > 0$ when $p >_2 q$ and $\phi \in \Phi_2$.

A Correlational Inequality

Our final inequality comes from the theory of partially ordered sets. Suppose $<$ is an asymmetric partial order on $\{1, 2, \ldots, n\}$ with $n \geq 3$, and define $i \sim j$ if neither $i < j$ nor $j < i$. A *linear extension* of $<$ is a linear or total order $<_0$ on $\{1, \ldots, n\}$ for which $i <_0 j$ whenever $i < j$. In general, unless $<$ is itself a linear order, it will have many linear extensions. In fact, if $<_1$ is any linear order on a subset of $\{1, \ldots, n\}$ such that $i \sim j$ for all i and j in the subset, then some linear extension of $<$ includes $<_1$.

Suppose it is known that $1 \sim 2 \sim 3 \sim 1$. Let $P(1\ 2)$ denote the probability that 1 precedes 2 ($1 <_0 2$) in a randomly chosen linear extension of $<$, where each linear extension has equal probability. Also let $P(1\ 2 \mid 1\ 3)$ be the probability that 1 precedes 2, given that 1 precedes 3 in a randomly chosen linear extension of $<$.

Which of $P(1\ 2)$ and $P(1\ 2 \mid 1\ 3)$ is larger? Intuitively, 1 seems more likely to be near the beginning of $<_0$ when $1 <_0 3$, so we suspect that $P(1\ 2) < P(1\ 2 \mid 1\ 3)$. But is this always true? In particular, if I can construct $<$ however I please so long as $1 \sim 2 \sim 3 \sim 1$, and you can bet on either $P(1\ 2)$ or $P(1\ 2 \mid 1\ 3)$ being larger before you know my construction, would you always be better off in expectation by betting on $P(1\ 2 \mid 1\ 3)$?

The answer turns out to be yes, but it is very hard to prove. Shepp (1982) showed that $P(1\ 2) \leq P(1\ 2 \mid 1\ 3)$, but the question of strict inequality remained open until I was able to verify it.

If the connection between this correlational inequality and section 1 seems slight, I can only say that, had it not been for Russ's example, you would not be hearing about $P(1\ 2) < P(1\ 2 \mid 1\ 3)$ from this author.

References

Ackoff, R. L. (1962). *Scientific Method.* New York: Wiley.

Allais, M. (1953). "Le comportement de l'homme rationnel devant le risque: Critique des postulats et axiomes de l'École Américaine." *Econometrica* 21:503–46.

Bawa, V. S. (1982). "Stochastic Dominance: A Research Bibliography." *Management Science* 28:698–712.

Chew, S. H. (1983). "A Generalization of the Quasilinear Mean with Applications to the Measurement of Income Inequality and Decision Theory Resolving the Allais Paradox." *Econometrica* 51:1065–92.

Fishburn, P. C. (1961). *A Normative Theory of Decision Under Risk.* Ph.D. thesis, Case Institute of Technology.

———. (1964). *Decision and Value Theory.* New York: Wiley.

———. (1970). *Utility Theory for Decision Making.* New York: Wiley.

———. (1980a). "Continua of Stochastic Dominance Relations for Unbounded Probability Distributions." *Journal of Mathematical Economics* 7:271–85.

————. (1980b). "Stochastic Dominance and Moments of Distributions." *Mathematics of Operations Research* 5:94–100.

————. (1982a). *The Foundations of Expected Utility.* Dordrecht: Reidel.

————. (1982b). "Nontransitive Measurable Utility." *Journal of Mathematical Psychology* 26:31–67.

————. (1983). "Transitive Measurable Utility." *Journal of Economic Theory* 31:293–317.

————. (1984). "Dominance in SSB Utility Theory." *Journal of Economic Theory* 36:130–48.

————. (1985). *Interval Orders and Interval Graphs.* New York: Wiley.

Gilmore, P. C., and A. J. Hoffman. (1964). "A characterization of comparability graphs and of interval graphs." *Canadian Journal of Mathematics* 16:539–48.

Golumbic, M. C. (1980). *Algorithmic Graph Theory and Perfect Graphs.* New York: Academic Press.

Kahneman, D., and A. Tversky. (1979). "Prospect Theory: An Analysis of Decision Under Risk." *Econometrica* 47:263–91.

Loomes, G., and R. Sugden. (1982). "Regret Theory: An Alternative Theory of Rational Choice Under Uncertainty." *Economic Journal* 92:805–24.

Luce, R. D. (1956). "Semiorders and a Theory of Utility Discrimination." *Econometrica* 24:178–91.

MacCrimmon, K. R., and S. Larsson. (1979). "Utility Theory: Axioms Versus 'Paradoxes.'" In M. Allais and O. Hagen (eds.): *Expected Utility Hypotheses and the Allais Paradox.* Dordrecht: Reidel, pp. 333–409.

Machina, M. J. (1982). "'Expected Utility' Analysis Without the Independence Axiom." *Econometrica* 50:227–323.

Marshall, A. W., and Olkin, I. (1979). *Inequalities: Theory of Majorization and Its Applications.* New York: Academic Press.

Roberts, F. S. (1969). "Indifference Graphs." In F. Harary (ed.): *Proof Techniques in Graph Theory.* New York: Academic Press, pp. 139–46.

Savage, L. J. (1954). *The Foundations of Statistics.* New York: Wiley.

Scott, D., and Suppes, P. (1958). "Foundational Aspects of Theories of Measurement." *Journal of Symbolic Logic* 23:113–28.

Shepp, L. A. (1982). "The XYZ Conjecture and the FKG Inequality." *Annals of Probability* 10:824–27.

Von Neumann, J., and O. Morgenstern. (1944). *Theory of Games and Economic Behavior.* Princeton: Princeton University Press.

Whitmore, G. A., and M. C. Findlay (eds.). (1978). *Stochastic Dominance.* Lexington, Mass.: Heath.

Chapter 18
Priorities and Decisions in Hierarchic and Feedback Systems

Thomas L. Saaty

Introduction

There are two prevailing views about people and their world. One is that the universe is an orderly place satisfying a set of laws operating through forces that shape everything including our bodies and minds. We learn about occurrences by observation, intuition, and causal thinking which aligns our thought with what is actually happening in nature. We tend to assume that our minds and our senses are faithful and adequate instruments for capturing the essentials of the laws operating behind the scene. We believe that we can really discover an objective order behind everything. With it we can construct a mosaic of the unknown.

The other view is that we exist in a slowly and chaotically changing benign universe into which we bring our own sense of order derived from our "neatly structured" brains (or from those of animals and from plant mechanisms) and that this order is only local and subject to change. The order of our brains is itself more or less chaotic and subject to change. As it looks inward onto itself, our mind endows itself or hypnotizes itself, sometimes with innocent simplicity and at others with mind-boggling Byzantine complexity, into a loftier sense of order than there actually is. Sometimes change is sudden and catastrophic as it appears in our lives and contradicts our gentle and continuous expectations. We maintain our sense of rationality and sanity by giving up old ideas to live with the new order arranged from the latest chaos obsoleting the past. We are fortunate that we are limited and do not retain too much of the old order so that chaos and disorder can continually be reorganized by us into new forms carefully linked with the old to maintain a modicum of coherence. When our individual efforts are pooled into a collective effort, we obtain an even stronger sense of lasting order. The many facets of the order created and shared by a group are better understood through a logic and rationality that are nonlinear representing diverse attributes and points of view simultaneously and circumventing bullying and individual charisma as no single person really knows the answer.

The second view is less dogmatic and more tentative in the sense that as change comes we can accommodate it. It is more relevant than the present mode of linear thinking derived from the first view of the world. The analytic hierarchy process, based on observed conceptual construction of complexity and the measurement of feeling and preference, is our attempt to construct such a logic.

Complex problems involve not only an intractable number of factors but also time dependence and uncertainty. Multicriterion thinking requires a viable and accurate procedure to synthesize the many relations developed in the system. Understanding such a problem requires a special effort and may follow a number of different directions in surfacing and testing conflicting assumptions. An outside advisor would have to be at least as knowledgeable about the situation and about the abilities of the people involved and the feasibilities of the system and have substantial outside experience to assist in a new understanding of the problem, its solution and implementation. Let us see how this process relates to our equipment for problem solving.

Conscious thinking may be simply characterized in terms of three activities. The first is the awareness and identification of objects; properties of objects; and relations among objects, among properties, and even among relations. The second is the interpretation of these kinds of awareness according to intensity expressed in terms of feeling and preference. The third activity is the will, desire, or curiosity to extend awareness in purposeful directions and commit feeling and judgment to create a coherent understanding of what we are learning with what we already know. What is needed is a dynamic theory to help us speed up the process of increasing our awareness of new ideals and goals so we can better satisfy our diverse and sometimes conflicting needs in the new framework. This is self-realization on an ever-expanding higher plane.

All three activities can be enhanced by conscious practice and exposure in a concrete framework that offers room for experimentation. We now illustrate the analytic hierarchy process (AHP) with a simple example. Measurement of the elements represented in the framework is derived from paired comparisons and gives rise to ratio scales representing priorities of the elements. These priorities are then used to make decisions and direct actions (Ackoff 1974).

An Illustrative Example

An individual with a background in finance was concerned with investment. His recently retired father had asked him to determine an investment portfolio for him. We use his study as an illustration of how AHP can be used in decisions involving uncertainty and risk. He constructed a hierarchy to represent his problem, as shown in Figure 18.1.

Actually the second level of four criteria is a clustering of the following twelve criteria that involved duplication: dividends, interest, capital appreciation, insured savings, low risk, stable investment, positive tax effect, diversity, liquidity, low transaction cost, reinvestment of dividends, ability to add to portfolio in small amounts. The first group (return) includes interest, dividends, and capital appreciation. Although capital appreciation and short-term income are taxed differently, this difference is taken into account in another group. Estimated annualized returns were used when judging the individual securities. The next group (low risk) included criteria involving diversification and low perceived risk and volatility of return. The third criterion (tax benefits) assumes that capital gains are taxed lower than short-term returns and that tax-free investments such as municipal bonds would be rated high. The fourth criterion (liquidity) included small transaction costs, ease of withdrawal, and the ability to make small additions.

The third level is an aggregation of the following ten alternatives: blue-chip stocks, municipal bonds, AAA corporate bonds, BBB corporate bonds, treasury bills, saving accounts, high-growth speculative stocks, money market funds, options, and savings certificates. The ten were grouped into five types of alternatives. The first (tax-free bonds)

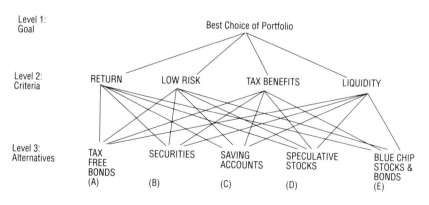

Figure 18.1.

are low-return, low-risk securities with great tax advantages. The second (securities) are tied to the treasury rate with medium return, low risk, and relative liquidity. The third (saving accounts) involve low return, but their liquidity and very low risk are their advantage. The fourth (speculative stocks) involve high-return and high-risk investments and include the options market. The fifth (blue-chip stocks and bonds) are a medium-return low-risk investment.

It is only to simplify the problem and prevent duplication that the grouping was done. The theory described here is sufficiently general to deal with situations of dependence within and between levels of the hierarchy (Saaty 1980), although space limitation prevents us from discussing it here.

The next step after structuring the hierarchy is to carry out comparative judgments. The elements in the second level are arranged in a matrix, and judgments are elicited as to the relative importance of each criterion when compared with another one of the criteria. The question here is: for a best choice of portfolio for the particular individual's circumstances (which give rise to his or her judgments), which criterion does he or she consider more important and how strongly more? A criterion X represented on the left is compared with respect to a criterion Y represented on the top of the matrix. If X is more important than Y then a numerical value greater than one is used in the (X, Y) position. If Y is more important than X, then the reciprocal of this value is used. The reciprocal of whatever value is entered in the (X, Y) position is automatically entered in the (Y, X) position.

The paired comparisons give rise to a ratio scale of the relative importance of the criteria. Similarly, the alternatives are compared in pairs with respect to each criterion in a separate matrix, and the resulting scales from the five matrices are each weighted or multiplied by the importance of the criterion just derived above and then added to obtain the overall importance of the alternatives. AHP does not insist on consistent judgments and provides an index for measuring inconsistency, both for each matrix of comparisons and for the entire hierarchy. It is also possible to find out where the most inconsistent judgments are and to change them, if desired, to improve the consistency, although this is not required.

An interesting area where AHP has found many uses is when a group must interact to arrive at a decision together. In that case the group structures the hierarchy and provides the judgments. Elaborate discussion is required. A collective vote is synthesized from the individual judgments so that the reciprocal property is satisfied for the group. It says that if the group judgment is that stone A is five times heavier than stone B, then the synthesis of individual reciprocal

TABLE 18.1. Scale of Relative Importance.

Intensity of Relative Importance Expressed Numerically	Definition	Explanation
1	Equal importance	Two activities contribute equally to the objective.
3	Moderate importance	Experience and judgment moderately favor one activity over another.
5	Strong importance	Experience and judgment strongly favor one activity over another.
7	Very Strong importance	An activity is favored very strongly and its dominance is demonstrated.
9	Extreme importance	Evidence favoring one activity over another is of the highest order.
2, 4, 6, 8	Intermediate values	When compromise between judgments above is necessary.

Decimal values: For comparing two activities when it is possible to make a finer distinction than allowed by the above numbers, e.g., by allowing a value such as 3.7. Human judgment is not so precise in general, but the theory allows it, if known.

Reciprocals of above: If an activity has one of the above numbers assigned to it when compared with a second activity, the second is assigned the reciprocal of that number when compared with the first. Thus a matrix displaying the judgments is reciprocal, with $a_{ji} = 1/a_{ij}$.

judgments must yield $\frac{1}{5}$ for stone B over stone A. It turns out that when the order of voting is not important, the geometric mean of the judgments gives the desired synthesis (Aczel and Saaty 1983).

Table 18.1 contains a scale of absolute values (not ordinals) that can be used to express judgments for the pairwise comparisons.

Remark: The validity of the scale to capture the variety of discrimination is borne out by many experiments. Here is one. We are given five figures to compare (Figure 18.2). We obtain the derived scale and compare it with the given actual values.

Our judgment matrix is:

	Circle C	Triangle T	Square S	Diamond D	Rectangle R	Derived Scale	Actual
C	1	7	3	4	5	0.499	0.471
T	$\frac{1}{7}$	1	$\frac{1}{4}$	$\frac{1}{3}$	$\frac{1}{1.5}$	0.056	0.050
S	$\frac{1}{3}$	4	1	$\frac{1}{2}$	$\frac{1}{3}$	0.224	0.234
D	$\frac{1}{4}$	3	2	1	$\frac{1}{2}$	0.140	0.149
R	$\frac{1}{5}$	1.5	3	2	1	0.081	0.096

Inconsistency Ratio 0.014

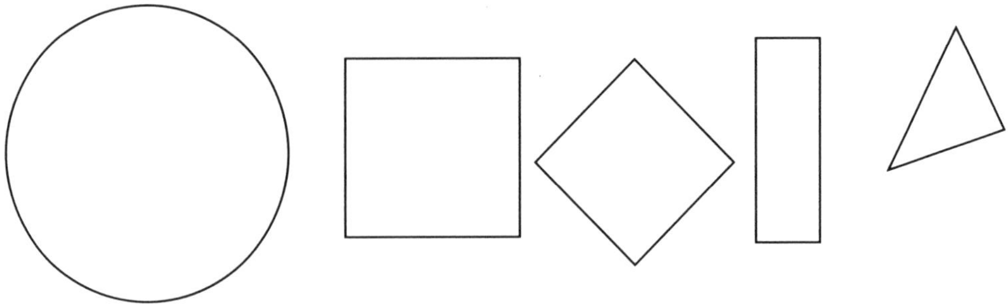

Figure 18.2.

Returning to our original hierarchy we have for level two with respect to the goal the following matrix:

	Return	Low Risk	Tax Benefits	Liquidity	Weights
Return	1	1/5	3	3	0.214
Low Risk	5	1	5	4	0.598
Tax Benefits	1/3	1/5	1	1	0.090
Liquidity	1/3	1/4	1	1	0.097
				Inconsistency Ratio	0.072

For level three with respect to level two we have the following four matrices:

Return	A	B	C	D	E	Wts
A	1	1/4	1	1/7	1/4	0.054
B	4	1	4	1/4	1/2	0.165
C	1	1/4	1	1/6	1/4	0.057
D	7	4	6	1	3	0.497
E	4	2	4	1/3	1	0.227
					Inconsistency Ratio	0.032

Low Risk	A	B	C	D	E	Wts
A	1	1/2	1/2	6	1	0.162
B	2	1	1	7	4	0.338
C	2	1	1	8	4	0.344
D	1/6	1/7	1/8	1	1/5	0.034
E	1	1/4	1/4	5	1	0.122
					Inconsistency Ratio	0.031

Tax Benefits	A	B	C	D	E	Wts
A	1	6	8	5	3	0.521
B	⅙	1	1	⅓	⅕	0.057
C	⅛	1	1	½	⅕	0.057
D	⅕	3	2	1	½	0.124
E	⅓	5	5	2	1	0.241

Inconsistency Ratio 0.023

Liquidity	A	B	C	D	E	Wts
A	1	⅕	⅐	½	½	0.051
B	5	1	½	5	4	0.298
C	7	2	1	7	6	0.487
D	2	⅕	⅐	1	½	0.068
E	2	¼	⅙	2	1	0.096

Inconsistency Ratio 0.025

The composite priorities or weights for level three are obtained by multiplying the weights of the alternatives with respect to each criterion by the weight of that criterion and adding, as shown in the following table.

	Proposed Portfolio	*Existing Portfolio*
Tax-free bonds	0.16	0.00
Securities	0.27	0.30
Saving accounts	0.27	0.20
Speculative stocks	0.15	0.00
Blue-chip stocks & bonds	0.15	0.50

Although the father makes use of the second and third investments appropriately, the bulk of the portfolio is tied up in medium-return, low-risk corporate securities. It was recommended that he sell a large part of these and reinvest in municipal bonds and more speculative issues yielding greater satisfaction from the investment. The overall hierarchic consistency was a low 0.025, obtained by composing the inconsistency ratios in the same way the priorities were composed and dividing by the same composition with random inconsistency ratios (see below for discussion of inconsistency). The father followed the advice and is happily prospering.

Brief Example of Benefits and Costs

In this example we consider the decision to choose the best word processing equipment according to benefits and to costs. Both hierarchies have the goal of choosing the best equipment. The benefits hierarchy has four levels whereas the cost hierarchy has three. The second level of the benefits hierarchy involves the following four criteria: time savings, filing, quality of document, and accuracy. The third level consists of five features: training required, screen capability, service quality, space required, and printer speed. The fourth level consists of three alternatives: Lanier, Syntrex, or Qyx. The costs hierarchy has the following criteria in the second level: capital, supplies, service, and training. The third level has the same three alternatives as above: Lanier, Syntrex, or Qyx.

One starts with the benefits hierarchy and sets priorities on the criteria as to their contribution to the goal, on the features according to each criterion, and finally on the alternatives according to the benefits of each feature. Similarly, one sets priorities on the cost criteria and on the alternatives for each cost criterion. The following two sets of relative values of benefits and costs for the three alternatives were obtained:

	Benefits	*Costs*	*Benefit/Cost Ratio*
Lanier	0.42	0.54	0.78
Syntrex	0.37	0.28	1.32
Qyx	0.21	0.18	1.17

According to this analysis the Syntrex word processing equipment yields the highest benefit to cost ratio and is the preferred choice. A company that sells this type of equipment may stock it in the ratio of $0.78/3.27 = 0.24$, $1.32/3.27 = 0.40$, $1.17/3.27 = 0.36$ where we have normalized the benefit-to-cost ratios.

This simple illustration has been used in a fairly elaborate form to make decisions relating to the allocation of incremental dollars to various research activities supported by the highest funding agency in a nation, to making a decision on the production of nuclear power generation plants, to making the right decision in conflict resolution, and so on. It has the advantage of representing complexity in as elaborate a fashion as desired. Later, I discuss how time horizons may be represented in the second level of the hierarchy and prioritized in terms of the elements of the third-level leading to a loop and appropriate scale derived from the feedback approach mentioned earlier. The decision in this case will be predicated on judgments taken with different time periods factored in the process for short- and long-term effects taken together.

Decision Making with AHP

Let us explain why we had to do what we did in the previous two examples. Almost every decision involves a number of intangible factors. To make a good decision we need to know these factors and what part they play in the problem. We also need to consider them simultaneously in making that decision and not one at a time which can lead to a less-than-the-best decision. A frequently cited example is that of a man buying a car. He asks his wife to decide the color while he decides what price he will pay, but he still wants a sporty-looking powerful car. The reader can guess the outcome: he buys a lemon.

Andrew Kingman decided to get married. On and off he had been courting two ladies Mary (A) and Jane (B). There were three important criteria that influenced this choice: beauty, character, and intelligence. His preference (>) for the criteria and ladies on each criterion is as follows:

Character	>	*Intelligence*	>	*Beauty*
A		B		B
V		V		V
B		A		A

Which one should he choose? Clearly the decision Kingman makes will affect him all his life (though maybe not from just these criteria), and it is very significant which girl he marries.

The Two Basic Hierarchies

Several hundred applications of AHP to a wide-ranging variety of problems by many people have confirmed my observation that there are two general hierarchic structures which the mind follows in understanding and problem solving (Ackoff and Emery 1972 and 1974, Saaty 1980). They are the forward and the backward hierarchies which combine in the planning paradigm. Let me explain. Planning is an iterative process that assesses in a forward process what is the likely outcome given the existing setup of material, relations, and people and in a backward process what is the most desired future and what must be done to attain that future, to overcome obstacles, and to take advantage of opportunities. The effective policies thus discovered are used in a second forward process to project the new likely outcome, thus testing the success of these policies to obtain convergence of the likely to the desired future. The process is repeated to close the gap. It appears that every decision problem involves a forward or a backward hierarchy. Sometimes two such hierarchies are used, one dealing with benefits and the other with costs as we showed in the example above. Here is a general itemization of the levels of these two types of hierarchies. They need not occur in such richness in every hierarchy, but they are helpful in guiding the reader to structure his or her problem along lines followed in many other formulations. Because of space limitation, I will itemize the levels on a line rather than in a column as a hierarchy is normally presented.

The levels of the forward hierarchy (most general pattern) include: (1) the goal, (2) time horizons, (3) macro environmental constraints or factors, (4) social and political constraints or factors, (5) external forces acting on the system, (6) the systems constraints, (7) objectives of the system, (8) the stakeholders, (9) the stakeholders' objectives, (10) the stakeholders' policies, (11) contrast scenarios as possible outcomes, and (12) the composite scenario as the most likely combination of the contrast scenarios. The contrast scenarios are characterized by a set of state variables which by appropriate weighting define the composite scenario and give rise to an index to show the effect of different control policies, particularly those introduced from the backward process in the planning paradigm.

The levels of the backward hierarchy (most general pattern) include: (1) anticipatory or desired future scenarios, (2) problems and opportunities presented by these scenarios, (3) actors and coalitions of actors who control the problems and opportunities, (4) actor objectives, (5) actor policies, and (6) particular control policies to attain the desired future. Note that time horizons may also be introduced as the top level (Saaty 1980 and 1982, Saaty and Kearns 1985).

Large Number of Elements

If in any level or cluster of our hierarchy there is a large number of elements and it is desired to compare them in pairs, we can decompose them into smaller clusters of a few elements each. We put similar elements together and arrange the clusters (say of four elements each) in descending order according to the size of their elements. To merge their scales into a single scale, we include in the comparisons of the second cluster the smallest element of the first cluster, and in the comparisons of the third cluster the smallest element of the second, and so on. To merge the scale of two such contiguous clusters, we multiply the weights of all the elements in the second cluster by the weight of the common element in the first cluster and divide by the weight of that element in the second cluster. In this manner the common element has the same weight in both clusters. The process is continued across all clusters. Should the elements be so disparate that it is not possible to share elements between two neighboring clusters, it may be necessary to decompose the larger elements in some fashion into smaller units, and use them for the common comparison and appropriate scaling. Alternatively, multiples of a smaller element may be used in the larger cluster. The process of clustering of elements reduces the number of paired comparisons considerably.

Let us assume that a cluster consists of three or four elements. Using a smaller number stands the risk of being unable to have adequate comparisons among the few elements to obtain refined values with the scale. If we start with 100 elements we would in theory need $(100)(99)/2 = 4,950$ comparisons. Dividing them into clusters of three (or four) each with an additional common element from cluster to cluster yields $(100/3)(3 \times 2)/2 = 100$, $((100/4)(4 \times 3)/2 = 150)$ comparisons, a considerably smaller number. This shows that decomposition is mandatory in practice so people can cope with their complex problems.

Deriving the Scale from Paired Comparisons

The scale is derived by solving the principal eigenvalue problem $Aw = \lambda_{max} w$. When $A = (a_{ij})$ is consistent so that the relationship of one element with all others automatically determines the numerical relationship between the remaining elements, the judgments a_{ij} are equal to the ratios of the derived scale values. Thus $a_{ij} = w_i/w_j$. In that case the solution is given by the sum of each row divided by the total sum of the rows. If A is inconsistent but satisfies the reciprocal property $a_{ji} = 1/a_{ij}$, then the scale cannot be obtained in this simple manner nor are methods of least squares (which yields non-unique answers) or logarithmic least squares (minimize $\Sigma_{i,j=1}^{n}(\log a_{ij} - \log w_i/w_j)^2$) or others any good (even though all methods yield the same answer when there is consistency) because although they minimize deviations they ignore the rank problem (Saaty and Vargas 1984) represented by the judgments in the rows which one works so hard to develop. Because A is inconsistent, the inconsistencies are obtained by taking the normalized sums of the rows of A, A^2, A^3, ..., adding these results for all the matrices, dividing by their number and passing to the limit with respect to that number. The result is the principal eigenvector of A and is the only way to surface the rank latent in the judgments.

In passing I note that the logarithmic least-square method produces results that are identical to the eigenvector for 2×2 and 3×3 matrices, but not for higher order ones. Although the practice should not be encouraged to use this method as an approximation to the eigenvector in the higher order cases because of the availability of software packages dealing with wide-ranging AHP structures, such as Expert Choice for the IBM PC compatible computer, sometimes one may be forced to do so in the absence of a computer. It can produce a different ranking for the elements than the eigenvector, which is unacceptable. Thus using the logarithmic least-square method as an estimate of the weights requires that one multiplies the elements in each row, takes their nth root, where n is the number of elements in the row, and then divides each result by the sum of these n nth roots.

The Measurement of Inconsistency

To find λ_{max} one takes the vector corresponding to the sum of the columns and multiplies it by the eigenvector or by its estimate as just described. The result is a single number that is λ_{max}. The inconsistency of a matrix is measured by taking $(\lambda_{max} - n)/(n - 1)$ and dividing it by the corresponding value for a matrix of that order with random and reciprocal judgments. This value is obtained by randomly assigning the scale values $1/9$, $1/8$, . . . , $1/2$, 1, 2, . . . , 8, 9 to an entry in the matrix and forcing its reciprocal in the transpose position which are the following for a matrix of size n:

n	1	2	3	4	5	6	7	8	9	10
Random Inconsistency Ratio	0	0	0.58	0.90	1.12	1.24	1.32	1.41	1.45	1.49

This ratio measuring inconsistency should generally be of the order of 10% or less for the following reason. The mind is primarily concerned with constructing a consistent account of complexity. But it must allow for new judgments for additional information. These judgments may be inconsistent with the earlier ones but they must not be too inconsistent. Still new judgments are needed for knowledge to grow, and hence, adjustment is always possible. It follows that the tolerance for inconsistency is neither as important as the concern for consistency, nor is it trivially negligible. Thus the measurement of consistency and inconsistency must differ by just one order of magnitude. A unit of effort to construct a consistent picture must give 90% to consistency and 10% to inconsistency so that significant adjustments can be made. It is clear that one should compare only a few elements so that their eigenvector scale values would be sufficiently high and that adjustment due to inconsistency would give rise to minor adjustment in their values. The larger the number of elements being compared the higher the inconsistency is likely to follow from the comparisons.

Time Dependence: An Illustration of Simple Feedback

Suppose we have three time horizons affecting an investment decision. These are placed at the top of the hierarchy as uncontrollable factors. Let us denote them by T1: 1988–1995, T2: 1995–2000, T3: 2000–2010. Suppose that the next level below this consists of four criteria: C1: return on capital, C2: obsolescence, C3: repair costs, C4: intensity of use. Now assume that the paired comparison matrices of the four criteria with respect to importance in each time period yield four scale vectors shown below. Also assume that the time periods are compared in four separate matrices according to the likelihood that a criterion would be most influential as the sole criterion during that time period yielding four scale vectors also shown below. The two sets of vectors may be exhibited in the following matrix which should now be self-explanatory.

	Time			Criteria			
	T1	T2	T3	C1	C2	C3	C4
T1	0	0	0	0.5	0.2	0.4	0.1
T2	0	0	0	0.2	0.6	0.2	0.1
T3	0	0	0	0.3	0.2	0.4	0.8
C1	0.7	0.3	0.25	0	0	0	0
C2	0.05	0.3	0.7	0	0	0	0
C3	0.15	0.1	0.05	0	0	0	0
C4	0.1	0.3	0	0	0	0	0

$A =$ (the matrix above)

The matrix A is a column stochastic matrix as its columns sum to unity. The steady-state priorities for the time periods and for the criteria are obtained by taking $\lim_{n \to \infty} A^n = \bar{A}$. The columns of this limiting matrix are the same in each block as follows:

	Time			Criteria			
	T1	T2	T3	C1	C2	C3	C4
T1	0	0	0	0.331	0.331	0.331	0.331
T2	0	0	0	0.328	0.328	0.328	0.328
T3	0	0	0	0.340	0.340	0.340	0.340
C1	0.415	0.415	0.415	0	0	0	0
C2	0.353	0.353	0.353	0	0	0	0
C3	0.099	0.099	0.099	0	0	0	0
C4	0.132	0.132	0.132	0	0	0	0

$\bar{A} =$ (the matrix above)

Thus the priorities of the three time periods and the four criteria are as indicated in the corresponding nonzero entries of this matrix. The time periods can be used to construct separate hierarchies, all using the same set of alternatives. The derived weights for the time period are then used to drive the system. Prioritization is continued down the hierarchy under each time period as if it is a separate hierarchy. The weights of the criteria derived for each time period are used accordingly. In the end the priorities of the alternatives over all the time periods are synthesized using the weights of the time periods. This is useful in making a decision that must take into account different time horizons.

Scaling, Measuring, and Scoring

Cognitive psychologists (Blumenthal 1977) have for some time been telling us that we learn by making two kinds of comparisons: the first is paired comparisons, and the second is absolute comparisons with a standard that has been learned and stored in memory. AHP is in agreement with these important psychological findings with scaling and scoring, defined below, corresponding to the first and second kinds of comparisons respectively.

An important observation about the pairwise comparisons of AHP is that they are always made between homogeneous elements whose weights are close with respect to a given criterion. Thus all the elements are considered relevant because they are included in the comparison, and we call the process of deriving a scale from fundamental paired comparisons *scaling*. Note that in this process, one does not arbitrarily introduce an alternative with small measurements assigned from thin air and claim that this is an irrelevant alternative. All alternatives fall in their appropriate set and level of the hierarchy.

If we wish to add a new alternative, such as a copy of an existing alternative, when the existing set has been previously recognized to be complete, we do this by comparing the alternative with one of the original ones and assigning it the appropriate multiple value of that alternative. The composite result over all the criteria would then retain the old ranking. In contrast with *scaling* by comparisons, we say that this added artificial alternative has been *measured*.

Thus by measuring we mean using the scale of the alternatives as a standard to assign a scale value to copies. A copy receives the same final value as the original and can be considered to be measured by it as the standard.

By *scoring* we mean scaling criteria and subcriteria or standards (which are often intensities such as very high, high, medium, low, very low) through pairwise comparisons and then identifying the subcriterion that best describes an alternative under each criterion and adding the scale values of the subcriteria thus chosen to obtain a score for the alternative.

Scoring is what one may wish to do in situations where alternatives are introduced in a steady stream one at a time. It is illustrated by a flow of applicants, for example, students applying for admission to a school. Ordinarily, we do not have them all present at the same time to carry out comparisons. (If they were all present at once, we could use clustering techniques to take care of an otherwise unmanageably large set of comparisons.) Here, rank reversal cannot occur. Why do we use scoring instead of paired comparisons? Usually because we do not have the other alternatives to make the comparisons or there are too many alternatives, or because the criteria no longer depend on the alternatives either functionally or structurally as their weights have evolved in practice.

Scaling has been illustrated in several examples above. We now illustrate how an alternative that is a copy of another alternative is measured. It is straightforward. Let us assume that as a result of scaling we have obtained weights for criteria and alternatives (candidates for professorship) with respect to the criteria of research and teaching. Thus to illustrate how measuring of alternatives is done, consider two criteria, research and teaching, with weights as shown in the following table:

	Research 0.68	Teaching 0.32
A_1:	0.667	0.250
B_1:	0.333	0.750

The overall priority of the two applicants, obtained by composition are:

A_1: $0.667 \times 0.68 + 0.250 + 0.32 = 0.533$
B_1: $0.333 \times 0.68 + 0.750 \times 0.32 = 0.466$

If a third applicant A_2 is considered with characteristics identical to those of A_1, we simply use the same weights as those of A_1 and we have:

A_2: $0.667 \times 0.68 + 0.250 \times 0.32 = 0.533$

Thus the copy A_2 has been measured by assigning it the same value as the original A_1.

To illustrate scoring we divide the two criteria above into standards of high (H), medium (M), and low (L) and carry out pairwise comparisons on these standards as to their relative importance with respect to their corresponding criterion. Let us assume that the paired comparisons of the standards with respect to the criteria give rise to the following matrices of judgments and their derived priority scales:

C	H	M	L	Priority		C	H	M	L	Priority
H	1	5	8	0.726		H	1	3	5	0.761
M	⅕	1	5	0.212		M	⅓	1	4	0.191
L	⅛	⅕	1	0.062		L	⅕	¼	1	0.048

Note that the first criterion, research ability, is regarded very highly, and to have a high capability for it is regarded as more desirable than to be medium or low. For teaching, the relative merits are not as distinct as in the case of research. Now suppose that A is H under research and M under teaching while B is M under research and H under teaching. Their scores and normalized results are as follows:

$$\text{Norm}$$
$$A: 0.726 \times 0.68 + 0.191 \times 0.32 = 0.5548 \quad 0.59$$
$$B: 0.212 \times 0.68 + 0.761 \times 0.32 = 0.3877 \quad 0.43$$

One can see how this generalizes to a stream of applicants. Scoring as described here is most useful in an open situation in which it is determined in advance that the weights of the criteria must not be affected by the structural information generated by applicants who apply to a well-established system. This is contrary to the case of buying a car where one's very criteria change with each new car seen. In the applicants' case neither the number of applicants nor their particular characteristics affect the importance of the criteria.

In closing we note that axioms have been developed for the AHP (Saaty 1986).

References

Ackoff, R. L., and F. E. Emery. (1972). *On Purposeful Systems.* Chicago: Aldine-Atherton.

———. (1974). *Redesigning the Future.* New York: Wiley.

Aczel, J., and T. L. Saaty. (1983). "Procedures for Synthesizing Ratio Judgements." *Journal of Mathematical Psychology* 27(1):93–102.

Blumenthal, A. L. (1977). *The Process of Cognition.* Englewood Cliffs, N.J.: Prentice-Hall.

Emery, F. E. (1969). *Systems Thinking.* Penguin.

Saaty, T. L. (1977). "A Scaling Method for Priorities in Hierarchical Structures." *Journal of Mathematical Psychology* 15:234–81.

———. (1980). *The Analytic Hierarchy Process.* New York: McGraw-Hill.

———. (1982). *Decision Making for Leaders.* New York: Van Nostrand Reinhold.

———. (1986). "Axiomatic Foundations of the Analytic Hierarchy Process." *Management Science* 32(7):841–55.

———, and Kevin P. Kearns. (1985). *Analytical Planning.* New York: Pergamon.

———, and Luis G. Vargas (1982). *The Logic of Priorities.* Boston: Kluwer-Nijhoff.

———, and Luis G. Vargas. (1984). "Inconsistency and Rank Preservation." *Journal of Mathematical Psychology.* 28(2):205–14.

Chapter 19
Measuring Process Creativity

Elsa Vergara Finnel

Introduction

In today's rapidly changing environment organizations are frequently faced with new and unpredicted problematic situations for which there are no ready-made answers. To deal with these situations it is necessary for decision makers to break away from the bonds of past experience and create new alternatives. In other words, managers need to learn how to be creative problem solvers and planners. The role of the planner is to facilitate and encourage the creative process by which organizations create their own futures (Ackoff 1978, Churchman 1968).

Summary of the Research

The research described here attempts to develop understanding of what creativity is and how it can be stimulated in group problem solving and planning. It is a report of an exploratory study that focused on how alternative creativity-enhancing techniques affect the creativity of planning.

A test of the creativity-enhancing techniques was designed using an experiment in which MBA students at the Wharton School were organized into six groups of three and given the task of redesigning the MBA program. After they had prepared their first design, two teams were instructed in the use of idealized design; two were instructed in the use of idealized design, dialectics, brainstorming, synectics, and several creativity-enhancing rules (all this in the same amount of time devoted to the instruction of the first two teams); and two teams were used as controls, receiving no special instruction.

The creativity of the designs was subjectively evaluated by otherwise uninvolved members of the faculty. A way of measuring the creativity displayed by the groups in their planning process was also developed. A significant association was obtained between the creativity of the products and the processes.

Instruction in idealized design increased creativity. The teams so instructed were able to use their intuitions and stretch their imaginations beyond self-imposed constraints. They were also able to use reality testing and logic in the development of alternatives to insure their operational viability.

No improvement in creativity was shown by either the control teams or those that had been instructed in multiple techniques. The latter, however, produced the largest number of creative ideas but were unable to translate them into workable alternatives.

It is not possible to address each of these aspects of the research and to report on the findings in this brief article. Therefore, I shall emphasize the methodological aspect of the research—the definition of creativity and its operationalization in the planning process.

What Is Creativity?

Although different schools—psychoanalytic, humanistic, associationistic, and information-processing schools—disagree about the origins of creativity, most researchers seem to agree that creative thinking requires overcoming barriers imposed by habit and tradition in order to find new solutions to problem solving and planning. I formulate this common insight using the concepts employed in the model of choice presented by Ackoff and Emery (1972). This model is composed of four components and three parameters, defined as follows:

COMPONENTS

A = The subject who displays choice.

C_i = The available courses of action determined by aspects of the problem situation which A can control: the controlled variables.

S = Those aspects of the problem situation which are perceived by the problem solver as both being uncontrollable and affecting the outcome of his or her choice: the choice environment.

O_j = The possible outcomes produced jointly by the problem solver's choice and the uncontrolled variables.

PARAMETERS

P_i = The probability that A will select C_i in S.

E_{ij} = The probability that O_j will occur if C_i is selected by A.

Subject A is said to be in a choice situation if the following conditions hold.

1. There are at least two exclusively defined courses of action available to A in S.
2. For at least two of the courses of action, the individual's probability of choice is greater than zero; these are called "potential courses of action."
3. Of the set of (exclusive and exhaustive) outcomes, there is at least one for which at least two of the potential courses of action have some but unequal efficiencies.
4. The outcome(s) relative to which the preceding condition holds has some value to A.

Subject A is said to have a problem if he or she has some doubt about the relative effectiveness of the courses of action and is dissatisfied with his or her present (purposeful) state (Ackoff and Emery 1972).

Note that an outcome may be pursued as a course of action for achieving some other outcome. Thus C_i and O_j link together in chains, such that any link (except an ideal) may be regarded as an end or as a means depending on the purposes of the observer.

Note also that a subject is frequently faced with several decisions at the same time. In such cases the course of action that is chosen depends on the way each course of action promotes or interferes with the achievement of other goals (Goodenough 1963).

It is important to emphasize that in a specific situation, a subject A_{max} be unaware (and this is usually the case) of all the courses of action and outcomes that are available. Thus his choice model is formed by what he *believes* are the courses of action available to him and the outcomes which these actions might produce (including the ultimate outcomes toward which his actions might progress). Let C^* and O^* be the sets of courses of action and outcomes respectively, believed by A to be available to him. The reason why A includes some C_i and O_j in C^* and O^*, respectively, rather than others is not arbitrary. The members of C^* and O^* share one or more properties which we will call the assumptions (constraints) in the subject's choice model. These assumptions involve:

1. Possible outcomes.
2. Controlled variables (which are fashioned into courses of action).
3. Relevant uncontrolled variables (which define the environment).
4. The relations among these three.

Changes in assumptions (reformulation) allow the individual to find and/or to develop new courses of action and new objectives. For example, consider the nine-dot problem: four straight lines have to be drawn (without lifting the pencil from the paper) which will cross all nine dots.

Figure 19.1.

If we assume that we may not draw a line outside the perimeter of the square, the only courses of action believed to be available will share that constraint, and the puzzle will be impossible to solve. However, if we deny this (self-imposed) assumption, other available courses of action will become apparent. For example,

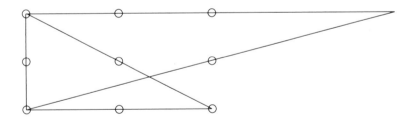

Figure 19.2.

Therefore, I define creativity as *the ability of a subject in a choice situation to modify constraints in his model of that situation (i.e., self-imposed constraints) so as to enable him to select courses of action or produce outcomes that he would not select or produce without such modification, and which are more efficient for, or valuable to, him than any he would otherwise have selected or produced.*

Constraints are adopted in the process of solving a problem. In attempting to develop a solution for a given problem situation, problem solvers generally start with consideration of a relatively large solution space. This space is reduced in size (i.e., alternative solutions are eliminated from further consideration) as problem solvers adopt constraints. One way of describing (Reitman 1965) the adoption of constraints is as the closing (defining) of properties which were formerly opened (undefined). According to Duncker (1945) these properties may be *general* in nature (relating to the general direction in which the solution will be sought), *functional* (relating to the specific functions to be accomplished by the solution), or *specific* (relating to the details of how functional requirements will be met).

The initial constraints (assumptions) a problem solver imposes on a problem situation are determined by his or her initial perception and conception of the problem, which are based on previous experience with similar situations. The choice model evoked by initial assumptions is a familiar one. In Duncker's (1945) terms we would have the most familiar branch of his solution tree:

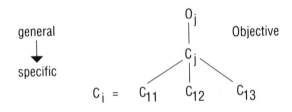

Figure 19.3.

C_{11}, C_{12}, and C_{13} all share the assumptions that define C_1 (for example, in the nine-dot puzzle, that lines connecting the dots must not fall outside the perimeter of the square). Once this assumption is removed, a new class of alternatives C_2 is "made possible." C_1 and C_2 may, of course, share a common assumption (e.g., the paper may not be folded while drawing the lines) and hence come into a node C_1. Removal of this assumption would open up a new class, C_{11}; and so on. Unless the assumptions that determine the nodes in the tree are made explicit, the subject may not be aware of the fact that he or she has narrowed the alternatives. "This can go so far that the S (subject) deprives himself of freedom of movement to a dangerous degree. He will therefore remain in the framework of this narrower problem, just because he confuses it with the original" (Duncker 1945, p. 11).

Most subjects are inclined to confine themselves to a familiar branch of the decision tree, to what Maier (1970) calls a "habitual direction." Familiar problems can be solved by using habitual directions. Other problems require the development of new directions, and therefore changes of assumptions. For this reason creative problem solving is characterized by Maier in terms of variability of direction. With each new direction, new facts are extracted and integrated into a new concept of the problem.

The ease with which the subject is able to remove constraints depends on whether or not he or she is aware of their presence and on the strength of belief that they are out of his or her control. The stronger the belief in the uncontrollability of the constraints, the more reluctant the subject is to modify them. Instead he or she tends to reconcile experienced inconsistencies by making further constraining assumptions (Festinger 1957, Goodenough 1963).

In some cases the intensity of belief in the uncontrollability of constraints diminishes with failure to produce the desired outcome. This corresponds, according to Maier, to problem-solving behavior. However, Maier reports a different type of change in problem-solving behavior of subjects after repeated failure to solve the problems (e.g., when the subject lacks the ability required). This type of change is characterized by lack of purpose, fixation (failures are repeated), aggression, regression, and resignation. Furthermore, the assumptions sometimes are such as to lead the subject to choose means which make future experiences consistent with his or her assumptions (Argyris and Schon 1976, Laing 1970, Waltzlawick et al. 1974, Goodenough 1963). In this way constraints and experiences become a closed self-reinforcing system, even if the constraints have little basis in fact. Such a self-sealing situation is called an "endless game" (Waltzlawick 1974).

Creative problem solving may involve finding alternative objectives, rather than alternative means. Duncker seems to have neglected this possibility, perhaps because the objective was given in the tasks he used in his experiments.

We can conceive of the solution tree as growing sideways at the level of objectives and upward to higher objectives.

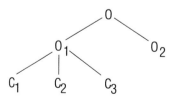

Figure 19.4.

The consideration of alternative objectives is especially relevant in group problem solving, as noted by Wertheimer (1959). Members of a group are likely to differ in the way they see a problem. They may value different possible outcomes as well as perceive different alternative means. Conflict between them may become an obstacle to effective problem solving because each member will try to pursue a different objective.

However, if there is tolerance and commitment within the group, problem solving can be enhanced by the variety of directions taken (Maier 1970). Differences among the members' objectives can lead the group members to attempt to understand each other's points of view, efforts that frequently result in a better understanding of the problem situation. Conflicts among group members can be dissolved by the creation of a new objective that either integrates or includes the differing points of view.

For example, suppose that in a living room *A* wants to read in a quiet environment and *B* wants to listen to rock music at a loud volume. These objectives appear to be in conflict because it is assumed that both cannot be pursued simultaneously. This assumption is denied by making a "head set" available to *B*. In this example, a "new" course of action is revealed. Consider a case in which a new common objective is found. *A* may favor increased income taxes and *B* decreased income taxes. Both, however, may prefer the same consumption tax to any income tax.

In conclusion, group problem solving can (but need not) enhance creativity by providing new directions and encouraging the development of alternative courses of action and the formulation of higher objectives.

Measuring Creativity in the Design Process

Several procedures for measuring creativity in individuals have been proposed (Guilford and Hoepfner 1974). These procedures are designed to assess the creativity *inherent in an individual* (very much like IQ tests) using the responses to a set of *independent well-structured* problems and tasks. However, none of the tests available evaluate the creativity displayed in such open-ended design and planning processes found in real-life organizations.

In addition, the definition of creativity used here calls for a procedure that captures the breaking of constraints in problem solving. No such measures are available; therefore, it was necessary to develop one. Specifically, the evaluation procedure has to be able to identify:

(1) the constraints under which the problem solver operates, (2) *if* and *how* these constraints are modified, and (3) how this affects the development of ideas for use in a final solution. The procedure that was developed relies on a graphical representation of a design process similar to that used by Duncker (1945).

Definitions

Creativity was defined above as the ability of a subject in a choice situation to modify self-imposed constraints so as to enable him to select courses of action or produce outcomes that he would not otherwise select or produce, and are more efficient for or valuable to him than any he would otherwise have chosen.

As discussed earlier, modification of constraints resulting in new objectives and new courses of action can be represented in terms of a change in the branches of a functional tree. The following definitions facilitate the use of functional trees in the measurement of creativity in design.

For coding purposes, an *objective* is defined as a statement of a desired outcome. A *course of action* is a statement describing means intended to produce a desired outcome. A *sequence* is an ordered set of courses of action $(C_i, C_{ij}, C_{ijk} \ldots)$ in which all members of the set share the same function (defined by C_i) with respect to a specific objective, O_m, and each member is a further specification of the preceding one $(C_i, C_{ij}, C_{ijk} \ldots)$. Each objective or course of action specified in a sequence is a *node* in that sequence. In such a sequence the highest node, O_m, represents the origin or formulated objective and will be called the *originating* node. The nodes diverging from the originating node $(C_i, C_{ij}, \ldots)$ are specifications of properties of what is to be done to achieve the stated objective.

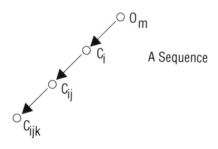

Figure 19.5.

The arrows in the diagram connecting the various nodes indicate the direction of the functional relationship between one node and another—from objectives to means. The numbers show the order in which ideas were stated in the design process.

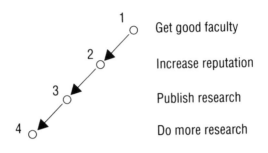

Figure 19.6.

A *class of sequences* of courses of action is the set of sequences diverging from the same objective O_m.

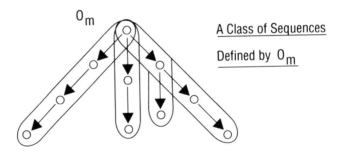

Figure 19.7.

A *subsequence* is a part of a sequence considered from a node other than the originating node.

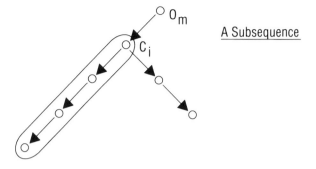

Figure 19.8.

A *class of subsequences* is the set of subsequences diverging from the same node.

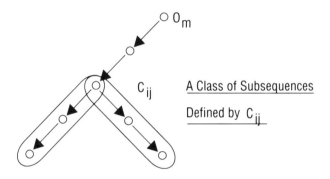

Figure 19.9.

The *final node of a sequence* is the most detailed specification of the way to achieve the sequence's objective. The *floor* of a sequence marks the point at which courses of action are sufficiently specified to be implemented or recommended. Therefore, a *complete sequence* is a sequence in which the final node "touches the floor"; that is, a set of nodes from the objective to a final formulation that is fit for implementation or recommendation.

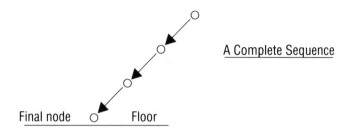

Figure 19.10.

An *incomplete sequence* is a sequence lacking a node which "touches the floor."

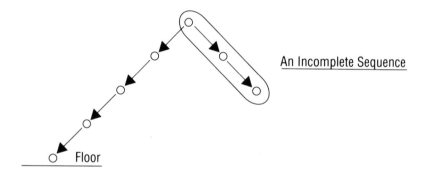

Figure 19.11.

An *overcomplete sequence* is a sequence that extends "beyond the floor." That is, nodes that go below the floor represent specification of properties that do not affect the probability of achieving the sequence's objective.

When a node is specified, it can be classified in terms of its role within the structure of the sequence of nodes of which the node is part. There are six types of specifications that can be classified thus.

1. *Originate:* to specify an objective that gives rise to at least one sequence.

Figure 19.12.

2. *Reclassify:* to specify an objective or course of action that serves as an alternative diverging node for an existing node or (sub)sequence.

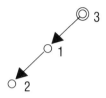

Figure 19.13.

3. *Generate:* to specify a course of action that creates a sequence.

Figure 19.14.

4. *Subgenerate:* to specify a course of action that creates a subsequent diverging from a node from which at least one subsequence has been built.

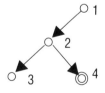

Figure 19.15.

5. *Extend:* to specify a course of action that creates a subsequence diverging from a node from which no other subsequences diverge.

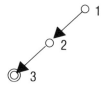

Figure 19.16.

6. *Complete:* to generate or extend a (sub)sequence in such a way that it touches the floor.

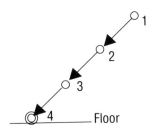

Figure 19.17.

Measures of Creativity

To be classified as a *creative move,* a node must either originate and/or reclassify a class of sequences or generate or extend a sequence, giving rise to two or more sequences itself.

Each creative move can be assigned a score that reflects the *level* at which it appears, its *generativity,* and its *elaboration.*[1] These criteria are defined for any particular node as follows:

Level: its distance, in number of nodes, from the originating node of the sequence;
Generativity: the number of (sub)sequences diverging from it; and
Elaboration: the average number of nodes in each of these diverging (sub)sequences.

These three variables serve individually as indicators of the creativity of a move. In the research presented here, they were combined into a single measure to yield an overall score for each creative move.

Scores for all creative moves in a design process were summed to yield an overall creativity score for the design process.

A creative individual or group was defined as one whose design process received a high creativity score. Is the measurement procedure outlined above a valid and reliable way of representing and evaluating creativity in the design process? This is the main methodological question addressed by this research. Results that justify use of this procedure are presented in the next section.

Effectiveness of the Evaluation Procedure

The main methodological question of this research was that the measurement procedure developed would prove to be adequate for representing and evaluating the creativity of the design process. To test this, the reliability and the validity of the procedure were calculated. The results were as follows.

Reliability

Using the same transcriptions, two coders were asked independently to draw the tree diagram for these protocols and to score them. Their results were compared for association using the Spearman rank correlation coefficient,[2] r_s. This is a measure of association between two sets of rankings of N objects or individuals. The resulting correlation coefficient is $r_s = 0.943$ indicating a strong association at the 0.01 significance level.

Validity

In order to determine whether the evaluation process really measures creativity, the process scores and product scores were compared using the Spearman rank correlation coefficient. This was done for the before and after training scores and for the difference between these scores. The results were $r_s = 0.8858$, $r_s = 0.8858$, and $r_s = 0.943$, respectively. These indicate strong associations at the 0.05 significance level.

In addition, a test was run using the process itself as the standard for comparison rather than the product. For this purpose, two judges were asked to evaluate the creativity of selected passages of the groups' protocols. These scores were compared with the scores obtained by the groups on those passages using the tree measurement procedure. This analysis was done using the Spearman rank correlation coefficient. The result $r_s = 0.9691$ indicates that the two series are associated at the 0.01 level.

Conclusion

It should be borne in mind that, although there was a high association between the process and the product evaluations, creativity in the process does not necessarily imply that the final product will be "more valuable or efficient" than one which is the outcome of a process in which constraints were not broken. A creative process does not have to have a creative output. Using the procedure suggested in this paper, the process that planners follow is considered creative when (1) ideas are proposed that challenge the assumptions that they bring to bear on the problem situation, and (2) these ideas are developed into a solution to the stated problem. Usefulness of the final solution proposed is not required.

On the other hand, for a solution to be considered creative it not only has to challenge self-imposed constraints but also to produce outcomes that the problem solver would not have otherwise selected or produced and that are more efficient for, or valuable to, him than any he would otherwise have chosen.

In addition, a creative solution results from the breaking of constraints that are held by the problem solver. Therefore, the same solution may not be considered creative by another person who did not share the problem solver's constraining assumptions.

In summary, the results reported show that the measurement procedure proposed in this paper is a valid and reliable measurement procedure for the creativity in the design process. In addition, this instrument can be used to analyze characteristics that distinguish creative from less-creative planning processes. Further work is required to extend use of the procedure developed here to organizational settings.

Notes

1. Originally it was hoped that the degree of completion of a sequence could be assessed. In practice, however, it was very difficult to assess with reliability if a sequence is completed or not. Therefore, this requirement on a creative move was left out and instead an "elaboration" index was calculated to indicate the degree to which a node is developed. This elaboration index substituted what I originally called a "productivity index," defined as the number of diverging (sub)sequences that include completion moves.

2. For a description of this technique, see Siegel (1956).

References

Ackoff, R. L. (1974). *Redesigning the Future*. New York: Wiley.

———. (1978). *The Art of Problem Solving*. New York: Wiley.

Ackoff, R. L., and F. Emery. (1972). *On Purposeful Systems*. Chicago: Aldine.

Argyris, C., and D. Schon. (1976). *Theory in Practice: Increasing Professional Effectiveness*. San Francisco: Jossey-Bass.

———. (1978). *Organizational Learning: A Theory of Action Perspective*. Reading, Mass.: Addison-Wesley.

Bales, R. F. (1970). *Personality and Interpersonal Behavior*. New York: Holt, Rinehart, Winston.

Churchman, C. W. (1968). *The Systems Approach*. New York: Dell.

Duncker, K. (1945). "On Problem Solving." *Psychological Monographs* 58(5).

Dunn, E. S. (1971). *Economic and Social Development: A Process of Social Learning*. Baltimore: The Johns Hopkins Press.

Festinger, L. (1957). *A Theory of Cognitive Dissonance*. Evanston, Ill.: Row, Peterson.

Goodenough, W. (1963). *Cooperation in Change*. New York: Russell Sage.

Guilford, J. P. T., and H. R. Hoepfner. (1974). "Structure of Intellect-Facters and Their Tests." In I. M. Stein: *Stimulating Creativity*. New York: Academy Press.

Johnson, S. M., and O. D. Bolstad. (1974). "Methodological and Naturalistic Observation—Some Problems and Solutions for Field Research." In Leo Hammerlynck et al. (Eds.): *Behavior Change*. Champaign, Ill.: Research Press Co.

Kantor, D., and W. Lehr. (1975). *Inside the Family*. San Francisco: Jossey-Bass.

Laing, R. D. (1970). *Knots*. New York: Pantheon.

Maier, N. R. (1970). *Problem Solving and Creativity*. Belmont, Calif.: Brooks/Cole.

Mintzberg, H., D. Raisinghani, and A. Theoret. (1976). "The Structure of 'Unstructured' Decision Process." *Administrative Science Quarterly* 21 (June): 246–75.

Mintzberg, H. (1978). "Patterns in Strategy Formation." *Management Science* 24 (May): 934–48.

Newell, A., and H. A. Simon. (1972). *Human Problem Solving*. Englewood Cliffs, N.J.: Prentice-Hall.

Normann, R. (1977). *Management of Growth*. New York: Wiley.

Reitman, W. R. (1965). *Cognition and Thought*. New York: Wiley.

Siegel, S. (1956). *Non-Parametric Statistics*. New York: McGraw-Hill.

Waltzlawick, P., J. Weakland, and R. Fisch. (1974). *Change*. New York: Norton.

Wertheimer, M. (1959). *Productive Thinking*. New York: Harper and Row.

Chapter 20
Innovation and Optimization
Britton Harris

Some Definitions and Assumptions

We are dealing in this context with a large number of related concepts that seem to defy clear-cut definitions and categorization. My own conclusion is that these ideas are closely related and in several cases virtually identical. I will hazard a few brief but perhaps sloppy definitions.

Planning is giving advice to those who might take action or, alternatively, taking such action aimed at controlling or guiding future decisions with a view to achieving certain objectives.

Optimization is the effort to make plans or take actions that will achieve the objectives in the best possible way. Explicitly to avoid a better solution if one is available is clearly irrational, and hence, all planning attempts to optimize.

Rational action may be regarded as a more general term for planning, implying the selection of means to achieve given ends, usually optimally. But rational action involves bounded rationality, since there may be obstacles to complete rationality, in ways to be discussed.

Design is the process or action of putting together schemes, plans, or designs. The term "design" might be regarded as synonymous with planning, except for two qualifications. First, and somewhat trivially, it may be regarded as concerned more seriously with aesthetic than practical concerns. Second, it may be regarded as a more subjective, less scientific, and less well-articulated process.

Operations research is a specialized form of rational action—or rather, a profession specialized in one form of rational action—in which it is assumed that problems can be solved and plans generated or actions recommended on the basis of a limited set of analytical and optimization techniques.

Innovation, strictly speaking, refers to the introduction of new, novel, or unaccustomed ideas and processes. "Invention" should be the preferred term to refer to confecting or originating the subject of such innovation. There may be reason to compromise in the fact that a new combination of innovative and possibly other elements could be regarded as an invention.

Organizations, which are the focus of most of Ackoff's recent work, can be planned, designed, or invented in the course of rational action, just like cities, transport systems, tax laws, constitutions, and religions. The positive theory of organizations, telling what will happen to them and how they will respond under different circumstances, is an important element in the practice of planning and innovation—but it is tangential to the present discussion.

Theories of planning and innovation ought to be largely independent of their subject matter, and in what follows I assume that this is so. In other words, I will speak mainly from the aspects of planning in urban areas and for transport systems with which I am most familiar, but I will assume on the basis of a good deal of thought and investigation that these ideas can be freely transferred into other areas.

The Nature of the Problems of Planning

Planning (or any of its surrogates defined above) can be regarded as a purposeful effort to solve problems. If a problem area cannot be identified, or if it can be shown that no actions can be found that will solve or ameliorate the problem, then there will be no motivation for planning.

Problems are usually identified only in very vague or general terms. Ackoff (1974) calls such typical problems "messes." Ozbekhan (1971) refers not to problems but to the "problematique." Rittel and Webber (1973) refer to "wicked problems" and suggest that these have the characteristics that we don't know what the problems are until we have found the solutions. In short, therefore, situations may often exist which generate social unease and unrest, or corporate uncertainty, and these may be recognized as problems in themselves. In other cases, the problem may be identified with a symptom that does not, in fact, define the problem at all. All of these are planning problems that demand "solutions," and this is the most common type of difficulty presented as a starting point to a practitioner.

The planner's or the consultant's brief may require a specific form of action that he or she deems inappropriate to the postulated problem. This possibility suggests that problem formulation and solution methods are not independent of each other.

Given a problem statement, however vague, the practitioner tries to find a solution method. A solution method cannot in fact be found inappropriate until it produces results that are themselves inappropriate—but the practitioner can to an extent look ahead to the outcomes of any particular method. The selection of a method therefore begins the process of redefining the problem by sketching the outcomes that might constitute an acceptable solution.

Any method, however, exists in an ideal form, and in a practical or applied form. Operations research (OR) for a long time assumed that these forms were identical: if a problem could be adequately and properly formulated as a problem in linear programming, then it could be solved in that form. It has come as a great surprise that some problems—and indeed the bulk of all planning problems—may be clearly formulated in mathematical programming terms but cannot be solved in a reasonable time. These intransigent problems, like the traveling salesman problem or integer programming, must most often be approached by approximate or heuristic methods. These are the essence of practical work.

Herbert Simon (1981) called these two solution methods substantive rationality and procedural rationality. Modern critics of optimization theory in planning would call both of them technical rationality, and would reserve the term "substantive rationality" for the formation of the goals of planning. There is no very good term for the real-world problem (including goals and the currently perceived difficulties in reaching them) in all its richness and complexity—and prior to its reduction to a mathematical programming formulation. In my view, however, this is the substantive problem; it is not limited to the normative choices prescribed by the critics just mentioned, nor is it circumscribed by the availability of formal problem statements as Simon would suggest.

I will take the position in what follows that solutions are found by trying to find them and that problems are redefined by these efforts. The most important feedback loop in the planning process is the comparison of the outputs of the process with the goals that were originally chosen for pursuit. This comparison may convince the decision maker that the goals were incompletely or incorrectly defined (that is, that the problem was incorrectly stated) or it may reflect on several other aspects of the process. We cannot investigate these implications without using a model of the planning process *in the abstract,* and the best such model seems to be mathematical programming, even though there may be grave doubts as to the appropriateness of this approach. Our disillusionment with OR, which has mathematical programming at its center, goes to the heart of this issue.

A Farewell to ORSA/TIMS

Operations research seems to have a half-life of about twenty-five years. It was originated during the last war, at a time when the consensus in Western nations on social goals was firmly established, and when the social costs of sacrifices needed to win the war were regarded as minor by comparison with the agreed benefits. At the first twenty years after the war, the transfer of OR techniques to peacetime social problems—led in part by Ackoff and Churchman—at first enjoyed unprecedented popularity and acceptance among decision makers. Then (under the same leadership) a disillusionment set in. We need to examine more deeply the causes of this disillusionment.

For my own part, I participated in the same process of optimism and its disappearance, but largely from outside of OR. Between 1955 and 1965, I was engaged in several forms of planning and analysis, most particularly transport planning. I engaged myself fully in the computer revolution, and in the early 1960s, I put forward the propositions that we could model most of the phenomena of urban activity and development with computers and, on this basis, proceed to the generation of good plans. Starting in about 1965, I began to investigate more thoroughly the theoretical and operational underpinnings of these propositions, staying much closer to the technical aspects of computer use and optimization theory than did Ackoff. With help and stimulation from Ackoff's views, I arrived at many of the same conclusions. These were undoubtedly also influenced by the growth of critical self-analysis in the field of planning. Similarly, legal theorists like Tribe and colleagues (1976) attacked the underlying premises and morality of analytical methods of decision making in ways which to a considerable extent parallel the later work of Ackoff and Churchman.

We thus see in this period not just a series of important defections from operations research, but a widespread questioning, on many bases in many professions, of the underlying concepts of OR, economics, planning, and rational action as practiced in public decision making. These questions arose despite the fact that, at a practical level, some form of mathematical programming seems to be the only game in town—and that to abandon it often seems to move backward into a mode of professional action that depends on internalized skills and that can be communicated only by example and guided apprenticeship and tested only by the results of practice.

In brief, we now know that formal rational action involves considerable difficulties. We also know that there is an overriding rationality of professional behavior that demands verifiability of the virtues of methods use in decision making, together with a democratic ethos that demands at least a commitment to openness and the minimizing of subjectivity in actions which serve the public. Avoiding the difficulties implicit in formal rational action may tend to drive the practitioner back into private and subjective modes of problem solving that violate the conditions of verifiability and accessibility.

It is my intention next to explore some of the reasons for this paradox, and some ways of fighting our way out of it. To do this I will consider three steps in the process of problem solving. The first step is translating a problem (however poorly defined it may originally be) into a mathematical program and examining the alternative simplifications that need to be made in this process. The second step is finding a method for solving a given mathematical program in a feasible manner: this corresponds to Simon's procedural rationality. The third step is looking for heuristic methods that connect solutions directly with the original problem without the intervention of mathematical programming. This third step is actually the first step in much professional practice, where for example, heuristics may more often be called "protocols." Here I would argue that any set of heuristics or protocols solves *some* mathematical program and that discovering what the implicit program is and deciding how well it is solved provide logically defensible methods of analyzing the protocols which are otherwise very difficult to come by.

We could regard these three steps as the sides of a triangle (Figure 20.1), connecting the three vertices which are the original problem

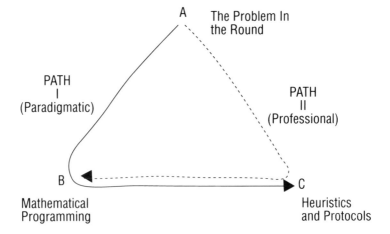

Figure 20.1.

(A), the mathematical program (B), and the heuristics or protocols (C). According to the analysis here, we might best proceed from A to C by way of B. In real life we often go from A to C directly, especially if there is a strong body of professional norms and rules of practice. But if we do this, then we ought to move back to B to test the validity of our practice at C. Once we have done this, we can pretend that our professional practice is in the mode ABC (rather than AC), and in an expanded view, this is exactly the professional mode of OR and management science. If this supposition is correct, we can then see whether we are doing better than these professions *at their own game*. And since we have honed our criticisms of them so sharply, we can apply that critique to ourselves.

If this approach seems "sharper than a serpent's tooth," there is a reason. Strictly rational action is vulnerable to criticism because it is fully open and fully specified. We cannot claim that an alternative method is superior without submitting it to the same kind of critical evaluation we give to others. The approach I have suggested is designed to place many different planning methods on the same footing. In discussing the actual steps we will see by example how some of these matters work out in principle and in reality.

The First Step in Problem Solving

Most of the practice of operations research, and of the construction of economic theory, revolves around formulating real-world problems as mathematical programs and solving the programs. Essentially, this is the process against which Ackoff and Churchman rebelled in their secession from OR, so that we see in their later work many of the criticisms that have been directed against rational action in a number of other fields as well. We will summarize these criticisms in general terms, largely without attribution, and we will see how many of the criticisms pose problems in practice regardless of the professional context or the proposed approaches.

The most sensitive issues revolve around values, subsuming the issue in particular of how the objectives of programming (or of planning) are chosen. All of this poses deep ethical, even religious, problems. The practitioner must be extremely aware of these problems, and of the fact that their ultimate resolution is in the field of politics. Any tension between the practitioner's own values system and that of the client creates a problem of choice for the practitioner as well as the client; this problem is largely unrecognized by many consultants.

As Ackoff has suggested, the ends-means dichotomy suffers from the fact that ends sometimes have extrinsic qualities, affecting systems performance, and means sometimes have intrinsic qualities, affecting the evaluation of an approach. The second of these difficulties is easily dealt with (in principle) by constructing an objective function, but the first is more troublesome. For example, the levels of equity may affect the productivity of an organization in various ways, but equity itself is indirectly affected by many decision variables, and even by the level of productivity. Thus we need to know both the levels of equity and the levels of productivity to predict each other, and the evaluation would have to be conducted interactively.

Those of us who are addicted to the systems view of planning object, with Ackoff, to the tendency of some analytic approaches to dissect a problem into its parts and to solve each part separately. This approach obviously leads to a gross neglect of the indirect effects of decisions propagated through other (and separately considered) subsystems. This leads to unintended and possibly undesirable consequences of plans. But the consideration of large systems complicates the programming problem and discourages a realistic view of these system interconnections.

Constraints, in mathematical programming concretely considered, turn out to be a means of biasing the solution in advance, by refusing to permit trade-offs in certain areas. Constraints are better entered into the problem as costs, or as penalty functions.

Many mathematical programming formulations are deficient in that they do not specify all of the available policy actions. Simon imagines that a principal activity of an architect, in the process of seeking (heuristically) an optimal plan, is to be constantly open to reminders about possible actions which might be taken but which have not previously been recalled. If we imagine that optimum-seeking is a sequential problem, as in, let us say, branch and bound programming, then changing the permitted actions at one point will invalidate many of the earlier decisions. This amounts to saying that finding measures which in combination may solve a problem is different from and prior to the search for actual solutions.

If we use mathematical programming to solve problems, we must be able to predict the effects of decisions upon the outcomes, so that these can be evaluated. Here there are many difficulties. Our understanding of behavior (especially in the field of organizational behavior) leaves much to be desired, and at best our predictions are probabilistic—but this complicates programming once again. Always, in the interests of finding a simple (and hopefully linear) programming formulation, we may tend to overlook or bypass behaviors that involve externalities and discontinuities. For example, there are linear programming models of residential choice that are quite reliable, as long as we can make the unrealistic assumption that people's choices do not depend on the choices of others—that there are no residential social preferences.

In all of these cases and many others, we can easily see that the translation of a real-world problem into a systematic problem-solving framework necessarily involves simplifications and that we have to choose the simplifications which do the least damage. Even so, this leaves us with one difficulty, which will later prove of enormous importance. Since we have left something out, if our optimization procedures were to throw up two or more plans of the same or similar "value," they might in reality be very differently valued by the decision makers, on the basis of the omissions and distortions. This fault is common to any plan-making process and is not to be attributed solely to mathematical programming and its practitioners.

The Second Step in Problem Solving

If we have a mathematical programming formulation of a problem, our immediate urge is to solve it, using more or less standard methods. Here, we encounter the difficulty that many of the most interesting such problems, and the bulk of the problems of planning and organizational design, are virtually insoluble in complete form and in reasonable time by formal methods.

Problems in this category include the traveling-salesman problem, machine scheduling, facility location (quadratic assignment), the K-median problem of public facility location, integer programming, network design, optimal clustering, and lots more. Typically, any problem where decisions interact strongly because of externalities, minimum facility size, decreasing costs, and so on, is apt to fall into his category. (Technically, all of the above problems are NP-complete, in the jargon of computer science—and computer science has become more knowledgeable in these matters than OR or economics, which are undermined by the existence of these problems.)

Problems of this type cannot be solved completely by exhaustive enumeration, or more seriously, by the kind of hill-climbing (or gradient search) that is typically applied in mathematical programming. NP-complete problems have very many local optima, and hill-climbing or improvement methods typically find only one of them. Constructive methods (like the greedy algorithm) also usually find single solutions, which may be subjected to improvements—once again, with a deterministic outcome. Taking sample starting points introduces the possibility of finding more than one local optimum, but the method works blindly, and is not in any sense guaranteed to produce useful results.

All of this is of overriding importance because local optima even for a well-defined mathematical program can be located in very different parts of the policy space yet have very similar values of their objective function. Since they are in different parts of the space, the omitted elements may make decisive differences where the program itself finds none. Most heuristics for solving mathematical programs do not provide for wide explorations in the policy space and consequently cannot provide suitable alternatives for decision making.

The Third Step in Problem Solving

Professional protocols, we have suggested, try to go directly from a problem statement to a heuristic solution method, without in the meantime providing a systematic formulation of the problem such as mathematical programming. Nevertheless, these protocols actually pursue two goals that become confounded in their specification. Good professional protocols sometimes follow textbook methods of constructing solutions according to a prescribed method. But wherever there is more uncertainty, as there is in medicine, law, and public policy (as well as in corporate strategic planning), then good protocols try to provide for more alternatives. Within this purposeful generation of variety, these protocols are in addition always found to be aiming at good solutions approaching the optimal.

In very broad terms, the informal protocols used to generate variety are creative in nature, but they are subject to disciplines that arise out of mathematical programming. Even if we assume that all of the alternatives which can be generated are generated (as, for example, by brainstorming), it is apparent that the overwhelming majority will be rejected immediately: there must thus be a quick, accurate, and appropriate rejection mechanism. Indeed, since the alternatives in some problems number in the billions, this mechanism obviously operates even in the process of creation. Only potentially useful candidates are thrown up, and even these are rapidly rejected in most cases. The survivors can be improved to various levels of completeness, pending further rejection along the line.

These levels of censorship should conform with a strong definition of optimality as defined by the original problem and its goals, but we have seen that there are many obstacles to such conformity. The more informal the criteria, and the processes of generating and rejecting schemes, the more likely that the censorship will be biased by the views, preferences, and prejudices of the individuals and groups engaged in planning. But the more formal and complete these criteria and processes are, the more likely they are to choke off the free play of imagination and to extend the investigation or limit its scope. Formal methods, as we have repeatedly seen, introduce their own biases.

The creative planner can articulate this process in many different ways to try to ensure that the planning is effective and unbiased. For example, if it is possible to specify a small set of highly influential variables, then the number of initial alternatives may be reduced in extent. But this then demands more discrimination in the perception of contradictions and unforeseen consequences. Detailed knowledge of many previous experiments is of great help in both suggesting and rejecting schemes and in specifying the decision variables that are available. Participation by those affected may help to clarify the objectives, to deduce the outcomes from possible decisions, and to suggest either new schemes or new protocols. Of course, such inputs may be biased, and care must be taken on occasion to discount such bias.

A Homely Example

We have now laid out more than enough material to outline my position in what may be hoped to be an understandable way. I have shown how I believe that planning and plan-making are optimum seeking processes, and I have shown that there are two types of difficulties in pursuing them systematically. The first of these, on which Ackoff and others have focused many criticisms, is the reduction of a real-world problem to a mathematical program. There are several separable reasons for this difficulty, and I should emphasize at this point that they form the basis for criticism not only of operations research but of all systematic problem solving. In setting up a problem-solving procedure, one must try to make only the least damaging simplifications. The second type of difficulty arises out of the fact that most planning problems are too complex to be solved by complete enumeration, so that heuristic or approximate methods must be used. This leads finally to the conclusions that heuristics and professional protocols are very similar, and that in most cases they attempt to solve a mathematical program. Working backward from professional protocols we could find these programs, and compare them with the original problem to see what has been sacrificed in their implicit formulation.

When we examine a competent professional approach like Ackoff's use of ideal planning in corporate strategic planning, we may see concretely how these ideas might be applied. I hope I may be forgiven if, in the brief space available, I am led to turn a sympathetic examination into a caricature.

As I understand matters, ideal planning starts by sketching a desired future state without regard to constraints or costs. A cautious view of this suggests that there are built-in constraints in the present situation of the corporation—so that the Flexible Flyer company would not sketch an ideal future in which it produced and sold half the cars in America. Neither very probably would Lee Iacocca for Chrysler. The consultant must use this idea to shake the client free from limiting preconceptions—but who decides which preconceptions are truly limiting and which not?

Given an ideal future state, an effort is undertaken to reach it at minimum cost but with cost having many dimensions. Cost is not only monetary but psychological, and there are costs that damage the goals themselves, as well as hinder their achievement.

The effort to get from here to there must deal with a large number of organizational variables and with many different kinds of uncertainty. It thus becomes a form of dynamic programming, which in cases like this is notoriously difficult even when well-conditioned. The heuristics and protocols used to solve such difficult problems must be very open to criticism and would require continual review and adjustment to the current problem.

When, as must often be the case, the outcome of this exercise proves that the ideal future is too costly to reach, a new enterprise must be undertaken. This is reducing the scope of the ideal future to make it achievable in a practical sense. Since these goals interact in their achievement with each other, and with the determination of costs in the dynamic programming analysis, this becomes a very nasty combinatorial problem. If there are ten components of the ideal plan, each of which may be achieved at any one of four different levels, then there are really a million such plans, each of which must (at least implicitly) be separately evaluated. The evaluation has two dimensions which must be traded off against each other: first, the closeness to the ideal, measured perhaps in generalized effectiveness; and second, ease of achievement, measured perhaps in terms of monetary cost, uncertainty, risk, and general appeal to the decision makers.

Obviously, no one will in this incompletely defined context explore in detail all of a million plans, and the branch and bound nature of this problem will suggest ways in which combinations of goals and their descendants can be shown to be unproductive. However, the temptation to make sweeping judgments can rule out potentially valuable schemes and must be tempered by a desire to achieve the best possible results.

One way of looking at all this is to point out that the ideal planning approach has one very great advantage: even if the ideal plan is infeasible, it may be expected to *contain* a large number of very good plans. In this sense, it preserves a creative approach. As I perceive matters, a major problem that then persists is to use our knowledge of the structure of the problem and of optimization of similar problems to guide the final planning activity in constructive ways. Such an approach will improve the chances of success, but it will not in the final analysis do away with creativity and imagination.

There is at least one very simple reason why this is true. Systematic approaches (and all attacks on these problems claim to be systematic to the extent that they can claim to give the best advice possible under the circumstances) can easily leave out plans or ideas that might be immediately accepted if they were known. If this were not so, there would be no fame in the names of Napoleon, Murphy, or Rockefeller. We therefore need extensions of dynamic programming and branch and bound programming that will produce surprises, and to an extent this is a contradiction in terms. The best heuristics for this purpose are still people.

References

Ackoff, R. L. (1974). *Redesigning the Future*. New York: Wiley.

Ozbekhan, H. (1971). "Planning and Human Action." In E. Jantsch (ed.): *Perspectives of Planning*. Paris: Organization for Economic Cooperation and Development.

Rittel, H. H., and M. M. Webber. (1973). "Dilemmas in a General Theory of Planning." *Policy Sciences* 4:155–69.

Simon, H. A. (1981). *The Sciences of the Artificial*. Cambridge, Mass.: The MIT Press.

Tribe, L. H., C. S. Schelling, and J. Voss (eds.): (1976). *When Values Conflict: Essays on Environmental Analysis, Discourse and Decision*. Cambridge, Mass.: Ballinger.

Chapter 21
Is It the Right Problem?

K. Brian Haley

Experience in operations research (OR) has shown that it is essential to ask and answer the question of the chapter title. There have been many examples of good work going to waste because it was not directed toward the relevant problem. This fundamental error forms the basis of warnings given to new practitioners and is so critical that further examples are given here to emphasize the point.

The examples are all concerned with the classical problem of dividing bulk material into separate smaller quantities. Various choices usually face the analyst, and it is sometimes necessary to consider intangible elements of the problem to achieve an appropriate solution. The problem has been known and its solution understood for over thirty years.

One of the earliest references to work involving the rational use of bulk material is by K. Eisemann in 1955 to the so-called paper trim problem. I also first met the problem in 1955 in the context of slitting rolls of copper strip and very soon after in the special version of cutting rolls of cellophane. As the techniques became more refined and the ideas of the "knapsack problem" were developed, so the solutions became more tractable and the difficulties of handling large numbers of variables were largely overcome. Many materials gave rise to their own individual modifications. For example, cutting glass sheets demanded "guillotine cuts" only, whereas cutting photographic film had to take account of minor but serious flaws in the surface finish.

It is not my intention to repeat any of the well-understood and documented standard approaches. Nor is it necessary to describe the special technical tricks or unique computer needs. This paper concentrates on a simple numerical example illustrating how different results are optimum in the context of particular company situations.

Company Profiles

Five companies are considered, each with slightly different requirements, but each posed the same question, viz., produce an operation system that gives the least scrap or waste material.

1. *Motor car exhaust systems:* A large company manufactures a range of exhaust systems using pipes of specified lengths cut from long lengths of tubes of a standard length. The tubes are purchased from a steel stockholder and the company pays for material actually consumed. During any one week, several hundred exhaust systems of a particular type will be made, and they require a set length and diameter of pipe. The same diameter of pipe (but differing lengths) is required by several different systems. It was felt that considerable benefit could be obtained by reducing the trim loss of the unused portions of tube, most of which were too short for any exhaust pipe.

2. *Steel springs:* The company manufactures spring by coiling very fine wire of 0.1 mm in diameter or bar steel of up to 30 cm in diameter. Each spring is made by cutting the appropriate length of steel from a long bar, smoothing the ends, and forming the spring of the required overall length, diameter, and number of coils. The material used is very expensive but has a low scrap value. Ideally, there should be no waste because for a given diameter of material leftover pieces cannot be utilized to make a spring of even one coil.

3. *Window frames:* A very small company makes double-glazed windows in a sealed unit to fit directly into customers' houses. Most of the work is carried out to the exact requirements of the homeowner, and very few standard orders occur. The windows are made by first forming a rectangular surround cut from a plastic extrusion that is purchased in a fixed length. Two sheets of glass are cut to size, separated by appropriate spacers, and the surround glued into place. Once fixed, it is not possible to alter the size of glass or surround, and if the assembly is not right, it can only be scrapped. The framework is cut by one person, and its lengths are matched up with the glass sheet. The glass is cut by hand and the cutter preserves any suitable sizes of sheet not immediately required. There are only sixteen alternative types of glass. Leftover lengths of plastic extrusion are usually thrown away, and the company wondered if they could—or should—be retained for later use.

4. *Copper slitting:* A rolling mill produces a strip of copper from a slab. The strip is rolled into a coil but has to be divided into narrower widths according to the needs of individual customers. At any one time, only a limited number of knives are available to carry out the slitting which also has to incorporate an edge-trimming facility. Orders

for the same thickness of material can be matched to reduce the waste, but any not immediately required is scrapped by incorporating it into the edge trim.

5. *Cellophane:* (a) The material is manufactured in a standard roll width and is demanded by a limited number of customers. Orders are for a large number of a few widths, and hence, some variable matching of orders can be done. It is possible to store the material against almost certain future orders, and a limited quantity of unused pieces which are a normal small width are stored. Non-normal widths are not stored nor can they be cut at a later stage. (b) The company also made a similar material that was sold in very small widths of integer dimension cut from a large roll. In this case, there was no limit to the number of small widths that could be cut at any one time.

The General Problem

For each example, a number of small lengths or roll widths have to be matched up and cut from a standard stock length or master roll width. Leftover portions are wasted. The original paper trim formulation and various solution techniques and refinements appear to be appropriate. Factors that determine the appropriate approach include the sophistication of the company, time available to carry out calculations, computer access, and potential savings. All competent analysts would take these factors into account. Beginners might just forget the full implications.

For example, the orders that have to be met are not always known until a shift is about to start, and there is no time to contact the central data processing department before the first piece of work commences. It is not unheard of for the required orders to be changed part-way through a shift, although this usually means additions. The annual cost of computer runs (or purchase) must clearly not exceed any estimated savings. Such errors are never made by OR people!

The mechanics of providing working instructions in a cost-effective way can be determined, but the common problem statement still requires some modification. Let us determine a combination of orders which can be cut from a number of pieces of bulk material of standard size so that the unused material is a minimum.

A Numerical Example

It is desired to cut from 3-meter lengths of bulk material two pieces each of 60, 71, 72, 78, 79, 80, 90, and 105 cm. The total amount of material required is 1,270 cm and this can be provided by five full lengths; 230 cm will be unused. The problem is to fit the lengths into five standards and Solutions 1, 2, and 3 give ways of achieving this.

	Standard		Widths Cut			Scrap
Solution 1	A	60	71	79	90	0
	B	90	105	105		0
	C	72	72	78	78	0
	D	60	79	80	80	1
	E	71				229
						230
Solution 2	A	72	78	105		45
	B	72	78	105		45
	C	79	80	90		51
	D	79	80	90		51
	E	60	60	71	71	38
						230
Solution 3	A	60	60	78	78	24
	B	79	79	72		70
	C	72	90	90		48
	D	80	80	105		35
	E	105	71	71		53
						230
Solution 4	A	71	71	105		53
	B	105	60	60		75
	C	78	78	79		65
	D	79	72	72		77
	E	80	80	90		50
	F	90				210
						530
Solution 5	A	60	60	90	90	0
	B	71	71	79	79	0
	C	72	72	78	78	0
	D	60	80	80	80	0
	E	90	105	105		0

The Appropriate Solution

The three solutions quoted each represent the same amount of un-used material but do not reflect the main needs of each of the clients. They can be used to illustrate the unstated desires, and unless care-ful examination has been made of the actual problem situation, the wrong or, at least, a less satisfactory result could have been used.

1. The exhaust-pipe manufacturer found that it was possible to negotiate the size of standard tube purchased. He would—by paying a little more for his own standard and not the supplier's—be able to reduce scrap and, with it, the total bill. It was therefore necessary to consider the best way of putting orders together to ensure the 230 cm scrap was as evenly divided as possible. This is achieved in Solution 2 where it is seen that a standard of $300 - 38 = 262$ will meet all his needs and reduce the amount of unused material by 190 to 40 cm.

2. The very expensive scrap means that the spring manufacturer wishes to utilize the material fully and to obtain the greatest flexibility by ensuring that leftover pieces stored are as long as possible, small sizes being almost useless. He therefore seeks to ensure that the maximum sized "lumps" are retained. Solution 1 leaves a piece as large as 229 and is of greater use than any of the other combinations.

3. The framework for the window required two heights and two widths, and the order sizes are grouped according to the window needs into, say, (60×78), (71×105), (72×79) and (80×90). The very small company size and the impossibility of carrying out any renovation work means that special precautions need to be taken to avoid incorrect surrounds being put together. In order to assist, the policy is to arrange that the four pieces for each window are cut together. The choice is therefore in which order to cut the windows, not the individual pieces. The cutting pattern of Solution 3 gives an appropriate solution. It is worth observing that Solution 4 represents a similar cutting pattern keeping the windows together but which requires a sixth standard length and therefore an extra 300 cm of scrap.

4. The copper slitting problem is totally dictated by the number of cuts possible, and if there are only three knives available, Solutions 1 to 3 could not apply. The amount of scrap must take second place to sixteen orders that require a minimum of six lengths.

5. The cellophane has a continuous value, and it is in this context that the number of orders of a particular size can be exceeded. Almost certainly, combinations can always be found that, if not reducing the scrap to zero, very nearly does. In this case, Solution 5 shows how to meet a demand of two widths minimum of each size, producing exactly two of every size except 60 cm, 80 cm, and 90 cm, where one extra has to be stored. The smaller the widths that have to be cut, the greater the number of combinations that can be found with zero or very little scrap. The problem is then to determine why one particular combination with zero scrap is better than any other also with zero scrap.

Although only five examples have been given of how a minimizing problem with the same numbers can be different, it is hoped that they do illustrate the importance of asking "What is the problem?"

Summary and Justification

I first came under the personal influence of Russell L. Ackoff in 1960, although we had met three years earlier. One memory is of attending a series of lectures based on a manuscript of "The Scientific Method" which in its published form includes, in the last chapter, the sentence "A problem never exists in isolation; it is surrounded by other problems in space and time."

The purpose of this article is to show that at least I have learned from him the necessity of considering the client as much as the stated problem. Even if I have been very inadequate in applying this principle, I will always be grateful for the encouragement, interest, and support of a friend, confidant, and mentor.

Chapter 22
How Management by Consensus Is Bringing the Kingdom Down

Ian I. Mitroff

A Fable

Once upon a time, there was a king who was determined to avoid as much as was possible the errors of all the kings who had come before him. He vowed that he would listen to as many voices as possible before he took action on any matter of great importance. He was determined to seek and to form as wide a consensus as possible before any action was taken even though he knew that as king he was not required to do so. But then the new king was wise enough to know that what was prudent and what was required of him were two very different things. His would be a reign of reaching out, good will, and involvement, not one of mere obligation and necessity.

The king widened his councils to include persons and voices of all kinds. People appeared regularly in court who had never come close to one before. They advised him on everything from the mysteries of the soul, to why birds fly, what women really want, and last but not least, the intricacies of the coin of the realm.

No one really knows why or how, but strange things began to happen. Huge scoreboards were erected everywhere. They flashed instantaneously and at all hours of the day or night the exact percentage of agreement between the king's advisers on all matters that were of importance to the realm. Thus, messages like "the king's advisers are 98.6% in agreement on the realm's fiscal policy" appeared regularly. The people constantly scanned the boards for direction. The very essence of their lives was bound up with them. Woe unto him who failed to be in tune with the pulse of the king and his advisers. The closer the percentage of agreement approached 100%, the more the people shouted great sounds of approval.

No one knew better than the new king a fundamental law of human nature: people feel safer and function better when they huddle together in agreement. He also realized that the people needed a great enemy to bind them together even further. And so the preceding king and all the members of his family were declared official enemies of the people. Anyone who deviated too far from the general consensus of the people was branded an enemy along with the former king.

No one denies that in the beginning and for a long, long time afterward (some say for a thousand years) this strategy worked beautifully. The king's advisers had their disagreements, but they were never serious. In the end they always came to see things in the same way, even though it often took a great amount of time for this to happen. But as a consequence, they were always able to present a unified front to the kingdom. In agreement lay their strength.

And thus it happened, ever oh so slowly, that the general belief in agreement became the kingdom's new god. And this god became so powerful that every problem in the realm was forced to submit to it, to pass it as a crucial test, before any pronouncement pertaining to it was approved by the king.

This strategy worked so well that at first nobody noticed when a strange, tiny, little bug—the disaffection bug—which visits all kingdoms began to infect everyone. In the beginning it popped out over the tiniest, most insignificant of matters concerning which no one really cared. For instance, whether the coats of the king's advisers should have four or five buttons. But then it began to spread to the most important matters. It affected everyone and every issue.

Something occurred that had not happened in a long, long time. The people began to disagree. A thousand years of paying exclusive homage to the god of consensus had rendered the people totally incapable of handling disagreement. They were horribly frightened of it. They attempted to run from it. But this only made matters worse. As a result, small disagreements soon grew into large ones. They became so pervasive that they infected everything. The people not only disagreed over what should be done to solve important problems, but far more basic, they disagreed over what were the important problems of the realm.

Some said the basic problem was that the people didn't work hard enough anymore. Others said it was because people no longer believed in anything. Others said it was the younger generation. Others still said it was the fact that the coin of the realm had been debased.

Nobody knows how it happened, but over time the new king began to look more and more like the king before him. True, he had listened more to the people than the old king ever had; he had involved them in important decisions more than before. On the surface at least, he did not use the same language as the previous king, but the people began to see that the music and the end results were the same nonetheless.

One day the new king appeared in public with a very shiny crown that was fashioned in the form of a giant screw. Every disagreement only served to drive the screw deeper and deeper into his brain. Like the people he was powerless to know what to do with disagreement. And thus, like the old king before him, in his own unique and distinctive way, the head of the new king began slowly to wedge apart and part company with his body.

Moral

1. Where the spirit is willing, there is a never-ending series of ways to cut off one's head and that of others.
2. One is advised to choose very carefully one's opposition and one's enemies. For they are precisely the things one is most likely to become.
3. The person who learns only how to sail in calm waters via one method is not a sailor. He or she is unprepared to tackle the broader oceans and turbulent waters of the world.
4. It is more important to learn how to debate important questions without necessarily agreeing on their solution than it is to agree on their solution without learning how to debate them.
5. New times require radically new ways of managing perpetually recurring problems.
6. Even the best of kings cannot survive if they govern by means that are inappropriate to the problems of their age.

Commentary

Consensus forms one of the, if not *the*, essential cornerstones of Western civilization. It is used variously as: (1) a scientific and technical *method* for producing truth, e.g., supposedly the more the agreement between independent observers, the more they have approached the truth; (2) a philosophic *criterion* for knowing when one has achieved truth; (3) a *process* that operates in all groups to bind the members to each other and to erect clear-cut barriers between who's "in" versus "out"; and (4) a *process* that operates in all organizations and indeed constitutes the core of the culture of the organization; it binds individuals to the general will; it rewards those who honor this agreement and punishes those who violate it.

A lead article on the front page of the *Los Angeles Times* shows how deep and pervasive the notion of consensus is in our general culture:

> WASHINGTON—Martin Feldstein came under heavy pressure Wednesday either to stop publicly *disagreeing* [my emphasis] with parts of President Reagan's economic program or to resign as Reagan's chief economic adviser.
>
> After being excoriated privately by White House officials and admonished publicly by White House spokesman Larry Speakes, Feldstein insisted that there must be some "confusion" about his comments on the President's program which he said he supports "completely."
>
> Speakes said the President wants his economic advisers to "speak with one voice or not speak at all."[1]
>
> Top White House officials initially excluded Feldstein from a top-level luncheon Wednesday to discuss preparations for the fiscal 1985 budget, including the question of whether the President would propose a contingency tax—something Feldstein has advocated. Feldstein complained to White House counselor Edwin Meese III about being excluded and was invited at the last minute.[2]

The preceding story is far from being an isolated exception. Consider the following from an article in *Time:*

> Faced with a grinding recession that has driven the unemployment rate to 10.8% of the work force, the economics profession has dissolved into a babel of conflicting voices. Result: as the new year gets underway, economists seem further than ever from *agreement* on how to restore the economy to robust health [my emphasis].
>
> *That leaves policy makers with few clear guidelines to follow* [my emphasis]. Last month, for example, White House Adviser Edwin Harper briefed Reagan for an hour on the dismal state of economic thinking. Harper's conclusion: "The US economy is too complex and depends upon too many human decisions to be explained by any single theory."[3]

Now it is one thing for the popular press and the so-called person-in-the-street to prize consensus as much as they do. But it is quite another thing when one of our leading academic thinkers and top economists leans on it so heavily as well. I quote from Lester Thurow's generally excellent book, *Dangerous Currents, The State of Economics:*

> It certainly appears that as if the economics profession *knows very little* indeed when two economists can look at the same thing and one calls it "equilibrium" and the other "disequilibrium" [my emphasis].[4]

> If economists disagree that sharply, how can they possibly know *anything* [Thurow's emphasis]?[5]

> The problem with econometric relationships does not mean that econometrics should be abandoned, but the emphasis should be put on "robust-

ness." Econometric results should not be given great weight *unless similar results are produced by different economists* using different techniques, different control variables, different models, and different data sets over an extended period of time [my emphasis]. . . . Users of econometric results should demand . . . robustness, and producers of econometric results should make it their number one objective.[6]

The author both understands and empathizes deeply with those who would like to see more consistency or consensus operate in the world. However comforting such consensus would be for forging collective action, do we not have enough historical evidence to suggest that such widespread consensus may never occur? Indeed, why should we expect to find people of all persuasions in near or perfect agreement on the important issues of the day? Doesn't the historical evidence we have point to just the contrary? Namely, because of deep underlying differences in fundamental values, people can be expected to *disagree* strongly on important matters. Indeed, isn't the basic relationship exactly the reverse of ordinary thinking? Something isn't truly important unless people disagree about it.

The notion of consensus as a way to secure truth and bind commitment to action in human affairs is so ingrained in our culture that it prevents us from asking some very fundamental questions. Are there methods for managing complex affairs that do not depend on consensus or at least not to the same extent that traditional methods do? If one has to depend on consensus as a condition for handling important social issues, then one must be forced to conclude that we will never be able to handle them. For the plain fact is, one just doesn't get such consensus on important issues.

In general, one obtains consensus only for very simple exercises for which one can look up the single right answer at the end of a text. It does not hold for complex problems for which differences in values can surely be expected to operate. In the real world, there are no textbooks wherein one can simply look up the right answer. Social problems are fundamentally not like simple exercises. The trouble is we have raised generations to expect the solutions to complex problems to be like exercises.

Contrary to Thurow, the invention of methods that do not depend on consensus should be our number one objective. What the nature of these methods are has been the lifelong work of people such as Ackoff and Churchman.[7] Not only do such methods exist, but it is relevant to note that they were developed in the course of working on complex, messy, problems in the real world.[8] They were not developed as an academic exercise.

It comes as a terrible shock to those who have been brought up to believe in the traditional ways of securing truth and managing human affairs to find that they no longer apply in today's complex world. Worse still, given nothing else to fall back on, they are generally rendered helpless and hopeless in the face of the collapse of their earlier beliefs. This is the real tragedy behind such recent exposés as "The Education of David Stockman," not the fact that political shenanigans were involved in the setting of the federal budget. What else is news? The open revelation by important public figures that the old ways of managing things no longer work, now that's news!

> The budget politics of 1981 . . . was . . . based upon a bewildering set of numbers that confused even those, like Stockman, who produced them.
> "None of us really understands what's going on with all these numbers," Stockman confessed at one point. "You've got so many different budgets out and so many different baselines and such complexity now in the interactive parts of the budget between policy action and the economic environment and all the internal mysteries of the budget, and there are a lot of them. People are getting from A to B and it's not clear how they are getting there. It's not clear how we got there, and it's not clear how Jones is going to get there."
> These "internal mysteries" of the budget process were not dwelt upon by either side, for there was no point in confusing the clear lines of political debate with a much deeper and unanswerable question: *Does anyone truly understand, much less control, the dynamics of the federal budget intertwined with the mysteries of the national economy? Stockman pondered this question occasionally, but since there was no obvious remedy, no intellectual construct available that would make sense of this anarchical universe, he was compelled to shrug at the mystery and move ahead* [my emphasis]. "I'm beginning to believe that history is a lot shakier than I ever thought it was," he said, in a reflective moment. "In other words, I think there are more random elements, less determinism and more discretion, in the course of history than I ever believed before. Because I can see it."[9]

The simple fact of the matter is that human affairs have become too complex to be managed by either the simpleminded rules and formulas of the old rationalist kings or the false comfort of a simple consensus of the new empiricist king. When it comes to vital social issues, it's more important to know why people disagree and to learn how to learn from it than it is to attempt to fashion a fragile and inappropriate agreement. Indeed, as we should know by now, it is vital on important social issues to secure and even to produce systematic differences in views. Unless this is done, one cannot be said to be appropriately informed on important issues. Management by *systematic conflict* has become more important than management by consensus in today's world.

It is not that consistency and consensus are all wrong and should be abandoned entirely. It is not that they have no role whatsoever to play in today's world. Rather, it is that when they are used without reflection to suppress serious debate, then they are self-defeating. They narrow our options instead of expanding them. They restrict the scope of discussion instead of broadening it. At their very best, they are necessary. They are no longer sufficient in a world as complex as the one in which we now live. In short, we need new ways of thinking about and managing in today's complex, turbulent world.

Notes

1. Jack Nelson and Sara Fritz, "Feldstein Pressured to Quit Post, Top Economic Adviser Cited For Critiques of Defense, Tax Policies," *Los Angeles Times*, December 1, 1983, p. 1.

2. Ibid., p. 23.

3. John Greenwald. "Where Have All the Answers Gone," *Time* (January 17, 1983): 36.

4. Lester Thurow, *Dangerous Currents, The State of Economics* (New York: Random House, 1983), p. 14.

5. Ibid., p. 19.

6. Ibid., p. 121.

7. Russell L. Ackoff, *Creating the Corporate Future* (New York: Wiley, 1981); C. West Churchman, *The Design of Inquiring Systems* (New York: Basic Books, 1971).

8. See Richard O. Mason and Ian I. Mitroff, *Challenging Strategic Planning Assumptions* (New York: Wiley, 1981); Ian I. Mitroff, Richard O. Mason, and Vincent P. Barabba, *The 1980 Census: Policymaking Amid Turbulence* (Lexington, Mass.: Lexington Books, 1983).

9. William Greider, "The Education of David Stockman," *The Atlantic Monthly* (December 1981): 38–39.

Chapter 23
Innovation in Juvenile Justice

Thomas N. Gilmore and Burton Cohen

Introduction

As the unit of managerial work shifts from well-defined problems to complex, interdependent messes (Ackoff 1981), dilemmas (Gilmore and Hirschhorn 1981), and wicked problems (Rittel and Webber 1973), creativity and risk-taking become critical characteristics of leaders. Ackoff (1979) has argued that of the five necessary characteristics for effective managers, competence, communications, coordination, creativity, and courage, the last two are the scarcest and hardest to develop. Each requires that the manager question the existing reality and challenge the assumptions that most people have been taking for granted. The following paper describes an innovative program in juvenile justice that illustrates creativity and courage and discusses how these characteristics can enable key stakeholders to learn interactively in ways that reshape the conceptual frameworks that they bring to the issues of delinquency.

History and Project Description

In the spring of 1974, Herman Wrice, the founder and driving force behind the Young Great Society (YGS), a West Philadelphia community development group, participated in a state-sponsored evaluation of the Cornwells Heights Youth Development Center (YDC), a juvenile training school just outside of Philadelphia. He was struck by the underutilization of the physical facilities—playing field, swimming pool, basketball courts, etc. At that time, he was beginning to look for a site for a residential summer football camp for the Giants, a football league sponsored by YGS. The previous summer he had used a

YMCA camp some thirty miles out of town which had been isolated from medical services and stores and was in general an alien setting for urban youth. Furthermore, he was identifying work sites for a Neighborhood Youth Corps (NYC) program that YGS had sponsored for the past four summers. These streams came together in an idea of using the NYC workers to fix up some of the YDC accommodations and the facility for the camp (a benefit for YGS and the YDC). Briefly, the plan was to have the NYC youth spend two weeks painting and fixing up the dormitories, then have the 200 football clinic participants move in for the four-week training camp, returning home on weekends.

It was decided that the Philadelphia Youth Development Center would be preferable to Cornwells Heights, and that site was eventually chosen. The Philadelphia YDC is housed in a former tuberculosis hospital in North Philadelphia, consisting of numerous old buildings connected by a long corridor. Many of the buildings had not been in use for some time. The YDC operated a nonresidential day treatment program in cooperation with the Philadelphia School District for about 200 youths referred by the court or the schools and also ran a smaller residential program for up to thirty adjudicated delinquents who were moved into community-based placements after a three- to five-week evaluation and planning phase.

Wrice was intrigued with the possible benefits that could be derived through the interaction of members of his football teams with both the residents of YDC and those involved in the day treatment program. He noted that while all of the groups came from similar environments, and in fact many of them grew up together, the kids in YGS seemed to find it easier to stay out of trouble, while many of those in the institution would repeatedly come into contact with the juvenile justice system as soon as they were released. He was disturbed by the widespread inability to transfer behavior practiced in institutions back to the community. For example, rival gang members who worked side-by-side in the institutions would immediately resume their rivalries when they returned to their own turf. One of the goals of the program was therefore to bring the two groups together in a meaningful way such that some of those in the Youth Development Center would get involved in programs like YGS upon their release.

On May 30, 1974, a planning session was held at Philadelphia YDC, with staff from YGS, YDC, the regional office of the Department of Public Welfare, and the authors, to go over the proposed program and to rough out a budget. By putting together components of the regular YDC program, a Neighborhood Youth Corps program, which Wrice managed, and assistance from other public and private agencies, the additional cost for the summer program was only about $20,000, most of which was picked up by YGS.

On July 1, 1974, the program actually got underway with members of YGS going daily to YDC for two weeks, during which time they were paid for painting and fixing up the unused buildings in which they would soon be residing. The following four weeks constituted the residential phase during which time YGS members stayed at the institution from Monday to Friday, going home for the weekends. A typical day for the boys in YGS consisted of an early breakfast with the other YDC residents, painting and fixing up their quarters from 9:00 A.M. to 11:00 A.M., lunch with the YDC students, football practice in the afternoon, and then football with the YDC students from around 5:00 P.M. to 7:00 P.M. One day a week, Wrice took his teams to the Cornwells Heights YDC where they could use the swimming pool and engage in athletic events with the Cornwells Heights residents.

As positive relationships began to develop between the two groups, it was decided to broaden the mingling by planning a joint picnic for all of the youths involved and their families and friends. The picnic was held on the YDC grounds on Sunday, August 4, 1974, with about 3,000 persons attending from all over the city. Significantly, the only problems were caused by members of one of the few gangs in the city who did not have any of its members participating in YGS programs.

Project Attributes

This summer project, both in its conception and in the way it was executed, exhibit the following characteristics that are scarce in the public sector in general and particularly lacking in the juvenile justice system.

Creativity: DeBono (1970) has noted that one way of coming up with a creative idea is to take things as they are and then try "reversing" them or turning them around. The idea of bringing significant numbers of community youth into a correctional setting for an extended period of time is an inversion of the concept of deinstitutionalization, moving adjudicated delinquents out of institutions and into normal community settings. It resolves a severe problem in community corrections, namely, that the corrections element always wants to use the community's facilities but rarely had much to offer in return, therefore, making the relationship more parasitical than symbiotic. The concept employed here is an interesting inversion of Jerome Miller's strategy for closing Lyman Training School in which the entire institution was suddenly transported to the University of Massachusetts for a six-week period to plan their reentry. In this particular case, a large number of youth from the community were transported into a correctional facility for four weeks. For too long, many delinquency institutions have had many resources that were of equal relevance to nondelinquent youth, but they have not had access to those resources.

Risk Taking: This project exhibited a considerable amount of risk-taking on the part of the director of the YDC and his staff, on the part of the Young Great Society, and finally on the part of many of the families of the children that were in the program. The risk-aversive norms that obtain in most bureaucratic treatment institutions protect the system from trouble. Bureaucratic systems punish administrators for errors of commission but ignore errors of omission. By contrast, as Ackoff (1970) has noted, leadership in the ghetto has the reverse orientation. For example, it is almost inconceivable in a multilayered state bureaucratic system that a manager of a local delinquency treatment program would be sanctioned for passing up an opportunity for a significantly innovative program such as the one described above. It is all too conceivable that having tried, gambled, and suffered some ill consequences that his or her career could be jeopardized. The ethic of "don't make waves," "go by the book," has given us mundane programs that are clearly unequal to the task of solving our youth problem.

Symbolic Reframing: Trist (1983) has studied a number of projects that led to revitalization of once depressed and oppressed communities. He notes that the initial condition is often a negative label that has been imposed from without on the neighborhood, group, or community and that has unconsciously often been adopted by the insiders themselves. Trist suggests that the first step is to reject the negative stereotype and reframe what has previously been regarded as a liability as an asset. In this case, we see the institution being reframed. When Herman Wrice looked at it from the point of view of a community organization in an impoverished neighborhood, he saw resources and positive potential instead of the traditional view of a stigmatizing institution that should be used only as a last resort.

Speed: The speed with which this idea was carried to its fruition is remarkable. Herman Wrice's position as a member of the Department of Public Welfare's Advisory Board gave him access to some key figures in the state administration. These connections increased the speed with which he was able to move it through and helped protect state staff at the operating levels. By operating through informal channels versus the chain of command, Wrice was able to move from the initial conversations in the spring to an operating program by July.

Contrast the speed with the usual process of developing a grant proposal, submitting it, waiting months for feedback and revisions, and finally getting the award so that it can be implemented when the next fiscal year begins. Delay between conception and execution is a major contributor to the lack of innovation in the public sector. Wildavsky and Pressman (1973) have elegantly illustrated how delay decreases the probability of implementation as opponents have increased opportunities to organize against the project. Psychologically, delay begins to create estrangement between one's actions and any ultimate outcomes. Here, speed serves to rebuild the idea that one can make a difference. An idea becomes tested in action rather than by endless discussion (see Revans 1983).

Scope and Size: A conventional approach to such an idea would be to try it out on a small scale by either having a large number of kids involved for only a few days or trying it with only a few kids at a time and seeing how it works. The problem with such pilot programs are that their scale transforms the idea and makes any smaller comparison meaningless. It is analogous to the invention of antiseptic conditions in hospitals which took well over thirty years to become accepted because it was frequently tried out in a small half-hearted way with poor results (Crichton 1970). The problem is that antisepsis can only be demonstrated on a system-wide basis and is not amenable to a case-by-case basis or small experimental design. Similarly, institutions have certain overall characteristics that cannot be broken down on a small case-by-case basis but need to be tampered with at the requisite scale, at a scale that makes the new concept an effective counterforce. It was similar thinking that led to Dr. Jerome Miller's deinstitutionalization in Massachusetts. He perceived the capacity of an institution to devour small experimentation or tinkerings, all of which was very costly and yet never could produce any long-term results. The size and length of the program prevented encapsulation. The conflicts between the YDC and YGS staff, between the youth in the football clinic and the delinquents could not be ignored but had to be worked out in a mutually satisfactory fashion. The two groups of kids had to work out a modus vivendi rather than simply ignoring one another for a short period of time and waiting until the end of the period.

Use of Multiple Resources: Because of the low budget, there was a need to link together many different sources of assistance. This turns out to be a benefit in that different people get involved, and the overall effects are more pervasive than if it was done on a single grant. Cots for the dormitories were acquired from Civil Defense. The Neighborhood Youth Corps Program paid some of the residents in the day treatment program and the summer workers in the YGS program to paint the rooms and get the dormitories fixed up for the residential phase. For the major picnic, prisoners from Holmesburg, an adult prison, did the cooking and provided much of the equipment. Many corporations provided free food and drink for the picnic. Other corporate groups donated the funds to pay for T-shirts and clothing. Families contributed a significant amount as well. Transportation was put together using available YGS resources. The physical plant of the Youth Development Centers, both the Day Treatment Center and Cornwell Heights, were used for space, etc. This reaching out for assistance illustrates a way of building involvement from a wider group in the overall program.

Potential Effects on Key Stakeholders

This section lists the various groups involved in the program and examines the ways in which their perceptions or images of themselves and each other may have been affected by their participation. As noted above, this is not based on any rigorous evaluation of the program or in-depth interviews with the persons involved. It is merely meant to suggest the potential richness of the interactions and the types of learning which could result.

Youth Development Center Staff: The child-care workers at the Youth Development Center risk becoming institutionalized just as the residents do. The routine becomes unquestioned and lives on not because it is appropriate but because of bureaucratic inertia. A sudden massive influx of persons who do not share the norms of that particular environment stands an institution on its end and can force staff to think about what they are doing and how they label and react to the youth. The top administrators at the YDC commented that the program did engender a major staff crisis and triggered useful discussions. Particularly, the youngest outsiders, eight and nine years old, were into everything and questioning rules and procedures.

YDC staff were exposed to kids right off the street who had not come through the labeling and stigmatizing court process. They saw these youth engaging in many of the same behaviors as the committed youth. This comparison helps them question the interpretative framework that is often placed on normal adolescent behavior when it occurs in an institutional setting. Whereas one kind of behavior from a Young Great Society football player is regarded as healthy exuberance, the same behavior from a court-committed client is often the occasion for a note in a file that furthers the labeling of that individual as an acting-out delinquent. Therefore, the influx of these outsiders forces YDC staff to examine their assumptions about why kids get there and what explains their behavior.

The YDC staff, although not intimately involved with the football clinic, had to cope with children over whom they have no formal authority. As a result, they may better understand how their authority shapes the kinds of relationships that can develop. For example, the outsiders protested the inclusion of liver on the menu. Delegates were appointed from each of the various groups and they made the decision not to include liver on any future menus. In the regular program, this issue would have been a more serious power struggle.

YDC staff got to see how the athletic coach and the counseling staff in the Young Great Society related to kids. In some cases, the model may be inappropriate or based on different kinds of considerations. But it does expose them to the way in which a group of peers solve essentially similar problems relating to the needs of kids. From this there was some mutual learning of different ways of handling situations.

Youth Development Center Residents: There are relatively few overnight residents at the YDC, roughly twenty at any given time. For these individuals the sudden influx of people their own age or younger is a challenging and provocative experience. They get to see kids involved in an organized activity who have managed to work through some of the problems related to the mixing of different gangs and mixing of ages, sizes, etc. They see a group of kids that have worked out some kind of a positive relationship with the YGS staff. They are perhaps able to see that joining such a program is not only for suckers. Over the four-week period a lot of the residents hunted around on the fringes and stayed aloof from the formal activities perhaps getting involved at night in pickup basketball games. However, by the end, five of the twenty had actively joined some of the teams and, after their placement in the community, had stayed involved during the season despite serious transportation problems in getting to the area of the city in which their teams played. This ultimately led to only two individuals staying with the YGS football program throughout the entire season. However, their involvement was an added benefit as it was not intended as an integral part of the program.

Young Great Society Kids: The kids who came into the program got a great deal of learning from it. They were able to experience the inner workings of a delinquency institution. They got a chance to meet with kids like themselves who have perhaps engaged in similar activities except that they were caught or their family situations were such that they were formally processed. They, therefore, begin to get some appreciation for that process and the effects it can have on one's life. Some of the older kids, particularly the counselors, get an exposure to what it might be like to pursue a career in service work, either through seeing the YGS staff work with kids or through seeing the other staff interact with the residents.

Young Great Society Staff: The program was useful to the YGS staff in allowing them to see a group of peers interacting with kids under very different kinds of conditions, and in an environment where different norms were pervasive. It also involved YGS staff in the delinquency problem and led to other YGS programs involving delinquents in a more organized fashion. YGS staff at first thought there would be more of a difference between them than there turned out to be, with most of them finally realizing that the differences were in many cases insignificant.

Families of Program Participants: The families of the kids in the YDC and YGS program both profited from the intermingling. At first, the Young Great Society parents were apprehensive over the choice of a delinquency institution and were not amused when some of the younger kids called home early on in the program and announced that they were staying in a real prison. However, over time and particularly at the picnic, they got a real sense of community and perhaps learned a considerable amount about the operations of the Youth Development Center that could lead to some future involvement there.

Conclusion

Many of our social problems have become so complex and interrelated that they create despair about the possibility of change. Wrice's ability to integrate the multiple contacts in his life, to challenge the prevailing assumptions and ways of seeing things, and to act on his vision creates a sense of the possible. Weick (1984) has developed a theory of small wins as an important element in overcoming the despair that surrounds intractable social problems. This innovation of Herman Wrice's represents just such a small win that has the potential to kindle an ongoing process of creative change that would lead to the necessary richness in our juvenile justice system for it to be responsive both to the heterogeneity of youth in trouble and their commonality with children who have not been caught up in the juvenile justice system.

Schur (1973) has articulated a contingency theory of delinquency. Youth who get into trouble are not the victims of any kind of diagnosable psychological disease or do not have any innate characteristics but rather a series of accidents that may relate to being apprehended or their behavior with the police or the particular judge that they encountered or many other kinds of situational variables. It would seem appropriate then to begin to postulate a contingency theory of treatment. Such a theory would suggest that youth do not escape delinquent careers by any known methods, that most of our techniques are unproven, and that no one treatment modality works for all delinquents or even for all of a certain type of delinquent no matter how we choose to classify them. A contingency theory of treatment might suggest that kids escape delinquent careers in much the same way as they get into them, namely, through various kinds of random happenings such as being exposed to a certain key individual, falling in love with a girl who is particularly strong, having someone close die, getting involved with yoga, developing an interest in organized athletics, being involved in community theater, and so forth. If this is the case, we pay a great price for the drab sources that characterize many delinquency programs.

This might suggest that the best strategy for a juvenile correctional system is to greatly enrich the range of opportunities available to youth in the system, while not investing a great amount of resources in any particular modality. Then allow youths and their family to have as much say as possible in choosing the sequence or combination of experiences to which they will be exposed. This is similar to Jerome Miller's strategy for devising a service delivery system for youth in state care that closely resembles the system that already exists for children in the upper middle class. Such a system would have certain similarities to the "voucher system" that has been proposed in educational settings, in that it would allow relative freedom of choice and also provide a mechanism for eliminating nonproductive alternatives.

Wrice's ability to knit resources together and to question time-honored assumptions reflects the inventiveness and risk-taking that would be required to multiply significantly the positive opportunities for youth in trouble. These characteristics also exemplify the kind of behavior that Ackoff has said is so critical for today's organizational leaders.

References

Ackoff, R. L. (1970). "A Ghetto's Research on a University." *Operational Research* 18: 761.

———. (1979). "Creativity and Corrections." Unpublished lecture notes, Management and Behavioral Science Center.

———. (1981). "The Art and Science of Mess Management." *Interfaces* 11(1): 20–26.

Crichton, M. (1970). *Five Patients: The Hospital Explained.* New York: Knopf.

DeBono, E. (1970). *Lateral Thinking: A Textbook of Creativity.* Hammondsworth, England: Penguin Books.

Gilmore, T. N., and L. Hirschhorn. (1984). "The Downsizing Dilemma: Leadership in An Age of Discontinuity." *The Wharton Annual* 8: 94–104.

Revans, R. (1983). "Action Learning: Its Origins and Nature." In Mike Pedler (ed.): *Action Learning in Practice.* New York: Gower Publishing Company, pp. 9–21.

Rittel, Horst, W. J., and M. Webber. (1973). "Dilemmas in a General Theory of Planning." *Policy Sciences* 4: 155–69.

Schur, E. M. (1973). *Radical Non-Intervention: Rethinking the Delinquency Problem.* Englewood Cliffs, N.J.: Prentice-Hall.

Trist, E. (1983). "New Directions of Hope: Recent Innovations Interconnecting Organizational, Industrial, Community and Personal Development." *Regional Studies* 13: 439–51.

Weick, K. E. (1984). "Small Wins: Redefining the Scale of Social Problems." *American Psychologist* 39(1): 40–49.

Wildavsky, A., and J. L. Pressman. (1973). *"Implementation: How Great Expectations in Washington are Dashed in Oakland."* Berkeley: University of California Press.

Section V
Planning for National
Development

The notion of creating a desirable future for many systems scientists is not confined to the actions of individuals and organizations. It becomes a global issue, one that must be addressed on a national level. For Ackoff, the ideas of progress and development rooted in the pragmatic tradition are critical to understanding and improving the societal context in which other human systems function. By viewing countries and cultures as purposeful systems, an understanding of how internal factors such as infrastructure and value systems influence practices and policies begins to emerge. Likewise, the role of environmental factors, such as political and economic conditions, can be seen to influence a country's ability to survive and thrive in the world system.

These ideas have been widely explored by systems thinkers and practitioners in settings throughout the world. Indeed, the community of systems scholars is a diverse international body. Issues concerning societal progress, especially in the less-developed countries, has long been a major topic of study and advocacy.

In this final section, several of Ackoff's colleagues reassess current approaches to planning on the national level. Ignacy Sachs and Francisco Sagasti both call for a rethinking of the development planning process in ways that will make it more systemic. Sachs sees a need for incorporating noneconomic dimensions, while Sagasti discusses the institutional support necessary to meet the turbulent socioeconomic environment of the 1980s. Chevalier, Taylor, and Carden investigate the policies guiding existing development planning organizations. They conclude that they are based on an OECD model that does not take into account the cultural diversity of the nations in which it is implemented.

In addition, several former students contribute studies focusing on the application of Ackoff's ideas in actual development planning projects. W. E. Smith discusses the political aspects of development project evaluation carried on at the World Bank. Paramjit Sachdeva discusses potential contributions of the interactive planning process to development projects. This is followed by Jaime Jimenez's account of the application of this participative planning paradigm in rural Mexico.

Chapter 24
The Elusive Interdisciplinarity
of Development Planning

Ignacy Sachs

"I don't know what you mean by glory," Alice said.

Humpty-dumpty smiled contemptuously. "Of course you don't till I tell you. I mean there is a nice knockdown argument for you."

"But glory doesn't mean a nice knockdown argument," Alice objected.

"When I use the word," Humpty-dumpty said in a rather scornful tone, "it means just what I choose it to mean, neither more nor less."

"The question is," said Alice, "whether you can make words mean so many different things."

This passage from *Alice Through the Looking Glass* [1] conveys the present state of development studies. All the parties concerned use the same words to convey different meanings. The confusion becomes inescapable when well-meaning scholars from different social sciences decide to give a show of interdisciplinarity by sitting around the same table, as if it could be achieved by mere juxtaposition of disciplines.

Since 1980, the world economy has been in the throes of the most severe crisis since the Great Depression. The final statement of UNCTAD (United Nations Commission on Trade and Development) VI rightly stresses that this is a crisis in which the deeper underlying problems of a structural and systemic nature have been compounded by cyclical factors. The burden of the crisis has fallen most heavily on Third-World countries. The response of international institutions to the challenge thus posed has been up to now utterly disappointing. Even more so have been the policies followed by the industrialized countries and the banking system. The official stance taken by the

United States is that the reactivation of the growth process in the industrialized countries will trickle down to the Third World and bring prosperity to all the parties concerned. In the meantime, all forms of pressure are being used to force Third-World countries to take on their shoulders the entire burden of adjustment policies, even though the configuration of exorbitantly high interest rates, depressed commodity prices, and rampant protectionism in industrialized countries makes this an impossible task.[2] The high conditionality imposed by the International Monetary Fund (IMF) means in practical terms a further slowdown of the economy monitoring unemployment, falling real wages, and deindustrialization. Albert Bressand is right to say that the IMF conditionality is based on principles of sound short-term management of finances, while The World Bank conditionality aims at ensuring the proper implementation of individual projects. However, neither can be considered to meet the criteria of "conditionality for development."[3]

No wonder that the neoclassical and monetarist theories, on which the IMF policy package is based, have been subject to devastating criticism on part of a growing number of Third-World scholars and politicians. The economic profession is deeply split on this issue between neoclassicists and structuralists. The dialogue between the two camps, postulated by Paul Streeten,[4] does not look promising. The cleavage is too fundamental to be bridged.

Under the circumstances, it is difficult to pretend that development economics, in particular, and economics, in general, constitute a scientific discipline with a consensual hard core, accepted by all scholars and practitioners. In matter of fact, the scope and status of development economics is open to discussion.

Reflecting on the rise and decline of development economics, Albert Hirschman attributed its short-lived success to its heterogeneous ideological makeup and over-ambitious promise.[5] The ideological diversity may have been even greater than his essay suggests.[6] On the other hand, both the "monoeconomists" (i.e., the neoclassical economists who believe in the universality of their theory), the development economists, and even some Marxists and neo-Marxists, i.e., all the four categories in Hirschman's suggestive typology (Figure 24.1) shared in common the belief that development would come as the result of rapid economic growth. They were all guilty, in different degrees, of economic reductionism, even though they would not all subscribe to the "trickle-down" theory. A linear interpretation of history, be it in the form of Rostovian stages of growth or of the succession of modes of production as described in the Marxist vulgata, prevailed on both sides of the ideological barricade.

Two typologies of development theories

A.

Types of development theories		
	Monoeconomics claim:	
	asserted	*rejected*
Mutual-benefit claim: *asserted*	Orthodox economics	Development economics
rejected	Marx?	Neo-Marxist theories

B.

A tentative summary of orientations in development theory.

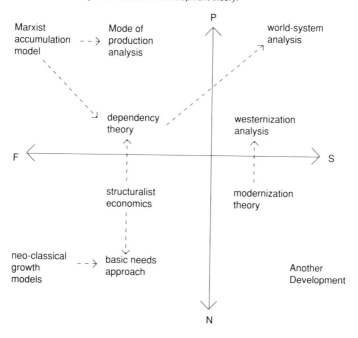

Figure 24.1. Two typologies of development theories: *A*, Hirschman (op. cit., p. 3; reprinted courtesy of Cambridge University Press); *B*, Hettne (op. cit., p. 240; reprinted courtesy of Longman Group UK).

The universalization of development theory

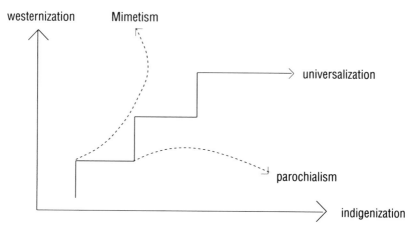

Figure 24.2. The universalization of development theory. From Hettne (op. cit., p. 242; reprinted courtesy of Longman Group UK).

The specificity of development economies, for those who admitted it, was the reflection of a different stage of growth, as compared with the developed countries today. The problem was then how to find a shortcut toward the stage already reached by the industrialized countries, which model to choose to become a new Japan, Soviet Union, or China, according to one's ideological preference. Implicit in this view was the virtue of mimetism. The concept of endogenous development emerged only in the seventies and does not enjoy, as yet, the favor of academe.[7] Only a minority of Western scholars would admit with Lisa Peattie that "the developed world is not a model; it is a group of peoples that have taken more than their share and have used it carelessly."[8] The challenge is then for the Third-World countries to find an original path refusing both the mimetism and the parochialism, transcending the Western paradigm and the indigenous values to give new embodiment to the universal aspirations of humanity. This point is suggestively made in Figure 24.2, from Hettne (op. cit., p. 242).

We know today that growth (and for that matter modernization) is not necessarily synonymous with development. It can be virtuous or perverse, bring about genuine social development or else maldevelopment, with the attendant social distortions and predatory patterns of resource use. In the latter case, the higher the rate of growth through inequality, the higher are its social and ecological costs.[9] Part of the present crisis involves the accumulated social and ecological costs for three decades of savage growth. The mere fact of externalizing them did not mean that they would vanish.

The criticism of using the conventional gross national product (GNP) as a yardstick of development has been aptly summarized by Robert Heilbroner: "Conventional GNP includes outputs that are malign, useless, or simply 'defensive'—war goods, superfluous advertising, or expenditures required to counteract the damage inflicted on the environment by the act of production itself. Meanwhile, GNP ignores the output of nonmarket services, including the work performed by housewives and the consumption of leisure." [10] No wonder that one of the most influential books of the last decade deals with the social limits to growth,[11] while an extensive and often polemical literature has developed around the environmental dimension of economic activity and the need to harmonize in the process of development social, economic, and ecological objectives.[12] Ecodevelopment stands for a socially desirable, ecologically sustainable, and economically viable development.[13]

The new environmental awareness has brought into the fore the concept of quality of life and, with it, a holistic conceptualization of development goals, and development styles that owes much to cultural anthropology and calls for new approaches based on human ecology and the concept of time-spaces of development (Figure 24.3).[14]

With "quality of life" we move clearly into the realm of "moral or-

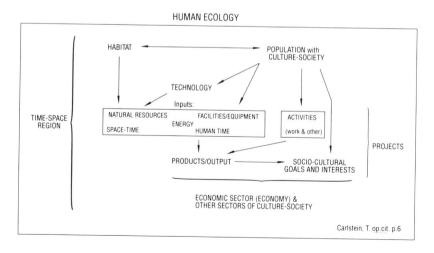

Figure 24.3. Human Ecology.

der." Hirschman's final chapter of *Essays in Trespassing* deals with morality and the social sciences and visualizes "a kind of social science that would be very different from the one most of us have been practicing: a moral social science where moral considerations are not repressed or kept apart, but are systematically commingled with analytic argument, without guilt feelings over any lack of integration, where the transition from preaching to proving and back again is performed frequently and with ease; and where moral considerations need no longer be smuggled in surreptitiously, not expressed unconsciously, but are displayed openly and disarmingly."[15] Exit economics; political economy is restored to its original preeminence. In a sense, institutionalists[16] and "open" Marxists, such as O. Lange or M. Kalecki,[17] are vindicated. So are those exceptional thinkers like Gandhi or Lebret who built their total development concept around the "human ascent," i.e., "the ascent of all men in their integral humanity, including the economic, biological, psychological, social, cultural, ideological, spiritual, mystical, and transcendental dimensions."[18] People do not live by bread alone. However, it is not enough to merely substitute ethics for an analysis of economic relations.[19] The political economy of development has both a normative and a substantive aspect.

The *retour aux sources* outlined above has deep epistemological consequences. Vijai Pillai traced back the methodological assumptions underlying conventional development thinking to a love affair with the scientific worldview that predominated from the seventeenth to the end of the nineteenth century. Its central tenets are reductionist and originate from Galileo's conviction that the Book of Nature was inscribed in mathematical characters.[20] As a result, the concept of social well-being is mechanistic and summative. A single linear causality between input and output is assumed with no regard to the social configurations in which the process is taking place. Pillai sees an analogy between this kind of analysis and the stimulus response model in mechanistic physiology. He then criticizes the attempts to apply the engineering-systems approach to development problems. It is bound to fail to the extent to which it is a closed system technique. "Now, the point about open systems, such as any given society, is that the interlinkages and blendings of various elements are so closely knit that they cannot be assigned orders of precedences. There is no way of judging what is 'relevant' and what is not."[21] This brings us back to the ideological stream of development thinking and the realm of values, the need for a new mythos (which is also an ethos and to some extent an aesthetic).

The realm of the political economy of development is situated a long way from elegant deductive models that account for most of the academic production in economics in Western universities and their doubles in the Third World. Fortunately enough, the dismal situation prevailing at present in economics is being challenged of late from within.

The main criticism develops on two fronts: the need to go back to systematic empirical inquiry in order to advance the understanding of the structure and the operations of the real economic systems,[22] and even more importantly, to recognize the limits of the economic science. The basic questions of our time, aggravated by the crisis, involve nothing less than the goals and the workings of the political and social system of the capitalist world. As Joan Robinson puts it, "they cannot be decided by economic theory, but it would be decent, at least, if the economists admitted that they do not have an answer to them."[23]

Hirschman's diagnosis on the decline of development economies rests on its pretense to slay the dragon of backwardness by itself ignoring or, at least, severely underestimating the challenge posed by dismal politics.[24]

What does political science have to say about development? From a planner's perspective neither the theories of revolution nor the theories of modernization, sharply criticized by the "dependency" school of thought fare significantly better than development economics. A contribution to the political economy of development can be expected from what Lindberg calls the "institutional disciplines": the central traditions in political science, organizational and historical sociology, and institutional economics.[25] The condition, however, is to broaden the field of analysis going beyond the discussion of the state and of the economic institutions so as to bring into the picture the civil society.[26]

The above considerations lead to three conclusions:

1. Development is clearly a multidimensional concept.
2. None of the monodisciplinary approaches has yielded satisfactory results.
3. A restructuring of the development paradigm is called for, debunking the conventional development economics and transcending the mystifying distinction between economic and noneconomic factors introduced in a simplified, if not caricatural, way into formal deductive models.

What matters is the elegance of the model; the ability to quantify becomes the criterion of relevance. Yet, as Celso Furtado rightly points out, "the more refined such models become, the larger the distance that separates them from the multidimensionality of the social reality."[27] The same author, a leading development economist, maps out the developmental field in the following way:

> For a long time the universally prevailing idea was that development is something quantifiable, supported by accumulation, investment, creation of productive capacity. However, experience has clearly shown that genuine development consists in a process of activation and channeling of social forces, increasing the peoples' capacity to associate themselves, to take initiatives, to show inventiveness. This is, therefore, a social and cultural process in which the economic aspect is only subsidiary. Development occurs when the society displays the energy capable of channeling in a convergent way the latent or dispersed forces.[28]

An interdisciplinary effort is the obvious answer to this challenge. But how to achieve it?

One way of not doing it, already mentioned, is by postulating some simple additive property of the social sciences. Adding one anthropologist or sociologist to a team of hard-nosed economists and engineers will be of no use, at least as long as the economists do not lose their arrogance and learn how to benefit from anthropological studies. The chances are pretty large that the anthropologist *de service* will introduce some innocuous considerations in the team's report, cautioning the recommendations reached on the basis of conventional economic wisdom. Judging by the experience of some international organizations and lending agencies, paying lip service to interdisciplinarity may be the easiest way to protect the monodisciplinary approach and the dominant position of conventional development economists.

Poles opposed to this conservative dynamism of traditional disciplines is the postulate of transcending them by means of creating a kind of integrative all-embracing metascience. Three Latin American scholars attributed the failure of the unified approach to planning to the lack of a unified social science: "A unified approach to development worthy of the name supposes a unified social science, which does not exist at present and which could only be constructed on certain philosophical postulates, derived from a general theory, which in turn could not count on general support for a long time to come."[29] Clearly such a course does not seem operationally viable in either the short or the long run.

Willy-nilly, however deceptive may have been up to now the experience analyzed by M. Wolfe, in spite of the elusive interdisciplinarity of development, we must strive to evolve some kind of unified approach to planning because interdisciplinarity really matters at this action-oriented level.

For inspiration we may turn to the integrative disciplines: history and ecology. Comparative studies with a historical perspective, as suggested by Marshall Wolfe provide the best crunch for our feeble social imagination, on the condition of not looking into history in order to find replicable models but, on the contrary, scrutinizing it for anti-models to be transcended. Two qualifications are in order here. The historian tries to interpret the past (or present) in order to understand it; the planner has the ambition of making history by promoting desirable transformations. He or she cannot help but be committed; the only planning worthy of its name is advocacy planning. On the other hand, the history that makes sense to the planner is *total history* of the kind produced by the *École des Annales* or open-minded Marxists.

As Eric Hobsbawn puts it, "Historians are by definition concerned with complex and changing ensembles and even their most specific and narrowly defined questions may make sense only within this context."[30] So are the planners.[31] "In this respect history resembles disciplines like ecology, though it is wider and more complex. While we can and must single out particular strands from the seamless web of interactions, if we were not interested primarily in the web itself we should not be doing ecology or history."[32]

Historians draw on many scientific disciplines, but history as such does not belong to the group of nomothetic social sciences. It is also part of humanities and arts. It differs in this from ecology, even though both are integrative disciplines, as distinct from interdiscipline studies, since they deal with supraindividual levels of organization.[33] Planning like history, albeit for different reasons, is in many respects, a soft discipline. Variant thinking[34] on society's values, goals, and means is too complex an affair to be subject to optimization, the more so if one refuses to treat people as if they were Pavlovian dogs; even higher mammals have a nonreductionist and nonmaximizing behavior.[35] Planning must build on the study of substantive and procedural rationality,[36] i.e., an *anthropological economics*, a discipline yet to be created. The planner's role is to prepare, inform, and organize the political decision-making processes and to ensure that suboptimizations are entered whenever possible.

Like an ecologist, the planner ought to take a global and fairly long-term view of development processes, but his or her usefulness will be evaluated by the capacity to influence a myriad of local and time-bounded decisions. The institutional problematique looms large here.

The above view of planning as the locus for the integrative elaboration of the development concept has little to do with actual planning, as we know it today. What should be done to put it one day into practice?

The dismal record of the quest for a unified approach does not allow any easy optimism. We can at best move slowly into the right direction by making the necessary changes in the way planners are being trained and recruited. Drawing from a limited experience of joint work between economists and environmental scientists, T. C. Koopmans pointed out the need to cultivate the skill in communication between disciplines. A beginning should be made by defusing the jargon. However, a more serious problem is that the universities do not seem to be the best place for gaining experience in interdisciplinary intervention.[37] The latter is in reality a mild understatement. A radical change in the teaching curricula and the widest opening of universities to real development problems of the surrounding societies are a precondition of any serious attempt at restructuring the development paradigm on an interdisciplinary basis. In one of my visits to Mexico, the students presented me with a poster featuring a shantytown right in front of the modern university building. The caption reads: "Reality is around the corner. The universities should deal with the problems of the societies that pay for them." This poster is quite a program.

Notes

1. Quoted by Chakravarthi Raghavan, IPS/IFDA Special correspondent at UNCTAD VI in a dispatch (dated June 25, 1983) on the strenuous efforts deployed in Belgrade to arrive at a final statement acceptable to all participants of this conference.

2. Compare the following assesment of the situation made by an outstanding Indian student of international finance: "I would submit that the position as it has evolved, particularly over the past three years, on the world economic scene is particularly ominous for the developing countries, more so for low-income countries, in that on pain of inaccessibility to external finance to cover their payments deficits they are being asked to shoulder the entire burden of corrective adjustment action even though it is generally accepted that the major part of the payments deficits which have currently emerged, have little to do with the domestic economic policies of those countries and are entirely attributable to extraneous circumstances," I. S. Gulati (1983). "International Finance. Asymmetries, Old and New," *Economic and Political Weekly*, 18(11): 895.

3. *RAMSES 82*, sous la direction d'Albert Bressand, 1982, IFRI-Economica, Paris, p. 178. For a critical analysis of the IMF conditionality, see I. S. Gulati, *op. cit.* and Sidney Dell (1982), "Stabilization: The Political Economy of Overkill," *World Development* 10(8): 597–612.

4. P. Streeten (1982), Development Dichotomies, Center for Asian Development Studies, Boston University, Discussion Paper, Number 17, Boston.

5. A. O. Hirschman, *Essays in Trespassing, Economics to Politics and Beyond* (Cambridge: Cambridge University Press, 1981), pp. 1–24.

6. For a critical review of new trends, off-Broadway and off-off-Broadway, see M. Wolfe, "Preconditions and Propositions for 'Another Development,'" *CEPAL Review* (vol. 3, second half 1977), and the pioneering book by B. Hettne, *Development Theory and the Three Worlds*, (London: Longman Scientific and Technical, 1990).

7. See in particular *What Now*, the 1975 Dag Hammarskjöld Report prepared on the occasion of the Seventh Special Session of the United Nations General Assembly, Uppsala; and I. Sachs, "Le Potentiel de développement endogène," *Cahiers de l'ISMEA* (1983).

8. L. Peattie, *Thinking about Development* (New York: Plenum Press, 1981), p. 30.

9. See I. Sachs (in press), "Développement ou maldéveloppement? Plaidoyer pour une économie qualitative" (Paris: EHESS/CIRED). *Science Economique et Développement endogène* (Paris: UNESCO).

10. R. L. Heilbroner (1977), "The False Promise of Growth," *The New York Review of Books*, 24(3, March 3).

11. F. Hirsch, *Social Limits to Growth*. (Cambridge, Harvard University Press, 1976).

12. Compare the following excerpt from R. Kothari (1981), "On Eco-imperialism," *Alternatives VII*, pp. 385–94: "There are two types of ecologists. There is, first, the eco-development school of ecologists who are concerned with making development both environmentally viable and socially equitable. Believing in the possibility of a steady, sustainable process of development for all within the outer as well as the inner limits of growth, they are convinced that a properly conceived model of development can reverse the structural characteristics of the present pattern of distribution of resources and power that is responsible for both maldevelopment of affluent societies and the underdevelopment of poverty-ridden societies. There is another school of ecology which believes in conservation pure and simple; it shows little or no regard either for the causes underlying the mindless ravaging of the environment by today's runaway technology, or for the need for the kind of planning for the future, which while providing for the basic necessities of all, would also ensure an ecologically sustainable strategy of growth. Neither is there much regard, in this school, for issues of equity and distribution. Indeed, it sees in these concepts the danger of further spoliation of nature consequent upon new demands made by the hitherto poor and underprivileged, who would feel encouraged to multiply without restraint. Such a growth in population of the poor in its view, will so overload the 'carrying capacity' of the earth that human survival itself will be at stake."

13. See I. Sachs, *Stratégies de l'écodéveloppement*, (Paris: Éditions Économie et Humanisme et les Éditions ouvrières, 1980); Hettne, op. cit.; and M. Wolfe (1982), "Elusive Development: The Quest for a Unified Approach to Development Analysis and Planning," *CEPAL Review*, August.

14. See Lisa Peattie, op. cit.; T. Carlstein, *Time Resources, Society and Ecology*, vol. 1, (London: George Allen and Unwin, 1982); I. Sachs (1980), "Styles de vie et planification," *Revue canadienne d'études du développement*, 1(2) and (1980), "Les Temps-espaces du développment," *Diogène* 112(October–December), and for the application of the concept of development styles, *The CEPAL Review*, passim.

15. Hirschman, op. cit., pp. 305–6.

16. For a contemporary definition of institutionalism, see K. W. Kapp (1968), "In Defense of Institutional Economics," *Swedish Journal of Economics*

70(1): 1–18, and G. Myrdal (1977), "The Meaning and Validity of Institutional Economics," in *Economics in Institutional Perspective*, ed. Rolf Steppacher, Brigitte Zogg-Walz, and Hermann Hatzfeld (Lexington, Mass.: Lexington Books), pp. 3–10.

17. See I. Sachs (1977), "Kalecki and Development Planning," *Oxford Bulletin of Economics and Statistics*, 39(1, February): 12–41.

18. D. Goulet (1980), "Development Experts: The One-Eyed Giants," *World Development* 8: 482.

19. For an assessment of Gandhi, see I. Sachs (1977), "Gandhi and Development," *Seminar* (New Delhi) 219(November): 16–21.

20. V. Pillai (1982), "Approaches to Development: A Critique," *Alternatives* 8(3, September): 372.

21. Ibid.

22. See in particular the devastating letter on academic economics, by W. Leontief (1982) in *Science* 217(4555, July 19): 104–5. Another Nobel prize winner, H. A. Simon, has the following to say on qualitative analysis in economics: "As economics expands beyond its central core of price theory, and its central concern with quantities of commodities and money, we observe in it this same shift from a highly quantitative analysis, in which equilibration at the margin plays a central role, to a much more qualitative institutional analysis, in which discrete structural alternatives are compared." (1978), "Rationality as Process and as Product of Thought," *The American Economic Review* 68(2, May): 6.

23. J. Robinson (1977), "What Are the Questions?" *Journal of Economic Literature* 15(4): 1337. At a more fundamental level, explored by K. Polanyi, it appears that instead of seeking in economics the meaning of social totality, we rather ought to seek in the social totality the meaning for us of economics. See L. Dumont's preface to the French translation of K. Polanyi's major work (1983), *La Grande Transformation* (Paris: Gallimard), p. xvi.

24. Hirschman, op. cit., p. 23.

25. L. Lindberg, "Economists as Policy Intellectuals and Economics as a Policy Profession," Paper prepared for the Twelfth World Congress of the International Political Science Association, Rio de Janeiro, August 1982, p. 23.

26. See on this point "The Third System Project," *IFDA Dossier 17*, May/June 1980. P. L. Berger (1974) makes the same point in a slightly different way by emphasizing the need for institutional innovation in the realm of *intermediate structures* between the modern state (be it capitalist or socialist) and the undifferentiated mass of uprooted individuals ("Pyramids of Sacrifice," Harmondsworth, England: Penguin Books, p. 14.). An excellent agenda for research in the political sciences of development is provided by Soedjatmoko (1983), "Political Systems and Development in the Third World: New Directions for Social Science Research in Asia," *Alternatives* 8(4, Spring): 483–99.

27. C. Furtado (1975), "El desarrollo desde el punto de vista interdisciplinario," *El Trimestre Economico* 46(1, January–March): 12.

28. C. Furtado (1982), "A Nova dependencia, divida externa e monetarisme," *Paz e Terra*, 149.

29. A. E. Solari, R. France, and J. Jutkowitz (1976), "Teoria, accion y desarrollo en America Latina," *Siglo XXI* 21: 621, quoted by M. Wolfe, 1982, op. cit., p. 41.

30. E. Hobsbawn (1981), "Historical Predictions," *Populi* 8(2): 42.

31. Compare the following statement by Joan Robinson (op. cit., p. 1319):

"In economics, questions cannot be isolated because every aspect of human society interacts with every other; hypotheses can be put forward only in the form of a 'model' of the whole economy."

32. Hobsbawn, op. cit.

33. Compare E. P. Odum (1977), "The Emergence of Ecology as a New Integrative Discipline," *Science* 195(4284, March 25): 1289–92.

34. The most concise definition of planning equated with variant thinking is M. Kalecki's.

35. See G. Bateson, *Steps into the Ecology of Mind* (Saint Albans, Vt.: Paladin, 1973).

36. See Simon, op. cit.

37. T. C. Koopmans (1979), "Economics Among the Sciences," *American Economic Review* 69(1, March): 13.

Chapter 25
National Development Planning in Turbulent Times: New Approaches and Criteria for Institutional Design

Francisco R. Sagasti

> Politics has been defined as the art of the possible. . . . Planning should be the art and science of the impossible.
> —Russell Ackoff

Introduction

This chapter examines some of the recent developments in the fields of planning theory and practice, focusing on the need for new institutional approaches to deal with long-term development issues. It has been motivated by the realization that, despite more than three decades of development planning efforts, most planning exercises appear to be rather isolated from the main concerns of policy and decision makers in developing countries. Furthermore, as the crisis of the early 1980s took its toll on economic growth, as the international context for development cooperation deteriorated rapidly, as the pace of scientific and technological change accelerated, and as the result of three United Nations International Development Decades appear disappointing, the need to reexamine development objectives and to reassess the prospects for developing countries has become increasingly clear. As a consequence, the once remote ideas of long-term planning and of futures research have acquired a new sense of urgency.

The main characteristic of planning is its concern with the future. Planning is a process directed toward guiding social change and generating a sequence of socially desirable future events by taking action at present. Future situations are conditioned not only by the present state of affairs or by a single event at some intermediate time between "now" and "then"; on the contrary, they are the result of a series of interrelated events and social processes that have taken place in the past, are happening at present, and will extend into the future. Moreover, note that the idea of socially desirable sequences of anticipated events is likely to change as the ever-shifting present transforms the future into the past. In addition, the process of imagining the future improves our understanding of the present and of the past; in this sense, the conception of future events and situations helps in actual decision-making tasks (Morin 1981).

In abstract terms, planning can be thought of as "anticipatory decision making." The generation of a sequence of socially desirable future events can be viewed as a process whereby decisions are made in advance and courses of action are selected in a series of interrelated situations that have not yet occurred but are envisioned to happen sometime in the future (Ackoff 1970, Sagasti 1973a and 1973b, Gharajedaghi and Ackoff 1986). This conceptualization highlights four important aspects of the planning process: first, its close relation to decision making, for anticipatory decisions may be considered the building blocks of planning; second, its orientation toward the future, for it seeks to shape events yet to come by taking anticipatory decisions at present; third, the transformation of anticipatory decisions that have the "putty-like" character of things to be done into actual decisions that have the "pottery-like" character of things done; and fourth, the continuous revision of anticipatory decisions which, as time advances, become actual decisions and slide rapidly into the realm of the past.

In this light a *plan* would consist of statements spelling out the anticipatory decisions, their interrelations, and the criteria employed in making them. A *planning methodology* would refer to the procedures followed in arriving at the commitments made in advance and to the ways in which actual decisions to be taken at present are derived from them. The total span of time covered in the planning process, i.e., how far it looks into the future, is the *planning horizon*. Finally, *national development planning* is the process concerned with guiding social change, with generating a sequence of desirable events and with making anticipatory decisions with reference to the future evolution of a country and with deriving present-day decisions from them.

There are many theories, ideologies, and perspectives on the process of development, but—with the exception of some extreme views that refuse to accept any social guidance but that provided by "market forces"—all of them consider a role for anticipatory decision making at some level of society. But even those extreme pro-market views must take into account that government intervention is required in order to establish and operate markets for factors of production and for goods and services and that individual agents and firms make anticipatory decisions in response to market signals. For example, Polanyi (1944) has showed how purposeful government intervention was necessary to establish national markets for land and labor in nineteenth-century England, and even economists who argue against state intervention in general agree that government action is required for the market to function effectively (Bauer 1984).

In short, as Myrdal (1970, p. 709) has described it, the basic ideology of planning is "essentially rationalist in approach and interventionist in conclusions. It is committed to the belief that development can be brought about or accelerated by government intervention." Nevertheless, this point is by no means universally accepted at present. Disenchanted with the planning experience of the last thirty years, some analysts are proposing a radical reappraisal of the planning ideology. For example, referring mostly to the Latin American experience, Zuzunaga (1986) has argued that "planning was an effort at rationality . . . in a world that has been and will continue to be irrational. . . . All our interest in rational planning, or in any other type of rationality, is a gigantic deception."

A Brief Background to National Development Planning

The roots of the current approaches to development planning extend back at least into the late 1940s and early 1950s. The work of Manheim (1940 and 1953) on freedom and planning, the Eastern European and Soviet experiences with central planning (Kantorovich 1965, Marczewski 1958, Lange 1949), the French indicative planning approach (Perroux 1961, Bauchet 1967, Meynaud 1963, Caire 1967), and the work of economists like Clark (1951), Kuznets (1941), and Lange (1961) set the stage for subsequent efforts. Development planning as a distinct area of concern was clearly formulated in the 1950s with the publication of a United Nations (1951) report on measures to promote economic development and with the work of leading economists such as Myrdal (1957), Prebisch (1953), and Hirschman (1958).

Since the early 1960s development planning has become an accepted practice in most developing countries (South Magazine 1985). What may be called the "conventional approach" to planning envisages the establishment of a central government planning agency; the formulation and implementation of global short-term (1–2 years), medium-term (2–5 years) and long-term (more than 5 years) plans; the disaggregation of the global plans into sectorial components according to the ministerial structure of the government; and the introduction of a geographical dimension by assigning responsibilities for projects to regional authorities. Implementation is supposed to take place by linking short-term global, sectorial, and regional plans to the budgetary process; by associating medium-term plans with the evaluation of investment projects; and by ensuring the commitment of political authorities to the development objectives specified in the long-term plans. Finally, plans are supposed to be revised periodically—usually on a yearly basis—updating them to incorporate new information.

Although this characterization of the conventional approach to planning is sketchy, it captures the main features of the proposals put forward by the leading figures in development planning during the 1960s, including Tinbergen (1964 and 1967), Lewis (1968), ILPES (1966), and Waterson (1965).

With financial and technical support from the United Nations, international development banks, bilateral development assistance agencies, and national governments, as well as from academic centers both in developed and developing countries, this concept of development planning was widely disseminated throughout the Third World during the late 1950s and early 1960s. Most developing countries established planning agencies and began to prepare plans earnestly, often as a result of requests from international funding agencies.

However, even as early as the late 1960s and early 1970s, there emerged some doubts about the effectiveness of the conventional approach to development planning. For example, Gross (1967) edited a volume in which he emphasized the need for "activating" national plans by transforming them into an integral part of a social learning process, and criticized the practice of planning that was directed at the elaboration of unattainable pies in the sky. Around the same time, the Organization of American States (1969) attributed the failure of planning in Latin America to the "conventional view of planning which emphasizes the plan as a collection of documents."

In addition, other authors were pointing out the limitations of development planning from some specific point of view. Pajetska and Sachs (1970) focused on the shortcomings of the process of implementation, particularly in the industrial sector; Hirschman (1967) criticized the emphasis on comprehensive planning and favored sector-specific plans linked to investment programs; Kornai (1970) advocated a move away from "fatalistic planning" and "planning as a special case of conventional decision theory" and into a more realistic "process of cognition and compromise"; and Griffin and Enos (1970) sought to provide a catalogue of practical tools and methods for development planners.

Probably one of the best early reviews of the theory and experience of development planning is found in the two volumes edited by Faber and Seers (1972). They observed the need for a shift away from an emphasis on the preparation of plans and on economic growth toward the execution of plans and the consideration of social objectives. They also indicated that the conventional approach to planning assumed the existence of political stability, economic certainties, political will, and administrative capabilities to carry out the plans. Needless to say, these assumptions seldom obtained in most developing countries.

During the 1970s Latin America was probably the developing region where the theory and practice of planning was most thoroughly scrutinized. Cibotti and Bardecci (1972) examined the ineffectiveness of planning organizations in Latin American countries and studied the different rationalities of planners, politicians, and bureaucrats. Cardoso (1972) dealt with the Brazilian experience and focused on the political realities that constrained the practice of development planning, an issue that Killick (1976) examined in a broader context. Solari and coworkers (1976) offered a thorough review of planning in Latin America by examining the different schools of thought that emerged, following their evolution, and contrasting the theoretical contributions with the achievements in practice. In a more radical vein, Zuzunaga (1977) dismissed all development planning efforts, stating that "planning is not useful for change" and that social advance "never takes place as a result of previous planning."

An interesting concept introduced during the 1970s was the idea of a "unified approach" to development and planning. The United Nations' (1971) International Development Strategy for the Second Development Decade called for a comprehensive and integrated view of development and emphasized social considerations that went beyond traditional economic concerns. This had important implications for planning, and the large number of studies and reports produced as a result of the new line of work sponsored by the United Nations introduced new ideas such as that of "development styles." One of the key issues that these efforts highlighted was the fact that the state is not a monolithic entity capable of choosing and following a single well-defined course of action, and that competing interest groups, political pressures, and international constraints intrude upon the process of development planning.

However, Solari and coworkers (1976) argued that such a unified approach to development and planning would first require a "unified social theory" and a "unified theory of development," two clearly unattainable intellectual utopias. Wolfe (1980 and 1982) reviewed the attempts to develop a unified approach, pointing out that those efforts left "something intact in the aspiration for rationally planned action" but that it is now necessary to transcend the "image of the State as a rational, coherent and benevolent entity," replacing it by a "more realistic frame of reference for policy-oriented interpretation of what the State does or evades doing, why, and how."

Two additional reviews of the national development planning experience have reiterated the shortcomings of the conventional approach to planning and have added a few others. After examining more than 500 projects oriented toward improving planning capabilities in developing countries, the United Nations Development Program (1979) concluded that "the strengthening of a self-reliant planning capacity is a process that requires much longer than was supposed until now." Mendez (1980) examined twenty years of development planning in Latin America identifying several different planning styles and emphasizing once more the need to move away from the concept of planning as aimed at producing "plans," and toward visualizing "planning as a process."

A further in-depth analysis of the past experience and future perspectives on planning in Latin America by Garcia D'Acuna (1982) revealed the serious problems that the concepts and practice of development planning are experiencing in the 1980s:

> The analysis of the Latin American experience leads us to conclude that while there were periods and instances in which planning played a significant role in orienting the development process in Latin America, it definitely did not manage to insert itself in the real process of decision making and of shaping economic policy. As a result, this led to the stagnation of the idea of planning, to skepticism regarding the possible contributions of planners and to a growing institutional disintegration. (p. 26)

Similar views have been advanced in the early 1980s by De Mattos (1981), Giordani and colleagues (1981), and Hodara (1983).

Finally, in his review of the planning experience of developing countries, Aggarwala (1983 and 1985) identifies three approaches to planning: comprehensive, as practiced by the centrally planned economies of Eastern Europe and some developing countries; indicative, as practiced by several Southern Asian and francophone African countries; and ritual, as practiced by several Latin American and

African countries. He concludes that the experience acquired during the last three decades indicates the importance of transcending the ritual approach to planning and of the "need to reorient efforts from the comprehensive planning of production to the planning of strategic policies." This involves striking a balance between analytical techniques and qualitative judgments, establishing and managing price and incentive systems, and harmonizing the requirements for widespread consultation with flexibility and rapid response capacity; in short, the need to adopt a "learning systems" approach to the planning process.

Thus, in spite of its shortcomings and problems of the last three decades, the idea of development planning during the 1980s is still generally accepted, as a review of national development plans in more than seventy Third-World countries clearly shows (South Magazine 1986). The belief in the possibility of rational intervention to guide national development remains in full force, although it has become clear that many changes are necessary in the conventional approach to development planning.

A Dilemma of Development Planning

The evolution of national development planning theory and practice has been accompanied by the emergence of several concerns that can be expressed in the form of "fundamental dilemmas." For example, issues such as "comprehensive versus sectorial planning" (Hirschman 1958) and "central planning versus market order" (Bauer 1984) have caught the attention of planning practitioners and theoreticians at different times. Even though it is clear that in reality these dilemmas do not present mutually exclusive choices, they have served as useful conceptual tools to focus the debate, to organize discussions, and to clarify the options faced in national development planning.

From this perspective, among the many persistent concerns that have remained on the agenda of development planning, this chapter focuses on two that merit special attention, both because planners and politicians refer frequently to them and because of their profound implications for the planning process. On the one hand, there is the preoccupation with the implementation of development plans, with influencing actual decision making and with having an impact on the "real world" of power struggles and political choices. On the other hand, there is the preoccupation with the ongoing problems, with generating long-term visions and ideals, with a desired outcome whose attainment is seen as being distant in time, with providing an overall direction to the development process, and with searching for new paths and ideas to transcend the limitations that characterize Third-World countries.

Putting these two sets of concerns together, it is possible to identify what may be considered as another "fundamental dilemma" that has emerged in the practice of planning. By paraphrasing statements that are often made by persons in authority in Third-World countries, this dilemma can be stated rather simply: *the more "relevant" or "practical" planning becomes, the farther it moves away from the central long-term issues and concerns that are crucial for the future development of a country.*

In order to avoid the "ivory-tower syndrome," i.e., the perceived isolation of the planning agencies from the centers of power—which are usually associated with day-to-day actual decision making—the heads of planning agencies have frequently sought to link their activities as closely as possible to the process of decision making at operational ministries and government agencies. This has inevitably led to power struggles over issues such as the responsibility for the allocation of financial resources through the national budget, in which the planning agency is usually pitted against the ministries of economics and finance; the responsibility for evaluating and approving investment projects, in which the planning agency confronts most government departments and public enterprises; and over responsibility for the evaluation of the performance of regional and sectorial government agencies, organizations, and departments, in which the planning agency faces virtually all the rest of the government apparatus. Additional conflicts are likely to emerge when the planning agency also plays the role of "technical secretariat" of the president or the prime minister, for this places it squarely at the center of short- and medium-term political controversies and political judgements.

It is seldom the case that a central planning agency preoccupied with these short-term immediate political concerns can at the same time deal with long-term issues in an appropriate way. Even if it does so, its credibility, impartiality, and technical competence are likely to be questioned as a result of the power struggles over short-term practical issues. The consequence has been either giving up the quest for relevance to actual decision making and taking refuge in the preparation of medium- and long-term plans for their own sake, or a concentration on providing technical support for short-term political decisions and the abandonment of any serious attempt at examining medium- and long-term development issues. This leads to a confusion of roles for the planning agencies, many of which have tended to move back and forth between these two positions. This creates a kind of "institutional schizophrenia," a disease to which planning agencies in developing countries are particularly prone.

When development planning gives priority to short-term and urgent issues, the institutional modality for the planning agency has generally been that of an operational ministry, with jurisdiction over the formulation and control of the national budget. A national planning commission—whose task is to coordinate and mediate between the conflicting demands for resources made by government agencies—usually complements the activities of the planning ministry. Long-term issues are left either to marginal government agencies—the National Research Council, for example—or to universities, independent research institutes, or even international organizations. On the other hand, when development planning leaves the short-term political arena to the operating ministries, in particular to the ministries of economics and finance, the planning agency usually adopts the form of an independent institute—attached nominally to the president's or prime minister's office—whose task is to prepare short-, medium-, and long-term development plans (even though these plans are likely to be ignored by other government agencies), to provide technical support to the president or prime minister, and possibly to explore a few multisectorial medium- and long-term issues such as population growth, employment demands, economic integration, and regional development.

In some cases the planning agency has oscillated between the horns of this dilemma: at some moment in time it may have focused on issues of great importance for the future of the country, played a leading role in the exploration of development options and strategies, and prepared technically sound plans, while at others it may have influenced short-term resource allocations, designed policies and measures to deal with emergencies, and placed itself at the center of power struggles.

Several authors have stated this dilemma of development planning in different ways. In their review of the Latin American planning experience, Solari and coworkers (1976) distinguish two main lines of thought that dominated the planning scene in the early 1970s: a global, integral, and long-term conception of planning that emphasized major social changes and a set of short-term concerns that focused on economic growth and income improvements. Similarly, Bryant and White (1982, pp. 233–34) indicate that "the tensions between the technician planner and the political decision maker grow out of the different mandates that each has and the different information with which each deals, and that sometimes they grow out of differences between short-term and long-term consequences." Moreover, they point out that:

The tension between planners and politicians goes to the heart of the dilemma about the nature of the political process and how to make decisions in the best interests of citizens. . . . Because politicians respond to short-term issues of necessity, public policy is further skewed away from dealing with broad public interests. This is the void into which planners have willingly stepped, on the claim that their insulation from political whims and their professional expertise enable them to better interpret public mandates.

According to Mendez (1985, p. 193), in Latin America this dilemma of development planning has usually been resolved in favor of approaches to address immediate problems and, since the early 1980s, in favor of short-term measures to deal with the worst economic crisis of the last fifty years: "The task of [alleviating the diverse aspects of the immediate crisis] is absorbing government efforts and does not allow breathing room to think about major statements regarding the future. Perhaps there has never been such an acute feeling of immediatism in the Latin America region." Pena-Parra (1984) states that some planning agencies in Latin America have tried to deal both with short-term urgent concerns and long-term important issues but that the result has been a preference to address those that appear closer in time.

Finally, Sachs (1983, p. 14) has focused sharply on the way this dilemma affects development planners: "the planner ought to take a global and fairly long-term view of the planning process, but his usefulness will be evaluated by his capacity to influence a myriad of locally and time-bound decisions."

In order to avoid what has been characterized as one of the fundamental dilemmas of development planning—choosing between the urgent short-term issues and the important long-term ones—it is necessary to adopt an integrative perspective of the different time dimensions involved in the planning process, to develop planning approaches and methods appropriate to this new perspective, and to suggest operational criteria for organizing planning efforts in this new light.

The main conceptual adjustment required is to view the long-term as an integral component of the process of actual and anticipatory decision making with a short-term horizon, while simultaneously accepting that the accumulation of actual and anticipatory decisions made with a short-term horizon generates constraints and opportunities that condition long-term options.

However, before exploring further these ideas on new approaches to planning, it is useful to examine the changed context for development efforts in the 1980s, as well as the demands that this new context imposes on planners and planning agencies. This new context requires major changes and adjustments in the conception and practice of the development and may also suggest the need for exploring new options for the institutionalization of planning activities.

The Changing Context for National Development Planning and Its Consequences

Most of the concepts, approaches, methodologies, and procedures for development planning, at least those of the conventional kind, were generated and began to be applied during the three decades following World War II, a period of unprecedented world economic growth and relative peace during which the United States economy loomed as the dominant and guiding force. In such an expansive economic context, many of the distributional problems and conflicts that emerged were rapidly accommodated and defused by the political powers at the national and international levels. In a sense, the world socioeconomic context approached what Emery and Trist (1965) have called a "clustered" environment, in which all kinds of social entities could pursue their own objectives and development paths without impinging on those of others.

However, as the 1970s unfolded, the international context for development began to change at a rapid pace—witness the two oil price shocks, the emergence of Japan as an economic powerhouse, the pressures for the New International Economic Order, the end of the Vietnam War, the culmination of the processes of political decolonization, the disenchantment with development assistance, and the emergence of new technologies such as microelectronics and informatics, among many other events. To use the concepts of Emery and Trist (1965), there has been a transition toward a "disturbed-reactive" environment in which it is impossible to ignore other social actors on the scene, and even toward a "turbulent" environment in which the very ground on which the actors stand is shifting. The newly emerging international environment is forcing a reappraisal of development objectives and strategies, and is also having a major impact on the nature of the planning process.

When facing a new and uncertain situation, the natural reaction is to take refuge in familiar concepts and accepted ways. The field of planning is no exception to this general rule, and some planners have argued that the reason why development planning did not live up to expectations is not because the concepts and approaches were wrong but rather because they were not fully applied, because they were not given enough support and a fair chance to succeed. Therefore, some voices are arguing for a "return to basics" in development planning where the conventional views are being reinstated, but this time, fully backed by the "political will," the "appropriate information," and the "adequate administrative and managerial capabilities."

A review of world trends indicates that the thirteen years that remain in this century will be quite different from the three decades after World War II (Sagasti and Garland 1985, Sagasti 1986). Economic trends that are expected to prevail during the next several years can be characterized by slower economic growth and a slow-down in the expansion of international trade, a continued decline in commodity prices, and deterioration of terms of trade for developing countries, increased foreign indebtedness, and changes in the structure of developing countries' debt, a restructuring of world industry in directions that are not at all clear yet, and continued experimentation with economic policies whose effectiveness is in doubt in an uncertain economic climate.

Social trends indicate that population growth will continue in most developing regions, associated with rural-urban migration and with the explosive growth of Third-World cities—twenty-one are expected to have more than 10 million inhabitants by the year 2000. The employment prospects appear rather dim for most of the new entrants into the labor force, and in many developing regions, the combined unemployment and underemployment rates exceed 50%. In addition, there are other social demands, such as food, housing, education, sanitation, health services, transport, and environmental protection, which will continue to grow and outstrip the capacity of most developing countries to satisfy them.

In the cultural sphere, the tensions between homogenizing pressures brought about by the mass media and the desire to assert a cultural identity will continue and even grow; in the political sphere it is likely that East/West tensions will continue, that cooperation with developing countries will remain as a relatively minor concern for the industrializing countries, and that political instability will continue to thwart long-term thinking and efforts in the developing countries.

In the fields of science and technology, the developments and advances are too numerous and pervasive to mention. It may be appropriate only to say that the very process of knowledge generation through the conduct of scientific research is undergoing profound changes and that many of the new advanced fields are virtually out of the reach of most developing countries. The emergence of new technologies—microelectronics, computers, telematics, robotics, space manufacturing, composite materials, fiber optics, biotechnology, and photovoltaic energy, among many others—is changing the shape of world industry, altering comparative advantages, and creating a most difficult challenge for all but a handful of developing countries (see Drucker 1986, Castells 1986, Perez 1984).

This emerging international context, which is likely to dominate the scene until the end of the century, requires innovative thinking and new approaches to development. It also imposes the need for a serious evaluation and reappraisal of development planning theory and practice: social values and objectives acquire greater importance; flexible time horizons and a long-term perspective become essential; contextual factors play an increasingly larger role; and new institutional arrangements must be brought into place. The conventional approach to planning, with its rigid time frames, its breakdown of planning tasks into sectors and regions, and its centralized and technocratic perspective on plan formulation and implementation is most unlikely to be effective in an increasingly turbulent environment. Indeed, as many critics have emphasized, this approach has not worked even in the relatively more calm and stable context of the 1960s and early 1970s.

Furthermore, as the environmental complexity becomes more visible in the 1980s and as rapid change becomes the norm, it is not possible to ignore several issues that challenge the conventional approach to planning. For example, the vastly increased amount of information on almost every aspect of social life—brought about by the advances in microelectronics, telecommunications and computers—is generating an "information onslaught" (Kerr et al. 1984) that requires new approaches in order to obtain access and processing information for development planning (Sagasti 1983). Moreover, conflicts of rationalities at different levels can no longer be ignored or easily accommodated in an increasingly interdependent world: what is rational at the level of individual behavior may be counterproductive at the level of a social group, and what is rational for a social group may undermine the objectives at the community, national, and international levels.

In a similar vein, the increased interactions among social groups have led to the interpenetration of the different spheres of human action and to the blurring of boundaries for decision making. For example, the emergence of new actors such as nongovernmental organizations, grass-roots groups, nonprofit research centers, and voluntary organizations is challenging the traditional division between the "public" and "private" spheres of action and competence; the formulation of policies and the performance of government functions are often assumed by these new entities and by the private sector, while public and government institutions intervene in activities that once belonged to the realm of private initiative. This is closely related to growing demands for "participation" at all levels of society and to the more complex nature of the process of government policy design and implementation. (See, for example, Bennis and colleagues [1985] for an analysis of these increased social interactions from the perspective of planning for change.)

Exploring New Directions

The new context for development is likely to sharpen what has been characterized as one of the fundamental dilemmas of planning agencies: emphasizing either the provision of responses to short-term critical problems or the generation of new visions and options for the future. The economic crisis of the early 1980s and the less favorable economic environment that can be anticipated during the coming years, the increases in social demands of all types, the political instability that is likely to afflict most developing countries, the cultural tensions that are now becoming more visible, and the challenges imposed by scientific and technological advances are making it necessary to move beyond the conventional approach to planning and to explore new ways of organizing the process of making and putting together actual and anticipatory decisions. This requires a reaffirmation of the belief that purposeful and rational human intervention has a place in the process of development and implies rejecting the views of those who argue that the inherent "irrationality" of human beings precludes any kind of planned or guided social change.

However, to avoid its being just an act of faith, this reaffirmation requires that the limitations of the conventional approach to planning must be recognized and that the characteristics of the new context for development be fully acknowledged. Development planning should not be viewed as a centralized and technocratic exercise but rather as a loose cooperative learning process that involves a multiplicity of actors throughout the whole fabric of society, that seeks to attain increasing levels of shared perceptions on objectives and goals, and that aims at agreeing on specific anticipatory and actual decisions on the basis of temporary consensus. Moreover, in this social learning process it will be impossible to eliminate all inconsistencies and to attain perfect rationality; it will be enough to agree on lines of action that provide a reasonably coherent framework for action.

This requires an exploration of new directions for development planning. Some of these directions may involve adapting existing ideas to the new context, while others will require creative efforts whose outcome cannot be anticipated yet. As an initial step, it is possible to identify the need for enlarging the scope of development planning decisions, the redefinition of the concept of time horizons, and the need to disperse planning capabilities throughout society.

The first requirement of a new approach is to *enlarge the scope of the anticipatory decisions involved in the planning process.* It is necessary to go well beyond the traditional concern of planners with economic issues and to cover as many aspects of the development process as possible. This implies adopting a synthetic perspective that seeks to provide an integrated and coherent picture of development prospects, options, strategies, and possible actions. The idea is to make sense out of apparent chaos in an increasingly turbulent environment in order to identify preferred sequences of future events and to derive actual and anticipatory decisions from them.

Table 25.1, adapted from Sagasti (1973b), presents five categories of anticipatory decisions that would enlarge considerably the scope of the conventional approach to national development planning: first, decisions that will define long-term ideals and the desired future for the country; second, decisions regarding the patterns of interaction with the increasingly turbulent international environment; third, decisions about the institutional structure and fabric of the country; fourth, decisions regarding the activities to be performed and the priorities attached to them; and fifth, decisions about the allocations of all types of resources. These five anticipatory decision categories are the domain of stylistic, contextual, institutional, activity, and resource planning. The interactions among these categories of decisions can be summarized by saying that *resources* are allocated to *activities* through *institutions* taking into account the *context* in order to approach the *desired future.*

The conventional approach to development planning focuses exclusively on the anticipatory decisions about economic and social activities to be given priority and on the allocation of all types of resources; that is, it only covers the categories of resource and activity planning. Consequently, it is necessary to develop, test, and disseminate methodologies and procedures for stylistic, contextual, and institutional planning.

An approach to development planning that incorporates the explicit identification of long-term ideals and the aspirations of various social groups in the country, that deals with the interactions with an increasingly turbulent international environment, and that also involves the design of institutions—in addition to the conventional concerns with activities and resources—would be more likely to avoid the dilemma between the urgent and the important and would also be more effective in a changing international context. The concept of "interactive planning" put forward by Ackoff (1981 and 1982), the ideas proposed by Sachs (1980), as well as the work carried out at GRADE (see Arregui and Sagasti 1987, Sagasti and Garland 1985, Herzka 1987, Sagasti and Felices 1986, and GRADE 1984) begin to offer specific methods and procedures for dealing with stylistic, contextual, and institutional planning.

The second requirement of a new approach to planning is to acknowledge the provisional nature of development plans as a collection of ephemeral anticipatory decisions, and the need to adjust them continuously to the changing circumstances (Beer 1972, 1974a, and 1974b). This involves nothing less than a *redefinition of the concept of "planning horizon,"* breaking down the conventional and rigid framework of short-, medium-, and long-term time spans. For example, "short-term" can be redefined as the period of time during which the inertia of historical processes in a given system limits its future evolution; "long-term" would be a time horizon in which historical forces and the inertia of a system do not limit significantly the range of possible future states; while in "medium-term" the inertia of historical process conditions the evolution of the system, but only up to a certain point.

Applied to development planning, these concepts would indicate that the "short-term" in issues like population growth may be a decade, while the "long-term" in issues like commodity prices may be a few months. Furthermore, each set of development issues will have its own different set of time horizons, and rather than forcing them into the procrustean bed of rigid time frames which characterize the conventional approach, the idea would be to deal with each development issue or problem on its own time-horizon terms, coordinating and interrelating their different rhythms as they evolve in time. The flexibility of time horizons that would characterize the planning would show clearly that many urgent short-term problems have profound long-term implications, and that the solution to these urgent short-term problems require making long-term anticipatory decisions.

The third requirement of a new approach to development planning involves building a broad and solid social support base to transcend the mostly technocratic character of the conventional approach. It is essential to *disperse and disseminate planning capabilities throughout society,* providing access to information, methodologies, and training to all social groups and individuals who are interested in exploring alternative development options and strategies. Development planning would thus become a social learning exercise in which the perspectives and rationalities of different actors could be contrasted and areas of partial and temporary agreement could be identified (see

TABLE 25.1. Characteristics of the Different Categories of Planning Decision.

	Stylistic	*Contextual*
Conditioning Influences	Value systems and preferences (stylistic constraints); long-term possibilities.	International setting; sociotechnical environmental constraints; interdependencies with other systems.
Emphasis	Alternative futures; desired images; identification of values and aspirations.	Insertion in international setting; convergence of different policies and plans; attaining overall coherence in plans and policies.
Type of Process	Exploratory; consultative; participatory; multiple-loop.	Monitoring; coordinating; negotiating.
Procedures Used	Establishing ideal standards; proposing broad directions; establishing dialogue with interest groups; involving "stakeholders."	Making explicit relevant implicit policies; resolving contradictions; use of indirect instruments for implementing plans and policies.
Dominant Time Horizon	Long-term.	Long/medium-term.

Source: Adapted from Sagasti (1973b).

Institutional	Activity	Resource
Institutional constraints and possibilities for development; organizational ecology.	Existing and potential capabilities; dynamics of processes.	Availability of resources; possibilities for directing resource allocations.
Defining entitlement claims and payment systems; establishing appropriate organizational structures (channels and clusters).	Defining areas for concentration of activities; evaluation of past performance.	Influencing or controlling resource allocation.
Structuring and texturing (setting the organizational fabric); legislative and regulative.	Diagnosing; target-setting; balancing; learning.	Allocative and distributives; experimental.
Institution building and renewal (creation and modification of institutions); defining performance measures; setting the "rules of the game"; establishing incentives, rewards and penalties.	Establishing objectives; defining orientation; setting operational procedures.	Acquiring and distributing resources; establishing priorities for resource allocation; defining specific aims and goals; generating data bases.
Medium-term.	Medium/short-term.	Short-term.

Dunn 1971, Michael 1973, Linstone 1972, Friedmann 1973, Emery and Trist 1973, Castells 1986).

Taken together, these three characteristics of a new approach to development planning would lead to a much richer planning process. Enlarging the scope of anticipatory decisions, making time horizons flexible, and dispersing planning capabilities through society would considerably improve social capabilities for dealing with an increasingly turbulent and uncertain environment, for transcending the limitations of the conventional approach to planning, and for avoiding the dilemma of planning agencies that perceive they have to choose between paying attention either to the "important" or to the "urgent."

Some Institutional Implications

The preceding sections have pointed out some of the problems that development planning is facing during the 1980s and will face in the next decade, and have also put forward some general suggestions that could overcome the limitations of the conventional approach to planning. It would also be interesting to explore the institutional implications of these ideas and to discuss the new organizational structure they would require for the planning process.

Perhaps the best way of addressing these issues is to derive a few implications to guide the design of organizational structures for the national development planning process. Although these implications would need reinterpretation within the specific context of each developing country, they provide guidelines for those interested in exploring further the consequences of adopting new approaches to national development planning.

The first three implications can be derived from the new directions for the planning process identified in the preceding section. In the first place, the institutional design for national development planning must be *flexible and encompassing enough to accommodate the enlarged set of anticipatory decisions* involved in the new approach. Dealing with anticipatory decisions that range from the desired future image for the country to the pattern of interactions with the international context and to the allocation of resources of all types requires a rather unconventional organizational setting.

In the second place, the institutional design *must be capable of dealing with each development problem and issue in its own time dimension and of achieving intertemporal coordination among these different time horizons.* This implies abandoning the organization of planning activities along rigid short-, medium-, and long-term time frames and structuring tasks around clusters of development problems or issues while preserving their inherent temporal complexity.

Third, *the institutional design for development planning must be open and capable of incorporating the contributions made by the widest possible variety of social groups and individuals involved in the development process.* This implies abandoning the technocratic and exclusive character of development planning agencies, designing procedures to ensure the participation of all interested parties, and enabling the largest possible number of government agencies, nongovernmental organizations, grass-roots movements, and professional associations, among other social groups, to become actively involved in the process of development planning (Wolfe 1982). Wider participation and dispersing planning capabilities are likely to highlight real conflicts of interest, and the institutional design must include conflict management mechanisms and procedures. As Del Valle (1986) has put it, planning must become a "process of social organization."

There are also other consequences for organizational design that can be derived from the changed context for development planning. For example, the planning organization *must be capable of processing a vast amount of information on the external environment and internal situation of the country,* which requires the development of synthesis and integration capabilities within the set of planning entities. In addition, the institutional design *must be resilient and able to cope with rapid changes and instabilities,* which requires an organizational structure that can monitor continuously external and internal changes affecting the development process. Finally, the institutional design *must have a high response capacity to restructure and recompose itself as the need arises,* which requires the possibility of discontinuing organizational units, creating new ones, and severing and forging links between the different components of the institutional structure for development planning.

At this stage, it is necessary to examine briefly the notion of who should apply these institutional design principles in a given context. The turbulent nature of the contemporary social environment and the requirement that planning capabilities be dispersed precludes the possibility of postulating a "central designer" who would put forward an institutional framework and oversee its implementation. While the initial impulse to structure the network of planning organizations will, more often than not, come from some government unit or group, it is essential that the initiatives, points of view, and concerns of a large variety of social actors be explicitly taken into account and incorporated into the institutional design and implementation process.

In consequence, there would be a dialectical interaction between the planning group that postulates the initial institutional design and the various agents at all levels of society that have a stake in the planning process. If the tensions and conflicts that usually accompany such intense interactions do not lead to destructive confrontations and power struggles, an overall institutional framework will gradually emerge and provide the basis for a participative planning process. The "central designer" would thus be complemented—or even re-placed—by a "synthesist" capable of articulating individual initiatives into coherent (but not necessarily totally consistent) lines of action supported by a series of provisional consensus.

The conventional approach has emphasized the role played by a central planning agency within the sphere of action of government organizations but without attempting actively to involve the productive sector (with the possible exception of public enterprises), academic institutions, professional associations, local grass-roots organizations, labor unions, peasant communities, and other similar entities that should take part in the process of development planning.

The picture that begins to emerge of the new institutional design for development planning is quite different from what has been the conventional practice. An organizational structure that is flexible, open, broad, issue-oriented, and organized as an evolving network contrasts sharply with the image of a "National Development Planning Agency" organized centrally either as an operating ministry or as an independent institute. The experience of Latin America (Cibotti and Bardecci 1972, Solari et al. 1976, Mendez 1980, Wolfe 1982, De Mattos 1981, White 1987), of Africa and Asia (Myrdal 1970, Bryant and White 1982), and of developing countries in general (Aggarwala 1983 and 1985) indicates that major changes will be required to adapt existing organizational structures to the new institutional needs.

Toward an Evolving Institutional Network for National Development Planning

The institutional design required for a new approach to development planning is that of an "evolving network" that should be flexible, open and capable of restructuring itself over time. The planning units that compose the network would not conform a hierarchical organization, and each would relate to the structure of political authority and power in a variety of ways that are also likely to change over time. Some of the components of such a network can be readily identified in a general way, even though it is clear that many more could be incorporated into the design for a specific country.

First, there is a *social intelligence unit* (Emery 1977, Dror 1980, Dedijer 1982), or *technoeconomic intelligence unit* (Sagasti 1983), a small group of highly qualified professionals with interdisciplinary training and broad experience in development problems. Working at the highest levels of government, this future-oriented intelligence unit would identify the key issues to be dealt with in national development planning; acquire, select, and process information about them; and suggest priorities for the work of the other units that conform to the planning network. The social or technoeconomic intelligence unit would be mostly concerned with anticipatory decisions that refer to issues of permanent interest for the developing country and to the evolution of the international context; would be involved in the generation of development options and strategies for the country; would report directly to the president or the prime minister; would not supervise directly any of the other planning units; and would not be involved in operational activities such as resource allocation. Its main instrument to influence actual and anticipatory decision making would be the provision of timely and accurate information and opinion.

Second, *specialized planning units* would be located throughout the government and would be concerned with anticipatory decisions within the purview of their specific government agency. These units would deal mostly with issues that have short- and medium-term consequences and would focus on institutional, activity, and resource planning. The specialized planning units would operate in the manner of Ackoff's (1982) "responsive decision systems" in which the planning function is fully integrated into the structure and functioning of the system itself. Bromley (1983) has described how these specialized units could function within the framework of an interactive and decentralized structure for development planning, while Kornai (1970) anticipated the need for these specialized planning units within the context of what he called "planning as a process of cognition and compromise." Of particular importance would be the planning units in the ministries of economics, planning, and finance, where the key decisions regarding resource allocation priorities and the national budget are usually decided. While these units have an intersectoral mandate, other planning units in government agencies, ministries, public enterprises, and regional or local governments have a more focused and specific mandate.

Third, *temporary issue-oriented task forces and commissions* would focus on a certain problem, usually with medium- and long-term implications. These task forces or commissions would seek to obtain the largest possible variety of inputs from all concerned parties, identify options and possible strategies, highlight areas of consensus and of conflict, and interact actively with government organizations, with other components of the planning network, with the mass media, and with the public at large. They would be established for a limited period of time, with a clear mandate and terms of reference and would have no operational function at all. However, it is clear that in some instances the mandate of these task forces and commissions is likely to enter into conflict with those of other planning units, and that this should be viewed as a possible source of creative tension rather than a problem to be avoided at all cost. There are many approaches and methods for organizing the work of such temporary units. Among them, the "search conference" technique and the procedures associated with it provide a useful tool for structuring the work of issue-oriented temporary task forces and commissions (Emery 1982).

In some countries there is a long tradition of presidential or royal commissions, of parliamentary committees that hold hearings and produce reports, and of specially appointed panels of experts to conduct specific inquiries. For example, the Royal Commission on the Economic Union and Development Prospects for Canada (1984), chaired by Donald S. MacDonald, provides a clear instance of a temporary organization whose task was to explore alternative futures and to build a consensus around a common vision. Moreover, as the book edited by Drache and Cameron (1985) shows, even before the official report was published, a spirited public debate followed the Royal Commission's interpretation of a supposed consensus view on the future of Canada. Other temporary commissions have been created recently in many developed and developing countries, particularly to deal with long-term issues. For example, Barney (1985) presents a list of more than twenty "Year 2000" commissions established during the last decade in developed and developing countries.

Fourth, *coordination committees to link planning units with all types of nongovernmental organizations* would have their own interests and mandates but could contribute with information, opinions, requests, and ideas to the planning process. The nongovernmental organizations may include grass-roots movements, associations of consumers, neighborhood organizations, cooperatives, religious groups, trade and professional associations, and similar entities, all of which should engage in planning activities and transmit their views through the coordination committees.

There are many examples of such organizations in developing countries, from the Sarvodaya movement in Sri Lanka and community kitchens in Santiago de Chile to associations of professionals in Peru, Brazil, and Kenya. In particular, the reports presented in the *IFDA Dossier,* published by the International Foundation for Development Alternatives at Nyon, Switzerland, contain a wealth of information on experiences of this type and, as Jenny (1981) has shown, with innovative institutional designs it should be possible to consider the initiatives of these "Third System" organizations as an integral part of the development planning process. Godard and coworkers (1985) have developed the idea of an "analysis grid for local development" as a framework to interpret a large number of experiences that deal with the mobilization of local resources and people for decentralized planning. Another example, although along more conventional lines, is provided by the National Planning Institute in Peru, which in early 1986 created several "Consultative Committees" to discuss long-term development objectives, the medium-term development plan, and the short-term financial and economic plans. Each of these committees involves representatives from trade unions, business associations, government agencies, the armed forces, and the intellectual community.

Fifth, *research and academic institutions* would be engaged in the description, study, and analysis of the situation in the country. These would include independent social science research centers, university departments and research institutes, government agencies in charge of natural resources surveys, statistical offices of ministries and other government departments, and technology research and development units in private and public enterprises. These institutions should be linked to the social or technoeconomic intelligence unit and to the various specialized planning units in order to channel the information and the results of their studies to facilitate and strengthen anticipatory decision making throughout the planning network. This amounts to providing a mechanism for mobilizing the contributions that the intellectual community can make to the process of development.

Research and academic institutions usually cover a wide spectrum of issues and concerns that range from short-term analysis of labor-management conflicts and assessments of the natural resources to anthropological surveys of rural areas and the compilation of macroeconomic statistics and projections, for example. It would be necessary to structure the ways in which they could provide inputs into the planning network in order to keep the development planning process and the anticipatory decisions it involves as close as possible to the reality of the country. Considering the instability of many government agencies, in order to ensure the continuity of planning efforts it may even be appropriate to replicate in an embryonic form some of the planning capabilities (such as approaches, methods, procedures, and information) in a nongovernmental research center, so that they could be transferred back to a government agency if the need arises.

Finally, an *international support network* is needed for all types of institutions including planning agencies in other countries, international organizations, international data bases, multilateral and bilateral funding agencies, and academic and professional associations. This is particularly important for the social or technoeconomic intelligence unit, which must monitor continuously the evolution of the international environment to assess its impact on the development prospects of the country and to suggest the anticipatory decisions to deal with them.

The evolving planning network envisaged here would be a loose confederation of the various components outlined in this section. They would use a variety of technological and methodological tools to function as a planning system: from microcomputers, advanced telecommunications and computer conferences (Beer 1974a and 1974b, Flores 1982, Barney 1985), to idealized designs (Ackoff 1974 and 1981), mathematical models (Sachs 1980, Sagasti 1976), formalized procedures for assessing the viability of a plan (Matus 1983) and search conferences (Emery 1982), complemented by opinion polls, statistical surveys, and the extensive use of mass media (GRADE 1984).

The large variety of components of the development planning network and the rich set of interconnections between them would allow tackling short-, medium-, and long-term issues at the same time, while also generating responses to a rapidly changing international environment. The dispersion of planning capabilities throughout the government apparatus, and ultimately throughout society, would empower people at all levels of society to address urgent problems in a concerted way; the linkages with academic institutions, with nongovernmental organizations, and with the public in general would allow society as a whole to confront the important and critical national development issues in a sustained manner.

Conclusion

This chapter has sought to explore possible new approaches to development planning that would transcend the limitations of the conventional approach, that would adapt better to the turbulent international environment of the 1990s, and that will overcome what was characterized as the dilemma of devoting planning energies either to short-term urgent problems or to long-term important issues.

It is clear that the new approach outlined here and the institutional design derived from it require additional work and elaboration. However, it provides a starting point and suggests new avenues for research; in particular, it is possible that many of the functions and components of the new approach to development planning put forward in this essay are already taking shape in many developing countries. A systematic survey of such unconventional planning efforts may prove a fruitful source of ideas and of inspiration.

Finally, as in all processes of social innovation and institutional renewal, the new approach to development planning outlined here requires new mindsets and attitudes on the part of politicians, technocrats, entrepreneurs, managers, professionals, researchers, workers, students, and people from all walks of life that are likely to elicit opposition from those who are not prepared to discard the habits of thought associated with the conventional planning approach or from those who reject any kind of planning effort. While accepting that planning is—by itself—no guarantee for national development, it is essential to reaffirm the belief that a process of social learning, of anticipatory decision making at all levels, and of defining lines of action through partial and temporary consensus can and will take place, thus empowering human beings to influence purposefully the direction of social evolution.

However, it is also necessary to acknowledge that the turbulent years ahead—with their increased social tensions and accelerated pace of change—will strain individual and social response capabilities to the limit. Moreover, in this turbulent context the relations between planning, democracy, and freedom—so well examined by Karl Manheim (1940 and 1953) half a century ago at another time of crisis— require a fresh reinterpretation and restatement. It could be said, in fact, that democracy is a process of participative planning.

This essay has focused on conceptual changes and institutional structures for national development planning, but in the final analysis, planning systems are designed and put into practice by people. In these uncertain times, planners in developing countries face a particularly difficult task: they must be able to filter out the noise and interpret the conflicting signals accompanying human actions on a social ground that is continuously shifting; they must be able to structure conceptual patterns to make sense out of apparently chaotic situations; and they must be able to identify positive directions for social change and devise ways of moving toward them. This calls for new attitudes and skills; development planning in the turbulent 1980s and 1990s requires the type of person whom Eric Trist (1976) has described so well: "We need flexible, resourceful, resilient people who can tolerate a lot of surprise and ambiguity emotionally while continuing to work on complex issues intellectually."

Acknowledgments

This essay is based on a report prepared at the request of the Population Division of UNESCO and subsequently presented at a meeting on "The Art and Science of Systems Practice" organized by Russell Ackoff at The International Institute for Applied Systems Analysis (IIASA) in Vienna. The work carried out at the "Grupo de Analisis para el Desarrollo" (GRADE) as part of a research program that explores long-term development options and strategies for Peru has provided the background material for the essay. The GRADE research program has received support from the Canadian International Development Agency (CIDA), the Ford Foundation, the Peruvian Foundation for the Development of the Public Sector (FUNDESARROLLO), the United States Agency for International Development (AID), The Tinker Foundation, the Peruvian Central Bank, the National Planning Institute in Peru, the United Nations Development Programme (UNDP), the United Nations Center for Science and Technology for Development, and from IBM del Peru and other private organizations. The essay was revised during my stay as visiting professor at the Social Systems Sciences Department of The Wharton School of the University of Pennsylvania.

I am grateful to Vally Kovary for the extensive review of the literature she prepared as an input to this essay during her stay at GRADE in 1985, and to Cecilia Cook for further bibliographic assistance. Jane King of UNESCO's Population Division provided me with the opportunity to organize my ideas on a rather difficult subject that has interested me for a long time. Russell Ackoff and Eric Trist, both of them emeritus professors in the Social Systems Science Department at The Wharton School, gave me comments on an earlier version of the essay. I am particularly grateful to Hasan Ozbekhan for his thoughtful criticism of the ideas presented here and for his many suggestions. Finally, my colleagues at GRADE and my students at The Wharton School have provided a most lively and stimulating environment in which to develop and test ideas on national development planning.

References

The following bibliography contains the main books, monographs, and papers reviewed during the preparation of this chapter. Not all the material consulted has been included here, and the text does not refer to all the items included in the bibliography. I am grateful to Vally Kovary and Cecilia Cook who helped with the literature review and prepared notes on the various texts and documents reviewed.

Acero, L., S. Cole, and H. Rush (eds.). (1978). "Conference Report: Issues and Analysis of Long Term Development," Science Policy Research Unit, University of Sussex.

Ackoff, R. (1970). *A Concept of Corporate Planning.* New York: Wiley.

———. (1974). *Redesigning the Future.* New York: Wiley.

———. (1977). "National Development Planning Revisited." *Operations Research* 25(2, March–April): 207–18.

———. (1981). *Creating the Corporate Future.* New York: Wiley.

———. (1982). "Beyond Prediction and Preparation," S³ Working Papers, Social Systems Science Department, The Wharton School, University of Pennsylvania.

Aggarwala, R. (1983). "Planning in Developing Countries: Lessons from Experience." Washington D.C.: World Bank Staff Working Papers, No. 576.

———. (1985). "La Planificación en los Paises en Desarrollo." *Finanzas y Desarrollo* (March).

Alford, R., and R. Friedland. (1985). *Powers of Theory: Capitalism, the State and Democracy.* Cambridge: Cambridge University Press.

Arregui, P. M., and F. Sagasti. (1987). "Futuros deseados para el Perú," Documento de Trabajo, Lima, GRADE.

Baran, P. (1986). *El Socialismo: Única Salida.* Mexico City: Editorial Nuevo Tiempo.

Barney, G. (1985). "Global Issues and Methodology: An Introduction." Arlington, Va.: Global Studies Center.

Bauchet, P. (1967). *La Planification Française: Vingt ans d'expérience.* Paris: Éditions du Seuil.

Bauer, P. (1984). *Reality and Rhetoric: Studies in the Economics of Development.* Cambridge: Harvard University Press.

Beer, S. (1966). *Decision and Control.* New York: Wiley.

———. (1972). *Brain of the Firm.* New York: McGraw-Hill.

———. (1974a). *Designing Freedom.* New York: Wiley.

———. (1974b). "Cybernetics of National Development, Evolved from Work in Chile," The Zaheer Lecture, New Delhi, Zaheer Science Foundation.

Bennis, W., K. D. Benne, and R. Chin (eds.). (1985). *The Planning of Change.* New York: Holt Rinehart and Winston.

Bettelheim, C. (1965). *Planificación y Crecimiento Acelerado.* Mexico City: Fondo de Cultura Economica.

Blair, C. P. (1980). "Economic Development Policy in Mexico: A New Penchant for Planning." *Technical Papers Series,* No. 26. Office for Public Sector Studies, Institute of Latin American Studies (ILAS), University of Texas at Austin.

Blancas Espejo, J. A., J. Flores Diaz, and M. Roman Enriquez. (1981). "La Planificación Prospectiva." *Cuadernos de la Sociedad Venezolana de Planificación* 153–155.

Boguslaw, R. (1965). *The New Utopians: A Study in Systems Design and Social Change.* Englewood Cliffs, N.J.: Prentice-Hall.

Branch, M. (1983). *Comprehensive Planning: General Theory and Principles.* Pacific Palisades: Palisades Publishers.

Bromley, R. (1983). "La Planificación del Desarrollo en Condiciones Adversas." *Revista Interamericana de Planificación* 17(66, June): 7–19.

Bryant, C., and L. G. White. (1982). *Management Development in the Third World.* Boulder: Westview Press.

Burchell, R. W., and G. Sternlieb. (1978). *Planning Theory in the 1980s: A Search for Future Directions.* New Brunswick, N.J.: Center for Urban Policy Research, Rutgers University.

Caire, G. (1967). *La Planification.* Paris: Éditions Cujas.

Cardoso, F. H. (1972). *Estado y Sociedad en America Latina.* Buenos Aires: Ediciones Nueva Vision.

Cartwright, T. (1981). "The Science and Art of Long-Range Planning." *Contact: Journal of Environmental Affairs* 13(1): 23–36.

Castells, M. (1986). "High Technology, World Development and Structural Transformations: The Trends and the Debate." *Alternatives* 10(3, July): 297–344.

Churchman, C. W. (1979). *The Systems Approach.* New York: Dell.

Cibotti, R., and O. J. Bardeci. (1972). "Un Enfoque Crítico de la Planificación en America Latina." In Avramovic et al. (eds.): *Transformación y Desarrollo: La Gran Tarea de America Latina.* Mexico City: Fondo de Cultura Economica.

Clark, C. (1938). *National Income and Outlay.* London: Methuen.

———. (1951). *The Conditions of Economic Progress.* London: Macmillan.

Comision Economica para America Latina (CEPAL). (1969). *America Latina: El Pensamiento de la CEPAL.* Santiago de Chile: Editorial Universitaria, Coleccion Tiempo Latinoamericano.

———. (1985). "Crisis y Desarrollo: Presente y Futuro de America Latina y el Caribe," vol. 3. Desafios y Opciones Para el Desarrollo Futuro, Santiago de Chile, Doc. No. LC/L.332 (Sem.22/L.3) Add.2, 11 de abril.

Cowan, T. (1981). "The Planner and His Adversary: A Dialogue," S³ Papers, Social Systems Science Department, The Wharton School, University of Pennsylvania.

Das Gupta, A. K. (1964). "Economic Planning in India." In Ignacy Sachs (ed.): *Planning and Economic Development.* Warsaw: Polish Scientific Publishers.

De Mattos, C. A. (1981). "Planes versus Planificación en la Experiencia Latinoamericana," *Revista Interamericana de Planificación* 15(59, September): 54–75.

Del Valle, A. (1986). *Planning as a Process of Organization,* Programa de Investigaciones en Energia, Universidad de Chile, Santiago de Chile.

Dedijer, S. (1982). "Intelligence for Development," Department of Business Administration, Lund University, Sweden, April.

Drache, D., and D. Cameron. (1985). *The Other MacDonald Report.* Toronto: James Lorimer and Company.

Dror, Y. (1980). "Comprehensive Strategic Intelligence for Rulers," paper presented at the meeting on "The Knowledge Industry and the Process of Development," organized by the Development Centre of the Organisation for Economic Cooperation and Development (OECD).

Drucker, P. (1986). "The Changed World Economy." *Foreign Affairs* 64(4, Spring).

Dunn, E. S. (1971). *Economic and Social Development: A Process of Social Learning.* Baltimore: The Johns Hopkins Press.

Emery, F. (1976). "Adaptive Systems for our Future Governance." *National Labour Institute Bulletin* (New Delhi) 2(4, April).

———. (1977). *Futures We Are In.* Leiden: Stenfert Kroese.

Emery, F., and E. Trist. (1965). "The Causal Texture of Organizational Environments." *Human Relations* 18: 21–32.

————. (1973). *Towards a Social Ecology.* London: Plenum Press.

Emery, M. (1982). *Searching: for New Directions, in New Ways, for New Times,* Toronto: Ontario Quality of Working Life Center, Ministry of Labour, Ontario, Canada.

Faber, M., and D. Seers. (1972): *The Crisis in Planning,* vols. 1 and 2. London: Chatto and Windus.

Faludi, A. (1973). *A Reader in Planning Theory.* Oxford: Pergamon Press.

Fedorenko, N. (ed.). (1976). *Desarrollo Económico y Planificación Perspectiva.* Moscow: Editorial Progreso.

Flores, C. F. (1982). *Management and Communication in the Office of the Future.* Berkeley: Logonet Inc.

Friedmann, J. (1973). *Retracking America: A Theory of Transactive Planning.* New York: Doubleday.

Friedmann, J., and C. Weaver. (1979). *Territory and Function: The Evolution of Regional Planning.* Berkeley: University of California Press.

Friend, J. K., and N. Jessop. (1969). *Local Government and Strategic Choice.* London: Tavistock Publications.

Garcia D'Acuna, E. (1982). "Pasado y Futuro de la Planificación en America Latina." *Pensamiento Iberoamericano,* 2(July–December).

Gharajedaghi, J., and R. Ackoff. (1986). *A Prologue to National Development Planning.* New York: Greenwood Press.

Giordani, J., C. Matus, M. Testa, and L. Yero. (1981). "La Planificación Posible en la Prospectiva Sociopolitica de America Latina." *Cuadernos de la Sociedad Venezolana de Planificación* Nos. 153–155.

Godard, O., J. P. Ceron, K. Vinaver, and S. Passaris. (1985): "Endogenous Development and Differentiation of Development Spaces: An Analysis Grid for Local Development." *Ecodevelopment News* (Paris) 35.

Griffin, K., and J. Enos. (1970). *Planning Development.* London: Addison-Wesley.

Gross, B. (ed.). (1967). *Action Under Planning: The Guidance of Economic Development.* New York: McGraw-Hill.

————. (1968). *Organizations and Their Managing.* New York: The Free Press.

Grupo de Analisis para el Desarrollo (GRADE). (1984). "Long-Term Development Strategies and Options for Peruvian Development: A Programme of Studies and Research," Lima.

Herzka, C. (1987). "Condicionantes externas del desarrollo Perúano." Documento de trabajo, Lima, GRADE.

Hirschman, A. (1958). *The Strategy of Economic Development.* New Haven: Yale University Press.

————. (1971). *A Bias for Hope: Essays on Development and Latin America.* New Haven: Yale University Press.

Hodara, J. (1983). "La planeación económica observada por un sociologo." *El Trimestre Economico* 50(199, July–September): 1425–36.

Horowitz, I. L. (1978). "Social Planning and Social Science: Historical Continuities and Comparative Discontinuities." In Burchell and Sternlieb (eds.): *Planning Theory in the 1980's.* New Brunswick, N.J.: Center for Urban Policy Research, Rutgers University.

Instituto Latinoamericano de Planificación Economica y Social (ILPES). (1966). *Discusiones sobre Planificación.* Mexico City: Siglo XXI.

————. (1974). *Experiencias y Problemas de la Planificación en America Latina.* Mexico City: Siglo XXI Editores.

Jantsch, E. (ed.). (1968). *Perspectives on Planning.* Paris: Organization for Economic Cooperation and Development (OECD).

Jenny, B. A. (1981). "Planning in the Third World: Issues of the 1980s." *TIMS Studies in the Management Sciences* 17: 395–408.

Jensen, A. (1974). "Adaptation to Change," Institute of Mathematics, Statistics and Operations Research, Technical University of Denmark, Copenhagen.

Kalecki, M. (1963). "Bosquejo de un Método Para Elaborar un Plan Perspectivo." In J. Benard et al. (eds.): *Programación del Desarrollo Económico.* Mexico City: Fondo de Cultura Economica.

Kantorovich, L. (1965). *The Best Use of Economic Resources.* Cambridge: Harvard University Press.

Kerr, D., K. Braithwaite, N. Metropolis, D. Sharp, and G.-C. Rota, (eds.). (1984). *Science, Computers and the Information Onslaught.* New York: Academic Press.

Killick, T. (1976). "The Possibilities of Development Planning." *Oxford Economic Papers* (June): 7–28.

Kohler, H. (1966). *Welfare and Planning.* New York: Wiley.

Kornai, J. (1970). "A General Descriptive Model of Planning Processes." *Economics of Planning* (Norway) 10(1–2): 1–19.

Kothari, R. (1974). *Footsteps into the Future.* New York: Institute for World Order.

Kuznets, S. (1941). *National Income and Its Composition 1919–1938.* New York: National Bureau of Economic Research.

Lange, O. (1949). "The Practice of Economic Planning and the Optimum Allocation of Resources." *Econometrica* (Suppl. July): 166ff.

———. (1961). *Economic Development, Planning and International Cooperation.* Cairo: Central Bank of Egypt Printing Press.

———. (1970). *Ensayos Sobre Planificación Económica.* Barcelona: Editorial Ariel.

Legna, C. (1981). "La Planificación posible en America Latina: Un análisis sistemático." *Cuadernos de la Sociedad Venezolana de Planificación,* nos. 153–55.

Lewis, A. (1968). *Teoria de la Planificación Económica.* Mexico City: Fondo de Cultura Economica.

Linstone, H. A. (1972). "The Nation-State—Magister Ludi? Reflections on the Role of Planning." Paper prepared for the Third World Future Research Conference, Bucharest, September 3–10, Systems Science Institute, Portland State University.

Marczewski, J. (1958). *Planification et croissance économique des démocraties populaires.* Paris: Presses Universitaires de France.

Manheim, K. (1940). *Man and Society.* London: Routledge and Kegan Paul.

———. (1953). *Essays on Sociology and Social Psychology.* London: Routledge and Kegan Paul.

Matus, C. (1976). *Planificación de Situaciones.* Caracas: CENDES, Libros Alfar.

———. (1983). "Planeación Normativa y Planeación Situacional." *El Trimestre Economico* 50(199, July–September): 1721–82.

Mendez, J. (1980). "El Estado de la Planificación en America Latina y el Caribe." *Cuadernos de la Sociedad Venezolana de Planificación,* Nos. 153–55.

———. (1985). "Las Estrategias de Desarrollo en America Latina." In F. Cepeda Ulloa et al. (eds.): *Democracia y Desarrollo en America Latina.* Buenos Aires: Grupo Editor Latinoamericano.

Meynaud, J. (1963). *Planification et Politique*. Lausanne: Études de Science Politique.

Michael, D. (1973). *On Learning to Plan and Planning to Learn*. San Francisco: Jossey Bass.

Monti, A. (1967). *El Acuerdo Social*. Buenos Aires: Edicones de Politica Economica.

————. (1972). *Proyecto Nacional: Razón y Diseño*. Buenos Aires: Paidos.

Morehouse, W. (1985). "Social Intelligence and Advanced Technology Alert Systems." Paper presented at the International Workshop on Advanced Technology Alert Systems, United Nations Center for Science and Technology for Development, West Berlin, 15–20 December.

Morin, E. (1981). *Pour sortir du vingtième siècle*. Paris: Fernand Nathan.

Motta, P. R. (1976). "The Incompatibility of Good Planning and Bad Management: Implementation Problems in Development Administration." Technical Papers Series No. 3, Office for Public Sector Studies, Institute of Latin American Studies (ILAS), University of Texas at Austin.

Myrdal, G. (1957). *Economic Theory and Underdeveloped Regions*. London: Duckworth.

————. (1970). *An Approach to the Asian Drama: Methodological and Theoretical*. New York: Vintage Books.

Organization of American States. (1969). *Status of Planning in Latin America*, Washington, D.C.: Inter-American Economic and Social Council.

Ozbekhan, H. (1971). "Planning and Human Action." In Paul Weiss (ed.): *Hierarchically Organized Systems in Theory and Practice*. New York: Hafner Publishing Company.

Pajestka, J., and I. Sachs. (1967). "Three Papers on Planning and Plan Implementation." Warsaw: The Advanced Course in National Economic Planning, Teaching Materials, Vol. 30.

Peatty, L. R. (1968). "Reflections on Advocacy Planning." *Journal of American Institute of Planners* 34(2, March).

Pena-Parra, I. (1984). *El Pensamiento Económico Latinoamericano*. Bogota: Plaza y Janes.

Perez, C. (1984). "Microelectronics, Long-Waves and World Structural Change: New Perspectives for Developing Countries." Science Policy Research Unit, University of Sussex.

Perroux, F. (1961). *L'Économie du XXème Siècle*. Paris: Presses Universitaires de France.

Polanyi, K. (1944). *The Great Transformation: The Political and Economic Origins of our Time*. Boston: Beacon Press.

Prebisch, R. (1953). *Problemas Teóricos y Prácticos del Crecimiento Económico*. United Nations Economic Commission for Latin America, New York and Santiago de Chile.

————. (1981). *Capitalismo Periférico: Crisis y Transformación*. Mexico City: Fondo de Cultura Economica.

Rweyemamu, J. F., J. Loxley, J. Wicken, C. Nyirabu, et al. (1972). *Towards Socialist Planning*. Dar es Salaam: Tanzania Publishing House.

Rosenberg, N., and L. E. Birdzell, Jr. (1986). *How the West Grew Rich: The Economic Transformation of the Industrial World*. New York: Basic Books.

Royal Commission on the Economic Union and Development Prospects for Canada (Donald S. MacDonald, Chairman). (1984). *A Commission on Canada's Future: Challenges and Choices*. Ottawa: Ministry of Supply and Services.

Sachdeva, P. S. (1984). "Development Planning—An Adaptive Approach." *Long Range Planning* 17.

Sachs, I., and J. Pajetzka. (1970). *Three Essays on Planning and Plan Implementation.* Warsaw: Institute of Developing Economies.

———. (1977). *Pour une économie politique du développement.* Paris: Flammarion.

———. (1983). "The Elusive Interdisciplinarity of Development Planning." Document de Travail 83/10, Centre International de Recherche sur l'Environnement et le Développement (CIRED), Paris.

Sachs, W. (1980). *Diseño de un Futuro para el Futuro.* Mexico City: Fundacion Javier Barros Sierra.

Sagasti, F. (1973a). "A Conceptual 'Systems' Framework for the Study of Planning Theory." *Technological Forecasting and Social Change* 5: 379–93.

———. (1973b). "Towards a New Approach for Scientific and Technological Planning." *Social Sciences Information* 12(2, April): 67–96.

———. (1976). "Thoughts on the Use and Abuse of OR/MS in Development Planning and Management." *Operational Research Quarterly* 27(4): 937–48.

———. (1983). "Technoeconomic Intelligence for Development." *IFDA Dossier* 35(May/June): 17–26.

———. (1986). "Perspectivas Futuras de la Ciencia y la Tecnología en America Latina." Lima, GRADE, July.

Sagasti, F., and E. Felices. (1986). "Hacia un Fondo de Apoyo a la Gestion Pública." Lima, GRADE, November.

Sagasti, F., and G. Garland. (1985). "Crisis, Knowledge, and Development: A Review of Long-term Perspectives on Science and Technology for Development." Lima, GRADE, January.

Sen, A. (1983). "Development: Which Way Now?" *The Economic Journal* 93(March): 745–62.

Sheahan, J. (1977). "Aspects of Planning and Development in Colombia." *Technical Papers Series,* No. 10, Office for Public Sector Studies, Institute of Latin American Studies (ILAS), University of Texas at Austin.

Sociedad Venezolana de Planificación. (1981). "La Planificación Posible en la Prospectiva Sociopolitica de America Latina." *Cuadernos de la Sociedad Venezolana de Planificación,* Nos. 153–55.

Solari, A., R. Franco, and J. Jukowitz. (1976). *Teoria, Accion Social y Desarrollo en America Latina.* Mexico City: Siglo XXI.

South Magazine. (1986). "Third World Development Plans: Strategies for a Decade." *South* 63(January): 67–84.

Stolper, W. F. (1966). *Planning Without Facts: Lessons in Resource Allocation From Nigeria's Development.* Cambridge: Harvard University Press.

Tinbergen, J. (1964). *Central Planning.* New Haven: Yale University Press.

———. (1967). *Development Planning.* New York: McGraw-Hill.

Trist, E. (1976). "Some Concepts of Planning." Paper presented at the seminar on Long-range Planning sponsored by The Extension Service of the University of Western Australia, 21 July.

United Nations. (1951). *Measures for the Economic Development of Underdeveloped Countries.* New York: U.N. Department of Economic and Social Affairs.

———. (1971). General Assembly Resolutions Nos. 2626/XXV and 2681/XXV, 25th Period of Sessions, New York.

United Nations Advisory Committee on Science and Technology for Development. (1984). "Discussion of Issues Relating to Science and Technology for Development: Long-Term Perspectives on Science and Technology for

Development." Report of a Panel Meeting held in Mbabane, Swaziland, A/CN.11/AC.1/V/3, 17 December.

United Nations Development Programme. (1979). *Estudio de Evaluación No. 1: Planificación General del Desarrollo.* New York.

United Nations Economic and Social Council (1974). "Report on a Unified Approach to Development Analysis and Planning," Doc. No. E/CN.5/519, 5 December, New York.

USSR Academy of Sciences. (1980). *Planning in Developing Countries: Theory and Methodology.* Moscow: Progress Publishers.

Varsavsky, O. (1971). *Proyectos Nacionales: Planteo y Estudio de Viabilidad.* Buenos Aires: Ediciones Periferia.

Vickers, G. (1965). *The Art of Judgement: A Study of Policy Making.* New York: Basic Books.

Waterson, A. (1965). *Development Planning: The Lessons of Experience.* Baltimore: Johns Hopkins University Press.

White, G. (1987). "Cuban Planning in the Mid-1980's: Centralization, Decentralization, and Participation." *World Development* 15(1): 153–61.

Wiles, P. (1967). "Some Fundamental Questions on National Planning." In B. Gross (ed.): *Action Under Planning.* New York: McGraw-Hill.

Willig, R. L. (1980). "Modelos y Estrategias de Participación para Cambio Social en America Latina." Ponencia presentada en el XIII Congreso Interamericano de Planificación, Caracas, 26–31 de octubre, organizado por la Sociedad Interamericana de Planificación y la Sociedad Venezolana de Planificación.

Wolfe, M. (1980). "An Assessment." In United Nations Research Institute for Social Development (UNRISD): *The Quest for a Unified Approach to Development.* Geneva: United Nations Research Institute for Social Development (UNRISD).

———. (1982). "El desarrollo esquivo, la bursqueda de un enfoque unificado para el analisis y la planificación del desarrollo." *Revista de la CEPAL* 17 (agosto).

Zuzunaga, C. (1977). "La Frustración del Desarrollo Planificado." *International Development Review* 1: 18–21.

———. (1986). Personal communication.

Chapter 26
Redesigning Western Foreign Policy

Michel Chevalier, Glen Taylor, and Fred Carden

Ethnocentrism in Western Foreign Policy

Introduction

Foreign policy in countries belonging to the Organization for Economic Cooperation and Development (OECD) is guided by a strong belief that the OECD system is the most desirable and that it should be the basis for the entire global system. Western countries approach our relationships with other parts of the world on that basis: transferring technologies and management styles to Africa so they may modernize in our image, challenging the East bloc on an ongoing basis on ideological grounds, and transferring technology to China to help speed their adoption of a more Western style. In effect, the OECD view would appear to be that, if the rest of the world could operate in our style, we would have a more stable and better world. And our global relationships are based on this assumption.

But modernization has not demonstrated any capacity to assist in development in Africa. Conditions there are worse now than they were thirty years ago, and slight movement toward improvement in the East-West situation only begins to emerge when the leaders talk about mutual respect and building some understanding of each other's system. China has its own path for development; it is exploring the role of technology and at the same time its relationships with the OECD system. To assume that this implies China is embracing the Western system is to ignore China's history and its demonstrated willingness to reject both Soviet and OECD influences if they become too overpowering. It is a smug ethnocentricity that permits us to believe our system is the best and the one to which all others should ultimately converge.

Ethnocentricity is essential in the national context. Our system is perhaps the best one for us, but it is not necessarily the only or best system in other cultural or economic contexts. What we will be exploring here is the development of strategies for integrating ethnocentric approaches with more polycentric international relationships, which are based on mutual respect for and learning from other cultures and systems. We are suggesting that the only way to begin to evolve a stable global environment is to develop the capacity to work with different systems, to increase the variety of acceptable operational styles and, indeed, to foster developmental alternatives. Global stability will not be achieved through a convergence to a monolithic world state but through an increased acceptance of diversity in political, economic, and social systems—an increasingly polycentric, or multicentred, world perspective.

We will develop this idea through a discussion of OECD relationships with Africa, China, and the East bloc, and we will develop a framework for polycentric approaches to international relations. In the last part of the paper we will explore joint design of new patterns of relations in each of the three settings, and we will look at the role of the university in stimulating change. The three examples are considered to be part of a larger metaproblem of foreign relations; they are not isolated areas of activity that can be dealt with individually. How we deal with relationships in one part of the world has significant impact on our capacities to deal with other parts of the world.

Our perspective on the OECD system is primarily Canadian, and we will generally focus on the Canadian role in presenting new perspectives. Of course, one cannot ignore the central U.S. role in the OECD system, but for the purposes of this paper, we have made some choices based on our work to date.

The Invisible Ethnocentricity of the Western Perspectives

The Western world can be loosely defined as OECD countries. Countries that were under Western colonial rule, such as those in Africa, the Middle and Far East, India, and Latin America, have continued to exist at the periphery of the Western world. Almost all these countries lean more or less toward the Western form of democracy and free enterprise. They explicitly or implicitly strive toward Western social and economic patterns—from clothing to consumer goods.

The implicit premise of most OECD initiatives, be they diplomatic, economic, or academic, is a profound, though usually unrecognized, ethnocentricity. The result of this ethnocentricity is an inability to fully appreciate other perspectives. The general OECD view is clearly that Western patterns of democracy (and free enterprise in American terms) are superior. The notion of "developing" countries is based on the assumption that less industrial countries will modernize in our Western sense. This is the justification of the massive global effort called international development.

The generally held view that the developing countries on the periphery of the Western world can and indeed should organize themselves in the "developed" country pattern is a major reflection of what we call the invisible ethnocentricity of Western perspectives of international development. These perspectives have been useful to a handful of developing countries such as Singapore, Malaysia, and South Korea which managed to gain access to OECD markets. These success stories may or may not prevail over the longer term, but for now, they clearly reinforce the assumption that developing countries can (and must) in the end integrate with the "developed" OECD system. This, in turn, reinforces the invisible Western ethnocentricity—the view that in time, *all* countries will cleave to its democratic and free enterprise ideals.

Within the West, relationships between countries are polycentric. Mutual respect among cultures, races, and languages continues to evolve. The internal polycentric character of OECD countries reinforces their ethnocentric attitude toward the rest of the world. In effect, the West is waiting for the rest of the world to join the club.

There are at least two global boundaries or fault lines along which tensions between the OECD system and the rest of the world are increasing: *first,* the East-West confrontation between NATO and the Warsaw Pact and, *second,* the increasing North-South gap in human well-being between OECD and most less-industrial countries, notably in sub-Saharan Africa. Furthermore, these two global fault lines intersect, increasing the tension on each fault line. This intersection is exemplified by East-West competitions in Third-World military and ideological arenas.[1]

The intolerance of the West, proselytizing its institutional and economic patterns as the exclusive means for socioeconomic development in the face of the two global fault lines—North-South and East-West—would appear to be dangerous, if not futile. In the end, pursuit of our ethnocentric strategy can only lead to East-West military confrontation and to an escalation of the already rampant human and ecological breakdown in many countries on the periphery of the Western world. We believe that this exclusivity (or the intolerance for other modes) should be modified. Otherwise, East-West tension with its ever-present potential for "final confrontation" will continue and probably grow. Neither arms control negotiations nor token academic exchanges are sufficient.

Instead of the exclusivity of ethnocentrism, we should work toward a greater measure of inclusivity, or tolerance for other modes based on a more polycentric view. This, in turn, should lead toward greater mutual respect, both to existing conditions and to clearly understood and respected different paths of evolution. Polycentricity in operations that occur to some extent *within* the OECD system (as discussed later in this paper) does not characterize foreign policy with respect to other parts of the world and other possible paths of evolution.

The focus of the present argument is on OECD organizations and their perspectives of other world systems such as those in Africa, China, and the Soviet Union. It does not attempt to represent the perspectives of African, Chinese, or Soviet organizations. As the argument is developed, these views must necessarily be put forward by those countries and people within them rather than by participants from the North, or the OECD system.

Major International Boundary Relationships

Introduction

This section will describe three of the major international boundary relationships critical to foreign policy: (1) the East-West and North-South boundaries, (2) the OECD-Africa boundary, and (3) the OECD-China boundary. In all three cases we will illustrate the impact of ethnocentricity on the current relationships.

There are of course other critical boundaries. These three were chosen because each exemplifies a major aspect of the metaproblem[2] of Western foreign policy. They are interrelated in several ways: *first,* they all have the potential for significant improvement in terms of OECD relationships; *second,* all three are rooted in the same ethnocentricity that characterizes Western foreign policy; *third,* changes in each or any of these relationships will have a major impact on the others.

East-West and North-South Boundaries

The existing pattern of relationships between East and West is linked to the pattern of relationships between North and South. While there are direct instabilities between East and West, especially the arms race, political boundaries are, for the moment, essentially stable. In North-

South terms however, the relationship between the East and West blocs as to spheres of influence is unclear. The instability of Eastern and Western spheres of influence in less-developed regions of the world is the broader context in which East-West relations need to be evaluated.

These conflicting spheres of influence are reflected in what could be defined as "negative linkage" between East-West and North-South relationships. For example, Afghanistan and Central America fundamentally affect both the East-West military confrontation and the pattern of international development. Moreover, these hot spots reflect a much broader pattern of East-West positioning, in both military and economic terms. This widespread jockeying for position in the Third World both aggravates East-West tensions and distorts social and economic development in Third-World countries.

A major distortion, for example, is the tendency of OECD international aid programs to tie the economies of Third-World countries to the donor country on one hand, and to the OECD market system on the other hand. This is not necessarily bad for the individual Third-World country, but in many cases, it has in fact been dysfunctional and even disastrous. The East bloc countries impose similar conditions in their relationships with Third-World countries, although the scale is much smaller.

There is no doubt that some characteristics of development patterns in both the West and East have relevance in Third-World countries. These relationships are characterized by the integration of economic with strategic military concerns, to the detriment (and potential breakdown) of national economic and social development in Third-World countries. At the macro level, this is reflected by the debt crisis and by growing militarization. At the micro level, this can be seen in the widespread transfer of inappropriate technologies, which are neither economically nor socially viable. The point is that each bloc is competing across the board to reinforce its own system in the Third World and to destabilize the other system.

This negative pattern of relationships between East-West and North-South is a salient, if not *the* salient, feature of East-West tensions because it is the most volatile and unpredictable sphere of East-West relationships.

Breakdown in Sub-Saharan Africa

In Africa the ethnocentrism of international development is a central factor of the current socioecological breakdown. The symptoms of the crisis are frequently reported and discussed. In many African countries, conditions have deteriorated in both absolute and relative terms after twenty years of massive development assistance.

- Drought and famine are widespread. Twenty-four countries in Africa aside from Ethiopia suffered food shortages in 1985. The environmental degradation that is exacerbating the problem is already severe and escalating. While the publicity is declining, the problem has not been resolved.
- Africa has little capacity to repay international debt, now at $200 billion. More money is flowing out of less industrial countries to service their debt than is being received in development assistance.
- Rising military expenditures have detrimental effects on large parts of Africa.
- The existing urban infrastructure is deteriorating while urbanization is occurring at an increased pace.

This breakdown is reinforced by the international development process that plays a significant economic role in most of sub-Saharan Africa. One example of the way in which North-South relations distort the development process is that the funds from aid programs may only be used to purchase goods and services in the donor country. The economy of the recipient Third-World country becomes a dumping ground for goods and services from donor countries. To suppliers in the North, the South represents a means for extending the life of mature products and services. The South is not seen as a place for Northern suppliers to create innovative new products and services geared to their special needs.

While the stated aim of development is to increase the self-sufficiency of the recipient countries, in the long run, the recipient of aid becomes more rather than less dependent on the OECD system as imported goods and services replace or deter indigenous goods and services. Depending on the number of donor countries involved, the recipients are locked into a multitude of self-reinforcing negative linkages that subordinate them to the OECD system. South-South relationships are distorted or smothered by the primary North-South pattern of exchange.

A Breakthrough in Relations with China

The recent reopening of the Chinese economy portends perhaps the largest intercultural transfer of both physical technologies and organizational structures ever undertaken. There will undoubtedly be turbulence generated by this transfer process over the next ten to twenty years, based as it is now to a considerable extent on a one-way transfer of Western technologies, entrepreneurship, and patterns of consumption. There could even be a backlash against Western ethnocentrism, visible already to some extent in the form of a backlash against the growing Japanese role and rampant consumerism in China.

The Chinese are aware of the potential for turbulence and are looking for ways to maintain a strong development momentum yet still manage the inevitable dislocations and strains that this development will generate. Turbulence will be generated in various ways. For example, the growth of independent enterprise with its comparatively decentralized mode of decision will create tensions within the overall context of the established socioeconomic system. The growth of income disparity, the unaccustomed pressures of market prices for agricultural goods, the social pressures of consumerism, and the inevitable pressures for urbanization that result from higher agricultural productivity, along with other unforeseen development issues, could rend the social fabric.

There is also the inevitable fragmentation caused by multiple external sources of technological and organizational inputs from international development.

In recognition of the mounting costs and risks of rapid development, the Chinese are beginning to rethink their priorities and retrench their economic objectives. This is a signal to OECD countries that future opportunities require a realignment of OECD attitudes to technology transfer and international development. A parallel with Sino-Soviet relations of the 1950s may emerge. It has been unrealistic to approach China as an extension of the Soviet pattern of development. It is equally short-sighted for OECD countries to expect China in the 1990s to move steadily toward the OECD pattern. The real opportunity is for an OECD country to take the lead in developing a new joint approach to international development based on the principle of design for scanning, selecting, and integrating suitable technologies into the Chinese socioeconomic system.

Conclusions

In its relationships with other parts of the world, the ethnocentricity of the OECD system is an overriding influence on both the pattern of international diplomacy and the international economic development process. In each case, ethnocentricity limits the scope for reorienting foreign policy. Africa is in a crisis to which the North has made a significant contribution, both through East-West jockeying for advantage in Africa and through efforts to "modernize" Africa in the European mode. China's bid for economic reform and a more open posture in the international economy presents significant potential, but it is also open to misinterpretation. A lack of regard for the integrity of China's own emerging pattern could force China off the path of closer ties to the OECD system.

The question remains whether and how we will redefine our international relationships. So long as foreign policy does not take into account the interests of both partners in each relationship, it is unlikely we will be able to address the crisis in Africa, the opportunities in China (beyond a short-term economic boom), or the diplomatic stalemate and military escalation in East-West relations.

A Framework for Redesign

Introduction

Ethnocentricity, which is always present in international development and foreign policy, has the potential to be a positive factor when it is recognized and well deployed. Every individual, organization, and society has its own values and perspectives about the world as it is and should be. Ethnocentrism creates problems when it is so dominant that other viewpoints are dismissed as antiquated or misguided. For example, most OECD countries share the policy perspective that the world is becoming and should become, one large integrated and homogeneous market, based on an increasingly homogeneous world culture. A polycentric view not only respects differences among cultures and questions complete integration but also recognizes the desirability of cultural diversity and multiple markets that may be only partially integrated on a worldwide basis.

For example, within the OECD system polycentric characteristics increasingly shape relationships among OECD countries. There is a more open and homogeneous European market, but one in which the cultural diversity of member countries is respected. In North America the strong trade and communications links between Canada, Mexico, and the United States have not eliminated the desire on the part of Canadians and Mexicans to develop their own distinctive values and international perspectives. Japan's distinctive but homogeneous culture, which is relatively isolated from other OECD countries, has not prevented it from playing a prominent role in the OECD system.

OECD countries however, in their dealings outside the OECD system, project an ethnocentric view of the world. There are many examples: Japan, North America, and Europe all tend to view China in terms of their own values about free markets and industrial development; Canadian development aid to sub-Saharan Africa is shaped in the belief that African underdevelopment is largely the result of their failure to adhere to "proper" fiscal and monetary policies, to promote private enterprise, and to espouse "democratic" ideals. Relationships between Council for Mutual Economic Assistance (COMECON) and OECD countries reflect politically stable boundaries in East-West terms, but as both OECD and COMECON countries attempt to project their values and economic system on developing countries, they have created instability in North-South terms.

In each of these three areas of Canadian (and OECD) foreign policy, Western perspectives and values have both ethnocentric and polycentric characteristics. A combination of these two characteristics is present in all foreign policy decisions and operations. Canada manages its relationships (as a member of OECD) with the three other major world systems referred to above, much more in terms of ethnocentric than polycentric characteristics.

The question is how to redeploy ethnocentricity on both sides of a relationship. First of all, ethnocentricity is neither bad nor good. But it is always there, even though individual and organizational actors often deny that it is a key aspect of *their* perspective. Second, it is always tied in some way to polycentricity—a dual perspective. Third, there are ways of redeploying the profile of decisions of the dual perspective to progressively move, for example, from deterrence toward détente in East-West relations. But the relationship between ethnocentricity and polycentricity must be more clearly understood.

Competing Interests and Conflict

Organized interests in international development include governmental, nongovernmental, and profit-making organizations. Each of these organizations can view itself as an autonomous entity, with its own distinct individual interests. Ethnocentric development is designed to optimize the objectives pursued independently by each organization that stands to benefit as an individual entity.

Governmental objectives express national interests in areas such as trade, defense, external debt, growth, employment, foreign ownership, and technology acquisition. International development objectives overlap with the achievement of national objectives. Some relationships will more effectively maximize national and international objectives than others. This requires looking for ways to manage interdependence and uncertainty. The ethnocentric ideal is to

A FRAMEWORK FOR FOREIGN POLICY AND OPERATIONS

	ETHNOCENTRIC	POLYCENTRIC
DESIGN	COMPETING INTERESTS Self-analysis of one's position in a pattern of relationships to optimize one's objectives – optimize objectives – solve problems – research existing pattern of relations	JOINT DESIGN Interactive definition and assessment of a pattern of relationships to dissolve a meta-problem. – idealize relationships – dissolve problems – identify stakeholders
OPERATIONS	CONFLICT Satisfy constraints and resolve conflict to maintain or improve one's position in a given pattern of relationships. – satisfy constraints – resolve problems – mediate conflict	JOINT OPERATIONS Construct and test new patterns of relationship – synthesize ideas and interests – progressively link interests into new pattern of relationship

Figure 26.1.

position oneself to the best advantage within the existing pattern of relationships (Figure 26.1).

Ethnocentric conflicts arise among interests competing for position in the system. Conflict management extends or defends organizational boundaries. It tends to reinforce status quo relationships rather than attempt to change the pattern of relationships and risk conflict.

Conflict resolution rests on power: who has it and how it is used. Where the difference in power between the parties is very large, the relationship can have a friendly character, with the weaker parties currying favor of the powerful. One way of viewing the ongoing crisis in African development is to see it as a product of friendly relations between powerless African and powerful OECD countries. Continuing the relationship on friendly terms requires reinforcing the status quo and the dominance of OECD objectives and values.

In cases where power is more balanced, the potential for overt conflict is high. In the international arena the escalation of conflict between major world powers poses the danger that equally matched contestants will be inclined to destroy each other sooner than look beyond the status quo for new relationship patterns.

In a polycentric approach, individual interests are building blocks for developing higher levels of understanding and agreement, as well as creating arenas for joint interorganizational operations. Western societies currently lack the necessary institutional infrastructure to take a polycentric perspective and make it operational. The United Nations concept, which is perhaps as close as we have come to the polycentric ideal, has not been an effective operational instrument, tending to bog down in bureaucracy and conflict management. What it and other organizational forms have failed to achieve is a redesign of the relationships so that ethnocentric objectives are incorporated through a process of joint design and operations.

Joint Design and Operations

The polycentric ideal is to design relationships that are mutually reinforcing and capable of opening new patterns. The system principle employed here is redundancy of potential command, introduced by McCulloch.

> According to this concept, brains and brainlike systems make their decisions wherever the information relevant to those decisions comes together. Therefore, it is unphysiological to appoint permanent centres where the decisions must lie. Any concatenation of logical elements may acquire the information relevant to the decision; therefore, any such concatenation is potentially in command. And since the combinatorial properties of a brain or a brainlike regulator are exponentially explosive, such potential command is highly redundant. (Stafford Beer 1975, pp. 425–26)

The purpose in polycentric design is to support a brainlike system of global management, not the creation of a monolithic international system. In this view, the world can be treated as an open, evolving, multicentred system.

A starting point for joint design is the recognition that solving problems one by one is less effective than dealing with sets of related problems. Joint design sees problems as systemic, as part of a larger "system of problems," metaproblems, or "messes," as Russell Ackoff (1974) calls them. By redesigning the system, these metaproblems can be dissolved (Ackoff 1981). Metaproblems are not solved by fixing the parts of the system but by changing the pattern of relations in which the metaproblem arose in the first place.

Joint design is a participative process (see Figure 26.1). It is not based on extensive research and problem analysis but on interaction among the actors. Meetings convened to organize those who have a stake in solving the metaproblem are used to progressively redefine the metaproblem as well as progressively link and redefine the interests involved. This is a selective process, with an emphasis on defining and addressing issues critical to the parties involved. By dissolving the metaproblem into a new set of issues, a common ground is created for action that is based on the interests of the parties involved as well as on building their institutional and international relationships.

The challenge is to move from joint design to joint operations, making the necessary connections between policy and operations, or idealized and strategic planning (see Figure 26.1). Going from design to operations requires descriptive and normative judgments about the pattern of relations among the interests involved. The aim is to do more than create better feelings among the stakeholders and a sense of commitment to take some joint action. The aim is to create and test some options for implementation to generate positive working relationships through system redesign. Joint operations explicitly move beyond the status quo to create new patterns of interaction. Joint operations are only sought when existing patterns of relationship become dysfunctional.

The connection between design and operations is made when one or more key actors takes a *position,* acting as a catalyst in the process of transforming a pattern of relationships. Polycentric strategy differs from ethnocentric strategy in that the latter takes a position within the pattern of relationships as given, whereas the former is a means for proposing and testing new patterns. In practice, not everyone is prepared to take a polycentric position. Nor is it necessary. What is needed is merely a catalyst, or a kick in a new direction. New patterns of relationship need not be precisely defined at the outset and are better left unfinished to be further developed in an ongoing participative design process. In this way, design and operations are not sequential, as in a linear planning model, but rather concurrent.

Implications for Western Foreign Policy

Introduction

Incorporating a polycentric approach into a rethinking of Western foreign policy offers some new directions for OECD relationships with the rest of the world. It opens the door to improving our capacity to assist in the crisis in Africa and generates alternatives for negotiating with China in ways that will be more effective in the long term—China is offering a polycentric opening, and so far, we are responding in an ethnocentric way. It also signals some contributions to building a positive East-West relationship, even extending current initiatives. The goal of joint design of new patterns of interaction stresses the need to do much more than extend and strengthen existing patterns. If all we do is strengthen existing patterns, conditions of famine in Africa will recur, a Chinese retrenchment is a strong possibility, and the potential for East-West conflict remains high.

OECD-Africa Relationships

The negative consequences from attempts to modernize are apparent in the traditional rural sectors of sub-Saharan African societies. Rural people are alienated by efforts at modernization to which they are not party to the decision making and from which they do not benefit. Of course, not all aid programs have concentrated on urban modernization. But even when aid is directed to rural development, it has been geared to increasing agricultural productivity to the exclusion of peasants who have no real incentive to voluntarily participate. By emphasizing modern agricultural practices, cash crops, and large-scale farming, the skewed benefits of aid have resulted in agricultural development that does not meet local needs for food self-sufficiency and that, by displacing agricultural workers, accelerates migration to urban areas.

The conflict between rural and urban interests and between those in the modern and traditional sectors is the outcome of underdevelopment, not its cause. The answer lies in developing the organizational infrastructure needed for the modern sector, and the incentives and opportunities for the traditional sector to "buy into" the drive to develop. Policies that continue to attack the symptoms of breakdown in Africa will, like food aid, remain critical short-term concerns in famine situations. But stop-gap measures must not be used to postpone a shift in emphasis to long-term development.

The neglect of the modern-traditional boundary has resulted in disincentives to peasant participation. Lacking open market institutions to trade in locally produced goods and in the absence of the commercial organizations built on local trade, peasants have had little choice but to pull away from development. It is logical for peasants under these circumstances to dissociate themselves from the development process. This creates a barrier between the modern and traditional sectors of the economy.

Aid to reinforce the organizational development of Southern countries is still rare. Any hope of building the necessary infrastructure will require a deep reorientation of the foreign policy establishment in OECD countries. Tied aid, technical assistance, food aid, physical infrastructure and commodity aid all have undesirable side effects. Each type of these aid programs displaces local interests, and the organizations they are capable of building. Further, each aid program has a certain degree of inertia, with special interest groups in OECD countries favoring their continuation. But although the interests of the international development community are closely related to the current pattern of aid activities, it is the same aid community that is increasingly aware of the shortcomings of the ethnocentric thrust of OECD aid policies. The stage is set for a reorientation in the direction of polycentric aid, building a new capacity for development which bridges the modern and traditional sectors and which sets about developing organizational infrastructures.

Development geared solely to the modern sector is an extension of the colonial era. African governments too often find themselves in the middle of the picture, trying to maintain a viable relationship between OECD countries and the African modern sector. This turns attention away from building a viable relationship between urban and rural as well as modern and traditional sectors. Aid continues to be tied to the short-term and ethnocentric policies of the donor country, which as a practical matter, means aid projects can only provide assistance to the modern sector. This is not the way to harness the productivity of the traditional sector.

In a polycentric policy framework, development is a process of building the organizations and institutions that will serve as the operational instruments of development. OECD countries would jointly design initiatives, respecting the legitimacy of putting African organizations at the forefront of development alongside OECD organizations. But perhaps more importantly, it would put the relationship between modern and traditional sectors at the center of development patterns. By stimulating polycentric development and thus an improvement in overall trade relations, not to mention the total incomes of all countries concerned, the international economy could begin to turn in a new and more productive direction.

Reorienting international development aid means that the established criteria of international development, both explicit and implicit, be changed. In the North-South pattern of relationships, the new criteria represent a change from colonial times when there was a direct relationship between individual colonial powers and each of their African colonies. Compared with this simple one-to-one hierarchical and authoritarian relationship, aid is currently mediated by a host of multicountry institutions organized around the North-South boundary. In operational terms, aid is measured by criteria that are more appropriate for projects focused exclusively in the modern sector. If effective aid must include both the North-South and modern-traditional boundaries, then the criteria for international development programs must be redefined accordingly.

Polycentric aid will be less easily evaluated and managed by centralized OECD governmental aid structures. The multiplicity of smaller projects, linked together in operational networks, points toward a leaner and more flexible form of organization. There will be less of the "development bank" style of operation, funneling money on a project-by-project and country-by-country basis. Instead, the emphasis will gravitate toward international project teams working to link all sectors of development. This linking role has characteristics similar to venture capital and merchant banking functions in OECD countries.

Some aid organizations, particularly non-governmental organizations (NGOs), attempt to deal directly with the traditional sector. By virtue of their small size and multiple projects, NGOs tend to adopt a more open and flexible style of organization. Well-intentioned attempts to deal with the needs of the traditional sector tend to circumvent the host government. Naturally, this raises tension and limits the potential of NGOs to integrate and extend themselves and help to build local organizational infrastructures. In many circumstances, NGOs distort their role by substituting for local organizations.

The development of African-based organizations has implications for both the North-South and modern-traditional boundaries. It necessitates the use of institutional mechanisms to assess, design, and initiate new organizations and new organizational forms to act as a middle ground.

Canada could take a leadership position in shifting the pattern of international development in Africa. As a middle-level power, bilingual in the two lingua francas of Africa and with a strong agricultural base, it has the experience and capacity to shift from a development process based on modernization and on the stability of the aid organizations themselves to one based on building the internal capacities in Africa to cope with the turbulence on the continent. This would require a fundamental cultural shift in international development patterns from a modernization perspective focused on the North-South boundary to a development perspective focused on the modern-traditional boundary. This requires as well a shift to a more negotiated approach to development—a shift to joint operations. It implies policy shifts in areas such as tied aid, the project design process, NGO roles, project funding, and leadership, among others. It could lead to a more balanced—and effective—development process in Africa, which would increase Africa's capacity to integrate into the world economy (as well as our capacity to integrate with the African economy more than as simply a supplier of raw materials).

OECD-China Relationships

The pattern of OECD relationships with China is based largely on the initiatives that China has undertaken to change the previous pattern of isolation. In our terms, we would say that China has taken a poly-centric position in relation to the OECD. The OECD response to date has been predominantly ethnocentric. We have wrongly assumed that the Chinese have decided to adopt "our" system and have wrongly concluded that this proves the superiority of the OECD system.

In its new drive to modernization, China has not turned its back on the rural and traditional sectors. On the contrary, incentive pricing for agricultural goods has strengthened food production, albeit with only a small overall surplus. Even though many farm workers will become redundant as productivity rises in the fields, the modernization of agriculture is of major benefit to the peasants as a group. The modern industrial sector is where China's population will now turn to seek employment. By balancing the pace of industrial and agricultural development, modernization can be a success. Unbalanced development could break its momentum, possibly leading to a reaction against further development and hostility to outside influences. Bridging the modern and traditional sectors in China as well as bridging the modern OECD and Chinese sectors is the critical factor.

The history of China does not suggest that it is prepared to imitate any of the other major socioeconomic systems, although it does suggest that China is prepared to deal with OECD countries if it can stand on an equal footing. In its recent past, China has cut itself off from both the OECD and COMECON systems when it felt they were exerting too much influence. Attempts to restructure the Chinese system to more closely reflect an ethnocentric OECD or COMECON view of how China should organize itself are bound to be less fruitful than dealing with China on a partnership basis.

The initial approach among OECD governments and private sector organizations was to deal with China as an extension of the OECD system, opening the world's largest untapped market for Western goods and services. The technology and entrepreneurial "experts" could come to teach the Chinese how to make the system work. Once it became clear that the vast Chinese market offered opportunities for the sale of Western technology and expertise, many OECD organizations began flocking into China to make their services available. The ethnocentricity of the OECD approach made it easier for China to "shop around." Some OECD organizations began to wonder if doing business with China was worth the effort. And the act of balancing various facets of development—juggling rural and urban, modern and traditional, domestic and international, agricultural and industrial sectors—has become increasingly difficult.

The Chinese seem to recognize the inherent constraints and risks of Western ethnocentricity. There is already some negative reaction against the rise of the consumer sector of the economy. Construction projects are cropping up everywhere causing concerns about the pace and quality of urban development. Foreign exchange reserves are being depleted, and the capacity for further growth may be more conditioned by China's capacity to export goods into OECD markets.

Western technology is a key component in China's drive to modernize. But the OECD countries have failed to come to terms with China's technological needs and interests in polycentric terms. Instead, they have followed the ethnocentric pattern of treating China as an operational extension of the OECD system of production. Major infrastructure plans now being discussed, including hydro dams, nuclear power, and offshore oil, closely resemble the postwar technology transfer programs that have left many Third-World countries deeply in debt and economically stagnant. In most cases, Western technology is adapted for reasons of geography, but not redesigned in view of differing organizational, social, or economic considerations.

In the short term, capital- and technology-intensive projects offer the path of least resistance where the OECD can be ethnocentric and still seem to play a leading role. But in the longer term, and in the wider sphere of economic development, China cannot modernize its economy merely by importing technology and capital. A deeper and more enduring relationship requires a polycentric approach based on joint design and operations. Rather than pursue the illusion that technology can be merely transferred on a massive scale, OECD relations would then center on the question of how OECD organizations could become partners with a willingness and long-term commitment to help China modernize itself.

By embarking on a more open foreign policy, China runs the risk of developing a fragmented relationship with the OECD system. Co-ordinating this relationship is proving difficult, and integration is presumably even more difficult to achieve. Instead of adding to the fragmentation, OECD countries could develop a relatively flexible and decentralized form of development administration. So far, they have not had to assume any responsibility for facilitating the situation. To do so might be misconstrued as interference. But it also provides a major opportunity to an OECD country willing to take the lead in developing a joint institutional design for scanning, selecting, and integrating development projects into the Chinese socioeconomic system.

Joint design and operations would also need to take into account the requirement for many small and medium enterprises that are essential for long-term viability. Such an approach could lead to the development of new technologies rather than using the Chinese market as a dumping ground for outdated technologies that can no longer be sold in OECD markets.

East-West Relationships

The boundary between East and West is the biggest threat facing the human race. Armed conflict between the superpowers would appear to be futile and self-destructive. Yet both East and West seem unable to break away from the escalating arms competition despite the implications. Our argument here is that the ethnocentrism of both East and West is the unwitting driving force behind this no-win relationship and that the arms race has merely institutionalized this conflict rather than resolved it. The arms race cannot be managed within the existing set of institutions and institutional arrangements. Instead, it must be dissolved by initiating new foreign policies on a broad range of fronts, with these policies reintegrated into a new polycentric framework.

Middle-level powers such as Canada can play a decisive role in reorienting foreign policy frameworks. This can be done at two levels: First by developing ad hoc polycentric initiatives such as those in relation to North-South and OECD-China relationships discussed above. Second, middle-level powers can play a role linking OECD interests in new collective patterns of relationship as well as linking OECD and COMECON interests. This can be accomplished by reorienting bilateral international development agencies: NATO,

General Agreement on Tariffs and Trade, International Monetary Fund, the World Bank, and the system of United Nations organizations to name a few. It might be more directly accomplished through the establishment of linkage institutions that have a dual design and operational role and that could be founded primarily to initiate and strengthen polycentric relationships. As a practical matter, both re-orientation of existing institutions and the development of new ones is far more likely to be effective than an approach emphasizing merely one or the other.

Conflict and confrontation have been institutionalized in arms control negotiations and periodic summit talks. The overall logic of deterrence is reflected by mutual suspicion and lack of respect. The defense by each system of its own ideals seems to demand an attack of the other. This style characterizes most negotiations and relationships between East and West, from arms control negotiations to sporting events.

In our interaction with the Academy of Sciences of the Soviet Union, we have been discussing the development of joint research activities in terms of the interaction of two distinctly evolving systems, rather than assuming a convergence of the two systems (an inherent assumption in most interactions that presumes the ultimate primacy of one system or the other). This implies moving beyond the polite tit-for-tat academic exchanges of the past to a joint design process extending the common threads of our relationships, particularly in areas of instability, such as interventions by both sides in less industrialized countries.

This could be achieved through jointly focusing on selected critical issues and developing challenging positions for the leadership of both sides. In this process, we are not defending or attacking the ideals of either but recognizing them as mutually reinforcing within the global system. Actors can be assumed to support their own system and to be participating from a perspective of improving the pattern of relationships between them.

Acknowledgments

This chapter represents work in progress on international policy and institutional relations. It is based on ongoing research in three settings: in OECD-Africa relationships through a joint research project between the Cooperative College of Tanzania and York University, sponsored by the International Development Research Centre and the Canadian International Development Agency; in East-West relationships resulting from an invitation to visit the Institute of the USA and Canada of the Academy of Sciences of the USSR; in OECD-China relationships through an invitation from Qing Hua University's School of Economic Management, to conduct an exploratory seminar on the management of technology transfer processes with the School and senior officials from several departments of the government of the People's Republic of China (Ministry of Foreign Economic Relations and Trade, National Planning Commission, State Economic Commission, and the National Research Centre for Science and Technology for Development).

Notes

1. One could also address other critical fault lines, for example, the one between Latin America and the OECD, as epitomized by the Rio Grande River, and the fault line between the Moslem World and the OECD, as epitomized by Beirut and the West Bank.

2. The concept of metaproblem was introduced by Michel Chevalier and is elaborated in a paper prepared with James R. Taylor for the Royal Commission on Bilingualism and Biculturalism, *Dynamics of Adaptation in the Federal Public Service*. Study No. 9. 1971. See the section entitled "A Framework for Redesign," below, for further discussion.

References

Ackoff, R. (1974). *Redesigning the Future*. New York: Wiley.
———. (1981). "On The Use of Models in Corporate Planning." *Strategic Management Journal* 2: 353–59.
Beer, Stafford. (1975). *The Brain of the Firm*. New York: McGraw-Hill.
———. (1981). "On Heaping Our Science Together." In Fred E. Emery (ed.): *Systems Thinking*, vol. 2. New York: Penguin.
Chevalier, Michel, and James R. Taylor. (1971). *Dynamics of Adaptation in the Federal Public Service*. Studies of the Royal Commission on Bilingualism and Biculturalism, Study No. 9. Ottawa: Supply and Services, 1971.

Chapter 27
Power in the Design, Management, and Evaluation of Organizations

William E. Smith

Background

This paper provides a summary of a conceptual framework for designing, managing, and evaluating organizations. The framework, built on a concept of power, has been developed and tested over the last eight years.

The need for such a framework arose from a review of project performance carried out by the World Bank in 1978 that concluded 75% of the problems resulted from poor management. The author was asked to review these problems in the light of the most current organization and management theory and practice. He concluded that most of the problems were not those of management. Two categories contributed most to poor performance: external factors, such as price policy changes; and human factors, such as lack of motivation and personality clashes. For example, a population project failed because basic disagreements about objectives had not been addressed in the earliest phases of preparation. The organizers did not develop an effective strategy for marshaling available support and minimizing opposition. Political differences and personality clashes between donors and government agencies were never dealt with effectively. Under these conditions effective implementation by management was very difficult. The implicit model of organization used to design, manage, and evaluate projects does not deal adequately with such factors.

The Rural Development Division of the World Bank expressed interest in these findings and sponsored the second phase of the work, an action research program to develop and test a more appropriate approach. The results were published in 1980 (Smith et al. 1980). A more thorough review of the theory and methodology was provided in the author's dissertation (Smith 1983).

The third, or application, phase of the program is now underway. The framework is being used in a variety of applications at different levels of organization. At the highest level it is being used to determine policies to govern assistance to developing countries. Within a country it is being used to design sector strategies consistent with those policies, for example, energy and public administration. Within the sectors it is being used to develop institutions capable of implementing those strategies. Most recently, it has been used to develop a new concept and approach to performance evaluation of public sector enterprises. In the private sector it is being used to design integrated programs of organization, management, development, and planning. The following pages trace the essential conceptual underpinnings of the framework.

The Implicit Framework

The implicit model is illustrated in Figure 27.1. An organization's performance results from two sources, internal factors it can control and external factors it cannot control, i.e., $P = f(C,U)$. Logically, there are four possible combinations of these two variables that express all possible causal relations between them: U-u, U-c, C-u and C-c. The first capital letters refer to the organization and the second small letters to the environmental agent.

External factors, uncontrollable by management include:

1. U-u, those factors uncontrollable by management (U), and uncontrollable by external agents (u); they are unknown or unpredictable in their effects on performance, for example, catastrophic climactic conditions, political and social upheavals, and unexpected technological breakthroughs or failures. The role of management relative to these factors is to react and adapt as the organization is affected.
2. U-c, those factors uncontrollable by management (U), but controllable by external agents (c), for example, price policies, taxes, predictable political interests, and social conditions. They affect performance in a predictable way and are known by the designers or managers. The role of managers is to predict the occurrence and state of these factors and prepare the organization to deal with them.

Internal factors, controllable by management include:

1. C-c, those actions that designers or managers can take (C) in response to factors controlled by external agents (c) or known

THE IMPLICIT MODEL

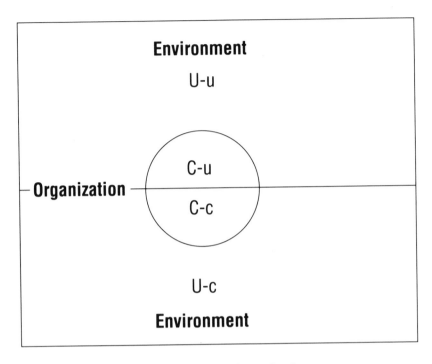

Environment

U-u

Organization

C-u

C-c

U-c

Environment

U	Uncontrolled by Organization
u	Uncontrolled by Environment
C	Controlled by Organization
c	Controlled by Environment

Figure 27.1

environmental conditions. The manager's role is to position or adapt the organization to take advantage of known opportunities or avoid known constraints.

2. C-u, the direct actions of the organization or its management (C) that cannot be controlled by any external agency (u). The implicit model sees this category as the heart of organization and management where management has complete control of its own decisions and resources without influence from any external sources.

The reader familiar with Russ Ackoff's (1981) four modes of planning (inactivism, reactivism, preactivism, and interactivism) will recognize that the implicit model uses the preactive mode. He points out that preactivism assumes that the future is predictable, and the job of designers and planners is to predict and prepare for that future. It assumes the environment will remain constant during the period of design, planning, and implementation. However, the environment is not a static external entity that exists for all organizations but rather is a dynamic entity relative to each organization and consists of the activities of all other actors, organizations, and external agencies. It changes as they act and will not remain constant while the organization predicts and prepares. If evaluation is left till the end of the planned implementation period then changes in environmental conditions that occur during the planning and implementation periods are not taken into account.

The dichotomy between uncontrolled and controlled variables results in a separation of the process of design or planning, management, and evaluation. Designers are responsible for dealing with the uncontrollable variables, U-u and U-c; planners for adaptation to the environment C-c; and managers for implementation, C-u. It is not clear who has responsibility for evaluation. As all uncontrollable elements should have been removed by the first two steps, it is only the manager who has the power (i.e., control) to affect performance; therefore, only he or she can be blamed for problems of implementation. Since evaluation is not carried out till the end of the planning period, the manager is not aware of any changes in the state of the uncontrolled external variables and so cannot make adjustments.

Evidence of this thinking is found at each level of development assistance organization. There is often a gap in the process of translation of macro economic objectives into implementation. Policy decisions are implemented through projects that cannot function adequately because of the lack of supporting sectoral strategies or institutional capacity. For example, in several countries energy policies have been translated into project assistance for specific utilities. The lack of strategies and institutional capacity at an intermediate level between the policy makers and the operating utilities resulted in excess national capacity at tremendous cost to the sector and lost opportunities for other sectors of the national economies.

Project organization itself, is a direct expression of the emphasis on the need for control. The chief characteristic of this form of design is its isolation from its external environment. The project attempts to control all elements, resources, etc., necessary for performance under the assumption that this is the only way the project manager can guarantee performance. Where evaluation exists it is carried out by a separate unit after project completion. Monitoring or supervision is carried out but only in relationship to internal or controlled variables.

At the micro level of problem solving, the model has its corollary in the tendency to jump from concept to blueprint, as attempts to find solutions foreclose adequate understanding of the problems and the development of alternative strategies for finding solutions.

The private sector suffers equally from this way of thinking. A recent *Business Week* article (March 3, 1986) summarizes a panoply of woes that result directly from an overemphasis on the controllable; for example, "impatient" capital has forgotten that finance exists to serve industry and not the reverse, and companies have abandoned manufacturing to foreign countries in order to raise profits. Both indicate the neglect of the longer-term strategic and policy issues in favor of short-term gains. A *Fortune* magazine article (May 2, 1983) showed how the worst companies in 1973 performed much better over the subsequent 10-year period than did those companies who had the best performance in 1973—an indication that even the best corporations have not yet learned how to sustain high performance.

At all levels of both the public and private sector, neglect of human factors is seen in the overreliance on objective rational thinking that precludes the subjective evaluation of political interest, and the role of personality. Politics and personalities are regarded as illegitimate for formal discussion. Yet these are regarded by practitioners as the most intractable problems affecting performance.

The primary objectives in building the new framework were to:

1. Place human actors with their political interests and personality differences at the center of the organizational stage.
2. Reflect more accurately the dynamic nature of interaction between the organization and its environment.
3. Overcome the barriers between design, planning, implementation, and evaluation.
4. Enable practitioners to understand and use the framework at any level of application, from the macro level of policy making to the micro level of individual, personal problem solving.

Building the Framework

The breakthrough in developing the framework came from two theoretical perspectives and from one blunt, but on-the-mark, comment from a frustrated practitioner.

The first insight came from David Silverman (1971) who argues that organizational theorists take too much of an observer's perspective. They stand outside of the organizational process and therefore have a very different perspective than the practitioners'. He argues that it might be equally valid to take an actor's perspective and view organizational processes from the inside. Organization would then be seen as an outcome of interaction between motivated people pursuing their own purposes and solving their own problems.

The second theoretical insight came from Trist and Emery (1975) who suggested the existence of three environments: the contextual, the transactional, and the internal. However, they, like the implicit model, distinguish only four environmental relationships: L_{1-1}, L_{1-2}, L_{2-1}, and L_{2-2}, where L_1 is an internal linkage and L_2 an external linkage. Each equates exactly to the implicit model's C-c, C-u, U-c, and U-u. The first refers to processes within the organization, the second and third to exchanges between the organization and the environment or the transactional environment, and the fourth to exchanges between parts of the environment providing the context for the organization and its transactions. The concept freed us from seeing only the duality of an organization and environment with controlled and uncontrolled variables.

The final link was provided by a frustrated practitioner, who in trying to link our concepts to practice in the field, said quite bluntly: "If you have to use terms like 'internal,' 'transactional,' and 'contextual' in the field to explain concepts, then they are no good for practice because they will never be used. What we want is language that people use, that relates to their experience."

How would a practitioner describe his or her action relative to the internal, transactional, and contextual environments? It was relatively easy to describe the actor's relationship to "internal" and "transactional" elements. He or she would "control" the internal and "influence" transactional. (This insight came directly from discussions with Russ Ackoff.) It was much more difficult to describe his or her action relative to the contextual. After much searching, the term "appreciation," borrowed from Vickers (1966), was decided upon. He, in turn, derived it from the British military who carried out "appreciations" of the enemy's position.

The choice of these terms was meant at first to translate academic language into that of the practitioner; however, once seen together, they gave new insight into environmental relationships. All related to a single concept: power. The three insights were then joined into a single framework.

1. Organization is seen relatively, that is, always from the viewpoint of a particular actor or group of actors (Silverman 1971), overcoming

the objective rational bias of the implicit model. The subjective aspects of motivation and personality are taken into account by including the central actors in the design, planning, or implementation process. It is not necessary to understand or treat all variables in an organizational situation equally, as a scientist might, but only to know those relative to the central actor's purpose. It is he or she who must act and can only do so from the basis of his or her appreciation of the situation. Action is governed by the limits of his or her personality, power, and competence. It is of little use to give the central actor a perfect scientific solution to the problem if he or she cannot understand it, does not like it, or does not have the power to implement it.

2. Complex organizational situations are understood as the interaction of the power fields of many actors. Stakeholder analysis (Mitroff et al. 1983) is helpful in developing an appropriate appreciation of the purposes of the actors and the appropriate mechanisms of mutual influence before deciding on specific actions to be taken.

3. The resulting language of control, influence, and appreciation, as experience showed, was immediately usable by practitioners.

(a) *Control* is the actor's highest degree of power; he or she can cause change directly without the assistance of any outside agent. For example, a manager can control the priority he or she gives to management activities, how to organize his or her time, and how much physical and emotional resources to devote to the work.

(b) *Influence* is a lesser degree of power; the manager can only cause change, or affect events indirectly. For example, he or she cannot control suppliers or customers but can influence them through the terms and conditions he or she negotiates for acceptance or delivery of goods or services.

(c) *Appreciation* is the lowest degree of power; it consists of understanding and valuing the impact of elements the actor does not control or influence in the organization or in achieving its objectives. For example, the likely impact of regulatory agencies, research institutes, and conditions of climate as well as general economic, social, and political events.

Environmental relations are power relations; the boundaries of the three environments define the limits of the actor's power. The internal environment defines the limits of the actor's control; the transactional environment defines the limits of his or her influence; and the contextual environments define the limits of his or her appreciation. The power of any actor or organization, relative to the achievement of an objective, consists of the sum of his or her appreciation, influence, and control: P = E (A, I, C). Performance is directly related to the organization's power over variables in all three environments. Programs of design, management, or evaluation must, therefore, deal with all three environments, not just the internal.

The weakness of the implicit model can now be described more explicitly. Performance is a function of appreciated variables (U-u and U-c), influenced variables (?-?), and controlled variables (C-u and C-c). Note that the uncontrolled variables (U) correspond to the appreciated variables (A). The implicit model omits the middle level or influence variables. It is precisely these variables that account for the constant level of interchange between the organization and its environment.

If there are three types of power of causal variables, then there are nine possible combinations of causal relationships between an organization and its environment, as opposed to four in the implicit model. These are depicted in Figure 27.2. The first capital letter represents the level of power of the organization relative to the environment, and the second small letter to the power of the environmental entity relative to the organization. The five missing relationships are the combinations of influence: A-i, I-i, C-i, I-a, and I-c.

The remainder of the paper develops the practical and theoretical dimensions of this insight.

The Organizing Processes

The dynamic interactive nature of the organization's relations with its environments suggested that understanding the process of organizing, rather than the structure of organizations as in the more traditional approach, would be more appropriate. For this purpose, the basic power map of Figure 27.2 was converted into a flow process Figure 27.3. The three environmental levels (represented by A, I, and C.) correlate with Parsons (1960) three levels of organization; institutional, managerial, and technical. The institutional level is concerned with relating the organization to its wider context, its appreciated environment. The managerial level is concerned with managing relationships between those who supply the organization with its inputs, and those who receive the organization's outputs, its influenced environment. The technical level is concerned with the internal transformation process, the technology for producing the outputs, the controlled environment.

The process of organizing moves from appreciation to influence and then to control—from institutional, to managerial, and then to

THE POWER FRAMEWORK

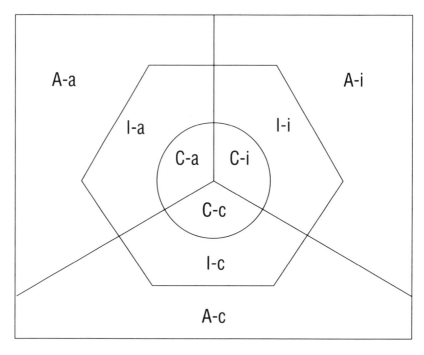

A = Apprec. by Organization   a = Apprec. by Environment
I = Infl. by Organization   i = Infl. by Environment
C = Controlled by Organization   c = Control by Environment

Figure 27.2

technical concerns. Each level is a complete process with its own inputs, transformation, and output. Just as the controlled or technical
level provides the output of the whole organizing system, so the output of each level is produced by a subprocess of control. Similarly, the
input and transformation functions are provided by subprocesses of
appreciation and influence. (The subprocesses within each level are
indicated by a, i, and c.)

Figure 27.4 translates the processes into their practical equivalents.
The appreciative or input processes at each level provide a *learning
system*. They provide both input and feedback to the subsequent
phases of organizing. The control or output process is the equivalent

SYSTEM OF PROCESSES

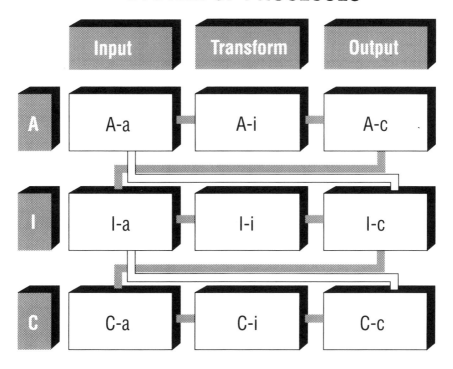

A,a = Appreciated
I,i = Influenced
C,c = Controlled

Figure 27.3

of a *planning system.* Its function is to reduce information to a form suitable for decision making or action.

The transformation process was the most difficult to name because it has no formalized equivalent in theory or practice. Its function is to transform learning through the priority filters of the organizers into the planning process. Priority in this sense determines how much energy or effort will be devoted to the particular aspects revealed by the learning or review process. After much discussion with practitioners and many trials, the term "political" was selected. The decision was made difficult by the negative connotations usually associated with

ORGANIZING PROCESSES

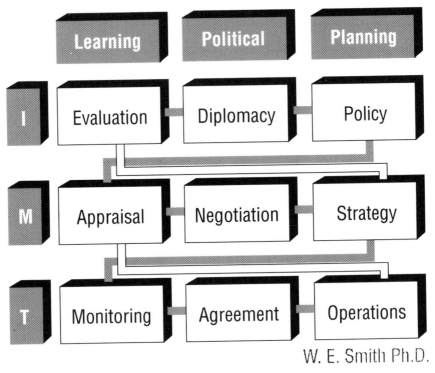

Figure 27.4

the word. However, once groups became used to using the term in the more neutral sense of the application of priority, then the term became accepted and useful. If it proves true, for example, that NASA space officials failed to give sufficient priority to warnings from engineers on the dangers posed by cold temperatures to the Challenger mission, then the incident would provide a dramatic example of the failure of the political process. Insufficient priority was placed in the planning process on the engineering information received from a review of previous flights.

The next task was to discover whether the sublevels of each process had counterparts in the practical world or, if not, whether their omission revealed an area of potential improvement in the organizing process.

Planning

To find the practical subparts of the planning process was not difficult because they already existed. Hasan Ozbekhan (1971) describes three levels of planning: normative, strategic, and operational. They correlate with the three levels of appreciation, influence, and control (Figure 27.4).

1. The concept of normative planning corresponds to the appreciative level of planning, A-c. Both are concerned with establishing a fit between the value premises of external stakeholders and those of the organization's internal stakeholders. The process produces the objectives that will guide subsequent levels of planning. The term "normative," however, was changed to "policy" because it fit better with the power concept of the framework and was more understandable to practitioners.
2. Strategic planning fit with the concept of influence. The strategic plan is the output of the influence level, I-c. After the appraisal of both policy and implementation level constraints and opportunities, the process selects and combines the most influential actors and technical elements into a strategy and structure for reaching the policy objectives. Seeing strategy as the selection and combination of the most "influential" elements is a very simple and practical way for practitioners to understand strategy.
3. Finally, operational planning fit with the concept of planning at the control level. The task of operational planning is to combine the activities of all implementers and to control all required resources into an appropriate technology to achieve the strategic goals.

Learning

A review of the learning process found existing practical equivalents for only two of the levels.

1. The controlled level of learning, C-a, is the equivalent of the monitoring process. The need for such monitoring processes has been well established both in theory (e.g., feedback loops and cyber-

netics) and recognized in practice (e.g., control systems, auditing, and quality circles).

2. Consistent with the hypothesis that the implicit framework omits the influence level, there was no formalized equivalent of learning at the influence level, A-i. Yet there is a genuine need for the function in practice:

> (a) To examine the output of the previous phase, the policy parameters in the light of the special knowledge of those responsible for formulating strategy (in large organizations these are often different people from those making policy in the previous phase).
>
> (b) To ensure that strategists consider all potential sources of influence on achieving objectives.
>
> (c) To look ahead to understand potential constraints and opportunities inherent at the implementation level, e.g., the competence of implementers, suitability of physical resources, and availability of appropriate technology.

The lack of this level of learning was a cause of failure in many of the projects and programs reviewed. Faulty strategic assumptions were not revealed till the postproject evaluation period, too late for changes during the life of the project. As a result of this finding, the Rural Development Division tried to introduce midterm reviews into the design of their projects. The term "appraisal" was selected because it captured the essential judgmental nature of the process.

3. The third level of learning is well recognized, if not well implemented, and corresponds to the appreciative level, A-a. It is the equivalent of an evaluation process. It literally draws out the value produced by the organization for its supporting external environment, whether its objectives fit within the scheme of priorities of its containing system. For example, in the private sector the market fulfills the evaluation function. In the public sector the evaluation function requires more conscious organization and is often provided by a separate unit or auditing entity. (To provide this function in a systematic way is the aim of the most recent application of the framework.)

Political

Again, consistent with the hypothesis, the influence process had no formalized practical equivalent. Invention was again required to name its sublevels.

At the appreciative level the influence task moves from a general evaluation of the purpose and interests of the stakeholders to establish general direction or policy. The task is a delicate political one because stakeholders at this stage of design are unlikely to reveal their real purposes, even if they know them. As the strategy is not yet developed, they are unable to estimate accurately the potential impact on their interests. Organizers have to infer, test, and guess in order to assess sources of leadership, likely support, opposition, and degree of commitment to the objectives. The process, when executed well, is very similar to the diplomatic process that governments use in establishing international policy, so the term "diplomacy" was, therefore, selected for the A-i process.

Once general direction is established and an appraisal of the factors necessary for implementation completed, the key political process necessary at the influence level, I-i, is one of negotiation between the various stakeholders to agree on a strategy. The purpose is to negotiate:

1. The roles of the various stakeholders.
2. Their position in the structure for organizing the effort.
3. The most influential elements that are to be included in the strategy.

The political problem at the operational level is not one of making decisions but of ensuring that decisions already made are actually carried out. The term selected to describe the C-i process was the establishing of "working agreements." Agreements are necessary to:

1. Carry out the activities necessary for completion of the strategy.
2. Use the resources allocated for the purposes indicated by the operational plan.
3. Use appropriate technology.

Roles in Planning, Management, and Evaluation

As indicated earlier, use of the implicit model leads to a separation between design, planning, management, and evaluation. The functions are performed separately and sequentially. Use of the power framework suggests that the three functions should overlap and be performed continuously—that management become a continuation of planning and evaluation part of the process of planning and management. The three levels of power help to explain how the roles of planners, managers, and evaluators can overlap in each phase.

When we think of designers, planners, and evaluators, we refer to those stakeholders in the influenced or even the appreciated environment who make policy, strategic, or evaluative decisions about the organization but who are not an operational part of the organization. In the case of a development project, they might be donors, sponsors, or superior level members of a ministry in which the project is to be housed. If the organization were the division of a corporation or other institution, then the design, planning, and evaluation function would be carried out by the next higher level of management.

During the policy phase, the upper level (designers or planners) controls the planning process, and operational managers play only an appreciative role (A-c). They provide information and need to understand the objectives (the output of the policy process) but have no decision-making power. In formulation of strategy, the upper managers retain decision-making control, but operational managers have much more influence on the choice of strategy (I-c). Finally, in the operational phase, managers control the plan, but final approval is still retained by upper levels (C-c).

Where evaluators are not part of management (e.g., where a separate evaluation or auditing unit exists), they have a role only in the learning process. They control the evaluation process, whereas the manager has only appreciative power. Evaluators and management have equal influence in the appraisal process. Their role is to negotiate for inclusion of the results of the evaluation process in the strategic planning process. However, evaluators have only an appreciative role in the monitoring process. They want to assure its effectiveness in providing valid and timely information into the appraisal process.

The overlapping roles of designers, planners, and evaluators (or upper levels of management, if they perform these functions) ensure continuity of learning and planning through all three environmental levels as well as within the organization itself.

Upper-level designers, planners, and evaluators, who know most about the appreciated environment, have the most power at the institutional (appreciative) level; however, their power declines at the managerial (influenced) and technical (controlled) levels, whereas operational managers exercise control at the technical level, influence at the managerial and appreciation at the institutional levels. The overlapping of the power fields of each of the levels avoids the dichotomous, discontinuous nature of the implicit model.

Summary and Conclusions

The framework takes as its starting point the existence of a human actor with a purpose. His power to achieve that purpose consists of his control, influence, and appreciation of factors necessary to translate that purpose into a realized outcome. To the extent that he does not control all the factors necessary to achieve his purpose, he has to organize, that is, to join his purpose and power with those of others to realize an outcome that would come as close as possible to his purpose.

Once the outcomes agreed to by actors become complex enough, multiple levels of organization are required. The outcomes of higher levels of organization become inputs to lower levels and vice versa. The relationship of appreciation, influence, and control can then be applied to whole levels of organization instead of only to factors necessary for achievement of purpose. The institutional level of organization provides an appreciative function, and the managerial level provides an influence function for the technical level.

The following framework maps out the nine major steps in a total organizing process. The processes at the appreciative level establish leadership, levels of commitment, and provide direction given the constraints of environmental variables over which the organization has no control or influence. At the influence level, the processes (1) appraise the operational implications of implementing policy, (2) negotiate roles, authority, and strategy between internal and external stakeholders, and (3) ensure maximum influence is brought to bear in the final strategy chosen. The final level of control can be effective only if the previous work of appreciation and influence has been adequately carried out. Processes at this level ensure that activities are carried out and that resources and technology are used appropriately.

1. Because the framework is based on the power fields of individual actors, it automatically includes consideration of human factors such as motives, personality, and competence. The actor's purpose is based on his or her personal and political preferences in the situation. Even though he or she may not fully be aware of them, or willing to reveal them, they still have to be considered as a legitimate part of the appreciative process. Appreciation of the purpose, role, personality, potential contributions, and commitment of stakeholders is an essential part of the organizing process.

2. The framework suggests that design, management, and evaluation of organizations must take into account the organization's relationships with its three environments: controlled, influenced, and appreciated.

3. Relationships to the influenced environment are omitted by the implicit model of organization and therefore offer the most scope for improvement. Greater attention to the influenced level ensures con-

stant interaction between the appreciated and controlled environments thereby increasing the organization's capacity for continuous learning.

4. Current theory and practice pay too much attention to the control processes and neglect influence and appreciation. In relation to Figure 27.4, they concentrate at the operational level (the control level) and on the planning process (the control process). In practice this means that more attention should be paid to the earlier phases of design and planning which deal with appreciated and influenced variables. Contrary to expectations, experience suggests that total planning time and costs are less, not more, when more time is spent on the appreciative and influence phases. Implementation is also more effective.

5. Strategic planning, i.e., planning at the influence level, is often omitted and results in insufficient options being generated, missed opportunities to gain support for objectives, and an underestimation of potential sources of opposition. The influence processes labeled appraisal, diplomacy, negotiation, and working agreements, if designed into organizations, would help overcome such problems.

6. The emphasis on control processes has minimized the need for learning. If poor performance is seen as the result of failures of control, the answer is too often a call for more and better controls. The framework suggests failures are more likely to result from poor appreciation of the environment and poor use of influence.

7. The design of improved learning systems provides better links both externally to the organization's appreciated and influenced environments and internally through the hierarchical levels of its own controlled environment.

8. The greatest barrier to the development of such learning systems is the inability of our organizational and management systems to overcome the power differences that exist between levels of the hierarchy. As interactions are based on concepts of control, it is difficult for appreciative information to be heard or given due priority. (The NASA incident dramatically illustrates this point.)

9. Organizations should be designed so that equal time and energy is devoted to the learning, political, and planning processes. (The current phase of our work involves designing the practical approaches for improving the performance of organizations in this manner.)

Overall, the framework suggests that we can improve our approach to organizing if we center our perspective on human actors and include their motives, personalities, and competences as major variables in the organizational equation.

We should remove the burden of control imposed by the implicit framework and broaden our thinking to include the influenced and appreciated factors involved in the problems we are faced with. We should understand that our relations with others, both personally and organizationally, are power relationships. We can be more effective if our attempts at control are based on appropriate prior levels of appreciation and influence.

Finally, we should recognize that organizing is a multilevel iterative process: we constantly repeat and recycle between levels of appreciation, influence, and control. In practice we need to keep asking ourselves:

1. Where are we in the process?
2. Have we completed the appreciative phase? Do we know all the stakeholders, and do we have commitment to a general direction?
3. Have we completed the influence process, and do all of the stakeholders understand their roles? Have we chosen the most influential elements for inclusion in our strategy?
4. Are we ready to control, to plan implementation, to develop working agreements with the implementers, to allocate resources, and to apply appropriate technology?
5. How will we know how well we did?

Acknowledgments

I would like to thank Francis Lethem, Ben Thoolen, and Turid Sato of the World Bank who, respectively, have been responsible for the development, testing, and application of the framework.

References

Ackoff, R. L. (1981). *Creating the Corporate Future*. New York: Wiley.

Mitroff, I. I., R. O. Mason, and Vincent P. Barabba. (1983). *The 1980 Census: Policymaking Amid Turbulence*. Lexington, Mass.: Lexington Books.

Ozbekhan, H. (1971). "Planning and Human Action." In Paul Weis (ed.): *Hierarchically Organized Systems in Theory and Practice*. New York: Hafner Publishing.

Parsons, T. (1960). *Structure and Process in Modern Societies*. New York: The Free Press of Glencoe.

Silverman, D. (1971). *The Theory of Organizations*. New York: Basic Books.

Smith, W. E., F. J. Lethem, and B. A. Thoolen. (1980). "The Design of Organizations for Rural Development Projects—A Progress Report." World Bank Staff Working Paper No. 375. (March).

Smith, W. E. (1983). *Organizing as a Power Process—The Creation and Testing of a Conceptual Framework and its Application to the Design of Development Projects.*

A Dissertation in Social Systems Sciences. University of Pennsylvania. University Microfilms International, Ann Arbor, Michigan, 1984.

"The Hollow Corporation." *Business Week*, 3 March 1986, pp. 56–86.

Trist, E., and F. E. Emery. (1975). *Towards a Social Ecology*. New York: Plenum Press.

Vickers, G. (1966). *The Art of Judgement*. New York: Basic Books.

Chapter 28
Toward Interactive Planning for International Development Projects

Paramjit S. Sachdeva

Introduction

Russell Ackoff's interactive planning approach has proven useful for redesigning the future in general and creating the corporate future in particular.[1] Its usefulness for national development planning is also expected to be considerable.[2] Since national plans and programs get translated into action through projects, these constitute a major part of international development assistance. Hence, if the relevance and applicability of interactive planning could be convincingly argued for international development projects (IDPs), the case for its wider use in Third-World development planning would be strengthened.

We compare below the planning needs of IDPs with what interactive planning has to offer and conclude that, in principle, the match between the two is remarkably good. However, adoption of the interactive approach by international aid agencies and national bureaucracies would require a redesign of the planning processes of both. The rationale and scope of the changes needed and their implications for planning IDPs are examined from a systems perspective based on Ackoff's interactive planning framework.

International Development Projects Defined

IDPs are projects undertaken by governments of developing countries with the financial assistance of international and bilateral aid agencies. They are thus a special kind of investment, flowing from and tied to the policies, programs, and procedures of the funding organization. The term "project" connotes purposefulness, some minimum size, a specific location, the introduction of something qualitatively new, and the expectation that a sequence of further development moves will be set in motion. A project also emphasizes immediate (rather than very remote) goals, is action-oriented and nonrepetitive, and generally covers nonroutine activities of a public organization or government agency for purposes of special emphasis and action.[3]

The State of the Practice

Since IDPs form an integral part of the larger set of development programs and projects undertaken in a country, their planning is basically the government's responsibility. Planning for IDPs is therefore generally undertaken by the same planning agencies that are responsible for locally funded projects. How planning is actually done depends in large measure on each country's institutional framework and its stage of development. Despite the diversity thus obtained, in most countries planning for IDPs suffers from the same general inadequacies that plague national development planning universally. As discussed by Albert Waterston on the basis of a comparative study of well over a hundred countries, the major unresolved planning problems are political and administrative rather than economic.[4] Besides other problems, the shortage of well-prepared projects remains a major impediment to implementing national development plans.

To help overcome some of the general deficiencies in national planning, aid agencies have established complex and detailed design standards for IDPs. The three primary instruments of control are prescriptive design frameworks; standardized proposal formats; and feasibility, appraisal, and supervision procedures, all of which are incorporated in comprehensive operations manuals for project staff.[5] These policies and procedures cover in great detail the various stages of the project cycle. The list of major planning and management functions covered is long and extensive and reflects a desire to use sophisticated systems analysis for prescribing and controlling project inputs.

Despite these painstaking and well-intentioned efforts, project implementation remains a difficult problem for both international aid agencies and the borrowing governments. Project evaluations document a mixed bag of achievements, with few projects rated as outstanding successes. Although internal audits by agencies such as the World Bank indicate that over 90% of their investments meet or exceed initial expectations,[6] these reports understate the complexity of the implementation process. Most development projects are affected by considerable initial ignorance and uncertainty and suffer through a host of unexpected problems during implementation.

The difficulties encountered and their sources are many and varied. Often included are the following: problems due to financial and material shortages; weak or nonexistent institutions and delivery systems; insufficient, untrained, or incompetent staff; inept or corrupt officials and politicians; outdated procedures and entangled red tape; inappropriate technology and careless design; unreliable administrative commitment and weak political will; and faulty planning and poor coordination.[7] These are well-known symptoms of the general malaise of underdevelopment. Therefore, to the extent that these afflict all government-managed development activity in the Third World, IDPs can hardly be expected to remain untouched. But aid agency procedures for disbursement and supervision are designed for the real world: they do a reasonably good job of preventing project resources from being dissipated unintentionally into the mainstream of national life, at least until such time that the government fully takes over for project completion.

But strict rules and complex procedures are double-edged: they constrain and isolate as much as they safeguard. The complex analytical requirements set by aid agencies impose a heavy burden on already weak national administrative capacities, intensify dependence on foreign experts and consultants, and obstruct rather than aid development planning. Worse, the side effects of planning in the aid control system have an unintended antidevelopmental bias, stemming partly from the impact of imperious rationality.[8]

According to Harry Strachan, much of the work of preparing a project is not inherently necessary but is done to satisfy the regulations of donor agencies. He feels that recurring problems in aid administration—long project lead times, high administrative costs, implementation delays, and managerial passivity and subterfuge— are due to the "rational" paradigm which places excessive emphasis on prior planning. Chambers and Belshaw concur, adding that the perfectionist planner and the intellectual academic are both susceptible to recommending yet more detailed planning with two unfortunate results: generating an insatiable appetite for planners, who are far from costless, and reducing the chances of anything happening on the ground.[9]

Despite such serious misgivings, aid agency and government planners apparently persist in their top-down, compliance- and control-oriented approach to planning, failing to redesign projects upon discovery of unanticipated obstacles to implementation. Some of them believe that problems are the result of not enough control being exercised rather than too much. Equally likely, some believe, as does James Emery, that a plan should serve as the basis for coordination, and that significant changes should be effected only through the same approval mechanism that first authorized the original document.[10] According to this view, failure to meet this stipulation could rob the plan of its integrity, thwart the objectives of the original planner, and allow the lowest levels to plan their own destiny unconstrained by higher-level considerations.

An alternative explanation based on power bargaining is given by Strachan, who notes that in the aid relationship the donor is overwhelmingly dominant until the grant is given, but once disbursement is made the recipient becomes more powerful.[11] The donor's requirements of detailed planning serve to bring many key decisions into the zone of negotiation where the donor has dominant power.

Strachan also finds fault with the great emphasis placed on prior planning. He feels that much of the failure stems from a fundamental misunderstanding of both the potential and limitations of planning. Though the long-term planning exercise could be useful for educating the decision makers, plans and projections quickly lose their accuracy. It is impossible to anticipate the future in the detail necessary for blueprint planning. Furthermore, any detailed planning years in advance by people who are neither going to be responsible nor involved in project implementation can only be ineffectual.

A similar view is expressed by David Korten and by Emery and Trist who question the assumptions that all obstacles can be foreseen and that local initiative is neither required nor desirable. They feel the present system is designed to maintain central control by encouraging uniform compliance and minimizing adaptive behavior.[12] It is inherently unworkable for the complex and uncertain tasks of development project management.

According to Rondinelli, a similar problem exists in the relationships between developing countries and aid agencies, making it almost impossible to plan, analyze, and manage projects in highly rational and systematic ways.[13] Any attempt to impose such procedures produces adverse results. Therefore, the challenge that still remains is to find more effective and relevant ways of dealing with the inevitable and sometimes irreducible uncertainty and complexity inherent in development projects. The planning approach tried thus far has not proved satisfactory.

Alternative Planning Approaches

In technical terms, planning for IDPs—as currently attempted—adopts the rational-comprehensive approach during the design phase and then proceeds with the blueprint planning approach during implementation.[14] In the rational-comprehensive mode of planning, programs put forward for evaluation cover the available action space, which itself has been derived from an exhaustive definition of the problem to be solved. Blueprint planning determines every detail of the solution to a problem (the master plan) and only then proceeds unswervingly toward implementation. Both approaches have their drawbacks. Not only is completely rational-comprehensive planning a practical impossibility, but it is based on the faulty assumption that the whole system can move forward in step and be maintained in balance. It also assumes—incorrectly—that all future system states are knowable and can be predicted and controlled.

The problems with blueprint planning are similar. Jon Morris, after a comprehensive review of development project management, feels that it is well-nigh impossible to anticipate all eventual organizational needs, exert firm control over field staff, and tackle in advance the effects of an unstable and changing environment.[15] The blueprint can only serve as an initial guide, but not as an instrument of control.

Alternative planning approaches are clearly needed, and a few have apparently been tried. When comprehensive planning was seen not to work, its opposite was tried in the form of disjointed incrementalism.[16] The latter approach relies on successive comparisons between a limited range of alternatives. This approach could perhaps be adequate if the environment were stable and the decisions made were effective from the start. It becomes much less appropriate when conditions are rapidly changing or the initial course set was wrong. In addition, if the ends being pursued have not been clearly articulated, there is a tendency to degenerate into "muddling-through incrementalism," which is no planning at all.

A more reasonable strategy is Etzioni's "mixed scanning approach," in which the general value direction is first set through interactions between the various stakeholders or decision makers, after which detailed planning is undertaken for the alternatives considered appropriate for reaching the goals selected.[17] This compromise solution does not, however, tackle the fundamental problems. In part because the strategy followed is determined neither by values nor by information but by the positions of and power relations among the decision makers. If the power balance is already a source of problems—which as was noted earlier is a definite possibility in planning IDPs—the status quo is unlikely to be a good starting point.

Moreover, mixed scanning is closer to "continuous blueprint planning" than it is to the "adaptive planning" approach needed for development project management.[18] It continues to rely more on external control than on organizational learning as a primary guarantor of project success and does little to modify the environmental factors that often are the source of a whole range of implementation problems. A more basic change is needed in how planning is done, by whom, when, and for what purpose.

Interactive Planning

As defined by Ackoff, interactive planning is the design of a desirable future and the invention of ways to bring it about.[19] Interactive planners want to do better in the future than they are capable of now doing: they idealize; they attempt to improve performance over time by maximizing their ability to learn and adapt; they use design methodology, and their focus is development. The planning approach is based on the operating principles of participation, continuity, and holistic planning and is undertaken in five interrelated steps: mess formulation, ends planning, means planning, resource planning, and design of implementation and control.

Each aspect is covered in considerable detail in Ackoff's publications. In broad outline, the main features are the following:

1. Continuous planning ensures that frequent modifications are made in response to emergent environmental and system changes.
2. Participation ensures the involvement of all stakeholders.
3. Integration means that all levels make their inputs from their own perspectives.
4. Coordination ensures that the lateral interdependence of decisions is considered.

The process of planning is more important than its product (the plan), and ends are considered as important as means. Only after what ought to be done is decided and the general direction set (Ozbekhan's normative planning step), are questions of what will be done (strategies) and what can be done (operations) entertained.[20] Moreover, the relations between these phases is not linear; they modify each other through feedback.

These and other features of interactive planning build upon a solid foundation of related systems concepts. For example, a key requirement is active adaptive learning, meaning thereby that the system be capable of changing itself or its environment or both in order to maintain or improve its performance in response to an internal or external threat or opportunity. This design specification recognizes the salience of the environment (open and nested systems), choice (purposeful, directed, and ideal-seeking behavior), and coproduction (fit and reciprocal interdependence with the environment). Similarly, the emphasis on participation follows from the systems view of development (no one can develop another, therefore, planning should be done by not for those affected). The principle of holism (i.e., integrated and coordinated planning simultaneously) recognizes that the system is more than the sum of its parts—it is the product of their interactions.

It is also stipulated that during the initial step of mess formulation, synthesis should precede analysis so that the system's role and functions are understood in relation to its containing systems. The process of idealization is considered important, placing emphasis on the ends of action before means are determined. This process also builds consensus and commitment and releases self-imposed constraints that restrain creativity. The overall purpose is to redesign the system and its environment so that the dynamic "mess" of problems is dissolved, and the focal system becomes development-oriented and ideal-seeking.

The interactive planning approach is therefore very comprehensive and full of challenge. Ackoff recommends it not because it is easy but because it is right! However, it is recognized that the formulation of interactive planning summarized above is idealized. It is a description of the kind of planning an organization should move toward, by successive approximations, in small increments. Although the adoption can be gradual, the integrity of the whole must however be maintained. It being a system of activities, the parts lose their essential properties when tried separately. Nevertheless, interactive planning is not a rigidly specified process: it is flexible and adaptable, and each of its applications is an adaptation of the version presented here.[21]

The next section outlines one such potentially useful adaptation.

Interactive Planning for International Development Projects

We begin by describing the characteristics of a well-planned international development project and then compare these with interactive planning. This leads to an expanded systems view of IDPs.

The Project Cycle

IDPs are time-bound and gradually move from birth to maturation and handover, passing through the following major stages of the project life cycle: (1) identification, (2) preparation, (3) appraisal and approval, (4) implementation and supervision, and (5) evaluation and policy review.[22] Each of these steps requires close collaboration between aid agencies and borrowers and is undertaken jointly. The standard operating procedures and capabilities of both parties to the exercise directly affect the outcome of each stage. Given the number and diversity of organizations involved and the broad scope of activities undertaken, each project's development experience is unique. However, there are some commonalities in the activities undertaken and the criteria used at each stage of the project cycle.

During identification, the main criteria used are desirability and suitability, so that a high-priority project is selected. The next step is preparation and requires a comprehensive and thorough examination of costs and benefits as well as feasibility. All aspects of the project—technical, institutional, social, economic, and financial—are examined in detail. During appraisal and approval, the project is again assessed for suitability, visibility, and implementability, given the particular contextual situation. Then funding approval is obtained, and project implementation and supervision begins. The focus now is on external effectiveness and internal efficiency so that the planned targets can be satisfactorily achieved. During the last stage of policy review and evaluation, the emphasis is on lessons to be learned from the project's experience. Evaluation attempts to measure goal attainment and compares final achievements with initial targets.

The various stages of the project cycle merge into each other. Even though the stages follow sequentially, the overlap is considerable. For example, issues of project viability often surface during identification and preparation in order to ensure that further design effort is spent only on feasible and implementable activities. As a result, one of the main objectives of policy guidance is to ensure that all project activities progress in step, and that the various interdependencies are managed as an integrated system. This important function cannot be effectively discharged without proper planning, and this "planning of planning" constitutes one of the major tasks of policy makers, both in aid agencies and government organizations.

The second critical task is the management of interdependent activities at each stage of the project cycle. The IDP manager must learn to manage intra- and inter-organizational relations very well. Even though the project organization is largely designed and controlled by project staff, the fitting together of tasks, structure, reward and information systems, and people into a coherent whole is not at all easy. Nor does this fit persist on its own: in the absence of constant attention, it quickly unravels, destroying any potential for effective action.

A similar problem is faced in inter-organizational relations. Various strategies such as bargaining, consultation, and joint problem solving are needed to reconcile competing interests. Here again, since the relative power and importance of various agencies changes over time, inter-organizational relationships require careful and continuous tending. This coordination task is therefore similar to the one within the organization: it is to achieve continuing coherence through flexibility and change, allowing for structural and functional evolution as the project moves through its life cycle.[23]

The "planning of activities" is the direct responsibility of project officers and field managers. It is as important as the "planning of planning" but requires different skills, techniques, time horizons, and personal dispositions. Not all policy makers are likely to be good at operational tasks and vice versa. Nor can headquarters staff ensure the project's future. Central policies and procedures can only be used as broad guidelines, leaving operational managers free to adjust plans on the ground as needed.

Furthermore, the issues addressed by planners change over time, as the project cycle unfolds. Normative concerns are of prime importance during identification and focus on the future that "ought" to be created. Strategic questions gain primacy during preparation and appraisal, with planners determining medium-term goals and ways of achieving them. During the next stage of implementation, operational planning is critical so that activities can be performed expeditiously and efficiently. Monitoring and control is done continuously but is especially important once implementation is underway.

Of course, questions of desirability, viability, and efficiency can never be fully addressed once and for all. They must be repeatedly raised during the course of the project, sometimes as part of a midterm evaluation or while preparing a follow-on project. However, the qualitative shift in perspective between normative, strategic, and operational concerns is important and must be consciously undertaken so that both the process and content of planning are adjusted accordingly.

Interactive Planning and the Project Cycle

The close correspondence between the project cycle and interactive planning discussed earlier is not difficult to see. The obvious commonalities are the following:

1. In both, normative concerns are important and precede strategic and operational questions.

2. Interdependence between various stages requires iterative decision making during the course of the project cycle.
3. Planning is a continuous activity.
4. The planning process used—both for "planning of planning" and for "planning of activities"—is of critical importance.
5. During project identification, determination, and prioritization of goals follows a thorough assessment of situational constraints and opportunities.
6. Effective planning requires the close collaboration and involvement of all major stakeholders.
7. Means planning, resource planning, and planning of monitoring and control are completed prior to implementation.
8. Environmental factors are taken into account at each step.

Not so obvious but much more important is that projects, to be successful, should be planned adaptively.[24] Project boundaries are hopelessly permeable to outside influences and uncertainties, and rigid adherence to any blueprint, no matter how well-prepared, can only hurt. Furthermore, the effects of a large, prestigious, internationally funded project on the local distribution of power, influence, and resource exchange cannot be anticipated in advance. When new political and administrative commitments get formed, project management has to respond quickly—to exploit fresh opportunities and reduce unexpected damages. Equally important, local staff can experiment with new ideas. This facilitates learning, without which there is little possibility of genuine development taking place, either of individuals or of institutions.

Therefore, deviations from the "master plan" are treated as opportunities for learning and redesign rather than as errors to be controlled. Initial project arrangements have the status of tentative hypotheses to be tested so that continual attention is given to obtaining and utilizing feedback for improving performance. In so doing, project managers actively seek change, both in their own system and in the environment, gradually gaining confidence and experience in "designing a desirable future and making it happen." This, as we have discussed earlier, is what interactive planning is all about.

An Expanded Systems View of IDPs

It seems clear that, in principle, interactive planning is more relevant and useful for international development projects than the rational-comprehensive blueprint planning approach now used. As discussed earlier, a major problem is the inappropriate policy guidelines and procedures enforced by aid agencies and government bureaucracies. These procedures seek to exercise control and compliance, and do not encourage the learning and adaptation necessary for managing complexity and uncertainty in turbulent Third-World settings. A major reorientation of control-oriented bureaucracies, both donor and recipient, is obviously needed but is unlikely to be achieved spontaneously. Nor should we expect that many opportunities for experimentation will exist in the "mess" of obstructions and social pathologies that dominate underdeveloped countries.[25] A gradual process of adoption (and adaptation) of new planning approaches is a much more likely occurrence and can be given a good start by undertaking an in-depth study of the nature and scope of modifications needed in current practice.

These changes are most clearly visible when contrasted with an idealized view of interactive planning and the development project cycle. The latter framework permits an examination of the interdependencies and process variables that are key considerations in planning IDPs. In addition, since international development projects are jointly undertaken by aid agencies and borrowing governments, IDPs can be viewed as an intersystem engagement.[26] Each collaborating organization can be examined as an open system, exchanging resources of various kinds with organizations in its transactional environment.

In an IDP the primary task of the overlapping systems is to create and maintain the relationship between them so as to achieve project objectives. In order to serve their common goals, the organizations must share information and action, each respecting the distinctive competence of the others and the complementary nature of their skills and interests. Unfortunately, because of the temporary nature of the relationship, few individuals in practice look to the rewards that emerge from the engagement itself. The point of reference for each set of individuals often remains their own system with its hierarchical superiors exercising power, exerting professional and informal influence, and controlling resources and rewards. However, the more clearly the personal and organizational rewards are linked with behavior produced in the intersystem engagement, the more the negative effects of an essentially transitory and partially opportunistic relationship can be overcome.[27]

The intersystem engagement can also be viewed from the sociotechnical perspective; the effects of the task, external, value, reward, and power subsystems on the overall planning process are important, as discussed by Alfred Clark.[28] The imagery of loosely coupled systems is also useful, since it draws attention to the identity, separateness, and boundaries of the elements coupled.[29] Loose coupling also carries connotations of impermanence, dissolvability, and tacitness—all of which are characteristics of an international development project.

These various viewpoints are complementary and together produce a unique systems perspective that is eminently suitable for examining both aspects of planning—the "planning of activities" and the "planning of planning" discussed earlier. This perspective, which builds upon Ackoff's interactive planning framework, is ideally suited for going beyond the symptoms of inadequate planning to the causes and can help identify the nature and scope of changes needed in the organizational and planning processes of concerned agencies.

Conclusion

A redesign of the organizational processes used by donor and government agencies planning IDPs is long overdue. There is a need to review procedures, reassess the presumed role of project preparation and design, and rearrange the relationships between headquarters, field staff, and beneficiaries in developing countries. The sanctity of blueprints is already being questioned as attention shifts from disbursement targets to development impact of projects. The time for moving toward interactive planning for international development projects has come.

The following major implications of interactive planning for IDPs bear reiteration:

1. The process of project planning is at least as important as its content. The guarantor of project success is not the adequacy of the blueprint but the appropriateness of the processes used to test and adapt it during implementation.
2. A "good" project design is not necessarily one that remains unchanged during implementation. Rather, it is one that allows changes to take place—through learning—in order that it remains viable and effective even under changing circumstances.
3. The emphasis given by aid agencies and governments to preparation and appraisal of detailed designs should be accompanied with the expectation that changes will be needed later on. The role of supervision should be to facilitate learning and redesign rather than to exercise control.
4. IDPs should be designed participatively by the key actors in the field, including project staff and beneficiaries. Flexibility of design is necessary and requires that those who are most affected by the project should be able to influence its redesign.

5. Project managers should resist the tendency to close options prematurely or to engage in unproductive overdesign of procedures that cannot be followed.

These lessons from theory, though obviously relevant, are seldom applied in the field, for reasons cited earlier. Present constraints on planning of IDPs and how these might be overcome are the subject of ongoing research by the author. It is expected that this research will, upon completion, provide further impetus toward interactive planning for international development projects.

Notes

1. Russell L. Ackoff, *Redesigning the Future: A Systems Approach to Societal Problems* (New York: Wiley, 1974); and Russell L. Ackoff, *Creating the Corporate Future* (New York: Wiley, 1981).

2. Jamshid G. Gharajedaghi and Russell L. Ackoff, *A Prologue to National Development Planning* (New York: Greenwood Press, 1984).

3. Albert O. Hirschman, *Development Projects Observed* (Washington, D.C.: The Brookings Institution, 1967), p. 1; and United Nations, Department of Economic and Social Affairs, *Administration of Development Programmes and Projects: Some Major Issues* (ST/TAO/M/55), 1971, p. 71.

4. Albert Waterston, *Development Planning: Lessons of Experience* (Baltimore: The Johns Hopkins Press, 1969), p. 249.

5. Dennis A. Rondinelli, "Designing International Development Projects for Implementation," in George Honadle and Rudi Klauss (eds.), *International Development Administration: Implementation Analysis for Development Projects* (New York: Praeger, 1979), pp. 23–26.

6. Operations Evaluation Department, *Annual Review of Project Performance Audit Results* (Washington, D.C.: The World Bank, 1982), p. ii.

7. Waterston, op. cit., pp. 249–365; Rondinelli in Honadle and Klauss, *ibid.*, pp. 26–31; Hirschman, op. cit., pp. 45–59; and various readings in Dennis A. Rondinelli (ed.), *Planning Development Projects* (Stroudsburg, Pa.: Dowden, Hutchinson and Ross, 1977).

8. Harry W. Strachan, "Side Effects of Planning in the Aid Control System," *World Development*, 1978, 6(4): 467–78; and Dennis A. Rondinelli, "International Assistance Policy and Development Project Administration: The Impact of Imperious Rationality," *International Organization*, 1976, 30(4, Autumn): 573–605.

9. Robert Chambers and Deryke Belshaw, *Managing Rural Development: Lessons and Methods from Eastern Africa* (Brighton, England: Institute of Development Studies, University of Sussex, 1973), pp. 63–64.

10. James C. Emery, *Organizational Planning and Control Systems: Theory and Technology* (New York: Macmillan, 1969), pp. 113–19.

11. Strachan, op. cit., p. 473.

12. David C. Korten, "Towards a Technology for Managing Social Development," based on a background paper presented at the *Caracas Meeting of the Management Institutes Working Group on Population and Development Management*, IESA, Caracas, Venezuela, July 22–23, 1977, pp. 12–17; and Fred E.

Emery and Eric L. Trist, *Towards a Social Ecology: Contextual Appreciations of the Future in the Present* (New York: Plenum, 1973), p. 203.

13. Dennis A. Rondinelli, "The Dilemma of Development Administration: Complexity and Uncertainty in Control oriented Bureaucracies," (mimeographed, 1982).

14. Andreas Faludi, *Planning Theory* (New York: Pergamon Press, 1973), pp. 131–70.

15. Jon R. Morris, *Managing Induced Rural Development* (Bloomington, Ind.: International Development Institute, 1981), pp. 19–22.

16. Andreas Faludi (ed.), *A Reader in Planning Theory* (New York: Pergamon, 1973), pp. 151–69; and Faludi, *Planning Theory*, op. cit., pp. 150–70.

17. Amitai Etzioni, "Mixed Scanning: A 'Third' Approach to Decision Making," in Faludi, *Reader*, op. cit., p. 227.

18. Paramjit S. Sachdeva, (1984), "Development Planning—An Adaptive Approach," *Long Range Planning* 17(5): 96–102.

19. See, for example, Russell L. Ackoff, *Creating the Corporate Future*, op. cit., in particular.

20. Hasan Ozbekhan, "Toward a General Theory of Planning," in Eric Jantsch (ed.), *Perspectives in Planning* (Paris: OECD, 1969). See also Eric L. Trist, "Action Research and Adaptive Planning," in Alfred W. Clark, *Experimenting with Organizational Life: the Action Research Approach* (New York: Plenum, 1976); and Eric L. Trist, "The Environment and System-Response Capability," *Futures* 12(April 1980): 122.

21. Ackoff, op. cit., pp. 76 and 240–41.

22. This section relies heavily on Sachdeva, "Adaptive Approach," op. cit. See also Warren C. Baum, "The Project Cycle," *Finance and Development* (Washington, D.C.: The World Bank, 1978); and Dennis A. Rondinelli, "Planning Development Projects: Lessons from Developing Countries," *Long Range Planning*, 1979, 12(June): 48–56.

23. The coordination requirements of development projects are discussed in Paramjit S. Sachdeva, "Work Division, Coordination and Intra-Organization Design," *Indian Journal of Public Administration,* Special Number of "Productivity in Public Administration—Concepts and Applications," 1982, 28(3, July–September): 573–87.

24. Samuel Paul, *Managing Development Programs: The Lessons of Success* (Boulder, Colo.: Westview Press, 1982).

25. Ackoff and Gharajedaghi, *National Development Planning*, op. cit.

26. Alfred W. Clark, "The Client-Practitioner Relationship as an Intersystem Engagement," in Alfred W. Clark (ed.): *Experimenting with Organizational Life: The Action Research Perspective* (New York: Plenum, 1976), pp. 119–34, takes a similar approach.

27. Alfred W. Clark, "Intersystem Engagement," op. cit., particularly the discussion of task and reward systems.

28. Ibid.

29. Karl E. Weick, "Educational Organizations as Loosely Coupled Systems," *Administrative Science Quarterly*, 1976, 21(1, March): 3.

Chapter 29
Surutato: An Experience in Rural Participative Planning

Jaime Jimenez

Introduction

A group of concerned parents in a small rural community decided to do something about a basic problem in their educational system: How can they provide their children with a better quality of education without having to send them away to urban schools where they lose their commitment to their community? This paper reports on their solutions to this problem and the applicability of Ackoff's model to it. Participative planning as proposed by Ackoff[1] has been successfully applied in urban settings. The importance of this study is the successful application of the model in a rural Mexican community. Federal education agencies sponsored the Community Education Project, an action-research program that features the implementation of the participative planning model in a number of rural communities. Surutato is an isolated community in the mountains of the northern state of Sinaloa, that had already begun its own self-development community program when the Community Education Project was introduced.

Ackoff's planning methodology helped the community reach their educational goals: they have improved educational quality at the elementary level, and are successfully experimenting with a nonconventional, postelementary education model, including the creation of a productive cooperative run by students. Since formal education is centrally designed in Mexico, it does not take the needs and desires of rural communities into account. In order to counter this, Surutato's Educational Planning Committee designed a program that, in addition to the standard core of secondary school subjects, emphasizes knowledge related to the region's economic activities. Their program includes two seemingly opposed concepts: self-learning and teamwork.

The entire project is embued with a philosophy of development similar to Ackoff's. In the words of Surutato's Educational Planning Committee: "The fundamental objective of basic education is to help human beings to understand their immediate problems, and provide them with the proper training to solve their problems by themselves."[2]

The Setting

Surutato is a small rural community in the mountainous sierra of the state of Sinaloa, in northwestern Mexico. Surutato has abundant natural resources. In addition to its forests, the climate favors cattle ranching as well as fruit and flower production. The climate also permits the storage and preservation of seeds. The natural beauty of the region makes it a potential tourist attraction.

Its population of about 2,500 (in 1980) lives on 29,000 hectares. Within the territory of the community, there are three main population centers, Surutato itself, El Triguito, and Santa Rita as well as about thirty smaller settlements. Land tenure is held communally as part of federally restituted *ejidos,* which are usufruct rights awarded to agricultural communities as part of Mexico's agrarian reform program. This land is held by the community as a body and is administered by it in a form of organization characterized by local level democracy with rights and obligations for all members. Continuity is guaranteed by the obligation to serve in cooperative labor and reinforced by community rituals.

None of the population centers has any urban services (electricity, piped water, sewage, telephone, mail, or telegraph). The nearest urban settlement, Guamuchil, is at least seven hours away over unpaved road.

Surutato's main economic activities are rainfall agriculture (corn, wheat, beans, and potatoes), animal husbandry (cows, pigs, and domestic fowl), forestry (a sawmill), and fruit production (peaches, apricots, and apples).

The agricultural land in the *ejido* is naturally irrigated by a series of seasonal arroyos. Surutato has a subhumid temperate climate with abundant rains from June to October; less rain during the winter months and frost from October to March occur. The annual average temperature is in the 64–68° F range, and annual precipitation varies from 800–1,000 mm. The winter is considered benign.

Species of pine, oak, and madrono make up 18,500 hectares of exploitable forest reserves (or 65% of the ejidal territory). Large grazing areas, good climate, and sufficient water make cattle raising feasible. Apple and peach production are also potentially important. Members of the *ejido,* or *ejidatarios,* have around 6,000 trees. Flower production is another potential resource, as preliminary experimentation has shown that soil composition and climate are suited to horticulture.

The many attractions of Surutato's streams, canyons, and scenery, as well as the hospitable nature of the climate and the population, make these developments a future possibility.

Background

Before the initiation of the Community Education Project, a process of community mobilization had already begun in Surutato. A review of the important characteristics of this mobilization is useful in explaining the success of the participative planning model.

Initial Steps

In 1977, Antonio Malacon, a civil engineer from the state capital of Culiacan, built a weekend home near Surutato. As he got to know community members, they told him about the problems they had with their children's education in the three elementary schools located in the three main settlements. There were not enough teachers, and not all grades were taught. Furthermore, teachers were frequently absent. The quality of education was far from satisfactory. In fact, these problems represented only the tip of the iceberg. Students who wished to continue their schooling beyond the elementary level had to leave their community and go to the nearest urban settlement, Guamuchil. Many families could not afford the costs implied by this. Those who did were not satisfied with the education their children received, because they tended to lose their community roots, developing new social and material needs that could not be satisfied in Surutato. In the parents' words, "Our kids come back home with different habits, if things go on like this, they'll become outsiders in their own community, even if they still live here."[3]

In sum, more education was not helping youngsters to live in their own community nor to learn skills useful in a rural setting. Sending children away to be educated meant alienating them from their community and family.

Malacon thus became involved in the educational problems of Surutato. He has played a major role in facilitating the process of discussion, design, and implementation of their own educational programs. Malacon held a number of preliminary meetings with various groups and informal leaders, with the help of Jose Luis Nansen, a rural education specialist. They wanted to be sure that "better education" was a felt need shared by many, not just the people they had talked to. From the beginning of the facilitation process, great respect was shown for community attitudes and decisions, allowing progress to take place at their own pace, without imposing their views and accepting suggestions on who should be invited to meetings. This was particularly important, because the *ejido* was involved in a very delicate problem at that time. The state government had funded a sawmill in order to introduce *ejidatarios* to lumbering. However, the sawmill was managed by outsiders who only hired a few men from the *ejido*, thus depriving the community of most of the benefits of their own lumber resources. This conflict had divided the community into two antagonistic groups.

After four months of preparation, a community assembly was held to let people express their thoughts about the most important community needs. Men, women, and children wrote down the single problem each felt was most responsible for obstructing community development. Those who needed assistance in writing were helped by youngsters who had just finished elementary school. Education was the most important problem expressed in various ways by 95% of the population. Most of the responses referred to the need for improving elementary education, both qualitatively and quantitatively. Others mentioned the need for some type of secondary education congruent with community economic activities. It was clear to all that something had to be done to improve the education system. Appropriate education would in turn enhance development, but real development would not come from the outside, it had to be generated from within the community, it must be a product of the community's decisions and actions. The community decided to create a committee, the Central Education Committee, to take charge of its project, called the Community Self-Development Program. The committee was made up of nine democratically elected members, three from each of the three main settlements. Malacon suggested that each local committee should have at least one woman member: "Women not only move the family, they move the whole community."

Creation of the School Center and Cooperative

In order to assess present and future educational demand, the committee carried out a census of the population. This information would be used to support demands for more teachers from the federal educational system. Each local committee organized workshops with parents to analyze the problem of education. A coherent set of demands was formulated from the conclusions reached by the workshops. These demands, which were basically for more and better elementary education, and the creation of an agricultural secondary school, were discussed with the Sinaloa representative of the Ministry of Education, who considered that the innovative nature of the demands deserved direct consideration by officials in Mexico City. A commission of three members of the committee went to Mexico City and spoke with the undersecretary for planning and his staff. The authorities readily agreed to supply more and better elementary school teachers. However, the unsuccessful history of agricultural secondary schools led them to reject that part of the petition. They agreed, however, to support as an experimental project any other alternative plan proposed by the community. The committee immediately proposed an experimental postelementary program with full community participation in formulating course content, and community control of the whole process. The authorities agreed, and appointed Malacon as a formal external advisor to the project. The ministry would also provide some funds for program expenses, which would be administered by the community.

The postelementary education program was initiated in November 1978 on a six-hectare plot near the sawmill, where its electric plant could also serve the school. The new school center was named the "Justo Sierra School Center" after the great Mexican turn-of-the-century educator. This name also contains an allusion to the geographical location of the school: *justo sierra* means "right in the hills" in Spanish.

The Central Education Committee and parents set up the following principles for running the center:

- To offer courses, with mandatory attendance, that make use of correspondence school texts already in existence. Teachers would be available for tutoring.
- To promote habits of self-teaching and teamwork among the students.
- To maintain manual skills to avoid alienation from the reality of their rural context.
- To establish workshops and technologies appropriate to the developmental needs of the community.[4]

In addition, Surutato decided to build the new school center with volunteer community labor, using local materials and know-how.

One year after the center was opened, a productive cooperative was set up on the same site. This cooperative is run by students so they can learn how to run a productive enterprise. Whereas individual *ejido* members cannot get loans because they don't have land titles to use as a guarantee since the land is communal usufruct land, the co-operative is eligible for loans.

The Community Education Project [5]

The Ministry of Education (SEP) began the Community Education Project in response to deficiencies in rural formal education. Generally, education in rural communities is limited to the primary level. However, as shown before, education at this level is designed more to prepare students for the next level of formal education than to provide a means of adapting to their environment. SEP defines rural communities as purposeful systems in the sense used by Ackoff and Emery.[6] A community is also an open system, meaning that it has an environment or context, which either affects or is affected by its behavior. Purposefulness is a real or potential community characteristic, which can be facilitated or inhibited by the environment. The key question here is how can purposeful behavior be activated in rural communities? SEP's answer is to involve them in their own participative educational planning process. This planning process, according to SEP's designers, must be systemic, participative, and prospective.

Systemic because, in order to produce a substantial contribution to community development, the educational program to be planned must take community economic, political, social, and cultural processes into account. The effectiveness of the education provided depends more on how well it interacts with all other aspects of the community than on its independent performance.

Participative because involving individuals in designing their own educational system makes it possible to relate it to collective and individual needs and goals. Also, those involved in the educational planning process become more efficient in obtaining better benefits from the education provided, and therefore, better able to improve their own quality of life. Furthermore, participation may mobilize local and institutional resources more efficiently and thus open the way to ensuring educational continuity and growth by increasing local commitment to the program.

Prospective because the education plan developed must open perspectives for the fulfillment of future collective and individual goals for increasing the quality of life in the community. Furthermore, it must also take feasible future opportunities for improving life in the community into account.[7]

Participative planning paradigms based on a systemic approach have been proposed and tested mainly in urban settings.[8] However, little or no work has been done in rural settings. SEP's project proposed to correct this deficiency by testing a participative planning methodology in rural areas. The hypothesis it tries to prove is that the greater the degree of participation of rural communities in designing and implementing their own educational system, the more education can contribute to improving rural quality of life.[9]

The project is formally constituted with a written agreement, renewable annually, between the SEP and the community, in which the community is responsible for setting up and supervising a democratically elected, volunteer planning committee. SEP, in turn, must provide the planning model to be adapted and tested, a promoter for advice and follow-up, and a small revolving fund for the committee's expenses. Committee members have control over this budget, with the stipulation that the money be spent for the benefit of all.

The initial model was derived from Ackoff's interactive planning paradigm.[10] The model has six interdependent phases:

- Community diagnosis: description of the current status of the community, the nature and origin of principal problems and future prospects.
- Goal planning: statement of desired futures.
- Means planning: formulation and selection of educational objectives and the appropriate educational strategies to reach them.
- Resource planning.
- Implementation.
- Evaluation and control.

SEP produced handbooks for each step in the planning process, kept track of progress in each community, organized meetings so project participants could compare experiences, and kept a record of the process in each community in order to enrich the general planning model with factual experience. One of the promoter's most important functions is to facilitate community members to learn and to put the planning model into practice.

SEP's design stage coincided with the initial stages of Surutato's Community Self-Development Program and was able to benefit from this experience.

Results

The community of Surutato learned and adapted the participative planning model supplied by SEP. As a result, they have successfully planned course curriculae at the secondary level, petitioned for better primary education, formed a productive cooperative, and in general, mobilized the community and taken control of community resources for the benefit of all. The model is currently being tried in other communities in the state of Sinaloa by student promoters from Surutato's School Center.

In April 1980, an agreement was signed between SEP and the community of Surutato that included the Self-Development Community Program in SEP's Community Education Project. Surutato's Central Education Committee became the Education Planning Committee, keeping the same nine representatives, and adding four new members. This committee is in charge of the organization, administration, and control of the whole community education process. The committee is the cornerstone of the entire project.

Ten other communities were added to the Community Education Project, all coordinated by SEP. This allowed other communities to exchange experiences with Surutato, which was very helpful for both parties.

The planning model was not only learned and put into practice by the Planning Committee of Surutato, but by students in the School Center as well. It helped make the organization of the cooperative more participatory. Instead of managing the cooperative hierarchically, the students proposed a horizontal structure. Cooperative tasks are carried out by student "brigades" under the command of a brigade leader. The Brigade Council is made up of all brigade leaders, who meet daily to make operational decisions. The Brigade Council depends on the Student General Assembly. All students must have experience as a brigade leader as part of their training. This allows each student to play a leadership role by speaking in public, conducting assemblies, negotiating with local officials, and in general, taking care of fellow students. Many benefits result from this rotational leadership scheme: students understand the goals and objectives of the entire project more clearly, they become more responsible toward their schoolmates and the community as a whole, they learn to overcome obstacles, individually and collectively, in order to reach middle-range objectives.

Adults have also benefitted from the planning methodology. They have successfully completed the design of a four-year secondary program and gone on to design a two-year preparatory school program, which is also a correspondence course. Where before there was only deficient primary education available in Surutato, today there are six years of postelementary education. Besides having experience in all of the technical specialties offered by the Center, students must master one specific ability by the end of their six-year period. Currently, those students who successfully complete the course are qualified to become promoters in other communities with self-development programs. In fact, state educational authorities have begun a program to promote development in other communities in Sinaloa. Some Surutato students are now working as promoters.

Another side effect of community organization has been the assertion of greater control over community resources. The sawmill is a case in point. As mentioned above, the allocation of resources from lumbering was a source of dissension because outsiders were getting all the benefit. In 1980, *ejido* elections put members of the Central Education Committee in the most important positions. This new board negotiated with state authorities until they obtained total control of the sawmill. By the end of the year, the sawmill reopened under new conditions: all employees are community members and profits go to benefit the community.

Conclusions

Participative planning is successfully practiced in Surutato by both adults and students. The community is aware that the future can be modified by communally made decisions and actions. They are in a process of development, not in the conventional sense of continuously acquiring more goods and services, but in Ackoff's sense of the "capacity defined by what they can do with whatever they have to improve their quality of life and that of others." [11]

The Community Education Project has come to an end. However, the Surutato project continues. The community's actions verify the project's central hypothesis that greater community participation in planning rural education leads to improvement in quality of life.

A note of caution should be added. In addition to a philosophy of participation, other "enabling conditions" appear to predispose the success of projects of this nature. Among them, the quality of the promoter is of paramount importance. Malacon, Surutato's main external advisor and community promoter, is a fortunate example. The community has not become dependent on his views.

In conclusion, Ackoff's model of participatory planning has proved to be very useful in applications in rural communities, permitting not only community level input in design, but innovation, adaptation, and modification of the learning experience to permit further local control of resources. This experience is being spread to other communities.

Funding for the Community Education Project should continue to support the application of the participatory model in other communities, with emphasis on opening channels of access of interested communities to the project. Future research should also consider the problem of how to adapt the model in communities where such "enabling conditions" as previous mobilization do not exist.

Notes

1. See for instance: Ackoff, R. L. *Redesigning the Future* (New York: Wiley, 1974), pp. 28, 39, 47, and 133; and Ackoff, R. L. (1977), "National Development Planning Revisited," *Operations Research* 25(2, March–April): 213–14.

2. Ackoff defines development in the following terms: "Development is the desire and ability to use what is available to continuously improve the quality of life. This ability cannot be given to others even by those who have it. It must be developed in and for oneself" (*Redesigning the Future*, pp. 221–22). Surutato's Educational Planning Committee is making an implicit reference to the same concept, in reference to basic education (Autodesarrollo Comunitario, Comite de Planeacion Educativa. Surutato, Sinaloa, 1980, p. 2).

3. Malacon's personal communication.

4. Autodesarrollo Comunitario, Comite de Planeacion Educativa, Surutato, Sinaloa, 1980, p. 19.

5. This section is based on Delgado, M., J. Prawda, and F. Ramon (1980), "Community Educational Planning in Mexico," a paper presented at the International Congress on Applied Systems Research and Cybernetics. Acapulco, December 12–16, 1980.

6. Ackoff, R. L., and F. E. Emery, *On Purposeful Systems* (Chicago: Aldine Atherton, 1970), p. 215.

7. Delgado et al., op. cit., pp. 3–4.

8. In addition to Ackoff, see Friedmann, J., *Retracking America: A Theory of Transactive Planning* (New York: Doubleday, 1972); and Ozbekhan, H. (1969), "Towards a General Theory of Planning," in E. Jantsch (ed.): *Perspectives of Planning* (Paris: OECD, 1969), pp. 97–158.

9. Delgado et al., op. cit., p. 4.

10. See for instance Ackoff, R. L., *A Concept of Corporate Planning* (New York: Wiley, 1970).

11. Ackoff, R. L. (1977), "National Development Planning Revisited," *Operations Research* 25(2, March–April): 212.

Contributors

Stafford Beer: Syncho Limited, Toronto, Canada.

Paul Broholm: Consultant, New Haven, Conn.

August A. Busch III: Anheuser-Busch Companies, Inc., St. Louis, Mo.

Fred Carden: Faculté de l'Aménagement, Université de Montréal, Canada.

Raúl Carvajal: Universidad Nacionál Autonoma de Mexico, Mexico City.

Michel Chevalier: Faculty of Environmental Studies, York University, Toronto, Canada.

C. West Churchman: University of California, Berkeley, Calif.

Burton Cohen: School of Social Work, University of Pennsylvania, Philadelphia, Pa.

Thomas A. Cowan: Busch Center, The Wharton School, University of Pennsylvania, Philadelphia, Pa.

William Evan: Department of Management, The Wharton School, University of Pennsylvania, Philadelphia, Pa.

Peter C. Fishburn: AT&T Bell Laboratories, Murray Hill, N.J.

John Friend: IOP Consulting, Tonbridge, Kent, U.K.

Ali Geranmayeh: Interact, Bala-Cynwyd, Pa.

Jamshid Gharajedaghi: Interact, Bala-Cynwyd, Pa.

Thomas N. Gilmore: Wharton Center for Applied Research, Philadelphia, Pa.

K. Brian Haley: University of Birmingham, U.K.

Britton Harris: Department of City and Regional Planning, University of Pennsylvania, Philadelphia, Pa.

Jaime Jimenez: Universidad Nacionál Autonoma de Mexico, Mexico City.

Erik Johnsen: Copenhagen School of Economics and Business Administration.

Aron Katsenelinboigen: Department of Decision Sciences, The Wharton School, University of Pennsylvania, Philadelphia, Pa.

Richard O. Mason: Southern Methodist University, Dallas, Tex.

Ian I. Mitroff: Graduate School of Business, University of Southern California, Los Angeles, Calif.

Leon Pritzker: Campbell-Taggart, Inc., Dallas, Tex.

Thomas L. Saaty: Graduate School of Business, University of Pittsburgh.

Paramjit S. Sachdeva: International Service for National Agricultural Research, The Hague, Netherlands.

Ignacy Sachs: Ecole des Hautes Etudes en Sciences Sociales, Paris, France.

Francisco R. Sagasti: International Bank for Reconstruction and Development, Washington, D.C.

Donald A. Schon: Department of Urban Studies and Planning, Massachusetts Institute of Technology, Cambridge, Mass.

William E. Smith: International Development Consultant, Washington, D.C.

Glen Taylor: Faculty of Administrative Studies, York University, Toronto, Canada.

Rolfe Tomlinson: University of Warwick, Coventry, U.K.

Eric Trist: Emeritus Professor, Social Systems Sciences Department, The Wharton School, University of Pennsylvania, Philadelphia, Pa., and former chairman, Tavistock Institute of Human Relations, London.

Elsa Vergara Finnel: Consultant, Toronto, Canada.

Subject Index

Name Index